Preface

Aim

The aim of this text is to provide a comprehensive course text for Business Studies modules or units which are part of non-business courses at degree level. It would also be useful as an introduction for students about to undertake a business studies course.

Need

Universities and Institutes of Higher Education are increasingly coming round to the opinion that specific academic studies should be put into their commercial context by the inclusion of a course or module on business as an integral part of the undergraduate programme, and this trend is likely to increase. As a result there will be a large number of students studying business who have little or no previous knowledge of the subject.

This text addresses the need of non-business students for a textbook that enables them to understand the fundamentals of business and to gain an appreciation of how the business world operates. It will give a sound basis of understanding upon which to build in subsequent studies. It is written in an easily digestible form, and there is no need for prior reading on the subject.

Approach

The text has been written in a structured form, with numbered paragraphs, self review questions, in-text questions and activities (with answers where appropriate), examples case studies and assignments. Material is laid out in a format that is easy to follow and, where appropriate, bullet lists and illustrations are included to summarise information. The chapter headings are planned to fit into a typical syllabus for the courses for which the book is designed. The text is designed to be easily read so that information can be taken in swiftly, and with a consistently high level of interest, and thus the book does not go into excessive depth on any single topic.

How to use the book

The book is intended to be used as a course text to support either a course with a high proportion of lecturer contact time or one that allows for less contact time and more directed self-study. For the latter type of course, students will find the numerous questions with answers allow them to test their understanding.

Students will find it useful to read the relevant chapters in this book in advance of lectures and seminars in particular subject areas. This will provide a theoretical basis upon which to build in classes, where issues raised can be discussed at more length in the context of the wider course of study that the students are undertaking. The book is equally useful for consolidating subjects covered in classes.

The chapters can be tackled in any order, and additional reading in the separate subject areas is indicated at the end of each chapter. These should be used if further clarification is required, or if students wish or need to go into a particular subject in greater depth.

Lecturers' Supplement

A free Lecturers' Supplement, containing answers to the end-of-chapter assignments is available on application to the Publishers in writing (on your college-headed paper) stating the course on which the book is to be recommended, the number of students on the course, and the probable numbers of books to be purchased by them.

Suggestions and criticisms

The author would welcome, via the publishers, any comments on the book. This will enable subsequent editions to be amended, if necessary, and made even more useful to students and teachers alike.

Genders used in the text

Throughout the book, the word *he* should be taken to mean *he or she* – the use of *he* in the text is entirely a matter of stylistic construction in order to help the flow of the text.

David Campbell, June 1994

Contents

Business

for Non-Business Students

David Campbell

BSc(Hons), CDipAF, DipM, MBA

David Campbell is a lecturer in Strategic Management at
Newcastle Business School, a faculty of The University of
Northumbria at Newcastle. As a graduate in chemistry, he held a
number of positions in the chemical industry before taking up his
academic appointment in 1992.

DP Publications Ltd
Aldine Place
London W12 8AW

1994

Acknowledgements

I wish to express sincere appreciation to the many members of Newcastle Business School faculty who supported me in a variety of ways during the writing of the book. Special thanks are due to Ron Beadle, Walter Fraser, Paul Lee, Pamela Graham, Ed Hyatt and Rev Dorothy Wilson, all of the University of Northumbria, for their editorial assistance, and to the helpful staff of the UNN library. I also gratefully acknowledge the contributions of Gavin Smith, Paul Collinson and John Montgomery, each of whom supplied 'ready made' case materials for the text, and to Jo Kemp of DP Publications.

This book would be much poorer without the helpful assistance of the many organisations that kindly provided information and case material for inclusion in the text. My particular appreciation to the following for their helpfulness in this regard:

AgrEvo UK Limited
BAT Industries Plc
British Aerospace Plc
British Gas Plc
British Gas Plc (Northern)
British Nuclear Fuels Limited
British Telecommunications Plc
The Central Statistical Office
Cray Valley Limited
Derwent Valley Foods Limited
The Department of Trade and Industry
Dewhirst Group Plc
Grand Metropolitan Plc
Hanson Plc
Nestlé UK Limited
Nissan
Philips Communication and Security Systems
Rover Group Motors
The RTZ Corporation Plc
Schering Agrochemicals Limited
Scottish and Newcastle Plc
Thorn Lighting Limited
Tor Coatings Limited
Toyota
The University of Northumbria at Newcastle

Disclaimer

The following names are used in this text book in fictional case scenarios. The names are entirely fictional, and any perceived similarities with existing or former companies is entirely coincidental.

Brown Industries Limited
Engonics (Engineering) Limited
Prime Burger Limited
Niff (Sportswear) Limited
Scirocco Plc
Warren (Electronics) Limited

A CIP catalogue record for this book is available from the British Library

ISBN 1 85805 082 0
Copyright D J Campbell © 1994

Typeset by Elizabeth Elwin

Printed by
The Guernsey Press Co Ltd
Braye Road, Vale, Guernsey

Section 5 Functions in a Business Organisation

Section 6 Markets and Market Structures

Section 6 Management of Business Organisations

Contents

Section 1
Business Basics

This section can be considered as an introduction to the concepts of business, the fundamental issues of business objectives and the factors that determine the location of business.

Although the chapters in this book do not have to be followed sequentially, it is advisable for students who are unfamiliar with business concepts to read this section first.

Contents   **Page**

1 Basic concepts in business

Objectives   After studying this chapter, students should be able to:

- ☐ understand what business is all about;
- ☐ define and explain the following terms:

  transactions, price and cost, revenue and profit, product and service, capital
- ☐ define and distinguish between *public* and *private sector* organisation;
- ☐ define and distinguish between *industry* and *commerce*;
- ☐ define and explain the difference between *primary*, *secondary* and *tertiary* industry.

1.1 What is business all about?

The question *'what is business all about?'* seems a logical starting point for a book on business. After all, it is a very complicated subject with many specialisms.

Around 75% of the working population of the United Kingdom are employed by businesses and earn their living from them. Everybody has an interest in the state of business as it affects their jobs, their incomes and their quality of life. Governments are constantly concerned with business and do all they can to stimulate a healthy business sector. There is a continual debate about all areas of business in homes, pubs, board-rooms and in the corridors of Government power. People talk about international trade, pollution, equal opportunities, fair pay and hundreds of other business-related topics. Can this complicated subject be distilled down to its essence? What *is* business all about?

The answer is that business is all about **money**!

In a modern industrial society, such as the United Kingdom, money is the currency by which all aspects of business are carried out, and it is needed at all stages in the business process. It is used in all sectors of business, and without it there would be no business at all. In less developed economies, business may rely in part on bartering and exchange of goods and services, but as money is the exclusive payment form in the developed world, we will confine our study to this area.

To broaden the issue a little, we might add that business is all about money and *trade*. Trade is the process by which money changes hands in exchange for goods and services. Businesses offer goods and services, usually for a relatively fixed price, and consumers pay money in order to enjoy the benefit of the offered goods and services.

Money takes a number of forms and is itself a subject of some debate. The study of money and the way in which money works in different situations is called *economics*, and the principles of economics underpin all aspects of business. We shall touch on this subject frequently in the course of this book.

1.2 The Basic Concepts of Business

As an introduction to the subject, we will benefit from considering a number of concepts that are used so frequently in business that it is usually assumed that everybody knows what they mean. The 'nuts and bolts' issues are best understood at the outset, and it is with this in mind that we shall consider them in turn.

1.2.1 Transactions

The transaction process begins when a seller is willing to sell a product and a buyer is willing to buy it. A shop on your local High Street displays goods because it is willing to sell them. If you go into the shop with an interest in one of the products, you are, potentially at least, willing to buy.

The seller has in mind a certain amount of money which he wants in exchange for the product. This is his opinion of its *value*. You, the buyer, have a notion of 'what it is worth to you' to possess the product.

Example   A local electrical retailer wishes to sell a video recorder. He wants to sell it for £300. You go into the shop with the intention of buying a video recorder. There are two possible scenarios.

1 You decide that to you, the video is only worth £150 (you don't want it that much). You offer the seller £150, and he declines your offer. You cannot agree on the value of the product and so no sale occurs.

2 You want the video and decide that you are prepared to pay up to £300 for it. The seller is asking £300 for the product. The two parties agree on the value of the video and so a sale occurs.

When a sale occurs after an agreement on value, it is referred to as a transaction. Business is based on transactions. Every time a purchase or a sale occurs, it signifies that buyer and seller have agreed on terms.

1.2.2 Price and cost

We all use these terms with great frequency, and they have generally understood meanings. Their usage in business is the same as in ordinary life.

A *price* is the amount of money the seller wants if he is to make a transaction with a buyer. Returning to our example above, the price of the video recorder is £300. The price becomes a *cost*, when you, the buyer, agree to pay the price. If you are the buyer, the video recorder will *cost* you the price of £300.

The terms are used in business in the following ways.

❏ A business will charge a price for the product or service it supplies. For example, a public house will charge a price of £1.40 for a pint of beer, a newsagent will charge 50p for a daily newspaper. Commodities such as chemicals will have a price of so much per tonne.

❏ The same business will have to pay for the goods that it sells. The pub will have to buy the beer it sells, and so will the newsagent. When it buys in these goods, the business will pay the price required, i.e. the cost to the business.
It follows that the business will attempt to maximise its price and reduce its costs.

1.2.3 Revenue

Revenue is sometimes referred to as turnover, sales or income. It refers to the total sales over a period of time (often a month or a year). We can express it as:

$$\text{Revenue} = \text{price} \times \text{quantity}$$

So the price charged multiplied by the number of units sold over a period of time is the total sales value, or revenue.

Example	A street trader is selling disposable cigarette lighters, at a price per item of 25p. He sells 146 on one particular day. The days revenue is £0.25 x 146 = £36.50.

1.2.4 Profit

Put simply, profit is the difference between the price charged for an item and the cost of the item to the seller.

$$\text{Profit} = \text{price} - \text{cost}$$

In business, profit is most frequently considered in terms of net or retained profit. This is the amount of money left over at the end of the financial year when everything has been paid for, including tax and interest payments.

$$\text{Net profit} = \text{revenue} - \text{total costs}$$

Profits, contrary to popular belief, are rarely used to 'line the pockets' of the owners of a business. They are used instead to reinvest in a business, to buy new machinery and to otherwise improve the future prospects of the business. In difficult times, retained profits from previous years are used to 'make good' losses until business improves.

1.2.5 Product or service

Businesses earn revenue by selling a product or service. Some organisations are seen as 'manufacturing sector' companies, whilst others are referred to as the 'service sector'. These distinctions are rather simplistic but are a useful starting point for thinking about these concepts.

A manufactured product is usually a good that is tangible and physical. It is something that can be seen and touched. Examples include consumer goods like cars and food, and also products like energy (gas and electricity) and large scale products like ships and aircraft.

A service is a special type of product in that it is not something that can be taken home and used. It can be considered as that which is *done* rather than that *is*. Examples include cleaning, laundry and car repairs and more commercial examples like auditing, health care and management consultancy.

The thing that a product or service have in common is that someone (the customer) is willing to pay in order to enjoy its benefit.

Activity 1	What do you think the products or services provided by the following organisations are?
	☐ Ford Motor Company ☐ Addenbrookes Hospital, Cambridge
	☐ Sketchley's Dry Cleaning ☐ The University of Northumbria at Newcastle
	☐ Barclays Bank ☐ Her Majesty's Prison, Strangeways

1.2.6 Capital

Capital is the money used by businesses to pay for plant, machinery, buildings etc. – those things that enable the company to begin doing business or to continue in business. Initially, capital is supplied by the owners of the business or through bank loans, but as the business develops, capital is provided by retaining profits that have been made as a result of successful trading. The *capital investment* in a business is the amount of money injected into it altogether and the size of a company is often measured by the capital investment.

The total worth of a business is defined by the amount of capital invested in the business.

Activity 2	*Understanding capital can be made easier when we consider our own personal wealth. Your own capital worth is made up of the value of all of the things you own. Make a list of all your main capital possessions, add up the values and that is your net capital asset worth. It might help to use the following format.*

> *Dwelling (=market value-value of mortgage)*
> *Car/Vehicle (=current value-value of any loans on it)*
> *Market price (current second-hand value) of*
> *   electrical equipment (TV, hi-fi etc.),*
> *   musical instruments,*
> *   computer,*
> *   books,*
> *Cash in bank (minus any debts or overdrafts)*
> *Investments (any shares you own)*
> *Other possessions*
>
> *Your total capital worth =*

1.3 Important Distinctions in Business

Business is a very wide field and embraces many sectors of work. Types of enterprise are divided up by a number of criteria, depending upon the purpose in mind. We will consider the most common ones.

1.3.1 Public and private sector

Put simply, public sector organisations are those which are part of the state (in all its forms) and are funded, at least in part, by the Government. It also implies that the Government has a high level of direct control over the organisation. They are called *public* because the Government is paid for and elected by the public and hence such organisations are accountable to the public. Good examples of public sector organisation are central Government, local authorities and Government departments like the Department of Health.

Private sector organisations are those over which the public have no direct influence. They are owned and controlled by private individuals or groups. This includes public and private limited companies and other forms of business organisations we shall encounter in Chapters 5, 6, and 7. For example, the local milkman, shops and pubs, manufacturing companies (e.g. British Aerospace, Ford) and accountancy practices are all in the private sector.

Activity 3   *If you are using this book as part of a course of study, it is likely that you are enrolled at a UK university or college. Is the educational establishment you are studying at in the private or public sector?*

1.3.2 Industry and commerce

These terms tend to be used together to describe that part of the economy that creates wealth. There is a difference between industry and commerce, but the dividing line can be blurred in many cases. Industry refers to enterprises that produce, convert, assemble or similarly modify materials that are then sold in a different form to that which they were originally in. So industries are concerned with a physical product, such as steel, cars, chemicals or food. Although this is the more usual meaning of industry, it is also sometimes used simply to mean 'business'. For example, people often refer to the tourism 'industry', meaning the tourism 'business'.

Commerce has become synonymous with what is sometimes called 'the service sector'. It does not produce a physical or tangible output, but is nevertheless a very large part of a modern economy such as the UK. Some areas of commerce deal with money (banking, accountants etc.) whilst others work with industry as advisors or consultants (architects, surveyors, management and recruitment consultants).

1.3.3 Primary, secondary, and tertiary sectors of industry

These terms are used to identify businesses according to the type of work they are involved with.

Primary industries are those that are concerned with the raw materials from which products are made. Included in this category are companies that are involved in mining, extraction, agriculture and fishing.

Secondary industries are those that take materials from the primary producers and *convert* them into products that are of use in themselves. Examples:

❑ motor manufacturers buy in sheet steel and make cars from it;

❑ companies that buy in oil products and produce plastic injection mouldings such as plastic computer cases.

In most manufacturing processes, there will be more than one level of secondary industry. See figure 1.1 for an example of this.

Tertiary industry is that part of the manufacturing route which is last to process the product before it gets to the end user. This may be retail shops or trade merchants, painters and decorators, motor mechanics (who fit parts to cars) or sub-contractors who carry out a whole range of tasks. Service organisations such as the education service, health, hotels and restaurants and the finance sector are also examples of tertiary industry.

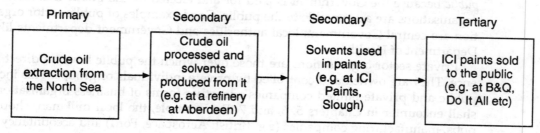

Figure 1.1: Primary, secondary and tertiary stages in a chemical process

Whilst most companies will be either primary, secondary or tertiary, it is possible for some companies to span all three levels. These are usually very large companies. A good example of this is British Gas Plc. It extracts gas, processes it and sells it directly to the end user – you and me. It will even sell you the fire or cooker through which to use the gas. British Gas is an example of what is called a 'deep' organisation. Other examples include most petrochemical companies such as British Petroleum Plc.

Review Questions

1. What is business all about? (1.1)
2. What is a transaction? (1.2.1)
3. What is a price and a cost? (1.2.2)
4. Define revenue (including a simple equation) (1.2.3)
5. Define profit (including a simple equation) (1.2.4)
6. What is a product or service? (1.2.5)
7. What is capital? (1.2.6)
8. Define and distinguish between *public* and *private* sector organisation. (1.3.1)
9. Define and distinguish between *industry* and *commerce*. (1.3.2)
10. Define the terms *primary*, *secondary* and *tertiary* as applied to industries. (1.3.3)
11. Explain what is meant by 'depth' in regard to a company. (1.3.3)

Answers to activities

Activity 1

Name of Company	Goods or Services	Product Offered
Ford Motors Co.	Goods	Motor cars, commercial vehicles, parts for vehicles.
Sketchley's	Service	Cleaning and conditioning of garments.
Barclays Bank	Service	Banking and financial services.
Addenbrookes	Service	Medical, surgical and other clinical and health services.
University	Service	Education, training, development, consultancy.
Prison	Service	Secure accommodation of offenders.

Activity 2

Here is a worked example of the capital 'calculation' for a real student at The University of Salford as at March 31, 1994.

Capital item	Current saleable value (£)
Dwelling	None
Vehicle (motorcycle)	400
Clothes	30
Jewellery	10
Guitar	300
TV	35
Hi-fi	100
Books	60
Computer	40
Cash in bank	200
Minus overdraft	(300)
Minus long term loan to relative	(250)
Total capital worth	**625**

For further thought

1. Next time you make a transaction, even if it is something as small as buying a packet of chewing gum, mentally go through the stages mentioned in 1.2.1. Consider that the shop is offering the product for a certain price, and observe that you agree with his estimation of its value when you part with your payment.

2. For most retailers, their 'mark up' is between 30% and 50%. This means that if you buy a product for a price of £1, the cost to the retailer of that item will be between 50p for a 50% mark-up and 70p for a 30% mark-up. Next time you buy a pint of beer or another common product, calculate the cost to the retailer for that product if the mark up is 30% and then 50%.

3. A paint company in the North of England had an annual turnover of £3.2 million. During the year, it sold 2 million litres of paint. Using the equation in 1.2.3, calculate the average price per litre of its paint.

4. Using the calculation you made in Activity 2, suggest ways in which you could increase your capital worth.

5. Find out whether the following organisations are in the public or private sector:

    Imperial Chemical Industries Plc (ICI)
    British Telecommunications Plc (BT)
    British Nuclear Fuels Limited (BNFL)
    The Department of Trade and Industry (DTI)
    British Rail (BR)
    Glasgow City Council
    Nuclear Electric Plc

6. Say whether the following organisations fit best into the primary, secondary or tertiary sector of industry.

    British Coal
    Kentucky Fried Chicken
    Imperial Chemical Industries Plc

2 The objectives of business

Objectives   After studying this chapter, students should be able to:

- ☐ define the term *stakeholders*;
- ☐ list the principal stakeholders in a business organisation;
- ☐ briefly describe the connection between stakeholders and business objectives;
- ☐ explain what is the most important objective of any business;
- ☐ describe the major purposes of a mission statement;
- ☐ describe the typical broad components of a mission statement.

Ordinary business are often referred to as 'for profit' businesses as (it is assumed) they exist to make profits. Profits, after all, are what keeps the business afloat from one year to the next and profit provides the necessary capital for investment and expansion. But is it the case that such businesses exist *only* for profit? This chapter discusses the objectives that a business has, which, we will see are wider than simply making a profit.

2.1 Stakeholders

The starting point in this discussion is to look at the question 'who does the business have to please?'. Or, more formally, it can be expressed as 'who are the *stakeholders* in the business?'. A stakeholder can be defined as:

> *any person or party who has an interest in the business, however tenuous that interest might be.*

So what type of persons or parties are stakeholders? Below is list of common stakeholders.

- ☐ customers
- ☐ employees
- ☐ shareholders
- ☐ trade unions
- ☐ management
- ☐ neighbours
- ☐ pressure groups
- ☐ suppliers
- ☐ auditors
- ☐ local authorities
- ☐ banks
- ☐ other lenders

- ❑ other local businesses (e.g. pubs, newsagents, housebuilders)
- ❑ regulatory authorities and QuANGOs (e.g. the Monopolies and Mergers Commission, etc. See Chapters 12 and 25)
- ❑ Government departments, e.g.

  Department of Trade and Industry
  Inland Revenue
  Department of the Environment
  Department of Employment
  Department for Education etc.

If it was simply the case that a company had to please its shareholders, then profit might well be its only objective. As it is, the business wishes to (or must) please many parties, and this shapes its objectives.

Activity 1	*Using the above definition of a stakeholder, apply it to yourself. Which people or groups have a stake (however tenuous) in **you**?*

2.2 The Prime Objective

Most of the stakeholders have one objective for the business over which there is rarely dispute, and that is *to survive*. This is consequently the most important aim of every business. This becomes paramount when the business endures difficult economic conditions such as in a recession. If there is no business there then:

- ❑ employees and management have no job;
- ❑ the Government gets no tax from the profits;
- ❑ customers must look elsewhere for their needs;
- ❑ suppliers lose a customer;
- ❑ local authorities lose local tax (council tax) and have a weakened employment base in their area of responsibility;
- ❑ trade unions lose members;
- ❑ shareholders lose their investment.

2.3 Other Objectives

Given that the first objective is to survive, there is much debate over other aims. The objectives that an organisation has will depend on who its stakeholders are. If the stakeholders are principally seeking a return on investment, then it is likely that profits will be an important objective. If, however, stakeholders are more concerned to benefit from value for money and to receive a service, then the objectives are likely to be very different from profit. The order of priority will depend on the relative strengths of the various stakeholders and will vary with economic conditions. Some objectives will be measurable, either financially or with some other numerical measure. Others will be more qualitative, social or environmental.

Examples of measurable/quantitative objectives

make profits

maintain a certain share price

maintain a certain level of investment

achieve a certain level of turnover

increase sales by so much year on year

achieve or maintain key accounting ratios (e.g. profit margin return on capital employed etc. See Chapter 18)

reduce toxic emissions by 3% per year for the next 5 years

reduce employees by a certain amount

begin a new product line

discontinue a product line

increase market share by a certain amount

establish a respected quality standard in the organisation (e.g. 'TQM' or ISO 9000).

Examples of qualitative objectives

be a 'good neighbour'

provide a good product or service

be seen as a 'good employer'

cultivate an image as a quality supplier

maintain good industrial relations

increase reputation as a good 'environmental player'

be a 'leading' supplier in the industrial sector in which the company operates

maintain a commitment to research and development.

Activity 2   *Examine your own personal and career objectives. Which of these are qualitative and which can be measured? Identify any connection between the objectives and the stakeholders you identified in Activity 1.*

2.4 Mission Statements

Some organisations express their objectives in the form of a statement. The term *mission statement* is used to describe this, as the mission is that which not only defines the broad objectives, but also the business the organisation intends to engage in.

Mission statements are meant to present a potted outline of an organisation's objectives. The way in which they are written is designed to communicate these objectives in a way that ordinary people can understand. This necessarily means that mission statements are general and can be rather vague. Rather than expressing specific financial objectives, they cover such things as:

❐ the market or business that the organisation is in,

❐ a realistic target market share/position that the organisation wishes to occupy,

☐ an indication/summary of the values and beliefs that the organisation feels it needs to adopt,

☐ specific and context – dependent objectives which are applicable to the organisation in question.

The purposes of a mission statement can be summarised as follows:

☐ To explain the essential purposes of an organisation to the various interested parties. These can include existing and potential employees, customers, investors, and other stakeholders.

☐ To achieve a common purpose in the actions of the various parts of the organisation.

☐ To influence actions and attitudes throughout all levels of the organisation.

☐ To provide cohesion (sticking together) and conformity.

☐ To influence and form the desired corporate culture.

A Mission Statement in Action: **Nissan Motor Manufacturing (UK) Limited**

Nissan's £900 million investment in its Sunderland plant in Tyne and Wear represented a significant expansion of the company's European business. As a 'greenfield' development and not a take-over of an existing business, it followed that all employees would be new. The stated goal from the outset was to introduce innovative new working practices into the British operation. The mission statement was well publicised and intended to summarise all of the key objectives and values of the organisation.

Nissan refers to its mission statement as **'Our Company's Philosophy'**. It reads as follows:

Nissan Motor Manufacturing (UK) Limited

As a Company, we aim to build profitably the highest quality car sold in Europe. We want to achieve the maximum possible customer satisfaction and ensure the prosperity of the Company and its staff.

To assist in this, we aim to achieve mutual trust and co-operation between all people within the Company and make NMUK a place where long-term job satisfaction can be achieved. We recognise that people are our most valued resource, and in line with this spirit believe that the following principles will be of value to all.

People

☐ We will develop and expand the contributions of all staff by strongly emphasising training and by the expansion of everyone's capabilities.

☐ We seek to delegate and involve staff in discussion and decision making, particularly in those areas in which each of us can effectively contribute so that all may participate in the efficient running of NMUK.

☐ We firmly believe in common terms and conditions of employment.

Teamworking

☐ We recognise that all staff have a valued contribution to make as individuals, but in addition believe that this contribution can be most effective within a teamworking environment.

Communication

☐ Within the bounds of commercial confidentiality we will encourage open channels of communication. We would like everyone to know what is happening in our company, how we are performing and what we plan.

☐ We want information and views to flow freely upward, downward and across our Company.

Objectives

☐ We will agree clear and achievable objectives and provide meaningful feedback on performance.

Flexibility

☐ We will not be restricted by the existing way of doing things. We will continuously seek improvements in all our actions.

These are tough targets and we aim high. With hard work and goodwill we can get there.

The statement is signed by Ian Gibson C.B.E., Managing Director and Chief Executive, Nissan's Sunderland plants.

(Reproduced with kind permission, Nissan.)

Mission statements vary greatly in length and complexity. The example of Nissan is one of the longest and most detailed. Others are shorter, more general, and arguably more 'punchy'.

Activity 3 *Find out if the college or university you are studying at has a mission statement. If it has, try to obtain a copy and identify the key phrases that inform the reader about its objectives.*

Shorter Mission Statements

1 British Telecommunications Plc

BT divides its mission statement into two parts. The first part is its Vision and the second, its Mission.

Vision

☐ to become the most successful worldwide telecommunications group.

Mission

☐ to provide world class telecommunications and information products and services,

☐ to develop and exploit our networks at home and overseas, so that we can...

☐ meet the requirements of our customers,

☐ sustain growth in the earnings of the group on behalf of our shareholders,

☐ make a fitting contribution to the community in which we conduct our business.

(Reproduced with the permission of British Telecommunications Plc)

2 Derwent Valley Foods Group Limited

Derwent Valley has been one of the major growth companies in the snack foods sector with both its 'own brand' products for some supermarket chains, and the Phileas Fogg brand of 'adult' snack foods. Its above industry-average growth and innovative marketing has made it a much studied company by business students and analysts alike. Its simple mission statement is:

> We will become the best UK adult snack company through dedication to quality, the bold use of new ideas, and the determination to succeed.
>
> As we strive to achieve this goal, it is important that we maintain an environment of friendship, co-operation and respect.

(Reproduced with kind permission: Derwent Valley Food Group Limited)

Review Questions

1. What is a business stakeholder? (2.1)
2. List some general types of stakeholder. (2.1)
3. What is the most important objective of a business? (2.2)
4. Define and distinguish between qualitative and quantitative objectives. (2.3)
5. Describe some of the purposes of having a mission statement. (2.4)
6. What are the typical components of a mission statement? (2.4)

Answers to Activity 1

Your list of stakeholders will be unique to yourself. It may include some of the following:

- □ your employer,
- □ family (parents, grandparents, spouse, siblings, progeny),
- □ friends,
- □ role-models (e.g. philosophers, religious leaders, actors or pop musicians, authors etc.),
- □ teachers and lecturers,
- □ your local authority (if they are paying your grant),
- □ bank manager,
- □ flatmates,
- □ nextdoor neighbours,
- □ clubs and societies you belong to,
- □ football team you support.

Assignment

Question 1

Consider two very different organisations, such as your local authority and a large British multinational company like Hanson Plc or ICI Plc. In what ways will their objectives be similar and in what ways will the business organisation differ from the local authority?

Question 2

Choose an organisation from the following list and answer the questions below.

> Guinness Plc
> Abbey National Plc
> ICI Plc
> British Gas Plc
> Sellafield Nuclear Reprocessing Plant, Whitehaven, Cumbria.

Questions

1. What is the business of the organisation you have chosen?
2. Bearing in mind the business, location and other features of the organisation, construct what you consider to be a thorough list of stakeholders in the business.
3. Which of the stakeholders you have identified do you consider to be the most influential (there may be more than one powerful stakeholder).
4. Use your list of stakeholders to suggest what objectives the organisation might have.

Sources

You may find the following sources helpful in completing this assignment:

❑ the annual accounts of the company,

❑ public relations literature that the organisation publishes.

These can be obtained either from your local business library or you could write directly to the organisation.

3 The location of a business

Objectives   After studying this chapter, students should be able to:

☐ describe the principal factors that determine where a business is located,

☐ comment on the relative significance of these factors for some types of industry.

3.1 Factors that Determine Business Location

The physical location of a business is very important. Some business organisations are located in rural areas whilst others are based in the City of London or other town centres. The question 'where shall our business be located?' is of immense significance.

There are many factors that determine business location. The degrees of influence that each factor has will vary from business to business and from industry to industry. The most important factors in business location are shown in figure 3.1.

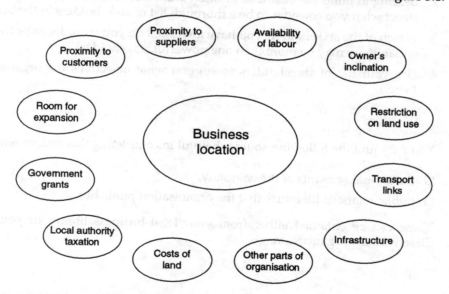

Figure 3.1: factors that determine business location.

3.1.1 Proximity to customers

Because the customers supply the business with its income, it is important that they have access to the company's products with the minimum of inconvenience. Businesses which have regular and frequent contact with customers find this factor particularly important. Generally speaking, this will be the most significant factor where customers buy little and often from the business. The costs of transporting goods to the customers' premises can make a significant difference to product pricing and the time taken to transport goods are issues very much linked to how near a business is from its customers. Two relevant examples follow.

Retail location

For retail outlets (shops), this factor is paramount. It has been said that there are three important aspects of retailing: location, location ad location. Whilst this is an obvious simplification, it underlines the importance of this factor. There are two aspects of location to customers that are relevant to retail outlets.

The first is the *demographic profile* of the customers in the geographical area of the shop. We shall see in Chapter 21 and 22 (marketing function) that markets are segmented according to what are referred to as *demographic variables*, such as social class, level of education and the stage of family life cycle. One need look no further than the main high street stores to see that they are located where the target profile group are in high concentration. Shops like Marks and Spencer would usually seek a location where a high concentration of quality conscious people have easy access to the shop. In contrast, the 'cash-only' chains like Aldi, Kwik Save and Netto are usually located out of town centres in suburbs predominantly populated by individuals and families who are principally concerned with value for money and price.

The second aspect of retail location is the *volume of traffic* that will regularly pass the shop. Traffic, in this context, does not mean cars and buses, but the number of individuals in the target market segment who will pass the shop frequently or who will find the shop convenient to get to. Retail outlets are concerned about location to the point where they will seek particular premises on a given street, and will decline to occupy a similar property on the same street because traffic volume is too low.

JIT supply

We shall learn about the JIT (Just In Time) manufacturing philosophy in chapter 20. One feature of JIT is that materials must be supplied to the customer at very short notice and often in relatively small quantities. For this reason, suppliers, particularly those who supply the majority of their output to one big customer, often set up close to the customer. When the large Nissan development (see section 3.2.4) began in Tyne and Wear in the early nineteen eighties, the JIT operation at Nissan demanded frequent supply of car components. Many suppliers located new plants close to the Nissan plant and one supplier even installed an internal rail linkage to the Nissan plant over the short distance to the car production line.

3.1.2 Proximity to suppliers (and other inputs)

Proximity to suppliers is the converse of the issue of proximity to customers. This is of especial significance when the materials bought from suppliers are expensive (or inconvenient) to transport or where supplies need to be gained at very short notice. For example, oil and gas refineries tend to be on the coast at the point where the pipelines come in. This is because the methods of transporting such materials from their source are very expensive. The same is true of fish processors but for different reasons, i.e. that fresh fish are perishable and must be cleaned as early as possible.

Proximity to customers and suppliers – summary

Proximity to **customers** will be most important when:

- customers buy little and often;
- a single customer (or small group of customers) buy a large proportion of output;
- the business needs personal contact with its customers;
- goods sold are perishable or expensive to transport;
- the major customers operate a low stock manufacturing policy (e.g. JIT).

Proximity to **suppliers** will be most important when:

- the organisation has a large requirement for material inputs;
- the organisation buys little and often;
- material inputs are bulky or expensive to transport;
- there are few choices of suppliers;
- a supplier (or group of local suppliers) supplies a large proportion of material input;
- goods inputs are perishable;
- the organisation uses a low stock manufacturing policy (e.g. JIT).

3.1.3 The location of other parts of the organisation.

This factor, whilst usually less important than the first two factors mentioned above, is a consideration for some types of enterprise. It is sometimes convenient for different parts of an organisation to be located within close proximity to one another, particularly if:

- ❏ a high degree of personal contact needs to occur between sections;
- ❏ one part of the organisation has spare capacity (e.g. land) on its site that would be cheaper to occupy than to build a new plant elsewhere;
- ❏ it would be of commercial advantage to be located in close proximity (e.g. so that customers can use more than one part of the organisation in one visit);
- ❏ when transport costs could be reduced by the location (e.g. distribution points may be located near to the manufacturing plant to avoid transport costs).

A good example of an organisation which is geographically concentrated is central government, which is largely located in and around Whitehall and Westminster. In recent years however, the various government departments have become more decentralised to other London locations (e.g. Canary Wharf) and out to the regional cities.

3.1.4 Availability of appropriate labour

All organisations need people, but labour requirements, both in terms of numbers and types varies enormously. Some companies, such as shipbuilders, require large numbers of skilled and semi-skilled trades people whereas others, such as a multinational corporation's head office may require accountants, clerical people and business managers. It is appropriate therefore that such businesses locate in an area that will provide the maximum possible supplies of the kind of labour they need. It would make little sense for an organisation with very large labour requirements to be located in the highlands of Scotland where population is of a very low density. The author knows of one chemical organisation in the rural North West of England who always have to relocate their management in from other regions -owing to the lack of local supply of key management personnel. This factor can sometimes work in reverse in that employers can attract people into a region.

3.1.5 Access to transport links and infrastructure

Manufacturing companies all have some need to transport materials, either as purchased parts inwards or finished goods outwards (or usually both). It would make sense therefore for a business who uses a lot of road freight to be within easy reach of the motorway network. There has been much development over recent years of business parks by local authorities in an attempt to attract new employers into their regions and one key location feature of such parks has been their accessibility from major trunk routes. Business park development often includes the improvement of roads from the business park location to the nearest motorway or main A road.

For industries like ship-building and power generation the key locating factor in this regard is to be near to a waterway. This may be for the docking of inputs such as sheet steel or coal or for the use of the water itself for use in the power generation process or for the launching of ships (it would be difficult to move a completed ship overland). Rail terminals are another key transport link which can be a factor to a business when deciding on its best location.

3.1.6 Access to other infrastructure

Other infrastructure includes reliable energy supplies (and in sufficient amount), such as gas, electricity or coal. Those companies who use complex telecommunications technology will also wish to be assured that they can access what they need from their chosen site. Some areas of the UK do not receive connection to gas and some telecommunications services. Such drawbacks would act as a disincentive for some organisations.

3.1.7 Costs of land

The costs of land, both to buy and rent varies greatly across the UK. It has traditionally been the case that land is more expensive in the South East than in say, the North East. Such disparities tend to be purely a function of the demand for land outstripping supply in the South East whilst the converse is the case in other parts of the country. DTI grants are available to assist in land purchase in assisted areas and this can affect its cost to the business by around 15% (see section 3.1.9).

Businesses who require a lot of land but who do not need to be located in an expensive area are unlikely to be so.

3.1.8 Local authority taxation

The amount of council tax charged by local authorities also varies across the country. High local taxation will deter possible businesses but some local authorities are prepared to offer discounts in an attempt to attract employers to the area. Local authorities have a conflict of interest when it comes to setting their tax charges. On one hand, more revenue can be raised if taxes are increased whereas low tax may attract new investment into the region.

3.1.9 Availability of government grants

The Government are keen to encourage investment in certain areas of the country. Part of the Government's strategy to reverse unemployment and to encourage regional regeneration is to offer grants to attract new and expanding businesses to set up in these areas. For the purposes of these grants, the Department of Trade and Industry (DTI – a government department) identifies certain regions of the country as *assisted areas*. These fall into three broad categories.

❑ Development areas (DAs)

❑ Intermediate areas (IA – IAs offer different types of assistance to DAs)

❑ Northern Ireland (seen as a special case due to its singular problems in attracting businesses to relocate into the region)

We can see from the map in figure 3.2 that the majority of assisted areas are in the North of the country and most centre around the major conurbations (such as Tyneside, Clydeside, Merseyside, West Midlands, etc.). In addition, the DTI offers to assist outlying regions such as parts of Cornwall, Wales and northern Scotland, which, due to their remoteness from the major cities, have suffered a lack of development and some deindustrialisation over recent years. Former coal-mining regions and other former 'heavy industry' areas are also included.

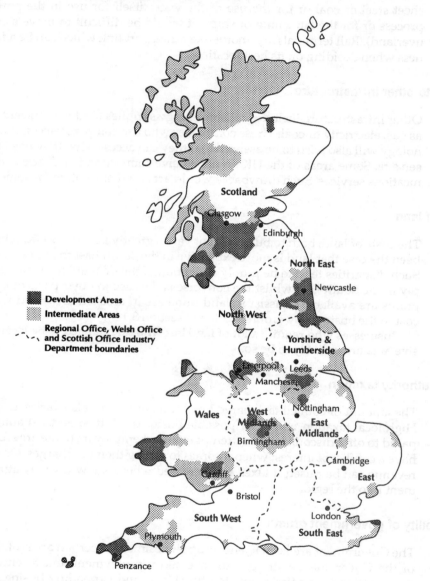

Figure 3.2: *Assisted areas from August 1993*
(Source: Department of Trade and Industry, 1993, Crown copyright. Reproduced with permission of GO-NE)

The number of grants available and their values (in money terms) change from time to time. The two main schemes currently in existence which seek to help businesses with the capital costs of starting up or expanding are:

1. **Regional enterprise grant** – available to small businesses (employment less than 25 on a group, world-wide basis at the time of application). Grant is at a fixed rate of 15% of acceptable costs up to £15,000 maximum grant.

2.   **Regional selective assistance** – open-ended in terms of business size but is not a fixed rate grant system – the level of the grant is negotiable, but is set at the minimum public sector assistance seen to be required to enable the project to proceed.

Both grant schemes are aimed mainly at manufacturing sectors of industry (together with some "industrial support" service sectors) and are of a discretionary nature. However, there are simplified procedures for Regional Enterprise Grant and for small (up to £25,000 grant) applications for Regional Selective Assistance.

Projects must be located in assisted areas to be eligible for consideration: Regional Enterprise Grant mainly in DAs; and Regional Selective Assistance in DAs and IAs. In addition, there may be some assistance to businesses who have projects to develop new products or processes.

3.1.10 Restrictions on land use

Both the Government and local authorities impose restrictions on the uses of land. This can vary from a 'greenbelt' around a town where planning permission for new building is greatly restricted to 'nuclear free zones' which do not allow industries who use nuclear technology in their processes. Other land issues concern the quality of land and its drainage, risk of subsidence etc. For horticultural and farming businesses, this factor will clearly assume special significance.

3.1.11 Personal inclinations of the owners

It is common for small to medium sized businesses to be located in the area where the owners are settled. Moving to a new area for the purposes of setting up a new business can be traumatic for the owners and their families and this 'human factor' is a very powerful one. Family businesses are invariably located near to the extended family home.

The sense behind locating locally need not just be subjective and 'sentimental'. It is often the case that owners have built up a number of key personal contacts in the locality which the business can use to the full if it remains in the region.

3.1.12 Room for expansion

One of the most compelling reasons for locating 'out of town' rather than in a town or city is that it is likely that there will be more room to build onto the existing premises. Additionally, some local authorities will be more willing to grant permission for such developments than others. We shall see later that for both Derwent Valley Foods Ltd and for Nissan, this factor was a very important one when considering possibilities for location.

3.2 Examples

Perhaps the best way to understand how the various factors vary in importance from business to business is to consider some examples.

3.2.1 Derwent Valley Foods Limited – Consett, Co. Durham

Derwent Valley Foods Ltd (DVF) began operating as an independent company in 1982 in Consett, a medium sized town not far from Durham city on the edge of the northern Pennines. The company was founded by four individuals who were experienced in the snack food industry, all of whom were already based in the North East region. Consett was renowned until 1979 as a steel town where the large British Steel plant employed a sizeable proportion of the towns workforce. The steel plant closed down in 1979 with the inevitable consequence of a large increase in unemployment and hence a large availability of labour to other local employers. In the late eighties, DVF increased the size of its operation in Consett by building a new 'greenfield' factory, thus further underlining its satisfaction with their initial choice of location. In a letter to the author, John Pike, one of the founding Directors who is still with the company, commented as follows:

> "You asked why we chose Consett. There were a number of reasons. Given that we were unprepared (nor in truth would any great advantage have been gained) to move house, we reviewed a number of locations within the North East which carried maximum grant support. Consett offered a suitable rent-free factory as well as space to expand. The support from DIDA (Derwentside Industrial Development Agency – then run at British Steel Corporation's cost) was a significant factor. There was a council and a town happy to welcome us who could provide the labour we required."

(Source: Derwent Valley Foods Limited – with kind permission)

Question 1   *From Mr Pike's comments above, attempt to 'rank' DVF's motivations for setting up at Consett. Which of the factors that Mr Pike mentioned do you think was the most important, which second and so on?*

3.2.2 Dewhirst Group Plc – Peterlee, Co. Durham

The Dewhirst Group is a manufacturer of a wide range of clothes including all types of men's, ladies and children's wear. It is a major supplier to Marks and Spencer. With its head office in Tunstall, near Stoke, Dewhirst has a group turnover of in excess of £180 million and it has manufacturing sites at over 20 locations throughout the country. The group employs around 6000 people.

Clothing manufacture involves individuals cutting materials whilst others use sewing machines to join the segments together. In the volumes that Dewhirst makes, there is a requirement for large numbers of semi-skilled labour. The location of its plants takes this labour requirement into account in tandem with the local transport infrastructure. It supplies retail outlets throughout the country and it follows that major transport routes must be easily accessible.

In 1964, the company opened a factory in Peterlee, Co. Durham to manufacture menswear items. Peterlee proved to be a most suitable location. This was for two reasons.

1. It provided a relatively plentiful supply of the key labour input. The company has found that women are the most suitable type of employee to perform repetitive cutting and sewing tasks. In consequence, the 'shop floor' at Dewhirst's Peterlee plant consists of around 700 women sitting behind sewing machines carrying-out relatively repetitive tasks. Peterlee, as a former coal mining region has a high concentration of semi-skilled manual labour of both sexes and this has worked to the advantage of the company.

2. Dewhirst buys rolls of woven fabric and other inputs which arrive by road and the finished articles leave by the same route. The factory is within a mile of the A19 trunk road which connects to the A1 via the A66 near Middlesbrough.

In consequence, the location of the Dewhirst factory relies not just on the good transport links, but also on ensuring an ongoing and reliable supply of women who are prepared to engage in repetitive machining work.

(Source: Dewhirst Group Plc)

3.2.3 Cray Valley Limited – Machen, South Wales

Cray Valley are one of the UK's major manufacturers of resins for the paint and fibreglass industries with several sites in key locations throughout Europe. When the company was sold to the multinational petrochemicals group Total in 1991, Cray Valley Ltd operated from three sites in the UK. The two manufacturing sites were located at Machen (pronounced *Maken*, to rhyme with *bracken*) in South Wales, where resins were produced for surface coatings, and at Stallingborough, South Humberside, where the company made polyester resins for fibreglass applications. The third site was at Farnborough in Kent where the company's administration and research and development was based. The Total take-over signalled a major review of the Cray Valley operation, including the use of the separate sites.

A re-structuring study by Total indicated that efficiency gains could be made in the UK operation. In 1991, a decision was taken to close the Farnborough site and move the accounts and R&D departments to Machen. Staff at Farnborough were offered transfers to Machen and a high proportion of the key intellectual staff (chemists, accountants etc.) accepted the move. The other staff were offered generous redundancy terms. The company describe the reasons for the move as including the following:

❑ as an assisted area, South Wales offered to possibility of grants to help with capital investment;

❑ staff costs were cheaper in Machen (i.e. staff could be retained for the same jobs at lower cost to the company);

❑ local authority taxation was lower;

❑ the Machen site offered almost limitless room to expand (which was certainly not the case in Farnborough – an area of relatively high population density).

❑ the technical (R&D) function could be nearer to the production site which would allow more technical supervision of operations, and chemists could be quickly in the factory to remedy any problems;

❑ the concentration of a higher proportion of the UK staff at one site meant that communications would be cheaper and in some cases, quicker.

The move was completed in 1992 and the Farnborough site was sold in 1994. The Machen site was enlarged to accommodate the functions which were previously located at Farnborough.

(Source: Cray Valley Limited)

Question 2   *Can you think of any other reasons why chemical manufacturers like Cray Valley might wish to be located in such regions as South Wales?*

3.2.4 Nissan Motor Manufacturing (UK) Ltd – Sunderland, Tyne and Wear

The story of the Nissan manufacturing site in the UK began in February 1984 when the Nissan company signed an agreement with the government to build a car plant in the UK. In March of the same year, the company announced the location for the investment – a large 'greenfield' site on the A19 trunk road, between the towns of Washington and Sunderland in Tyne and Wear. Construction began in July 1984 and the first car, the Nissan Bluebird, rolled off the production line in July 1986 (which was, incidentally, presented to His Royal Highness the Prince of Wales). Since then, the site has been developed further and a number of key suppliers have set up their premises adjacent to the Nissan plant. As at December 1993, the Nissan plant directly employed 4250, almost all of whom were local people.

The company describes its reasons for choosing the Sunderland site as follows:

1. The site is situated on what was once the old Sunderland Airfield, giving a large expanse of flat land allowing new buildings to be built easily and quickly. This is essential for a company that is rapidly expanding.

2. The site offers an excellent road infra-structure with the A19 and access to the A1 nearby.

3. The close proximity of a deep water port at Teesport. [Nissan have since changed their export port to the nearer River Tyne]

4. The area is well known for its engineering background and the excellence of its engineering colleges.

5. The very positive attitude of the local people and trade unions.

6. The existence of an enterprise zone. This was not, however, an overwhelming factor as grants only existed for one hundred million pounds on what has become close to a one billion pound investment by Nissan.

(Source: Nissan – reproduced with kind permission)

Question 3   *Attempt to prioritise the location factors that we discussed in 3.1 as far as Nissan is concerned. Which do you think was the most important factor, which second and so on?*

Review Questions

1. When would proximity to customers be a key determinant of business location? (3.1.1)

2. What are the two important factors that a retail organisation would consider when establishing an outlet? (3.1.1)

3. Why is it common for JIT manufacturing companies to be located near to customers or suppliers (3.1.1 and 3.1.2)

4. When might an organisation wish to set up a new plant near to other parts of the organisation? (3.1.3)

5. What are the major types of transport links that may be of importance to a business when considering its location? (3.1.5)

6. What is the difference between an assisted and a non-assisted area? (3.1.9)

7. Why has the government identified some regions as assisted areas and not others? (3.1.9)

8. What are the three types of assisted area? (3.1.9)

9. What is the difference between a discretionary and an enterprise grant? (3.1.9)

Answers to questions

Question 1: DVF

There are several possible locations in the North East which have a ready supply of labour with room to expand. It is therefore unlikely that this was their main motivation in choosing Consett. Mr Pike mentioned that they reviewed several sites which carried maximum grant support, so it is equally unlikely that this was the single deciding factor. The DIDA may have offered additional funds as well as the government grants and if so, these would have been unique to Consett. All of the founding directors live in the general region of the Derwentside area. Although this is not to be seen as a definitive answer, the author's opinion is as follows:

1. Grant support including DIDA grants,

2. Personal wishes of the founders to work near to their homes,

3. Plentiful supply of skilled and semi-skilled labour,

4. Room to expand.

Question 2: Cray Valley

Chemical manufacture often involves sites which are relatively spacious. This is one reason why the chemical industry tends to be concentrated in the North of England, in areas like South Wales, and in rural areas around the major regional cities, where land is cheaper then the South East. In addition, some sections of the public are suspicious of chemical companies, fearing that they may contribute towards the pollution of the environment. This is another contributing factor behind the location of chemical companies away from major population centres (of course, most chemical companies would argue strongly that they do not pollute the environment).

Question 3: Nissan

Although the company says that the availability of grants was not a major factor in its choice of location, it is unlikely that they would have entertained the thought of setting up in a non-assisted area. Given this though, they had many possible choices which would have offered such grant support. The question thus becomes: which assisted area offering grant support is the most suitable? The company say that the North East offered a work-force with a strong engineering background with an academic community which is capable of providing an on-going supply of skilled and semi-skilled engineers and operatives. This may have been the key determinant for the North East. The Washington site was thus a suitable location within the chosen region, which offered the large flat site, and a pool of potential employees within convenient commuting distance of the site.

The author's suggested (and tentative) list in order of priority is as follows. Students should understand that other answers may be equally correct.

1. availability of grant support,

2. room to expand,

3. access to transport infra-structure,

4. availability of appropriate labour,

5. access to other infra-structure (a suitable port for the export of cars).

Assignment

Question 1

Which would be the most important factors in the location of the following organisations?

☐ a coal mine

☐ a retail outlet of Burger King

☐ a tractor rental company

☐ a pub

☐ a road haulage company

Question 2

Choose an manufacturing, service or retail organisation within three miles of the University or college where you are studying. In a group, make an appointment to visit one of the senior managers in the organisation (for example the Company Secretary). Find out the answers to the following enquiries.

☐ The type of products or services they supply.

☐ The location of their major suppliers of materials (if appropriate).

☐ The location of their customers.

☐ The types of labour they employ.

☐ The number of people they employ.

☐ If the organisation is relatively new to the site, the type and size of grants that were available to them.

☐ Their requirements for transport and other infrastructure (e.g. energy, telecommunications).

☐ Any other factors that are relevant, such as being close to waterways etc.

Considering the type of organisation it is, rank the factors in order of significance as determinants of the organisation's location.

Further Reading

Beardshaw J & Palfreman D, *The Organisation in its Environment*, Pitman Press (Fourth Edition, 1992, Pages 179, 186, 180–186)

Section 2

Business Organisations

Essential to an understanding of business is an appreciation of the basics of organisational theory, and an awareness of the different types of organisation that exist.

In this section the various legal forms of organisation are discussed, with the key distinctions being made between incorporated and non-incorporated organisations, and 'for profit' and "not-for profit' organisations. Examples are used to illustrate the principles discussed in the text.

Contents   **Page**

4 General characteristics of organisations

Objectives   After studying this chapter, students should be able to:

☐ define what an organisation is;

☐ list the principal reasons why organisations exist;

☐ explain how organisations differ;

☐ describe the features that all organisations have in common.

4.1 What is an Organisation?

Buchanan and Huczynski's (1985) definition of an organisation is as follows:

> 'Organisations are social arrangements for the controlled performance of collective goals.'   (*Organisational Behaviour – An Introductory Text*)

We can see from this definition that there is an emphasis on both *performance* and the notion of collective *goals*.

There are certain things that all organisations have in common; distinctive features which separate them from 'groups'. Broadly speaking, we can describe several defining features of an organisation:

☐ All organisations involve *people performing* a role. Each member has a part to play, in collaboration with other members, to help the organisation achieve its objectives. This means that membership of an organisation does not rely on 'being' or 'joining' (such as in a family), but on 'doing' or 'performing'.

☐ The members of the organisation have *common purposes or goals*. The reason for members arriving at this common purpose may simply be that the organisation that pays their salary has a certain set of objectives which they agree with in order to get paid! Some organisations, such as charities or 'self help groups', will tend to have a common purpose arising more from the personal persuasions or needs of the members. Objectives may be anything from preserving hedgehogs to preserving national security and may vary from the overt, the urgent and the immediate, to the vague, the unstated and the nebulous.

☐ Within the organisation there are *divided responsibilities and roles*, and a *division of labour*. This means that different members are responsible for different parts of the organisation's functioning. This can clearly be illustrated by examining the internal structure of any typical limited company where there are different departments, each containing management and subordinate employees. The same point can also be demonstrated by looking at a less formal organisation such as a social club. Within a social club, there will be a number of ordinary members, but usually, there will also be a committee comprising such officers as Membership Secretary, Entertainments Secretary, Administrative Officer, Treasurer, Licensing Manager,

Chairman and Deputy Chairman. Each member of the committee will have different but clearly defined responsibilities depending upon his or her abilities or job remit. We see here a delineation of responsibilities designed to ensure that all the necessary work gets done, and that tasks are shared out fairly among the active members of the organisation.

❑ Most organisations, in addition to the above, also have a *defined hierarchy of authority*. This means that members each understand their position in the organisational structure regarding this hierarchy. The highest authority in an organisation might be anything from President of the United States to captain of the football team. The most senior member, as well as enjoying the authority over the organisations activities, must, of course, also assume the responsibility that attends such authority.

4.2 Why Organisations Exist

Now we have established *what organisations are*, we may turn our attention to *why they exist*. We are not talking here about the objectives of a business (as discussed in Chapter 2), but the advantages inherent in working as an organisation rather than as separate individuals. It is these advantages that lead people to form organisations.

4.2.1 Economies of scale

One major advantage for organisations is that they are able to achieve *economies of scale*. This means that tasks can be performed more efficiently and effectively when more people are involved in the work. A key concept in this regard is that of *synergy*, which means that *the whole is greater than the sum of the parts* (or, as popularly expressed, *2+2=5*). A way of exemplifying this is to look at the difference between the sole proprietor and the partnership. The sole proprietor performs all the functions of the business himself. Although he may be poor at, say, administration, the nature of his business is such that he must perform the administrative function regardless. The fact that he is not fully competent in this area may lead to:

❑ the administrative part of the business being done inadequately;

❑ the administrative function taking up a disproportionate amount of the sole proprietor's time, thus leaving less time for income-creating activities.

Within a partnership, the fact that more than one person is involved means that tasks can be shared out between members according to their abilities. Hence, one partner will concentrate on, say, the operations of the organisation whereas the other will be principally concerned with the desk and administrative functions. The effect of this *division of labour* is that *both* functions are performed more efficiently than would be the case if there was only one person involved in the business.

4.2.2 Goals and objectives

An extension of this idea is that *goals and objectives can be achieved* more easily. That which could not possibly be achieved with a 'one man band' can be accomplished when an organisation is established, with all its resources and commitment. Imagine attempting to achieve the objectives of a charity like Oxfam, if only one person was engaged in the task. Instead, a large number of individuals are employed, both in the administrative head office and in a number of countries around the world, both in fund-raising and in performing the relief work for which the charity is well known. Hence the structure of an organisation helps objectives to be achieved.

4.2.3 Authority and responsibility

Organisations are also formed in order to formalise relationships and to *establish a formal authority and responsibility network*. Such a formalisation enables members to recognise their own roles and it ensures that authority and responsibility are respected, thus enabling tasks to be completed with efficiency. An organisation in which a formal authority network doesn't exist can tend to be chaotic, with members continually having to establish what their roles and responsibilities are rather than carrying out the tasks for which the organisation exists. Some sort of structure is indispensable to organisations; there is an illustrious history of organisational failure when such a network is not fully understood or where it fails to be observed.

4.2.4 Co-ordination of activities

The structure of organisations enables activities to be *co-ordinated*. This theme is linked with the foregoing points in that authority must be respected before co-ordination can be implemented. Usually, this activity is carried out by managers and directors. In a typical limited company, the central co-ordination will be carried out by the Board of Directors. A natural extension of this concept is that the co-ordinators are aware of organisational objectives. This involves ensuring that:

- all necessary tasks are carried out;
- appropriately skilled staff are assigned to specific tasks;
- sufficient instruction and detail are provided by managers and directors to enable tasks to be performed;
- work is not duplicated by more than one person or department;
- feedback is provided to the co-ordinators on progress, problems and upon successful completion.

Managers and directors will modify requirements (e.g. time allotment) in the light of feedback from the other members of the organisation.

4.2.5 Communication systems

A formal organisational structure will enable *an efficient communication network* to be established. An organisation can be viewed as a body with many organs, each of which, according to the principle of division of labour, has a distinct function or purpose. Students of Biology will know that in order for separate biological organs to operate together, the body has a complex system of blood vessels and nerves through which information is communicated in electrical or biochemical form. Without this communication network, there would be no communication and there could accordingly be no co-ordination. The same principle applies to organisations – in order for them to survive they must have effective communication systems. The larger the organisation, the more important this network becomes, and in most large organisations, communication occurs through highly formalised channels.

4.3 What do Business Organisations Have in Common?

In order to examine business organisations – what they have in common and how they differ – we may consider two examples: a local plumber and a large company such as British Telecommunications Plc (BT). It might be thought initially that these two businesses have little in common. Further examination however, will reveal that they are both in business for a number of similar reasons. For example, they might both aim to create profits, provide a service, generate a worthwhile occupation for their respective employees or to establish for themselves a favourable reputation as a supplier of goods or services.

But more than this, there are a number of things that *all* business organisations have in common, and it is by looking at these things that we can also begin to understand how they differ from each other.

❏ The **first** thing that all business organisations have in common is that they all involve *people*. People do the work, monitor and manage, keep records, sell the product, invoice the customer and collect the money that keeps the business alive. Using our examples as before, we can readily see that the local plumber and BT both need people to run the business. A key difference though, is that the latter employ in excess of 150 000 people, and the former, just one. In BT, there is a massive corporate structure with many different jobs and responsibilities, whereas the local plumber performs all the business functions himself.

❏ The **second** thing all business organisations have in common is that they all need *money*. By using money, they can buy machines, materials, premises and hire staff in order to make more money by making business transactions. We saw in Chapter 1 that the type of money used to set up and maintain a business is called *capital*. There are a number of different types of capital, and we shall see this in more detail later in the book. Let us look at how much capital is needed to run our two businesses.

The local plumber requires a van, a telephone, his 'tools of the trade', perhaps a typewriter and he is in business. British Telecommunications Plc have a massive capital investment in offices, telephone exchanges, lines encompassing the entire country, fleets of motor-vehicles, complex computer systems etc. So, whilst the plumber has a capital value of maybe two or three thousand pounds (and for many businesses it is significantly less than this), for BT, it runs to over £11 billion.

❏ All businesses have *owners*. The owners are the people (or other organisations) who injected the capital to get the business going, or who bought the business as a going concern. Usually, the owners will expect a *return* on their investment, i.e. a part of the profits. Again we see a key difference here between businesses. The local plumber has one owner – the local plumber, and he owns *all* of the business. BT has hundreds of thousands of owners, the shareholders, each of whom own *only a part* of the business. It can be said that all of the owners share control of the company to a degree.

❏ All businesses need to provide a *product or service* for which there is a demand. It is by selling this product or service that money is generated that allows the business to continue. Some businesses have only one product or service (the plumber) and others have many thousands. Consider, for example, a large industrial company such as Grand Metropolitan Plc. The parent company owns a large number of subsidiary companies and brands including Burger King, Green Giant, Baileys and Le Piat d'Or. In consequence, it offers a range of hundreds of different products and services from which to generate money. Of course it is not just large organisations that offer a large product range – just think of the variety of different products on sale at the local newsagent.

❑ All businesses need *customers or clients*. These are people (or other organisations) who need or want the product or service being offered by the business. They are prepared to exchange monetary payment in order to enjoy the benefit of the product or service. The number and type of customers varies widely. At first glance it might appear that the Ministry of Defence buying a naval ship at a price of hundreds of millions of pounds has little in common with someone buying a newspaper for 45p. Both are customers however, in that they agree to pay the price being asked for the product and are providing money to the seller that helps to keep him in business. Without customers, the business could not generate any money and would quickly go out of business.

Activity	*We can readily see that for a shop like Marks and Spencer, the customers are those who go into the shop and exchange money for goods. Identifying the customer is not always so easy. Suggest who might be 'the customer' for the following organisations:*
	the police force;
	Her Majesty's Prison Service;
	the National Health Service;
	a University;
	the Army.
	(Hint: A useful point to consider is to identify who pays for the service and who it is designed to benefit.)

❑ All businesses need to *collect money* in exchange for their goods and services. This might seem obvious, but this forms a large proportion of the activities of many businesses. The local newsagent who sells you a newspaper will receive your 45p at the same time that you buy the goods. A milkman might have to wait a week for payment for a week's supply of milk, but in industry, a supplier might have to wait thirty to ninety days between delivering the goods and receiving payment. This time gap can be very important to the business as it affects its 'cash flow'. We will look at this in more detail when we come to look at the financial function of the organisation in Chapter 18.

So, having looked at what all businesses have in common and the ways in which they differ, we can turn to the distinct legal differences between them and examine the different types of business organisation that exist. All businesses, whatever their size, will fit into one of the categories that are described in Chapters 5, 6 and 7.

Review Questions

1. Explain three defining features of an organisation? (4.1)

2. Give details of three advantages gained by people working as an organisation rather than separately. (4.2)

3. Describe four factors that all business organisations have in common. (4.3)

Answers to activities

The customers of the mentioned organisations might include:

The mentioned organisations are all in the 'public sector' (see Chapter 1), and as such are paid for out of public funds, that are made up of tax revenues.

❑ The Police Force and Prison Service
the tax payer (who pays, indirectly, for the service),
the communities that are protected by the services,
employees of the services.

❑ The National Health Service
the tax payer,
patients,
employees.

❑ A University
the tax payer,
the students,
employers who benefit from the services of the graduates,
those who pay for students tuition (Local Education Authorities, sponsoring organisations and parents),
lecturers and other employees.

❑ The Army
the tax payer,
the country's citizens who benefit from the security the Army helps to ensure.

Assignment

According to the definition of organisations given in 4.1 above, it is possible for collectives of people to be something other than organisations (one might refer to them as groups). Based on the definitions, decide whether the following are groups or not:

❑ Carlisle United Football Club;

❑ The Macintosh family who live at 55 Boghead Street, Oldham (Mr and Mrs Macintosh and their two children);

❑ The Royal Victoria Infirmary, Newcastle;

❑ Orpington Baptist Church;

❑ Huntingtower Road Junior School, Grantham;

❑ The University of Cambridge;

❑ The local train spotters club;

❑ The cast of Coronation Street;

❑ The guests at a wedding reception;

❑ The RTZ Corporation Plc;

❑ A firm of chartered accountants.

Further Reading

Buchanan D.A. and Huczynski A.A., *Organizational Behaviour – An Introductory Text*, Prentice/Hall International (Chapter 1)
Luthans F., *Organisational Behaviour*, McGraw Hill (Sixth Edition, 1992)
Mullins L.J., *Management and Organisational Behaviour*, Pitman Publishing (Third Edition, 1993: Part One – Chapters 1, 2 and 3)

5 Non-incorporated organisations

Objectives   After studying this chapter, students should be able to:

❑ define the essential features of the *sole proprietor* and *partnership* as forms of business enterprise;

❑ explain the forms of ownership that these two forms of business demonstrate;

❑ describe the pros and cons of holding *sole proprietor* and *partnership* status.

5.1 Sole Proprietor

5.1.1 What is a sole proprietor?

A sole proprietor is usually, but not necessarily, a single person carrying out a business in a one-person (or very small) operation. Most self employed people will fit into this category, although there is no legal limit to the number of people that sole proprietors can employ (some are known to employ up to 100 staff). Common examples are as follows:

❑ tradespeople (joiners, plasterers, electricians, painters, roofers etc.);

❑ market stall holders;

❑ small independent retailers (e.g. fish and chip shops, newsagents, greengrocers etc.);

❑ 'cottage' industries (e.g. craft workshops.);

❑ farmers;

❑ window cleaners.

Question 1   *In addition to the examples given here, how many other examples can you think of for businesses which are usually carried out by sole proprietors?*

There are a number of features that are characteristic of sole proprietors. As they are not a legal entity as such (the sole proprietor *is* the business), they cost nothing to set up apart from the necessary capital. Anybody can be a sole proprietor simply by commencing business transactions in an informal manner. They have no legal requirement to keep books according to the conventional legal (accounting) standards. They must however, like everybody else who receives income, pay income tax on their pay from the business, so the Inland Revenue will require a certain amount of documentation to verify taxable earnings.

5.1.2 Pros and cons of holding sole proprietor status

There are advantages and disadvantages of holding sole proprietor status and these can be summarised as follows:

Advantages

❏ No legal or statutory setting-up procedures, hence cheap and quick.

❏ All profits and earnings belong to the owner.

❏ The owner is only accountable to himself therefore
   – decisions can be made quickly,
   – he has autonomy to arrange his own working schedule,
   – he has independence to act as he sees fit.

❏ No requirement to submit annual accounts to Companies House (see requirements for limited companies). This has the advantage both of saving on bookkeeping and auditing costs, and enables the sole proprietor to refrain from publicly disclosing the financial particulars of the business.

Disadvantages

❏ All tasks in the business must be performed by the owner/manager (i.e. operations, selling, invoicing, tax documentation).

❏ Skills and abilities are limited to those of the owner. Any key skill deficiencies are therefore to the detriment of the business. This is usually a key consideration as the owner, although he may be proficient in his trade, may be poor at administration, selling or any number of important business functions.

❏ Often, the work a sole proprietor does is labour intensive, and therefore, when he is not working, no money is coming in. This tends to mitigate against holidays and other reasons for time off.

❏ Poor economies of scale. This means that being only a small concern, the sole proprietor has little buying power, and will pay a higher price per unit (e.g. per nail, length of pipe, tin of paint, etc.) than the larger concern that will buy much more of the same materials at any time of purchase.

❏ A sole proprietor has what is known as *unlimited liability*. This is a major drawback of being a sole proprietor as opposed to becoming *incorporated* (see Chapter 6). As they have only an informal legal identity, sole proprietors do not benefit from *limited liability*. This means that the owner of the business (the sole proprietor) is liable for any or all of the business's losses from his own personal reserves, without limit. If for example, a customer successfully sues the sole proprietor for damages resulting from his work, then the sole proprietor will have to find the settlement entirely from his own resources. The implications of this are that he runs the risk of losing his house, savings etc. Many sole proprietors get round this apparent handicap by taking out insurance policies up to a certain value against loss. This drawback arises because the sole proprietor *is* the business and not an employee of it. Hence, while she may enjoy all the benefits of the profits, he must also personally accept the responsibility for losses.

Because there is no requirement for sole proprietors to submit annual accounts, no one knows exactly how many such organisations exist in the UK. There are, however, estimated to be around one million – many of these businesses are like those listed above, but there are also 'odd job' people who do occasional work for financial gain. Despite any apparent drawbacks to this type of organisation, it is quite obviously successful and popular and many people remain in this form of organisation for all of their working lives.

What is a legal entity? In law, the concepts of human and legal personality can be different. A *juristic personality* is any party that the law recognises, in that the law will enforce contracts made by that 'person'. A legal entity may therefore make contracts, carry out business, own property, employ people, and it is capable of suing and of being sued for breach of contract.

In the case of a sole proprietor, the law does not recognise the business entity of the sole proprietor, but it does recognise the human person who is the sole proprietor. The same is true of partnerships.

The issue becomes a little more complex when we consider limited companies (see Chapter 6). The law recognises the company and not the employees of the business as the legal personality. Hence, it is the entity of the company that makes contracts. The employees who make contracts on behalf of the business are called its *agents*, for example a Sales Manager is empowered to make contracts of sale of the company's goods. The company, and not the Sales Manager as an individual, is bound in law to keep the contract.

5.2 Partnerships

5.2.1 What is a partnership?

According to **The Partnership Act 1890**, such an organisation is defined as,

> '*the relationship which subsists between persons carrying on a business with a view to profit'.'*

Such a definition leaves room for interpretation, and hence there has been a number of formats for partnerships over the years.

A partnership is like a sole proprietor in that it is not *incorporated* and therefore has *unlimited liability*, but unlike him in that it can be a legally acknowledged form of organisation. It is an arrangement in which not less than two and (usually) not more than twenty people come together for the purposes of carrying out a business.

Partnership arrangements are occasionally found in the 'trades' (such as electricians or builders), but are more common among professional concerns such as:

- surveyors;
- architects;
- accountants;
- management consultants;
- lawyers and solicitors.

The professions that hold partnership status usually do so to enable clients to have the assurance that the lawyer (or other professional person) is professionally more accountable to the client than if the business were incorporated.

5.2.2 Pros and cons of holding partnership status

There are of course, a number of advantages and disadvantages to this form of organisation.

Advantages

- More capital can be raised when more than one person is investing in the business.

❏ There is no need to submit accounts as limited companies have to.

❏ Partners may divide profits between themselves without being accountable to anybody else, for example shareholders.

❏ Because there is more than one person working for the business, there is likely to be a breadth of skills and abilities from which the business can benefit.

❏ Work can be divided up so that individuals are less burdened by the weight of jobs to be done. this relieves the pressure on any one partner.

❏ Any liability losses are divided up between the partners, thus reducing the risk of personal bankruptcy for any one partner.

Disadvantages

❏ Like a sole proprietor, partnerships still have unlimited liability. This is a little more complex than the arrangement for a sole proprietor as the losses must be borne by all the partners, even if they are caused by the actions of just one.

❏ There are some setting up costs as a legal arrangement is usually entered into to prevent one or more partners conveniently leaving if a lawsuit is made against the business. A legal arrangement is also beneficial in that it ensures that profits are evenly distributed between partners.

❏ Because there is more than one person in a partnership, decisions are reached by consultation between partners. This could make decision making slower than if the business were a sole proprietor. It also introduces the risk of arguments and conflict between partners.

❏ The individual independence that the sole proprietor enjoys is lost. A partner does not have the authority to decide on days off, type of work taken, quality standards of work and so on that the sole proprietor enjoys. He must confer with his partners on such things if the partnership is to work effectively.

❏ In common with the status of a sole proprietor, partners *are* the business and not employees of it. This means that if one partner dies or in some other way becomes unable to continue with the business, then the partnership is automatically dissolved (although most partnerships make provisions for this possibility in their partnership agreement – usually set out by a solicitor).

Again, partnerships are fully liable for taxation on income, but apart from this constraint there is no legal obligation for keeping 'books' or accounts. This tends to reduce the administrative workload, and enables the partnership to refrain from publicly disclosing their turnover and other financial information. This may also be of advantage to the business.

Unlike sole proprietors, partnerships can grow to be relatively large organisations. The large accountancy auditing organisations (you may have heard of Price Waterhouse, and Coopers and Lybrand), have many employees in addition to the partners, with offices in every major town and city in the country as well as overseas.

Review Questions

1. Define the term sole proprietor (5.1.1)
2. Define the term partnership (5.2.1)

3.   What are the advantages of holding sole proprietor status? (5.1.2)

4.   What are the disadvantages of holding sole proprietor status? (5.1.2)

5.   What are the advantages of holding partnership status? (5.2.2)

6.   What are the disadvantages of holding partnership status? (5.2.2)

Assignment

Wood-u-like is the trading name of a Mr John Clarke of Upton, Wirral. John is a sole proprietor and has been in business for about three years. He earns a reasonable living by doing a wide range of home improvements including joinery modifications, kitchen fitting, decorating, plumbing and similar 'handyman' jobs. He works from home and he relies on an answer phone to receive business enquiries while he is out. The assets of *Wood-u-like* comprise a wide range of tools, a tiny quantity of stock (nails, screws, glue etc.) and a personal computer which is used for correspondence, accounts and invoicing. John uses the family car to transport himself and his tools to and from jobs.

John does not employ anybody on a full-time basis, but he is able to call on Roo, a retired carpenter, to help out during busy periods. Roo is paid according to the time he puts in helping John.

Tasks

1.   Inform John of the potential risks of holding sole proprietor status within the business sector in which he operates.

2.   John has a friend who is a qualified electrician, who also has experience in getting work and managing accounts. What would be the advantages to *Wood-u-like* if John were to join with him to form a partnership?

3.   John has been heard to say, "I like being a sole proprietor. I can work at my own pace, I don't owe anybody anything and I'm my own boss". What features of John's life might change for the worse (as John sees it) if he were to join with the electrician to form a partnership?

Further Reading

Beardshaw J. & Palfreman D., *The Organisation in its Environment*, Pitman Press (Fourth Edition, Chapter 3)

Bendrey M., Hussey R. & West C., *Accounting and Finance for Business Students*, DP Publications Third Edition, 1994. For a more detailed financial treatment of the subjects of this chapter: Sole proprietors – Chapters 10 and 11; Partnerships – Chapter 23)

6 Incorporated organisations

Objectives   After studying this chapter, students should be able to:

- ❐ explain why limited liability was introduced;
- ❐ describe how limited liability works;
- ❐ define the term *shareholder* and explain how ownership is organised in a limited company;
- ❐ describe the conditions placed upon limited companies as a condition of enjoying limited liability;
- ❐ explain the procedures by which limited companies are managed and operated;
- ❐ show how the management of a limited company are divided into departments;
- ❐ describes the advantages and disadvantages of holding limited company status;
- ❐ explain what is meant by a holding company;
- ❐ describe the ways in which holding companies generate money;
- ❐ define the terms *subsidiary*, *associated* and *related* as applied to company ownership;
- ❐ explain how a typical holding company is structured;
- ❐ describe the purposes that can be served by adopting holding company status.

6.1 Limited Company

6.1.1 The need for limited liability

The need to make provisions for businesses other than sole proprietors and partnerships first arose in the mid nineteenth century when it was realised that money needed to be injected into infant industries like engineering and chemicals. Quite understandably perhaps, investors were reluctant to enter into partnership with the knowledge that by doing so they might be putting all of their personal wealth at risk (especially if the investor did not intend to take an active part in managing the business). In response to this need, legislation was introduced that enabled businesses to be recognised as *entities in themselves*.

This meant that those who worked in such organisations would be *employees* of the business and hence they would not *be* the business. As a result of this, unlike sole proprietors and partnerships, there was a 'continuity of succession', meaning that in the event of an employee leaving the employment of the business, the entity of the company could appoint a replacement without having to dissolve the business as a result of the departure. The consequence, as far as investors and employees were concerned, was that if the business failed then, because the business was in law a person, they would not be personally liable for the businesses debts. The converse of this of course is equally obvious, that as employees and investors, they would not be automatically entitled to take all the profits out of the business as they are under the previous two arrangements. Profits would be divided up by the entity of the *company* (in the form of its agents – the directors), and this may or may not be to the desires of employees and investors.

The arrangement whereby the members of the company would not be liable for the business debts in the case of company failure was called *limited liability*. The way in which the principle works is as follows:

☐ investors pay an amount of money to the company, and in doing so, become one of the owners. It is said that they share the ownership with other investors and hence the amount they own is called a *share*;

☐ in exchange for the capital provided by the *shareholder*, the company agrees to return part of the money by dividing up some of the profits between the investors. The percentage of the profits set aside for this purpose is determined by the management of the company, depending on how much they think they can afford. The payment made to shareholders under this arrangement is called a *dividend*. This pleases the shareholders as they are receiving a *return* on their investment, much as they would if they put the amount on deposit in a building society and gained interest on their money;

☐ individuals agree to sell their time and labour to the company in exchange for an agreed sum of money per week, month or year, and they become *employees* of the company. Their income from the company is called remuneration, wages or salary;

☐ in the event of company failure, losses are paid out of the asset value of the business at the time of failure, in which of course, the shareholders have their investment. (The Assets of a business are the things it owns at any one time to which a financial value can be given – things like land, buildings, stocks etc.);

☐ the shareholders liability is limited only to the loss of the existing money they have in the business, that is, the value of their shareholding. This means that if the company fails, they lose the money they invested in the business, but they cannot be pursued further by people who want money from the company at the time of failure;

☐ employees (the other key 'members' of the company) will lose their jobs if the company fails, but in the same manner as the liability of shareholders, they also cannot be pursued further for the company's debts.

Case Study	Polly Peck Plc

Polly Peck was one of the major growth companies of the nineteen eighties. Among its corporate interests was the Del Monte canned fruit business, and a number of consumer goods and electronics companies including Sansui, Russell Hobbs and Tower. The group failed on 24 October 1990 when its creditor banks (those to whom the company owed money) refused to continue their support and to call in some of their debts.

At the time of the failure, the group had total debts of £1.2 Billion. Other concerned and worried parties included 35,000 employees and 20,000 shareholders.

Over the ensuing months and years, the creditors made every effort to recover their debts, but knowing they could not pursue the owners (shareholders) for monies owed, they tried to get the administrators to turn the company's assets into cash. Because the member companies of the group were largely sound, most employees kept their jobs. Shareholders lost their investment, but in keeping with company law, could not be asked to pay anything more towards the company in its time of crisis. It is consequently in the interests of everybody who has dealings with a company, that it remains afloat and in a good financial state.

6.1.2 Ownership of limited companies

It can readily be understood that those who own a company are those who injected the capital to allow the business to begin operating at its inception. Ownership can be transferred when an individual or organisation pays the owner the value of his share in the company, thus allowing the share of ownership to change hands.

The value of a company is divided up into small segments which we have already established are called shares. These can be of any value, but will typically be to the value of a small amount of money such as £1 or 25p. The owners, therefore, are said to have so many shares in the company. The ownership of shares confers on the shareholder, as a part owner of the business, the right to vote on certain aspects of company policy at the annual general meeting (AGM) of the business. The weight of the shareholders vote is pro-rata with the number of shares owned, and in consequence, the larger the shareholding, the more influential the shareholder.

Some companies have total share values of just a few pounds, all of which may be held by one person. Others, such as a large public limited company (see below) may have share values up to tens of billions of pounds, and these will typically be divided up between many thousands of shareholders. The number of shares a company has is referred to as the *share volume*.

The way in which the shares are divided also has a influence on the control of the business. Bearing in mind that shareholding is the same as part ownership, it follows that if any one shareholder has sufficient shares, then he can claim ownership of the company. However, due to the fact that (as far as influence over the company is concerned,) shares confer the right to vote, it will be appreciated that control over the company can be gained by holding 51% of the shares. To have 51% will mean that the dominant shareholder can automatically veto any other shareholder's motion and install company management or policies of his choice.

Limited companies can be classified according to who owns (or has access to own) the shares of the business.

❑ A **family business** is one in which the shares are owned either wholly or predominantly by the members of a family (either nuclear or extended). This is an example of a private limited company.

❑ A **private limited company** (abbreviated as 'Limited' or 'Ltd') is one in which the shares are owned by a number (usually a small number) of private individuals. The shares are not available for sale except with the permission of the shareholder and the Board of Directors of the company.

❑ A **public limited company** (abbreviated as 'Plc') is a company in which the public has access to the shares. These are bought and sold through the Stock Exchange. With a few minor exceptions, anybody can buy shares in the company to any value.

Case Study   **Tor Coatings Limited** is a small to medium sized company that operates from a single site in Birtley, Tyne and Wear. It manufactures a range of paints and specialised surface coatings. Its turnover in the year ended 31 March 1993 was £5.032 million, on a capital employment of just under £1.3 million. Because it is a private company, the shares are held by private individuals, in this case, substantially by three of the four directors. In 1994, the majority of the share volume of 1,002,000 shares was divided between them as follows:

Shareholder	Holding	Percentage
Mr G Readman	625 000	62.4
Mr A Turner	125 000	12.5
Mr R G Carr	80 000	8

In contrast, there are 4.323 billion shares in **British Gas Plc**. In the year ended December 1992, the company had sales of £10.254 billion on a capital employment of £20.36 billion. At June 1993 it had 1.9 million shareholders, a mixture of private individuals and financial institutions.

Activity 1   *Compare and contrast the level of control that a shareholder with 625000 shares would have over the affairs of the two companies described above. How will this affect the decision making process? Explain why this is the case.*

6.1.3 Conditions placed upon limited companies

In exchange for a company benefiting from the advantages of limited liability, the law requires that certain conditions are met. These are legally binding upon the business and to fail to comply with them would take the company outside of the law. The conditions as laid down state that all limited companies must submit the following documents. All of these are available for inspection by the public:

❏ memorandum of association;

❏ articles of association;

❏ annual audited accounts.

The memorandum and articles of association are filed at Companies House at the time of the company's foundation, but they can be changed later if the need arises.
The **memorandum of association** contains the following information:

❏ the company name;

❏ the address of the company's office;

❏ the purpose of the company;

❏ a statement that the 'members' are claiming limited liability in accordance with the relevant legislation;

❏ the value of the company's share capital;

❏ the way in which the shares are distributed among the members and the type of shares that each member holds (there are some shares that do not allow the holder to vote);

❏ a 'declaration of association' in which the members state their intention to form a company and to take up shares in it.

The **articles of association** are concerned with the internal affairs and rules of the company. They state the following:

❏ identity of shareholders;

❏ names and addresses of the directors (those appointed by the shareholders to operate the business on a day by day basis);

❏ identity of the company secretary;

- ❏ the name of the company that will be the auditors of the company's annual accounts;

- ❏ powers and responsibilities of directors;

- ❏ rules regarding the calling of meetings of shareholders.

The **annual audited accounts** contain the important financial information in the form of three statements. We will look at these statements in detail when we look at the financial function of the company later in the book, but in summary, this document must have the following characteristics:

- ❏ it must contain the following financial statements:

  profit and loss statement,

  balance sheet,

  cash flow statement;

- ❏ they must be *audited* (checked and commented upon) by a suitably qualified and accredited chartered or certified accounting organisation;

- ❏ upon completion, they must be submitted *annually* to Companies House in Cardiff.

It can be seen, therefore, that in exchange for the *privilege* of limited liability, a number of conditions are imposed which are legally binding.

Companies House

Companies House is an 'executive agency' of the Department of Trade and Industry – a Government department. For companies in England and Wales, Companies House is in Cardiff, and for Scottish companies it is in Edinburgh. It performs two key roles in the economy:

- ❏ it regulates and controls all limited companies, by approving their incorporation and dissolving them;

- ❏ by holding up-to-date records, including annual accounts on the companies, it acts as a source of information for the public. Anybody can inspect any company's records, and can obtain the company records for the payment of a small fee.

6.1.4 The management and operation of limited companies

There are a number of important people involved in the operation of a limited company. Their responsibilities and roles can be summarised as follows:

- ❏ **Directors**

  The directors of a limited company are chosen by the shareholders at annual meetings. They are responsible to the shareholders for the day-to-day running of the business – the control and maintenance of the company's assets and resources – and have responsibility to provide the shareholders, to the best of their ability, with a suitable return on their investment. The duties and constraints of the directors are determined by the articles of association. In most medium to large companies, there are a number of directors, (typically between two and seven) who each have a distinct area of responsibility within the operation of the company. One of their number is appointed in seniority over the others and he or she is given the title Managing Director or Chief Executive. This office oversees all aspects of company operation and reports directly to the shareholders. Directors are the *agents* of the company and as such are empowered to make contracts with outside parties on the company's behalf. They are required to assume managerial and planning duties, but as agents, they also have a number of legal responsibilities, among which are:

❑ to ensure that annual accounts are submitted in accordance with accounting standards and on time (usually via the company secretary);

❑ to approve any changes in the assets of the company;

❑ to approve the dividends paid out and any investments made;

❑ to attend Board and members' meetings;

❑ to comply with the British law in all respects (such as employment, health and safety, pollution etc.).

Directors fall into two categories. *Executive directors* are individuals who work full time for the organisation and who usually assume a role in the management of a function within the company. The second category is that of *non-executive directors*, who are not in the full-time employ of the business and are usually engaged in a part-time or advisory capacity. Non-executive directors are often specialists in a certain field, retired and respected former executive directors or famous or well established people who (it is believed) will bring a favourable image or a particular expertise to the company (an example of this is the appointment of former Chancellor of the Exchequer, Nigel Lawson to the Board of Barclays (Bank) Plc).

❑ **Company Secretary**

The company secretary is usually appointed by the directors. It is a professionally recognised position (not to be confused with the departmental or personal secretary) and usually attracts a senior management salary. The responsibilities of the post are concerned with the senior administrative functions of the company, often embracing a financial or operational oversight role. According to the various Companies Acts it is the company secretary who is made responsible for returning the audited accounts of the company, annually, to the Registrar of Companies at Companies House. In law, the company secretary is recognised as having the authority to act as an agent of the company and to make contracts on the company's behalf. He or she usually reports to the Managing Director. All limited companies must have at least one director and one Company Secretary. The Secretary can also be a director.

❑ **Management and Employees**

We saw earlier that one of the responsibilities of an executive director is to oversee the working of a particular function of the company. In medium and large companies, directors delegate the running of a function (or a department) to a number of *managers*. In turn, managers are responsible for a number of staff through whom they ensure that the required work is done. The managers report to the appropriate director and are held responsible for the work delegated to them. Managers who are not directors are often highly paid with highly responsible jobs, but a strict demarcation exists between them and the directors as they are not empowered in law to make contracts on behalf of the company unless authorised so to do by one who is, in other words, a director.

The typical organisational structure of a limited company is shown in figure 6.1. (structures will be discussed in more depth in Chapter 8)

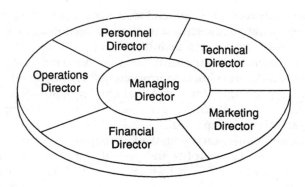

Figure 6.1: Typical structure of a limited company

6.1.5 Advantages and disadvantages of holding limited company status

Advantages

❑ More capital can be raised by having a number of shareholders.

❑ The shareholders have the benefit of limited liability.

❑ In the case of a Plc, shares are readily transferable between members of the public.

❑ Companies can raise extra money, under some circumstances, by issuing more shares for sale.

Disadvantages

❑ A number of legal constraints have to be adhered to. These involve expense and a substantial management commitment.

❑ The fact that investors have limited liability may mean that banks and other lenders may be more reluctant to lend money. This is especially applicable to smaller limited companies.

❑ Investors are not automatically entitled to all the profits of the business.

6.2 Holding Company

6.2.1 What is a holding company?

A holding company is a special example of a limited company. You will remember that those who have control of a limited company are those who own 51% of the shares, thus giving them majority voting rights in the company's affairs. It follows that a shareholding of more than 51% simply means that the owners receive an accordingly greater share of the profits in the form of dividends. They would not have any more control, even if they had 100% of the shares.

Shares can be owned either by individuals or by other organisations (for example, insurance companies and banks invest heavily in the shares of a wide range of public limited companies). Some companies, however, exist simply to own the shares of other companies, and where possible, these organisations own enough shares to control the companies in question. In consequence, you have a company that does not provide a product or service itself, but simply owns other companies who do. These organisations are called holding companies, so named because they 'hold' the shares, and hence the ownership, of other companies. This is a common form of organisation for very large companies – usually Plc's. Investors buy shares in the holding company, the total profits of which arise from the sum of the profits obtained from the businesses over which it has control. They tend to operate from a head office composed of a number of administrative personnel, including accountants, secretaries, strategists and other office staff, sometimes including lawyers. There are a number of well known companies that have this structure. You may not have heard of Williams Holdings Plc, BAT Industries Plc and Grand Metropolitan Plc, but you will be familiar with Cuprinol Wood Preservers, Eagle Star and Allied Dunbar Insurance, Smirnoff Vodka, Cinzano, Haagen Dazs Ice Cream and Burger King, which are all companies or brands which are owned by the above companies.

Holding companies can be viewed as the same as ordinary companies in that they are in business to make profits and provide attractive returns for their shareholders. But they are slightly different in that, instead of dealing in conventional goods and services, their way of doing business is by buying, selling and operating existing companies.

6.2.2 How do holding companies make money?

There are three ways in which holding companies can make money:

☐ by extracting profits from the companies over which they have control;

☐ by buying a company for a price, increasing its value and selling it at a profit;

☐ by acquisition and selective divestment. (This is the buying of a company which itself owns a number of companies, selling the bought companies to redeem the total initial purchase cost whilst still retaining part of the acquisition from which to make holding company returns.)

Case Study   Growth in holding company assets by acquisition and selective divestment.

The Acquisition of the SCM Group by Hanson Plc
The British company Hanson Plc bought 100% of the shares in the US based SCM Group in January 1986 for just under $1 billion. SCM were a large industrial 'conglomerate' (a company with a large number of companies operating in different market sectors) of 17 companies, with interests in chemicals, food, paper, paint and typewriters.
Because SCM itself was a collection of companies, the new owner (Hanson) was able to split the group up and dispose of any companies in the SCM Group that it felt it didn't need. What actually happened was this:

1986 – SCM bought for $930 million

Same year – Hanson sold off SCM companies for a total of $935 million.

1987 – Hanson sold off SCM companies for a total of $28 million.

1988 – Hanson sold off SCM companies for a total of $266 million.

1989 – Hanson sold off 52% of the shares of one SCM company (Smith Corona Typewriters) for $309 million.

1990 – Hanson sold off SCM companies for a total of $41 million.

Total receipts from divestments : **$1.579 billion**

Result – Hanson recovered more than the purchase cost of the SCM Group whilst still retaining one SCM company and 48% of the shares in Smith Corona Typewriters. The one company it retained from the SCM Group was SCM Chemicals, the world's third largest producer of white pigments for paints, paper etc. – a business capable of generating $300 million in profits each year. Hence, it got SCM Chemicals 'free' to retain in the Hanson group and a cash surplus on the total deal of **$649 million**. (Source: Hanson Plc)

Activity 2   *This practice (purchase and then divestment) is sometimes criticised for being unethical. Find out what the major arguments are against this approach to managing holding companies. Do you agree with the objections?*

6.2.3 Ownership of holding companies

There are a number of useful terms that are used to describe the degree of ownership that one company has over another.

❏   If a company owns more than 50% of another company, and hence has control over it, then *the company that is owned* is called a **subsidiary** of the larger business. Most of the companies which are part of a holding company will be subsidiary companies.

❏   If the larger company owns between 20% and 50% of the shares of a smaller company, then *the smaller company* is known as an **associated company** of the larger concern. This is a useful distinction, as a shareholding which is large but not controlling is nevertheless usually a highly influential holding in the smaller company. The precise degree of influence will be determined by who owns the rest of the shares. If, for example, one business owns 49% of a company's shares (which is hence an associated company) but another company owns the remaining 51%, then the company with the larger holding has control.

❏   If the larger company owns less than 20% of the share in a smaller concern, then *the smaller company* is referred to as a **related company** of the larger one.

There are specific accounting rules that dictate how each of these forms of ownership are dealt with in law and in annual accounts by the larger holding companies.

6.2.4 Holding company structure

A typical holding company structure will be as figure 6.2:

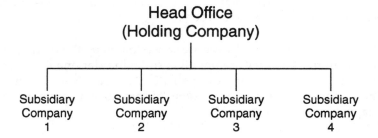

Figure 6.2: Typical holding company structure

Example   **Scottish and Newcastle Plc**

S & N Plc is a holding company which, at its year end of April 1992, had 107 subsidiaries. These add up to a total group turnover of around £1.4 billion. Its commercial interests, as one of the so called 'big five', are predominantly in the brewing sector, but it has recently made a number of acquisitions in the leisure industry. The structure of part of the company is:

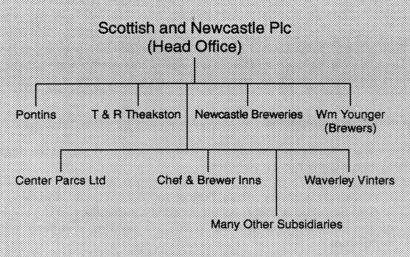

Figure 6.3: Holding company structure – Scottish and Newcastle Plc

Activity 3   *According to the strict definition of a holding company, when might a multi-company group, not be a holding company as such?*

What advantages would be gained by the group by merging two or more companies in the group into a single company?

6.2.5 Reasons for adopting a holding company structure

There are a number of purposes which can be well served by a company adopting this kind of structure. Among these are:

❑ it provides the holding company with a *'portfolio'* of business interests. This means that whilst a company that operates in only one market, for example, brewing, is highly dependent for its fortunes on the trends and influences in beer buying (such as the level of disposable income), a holding company, by spreading its *opportunity and risk*, can reduce the effects on itself of a downturn in any one of the market sectors in which it operates. It does this by holding interests in a number of different areas of the industrial marketplace (and sometimes in a number of countries of the world);

❑ because the subsidiary businesses are retained by the holding company as separate legal entities (i.e. they are not all absorbed under one homogenous company banner), any given company can be readily *divested* (sold off) from the holding company portfolio. The holding company provides a convenient structure for this to happen;

☐ as we have already seen, the rules of majority shareholding mean that a holding company can control a subsidiary by owning only 51% of its shares. This means that *control can be gained without holding all of the stock* (the name given to the shares in a company) – a significantly cheaper option than buying the company outright;

☐ for very large organisations, it is very hard to control everything from one head office location. In a holding company, the member companies of the group, are given a certain amount of autonomy to allow the management of the individual companies the right to manage their companies as they see fit. This means that for these large organisations, a holding company is a convenient way to devolve authority to individuals, making it a convenient structure under which to operate;

☐ in the same way that the structure allows for easy divestment of companies, the way in which companies are maintained as distinct entities in holding companies also allows for convenient *acquisition* (buying) of businesses. They can simply be bought and 'strapped on' to the group without the need to amalgamate them into existing group companies.

Review Questions

1. Describe what is meant by limited liability. (6.1.1)

2. What conditions must organisations meet to gain limited liability? (6.1.3)

3. You are a wealthy investor and you have just bought 49% of the shares in a public limited company. Will this large shareholding mean you can impose your will upon the organisation? Answer either *yes, no* or *depends* and explain your answer. (6.1.2)

4. Describe the principal pros and cons of having limited company status. (6.1.5)

5. What is a holding company and how do they differ from ordinary limited companies? (6.2.1)

6. Explain the ways in which a holding company can generate money. (6.2.2)

Answers to Activities

Activity 1

A shareholder in Tor Coatings will have a proportionately larger share of the company ownership than in British Gas. Mr Readman of Tor Coatings has 624 750 shares in the company and consequently has 63% of the issued shares in the business. Because he has over 50%, he has control of the company. If he had 624 750 shares in British Gas, he would only own 0.0144% of the issued stock – an imperceptible influence over the affairs of the company.

Activity 2

People sometimes criticise this practice because:

☐ They believe that it overlooks the needs of the individuals who work for the companies – acquisitions and divestments often involve redundancies.

☐ The acquiring company is said to be reaping the benefits ('milking the company') that previous generations of managers and owners have sown.

❏ It sometimes involves a 'hostile' take-over – buying the company on the Stock Market without the consent of the existing Board of the acquired company.

❏ The acquiring company sometimes does not develop the acquired company by investing in it. When this occurs, the company is 'milked' and sometimes run down.

Activity 3

A multi-company group is not a holding company when the head office is directly involved in running one of the companies in the group – i.e., the subsidiary is not an independent company.

By amalgamating two or more companies, the holding company can save costs by:

❏ joining together two production facilities in one place;

❏ reducing the duplication of tasks, such as purchasing;

❏ gaining economies of scale;

❏ prevent the two companies from competing with one another;

❏ reducing some personnel costs, particularly some of the expensive management levels.

Assignment

Choose a limited company with which you are familiar, or a local business that you know of. Find out the following information about the company:

❏ its turnover and profit at the last financial year end;

❏ the names of the Directors and the Company Secretary;

❏ the shareholdings of the Directors and their total share volume;

❏ the nature of the business from its memorandum of association;

❏ the number of employees;

❏ if the company owns other companies, find out how many there are and their names.

You could try the following sources in pursuit of the information:

❏ the company file at Companies House (will involve payment of a small fee and access to a microfiche reader);

❏ writing to the company;

❏ data sources at your local University or College library (e.g. Fame, Extel), company files;

❏ obtaining permission to visit the company and interview the accountant or another senior manager.

Further Reading

Beardshaw J. & Palfreman D., *The Organisation in its Environment*, Pitman Press, (Fourth Edition, Chapter 3)
Palmer A. & Worthington I., *The Business and Marketing Environment*, McGraw Hill, (First Edition, Section 2)

7 Other (not-for-profit) organisations

Objectives   After studying this chapter, students should be able to:

❏ explain what is meant by a *not-for-profit* organisation;

❏ describe the similarities between *for profit* and *not-for-profit* organisations;

❏ describe how co-operatives works and why they were initially set up;

❏ explain the pros and cons of co-operatives;

❏ describe the functions and purposes of government departments;

❏ explain the differences between central and local government;

❏ describe the functions of local government;

❏ explain why charities are unique *not-for-profit* organisations;

❏ explain how charities are funded.

7.1 Introduction

Many organisation exist for purposes other than the generation of profits in order to provide a return on investment for shareholders, owners etc. These are commonly referred to as not-for-profit. Their *raison d'être* may be anything from providing a necessary but uneconomical service, to helping the needy or preaching a religious message.

The question may be asked why they are being included in a general discussion of *business* organisations. The reason for this is that, although they exist for different objectives, they have a good deal in common with conventional business organisations, including:

❏ they all need money;

❏ they all spend money;

❏ they all need people;

❏ they all have a product or service (albeit in some unconventional forms);

❏ they all have customers, clients, or individuals they aim to provide a product or service for.

Like conventional business organisations, not-for-profit organisations can vary in size from the enormous to the minuscule. Their incomes can vary from just a few pounds to tens of billions of pounds.

They tend to use a different terminology to other organisations and the internal *corporate culture* (the 'feel' or 'morale' of an organisation – see Chapter 10) is usually very different to that in a business organisation. For example, once they have provided the product or service, any money left over is not called a profit (as would normally be the case), but a *surplus*. A technical loss on the year is called a *deficit*.

The common types of not-for-profit organisations are described in this chapter.

7.2 Co-operatives

7.2.1 Introduction to co-operatives

Co-operatives are worth an individual examination as they do not fit neatly into any of the other categories of business organisation. Since the first British co-operative was set up in the 1840's in T'Owd Lane in Rochdale, their popularity has grown and fallen.

The first co-operatives were set up in order to:

❑ circumvent the seemingly excessive profits of the early retail organisations;

❑ to ensure that goods were of a certain quality; and

❑ to enable profits to be redistributed more equitably among the factory workers and shoppers who at the time were predominantly members of the new industrial working classes.

Co-operatives are founded upon the basis that profits should be shared out, not among shareholders, but among the customers of a business. The co-operative principle is that at the year end, the amount of money that would be paid out in dividends to shareholders is paid out instead to the co-operative members – the customers – in proportion with the amount they have spent in the shop (and hence proportional to the amount they have contributed to the profits).

In the early days, every purchase by members was logged by an ingenious mechanical device involving a ball, troughs and pulleys! In later years, this idea was commuted to the giving of trading stamps in proportion to the value of the purchase, which could then be exchanged for goods in the co-operative shop. A person becomes a member of a co-operative by buying a share, but co-operative shares are markedly different from those in limited companies. In a co-op, each share entitles the member to one vote at meetings which appoint the management of the co-op, but unlike the limited company, if an individual owns more than one share, they still only have one vote.

7.2.2 Advantages and disadvantages of co-operative business

As with all forms of organisation, there are advantages and disadvantages associated with holding co-operative status.

Advantages

❑ Customers, in the long run, get goods at cheaper prices by benefiting from dividends.

❑ The customers (members) have control over the business as the shareholders. This means that the provisions of the business can be more closely allied with the requirements of the customer.

❑ Decisions are made democratically and therefore there are no powerful or autocratic leaders.

❑ Rewards are made equitably to members, in proportion with the level of their expenditure at the co-op.

❑ If co-operatives are registered, they can benefit from limited liability.

Disadvantages

❑ Because the customers control the organisation, there is less likelihood of the business achieving good profits. This means that there will be less money available for expansion and reinvestment.

❑ Less money will also be available for the expansion due to the fact that members will require a sizeable share of the profits.

❑ If the interrelationships between members and employees deteriorate, the co-op can be adversely affected.

❑ The fact that decisions are made democratically can mean that important decisions cannot be made as quickly as the circumstances may demand.

7.3 Government Departments

7.3.1 What do government departments provide?

Government departments are funded by central government, largely from taxation revenues. Government provides certain things that, for one reason or another, could not (or would not) be reliably provided by conventional 'for profit' organisations. The goods and services provided by government departments fall into two broad categories:

Public goods

These are goods and services that are provided for the population for the general good. They tend to be things that are needed by everybody, regardless of the individual's specific need. Among them are:

❑ defence;

❑ police and other services;

❑ transport infrastructure.

Merit goods

Merit goods are provided by the Government to be taken advantage of as and when the population has need of them. Common examples are:

❑ health service;

❑ social security and unemployment benefits;

❑ education.

We shall look at how the Government is organised in the UK in Chapter 12 of this book.

7.3.2 Government departments are large organisations

Money is channelled into the relevant departments by Her Majesty's Treasury and Exchequer and then allocated by the senior politicians and civil servants to the different parts of the department. The biggest government department, in terms of budget, is the Department of Social Security (DSS). In 1992, the DSS had an income from the Treasury of around £65 billion (a billion is one thousand million). If this were a business organisation, with a turnover of this magnitude, it would be one of the worlds biggest companies (in 1992, the worlds biggest company, Itoh & Co. Ltd of Japan, had a turnover the equivalent of £86.6 billion).

Figure 7.1 compares some government departments with Britain's biggest business organisations:

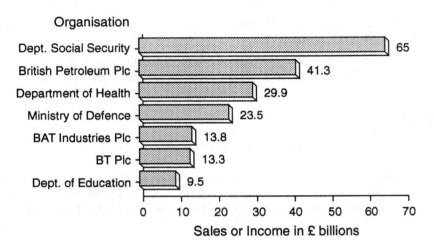

Figure 7.1: Some of Britain's largest organisations (by income or turnover, 1992)
(Source: The Times 1000 and the Chancellors Autumn Statement, 1992)

7.3.3 Emphases and locations of government departments

Because government departments are not designed to make money, the corporate emphasis is less on *profit and sales*, and more on providing *value for money*. In any department, there is only so much 'in the kitty' with which to provide the service to the public that is required of them by law. There may, in consequence, be much made of *efficiency* and the *reduction of costs*.

Because they each have such a large area of responsibility, government departments tend to be highly organised structures employing many thousands of employees (called civil servants). Whilst many are still based in London, there has, over recent decades, been a move of some departments to the regions where the jobs are more needed. Examples are parts of the Department of Social Security in Newcastle upon Tyne and the Driver and Vehicle Licensing Authority in Swansea.

Activity 2   *If you live in, or are studying in a town or city outside London, find out whether there are any parts of central government administration in your locality.*

The size and complex organisational structure of government departments, coupled with the large range of tasks they are required to undertake, means that they are often criticised for being somewhat 'flabby' and inefficient. It has been said that some of them represent bad value for money for the tax-payer (the people who pay, via the Inland Revenue and the Exchequer, for government departments). In recent years the Government has taken the view that costs must be kept down and standards of quality must be raised in these huge organisations. An example of this is the so called 'opting out' of health authorities, where, it is believed, better value for money can be achieved if an element of competition is introduced. The thinking behind this is that competition results in an upward pressure on quality and downward pressures on costs.

Two other types of organisation which might be thought of as types of government department are nationalised industries and QuANGOs (**Quasi Autonomous Non Governmental Organisations**). We shall look at these in more depth when we consider the structure of the UK Government in Chapter 12.

7.4 Local Authorities

7.4.1 What are local authorities?

Local authorities are a branch of the Government that is charged with maintaining a range of government provisions to a specific town, city or county. They operate from premises variously called town halls, civic centres, county halls etc., depending upon the level of local authority. There are a number of strata of local government, including borough, city and county councils.

Their structure and divisionalisation is not unlike central government, except on a much smaller scale. The executive decisions are made by elected representatives called *councillors*, and the administration is carried out by a staff of up to several thousand. Local authorities are largely controlled in what they may or may not (or must or must not) do, by legislation.

7.4.2 What do local authorities do?

Among the duties for which local authorities are responsible are:

☐ maintenance of local transport infrastructure (especially roads);

☐ local education services;

☐ environmental services (hygiene and licensing of pubs, clubs etc.);

☐ social services;

☐ refuse collection and disposal;

☐ provision of local authority housing and homes for senior citizens;

☐ care of homeless persons.

Local government is legally bound to maintain certain services, and in order to facilitate this, it receives funding from a number of sources. The majority comes direct from central Government, but money is also collected from other sources. The other sources of income include revenues from council house rents and leisure centre admission charges, but the majority of the extra money is raised in the form of a local tax. In 1993, the Conservative Government introduced a new format for local taxation called the council tax, which replaced the ill-fated community charge or poll tax. Many local authorities also raise finance in the form of loans and some engage in other financial arrangements.

7.4.3 Objectives of local authorities

It is clear that local authorities are not-for-profit organisations. Their objectives may be summarised as:

☐ compliance with the law regarding those services that a local authority **must** provide;

☐ getting the best possible services at the lowest cost;

❏ councillors are elected on the basis of their manifesto commitments and naturally aim to fulfil these and please those who elected them.

It can be seen that these objectives may, in certain circumstances, be in conflict with each other. Councillors must balance all three with the minimum of compromise on any one of them. This is the essence of local government.

If the Department of the Environment thinks that a certain local authority's council tax is too high, it has the power to *cap* the tax. This means that a maximum charge is imposed, and the local authority may need to cut back on some services in order to stay within the new capped financing limits.

7.5 Charities

7.5.1 Introduction to charities

A charity is an organisation that exists for a purpose that is essentially charitable ('charity' is an old English word for love, the implication being that a charity is a 'labour of love'). It implies a cause that is primarily based on compassion, sympathy or altruism. There is, of course, a wide interpretation of these terms in practice, and consequently, charitable organisations exist for an enormously wide variety of purposes from the relief of suffering in the third world to the prevention of the export of horses. Subsumed within this category are private schools and a wide variety of religious organisations including churches and missionary enterprises.

Britain's biggest charities

Name of charity	Voluntary income/year (£ millions)
National Trust	55.727
Royal National Lifeboat Institute	47.366
Oxfam	45.027
Imperial Cancer Research Fund	42.117
Cancer Research Campaign	40.284
Salvation Army	38.958
Save the Children Fund	38.610
Barnardo's	29.938
Help the Aged	24.508
Guide Dogs for the Blind Association	24.449

Source: Chambers Book of Facts (1992)

As there are a number of financial privileges extended to registered charities, there are also a number of conditions that organisations must meet before they are able to take advantage of charitable status. These include the submission of annual accounts, much the same as incorporated companies.

7.5.2 Features of charities

As organisations, charities have a number of features that distinguish them from other organisations. Certainly, as we have already seen, they exist for very different reasons, i.e. they have different objectives, compared to conventional business or Governmental organisations. In addition though, the following may also be said about them:

❏ They tend to be funded by voluntary contributions from private individuals or other organisations. Some make a little money from shops (where the stock is donated free of charge), but they do not qualify for any financial assistance from the Government purse except for the significant benefit of not having to pay any tax.

❑ Employees tend to be in sympathy with the objectives of the organisation. There are two factors that point to this, the first being that due to the cost pressures on charities, full-time employees tend to work for lower salaries than the going rate for a comparable job in industry or commerce. The second notable thing is that most charities rely on an amount of voluntary labour, where individuals donate work time to the charity for no financial reward. Both of these features indicate an intrinsic motivation on the part of employees to assist the charity purely on the basis that they agree with its objectives.

❑ They are granted exemption from the taxation laws that apply to conventional business organisations. Charities may claim tax money back from the Inland Revenue on contributions made by individuals who have paid their donations after tax on their incomes. A more formal method of doing this is called a *covenant*, where an individual covenants (agrees) to pay a certain amount, usually monthly, to the charity for a period of at least four years. Recent legislation has enabled those on regular salaried incomes to give regularly to charity directly from their monthly gross income before tax is taken off – a scheme called *pay-roll giving*. Money left over at the end of the charity's financial year, in common with other types of not-for-profit organisations, is called a surplus, and in the case of charities, this is also not liable to taxation (in the belief that it will eventually be used for charitable purposes).

Review Questions

1. In what ways are not-for-profit organisations like other business organisations? (7.1)

2. In what ways do they differ from conventional business organisations? (7.1)

3. What are the principal types of not-for-profit organisation?

4. What are the major features of a co-operative? (7.2.1)

5. Why were co-operatives originally set up? (7.2.1)

6. Government departments exist to provide *public* and *merit* goods. What do these terms mean? Give examples. (7.3.1)

7. What is the biggest spending Government department? (7.3.2)

8. What does QuANGO stand for? (7.3.3)

9. Which group of people make the important decisions in a local authority? (7.4.1)

10. Give examples of the essential services that local authorities must provide? (7.4.2)

11. Why are charities so named? (7.5.1)

12. What are the organisational features that are unique to charities? (7.5.2)

Answer to Activity 1

Conventional ('for-profit') organisations primarily exist to generate profits (although we saw in Chapter 2 that this is something of a simplification). Not-for-profit organisations exist primarily to provide a product or service to their 'customer' group without making financial gain in the process.

Within business organisations, the profits can be used for many purposes depending upon the wishes of the directors and shareholders. They can be left in the business for re-investment or extracted in order to pay a dividend to the shareholders. Not-for-profit organisations do not have these options. When they have an operating surplus, they must use it within the organisation or else repay it to the donors (e.g. the treasury, the tax-payer, the charity bene-factor). No dividends are payable. Hence, the not-for-profit organisation does not itself benefit from the surplus – its beneficiaries may, but not the organisation itself.

Assignment

Question 1: Central Government

Central UK Government is based in Whitehall, Westminster. There are many separate government departments. Find out the full list of departments, and the name of the Minister or Secretary of State who is currently in charge of each.

Question 2: Local Government

Find out the following:

the name of the local authority which covers the college or university at which you are studying,

the number of councillors the local authority has,

the political parties to which the councillors belong,

the political party which has overall control of the council (if any).

Further Reading

Palmer A. & Worthington I., *The Business and Marketing Environment*, McGraw Hill (1992, Sections 2.4 & 2.6)

Section 3

An Introduction to
Organisational Theories

All businesses are made up of people working together. In this section we discuss the various types of structure that usually exist within organisations, and the behaviour of individuals in an organisational context, both of which are issues that successful managers should be aware of.

Contents   Page

8 Types of organisational structure

Objectives   After studying this chapter, students should be able to:

❏ describe the factors that determine the structure that an organisation adopts;

❏ draw and describe the authority lines in the following general organisational structures: functional, product, customer, geographic and matrix structures.

8.1 Introduction

The shape that an organisation assumes will depend upon a number of factors such as the organisation's:

❏ objectives;

❏ size (in terms of personnel);

❏ operation (i.e., what it does);

❏ geographical coverage;

❏ economies of scale.

In one sense, there are as many organisational structures as there are organisations, but to simplify things, we can divide structures into a number of generic types. These structures generally describe business organisations, but they can be equally applicable to some not-for-profit operations. The structure of most organisations will be able to be subsumed within one of the following:

❏ functional;

❏ product;

❏ customer;

❏ geographic;

❏ matrix.

Whilst these are useful generalisations, they are just that. Some organisations, particularly large ones, may be a combination of more than one form. Let us look at each in turn.

8.2 Functional Organisation

This is the most common form for manufacturing companies as it enables optimal control and accountability. The company is divided up into departments, called functions, and a senior manager (usually a director) is responsible for both the internal oversight of the function and ensuring it is adequately co-ordinated with the other functions in the business. We shall look at the internal functions in a company in more depth in

Chapters 18 to 24, but to summarise, the organisational structure will be as that shown in figure 8.1.

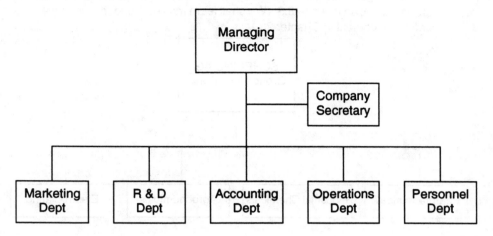

Figure 8.1: Functional structure

8.3 Product Organisation

Under a product-based organisation's structure, the products will be sufficiently different to warrant a different part of the company for each product area. Under each product, there will usually be operations and marketing functions, unique to the product. This structure is shown in figure 8.2.

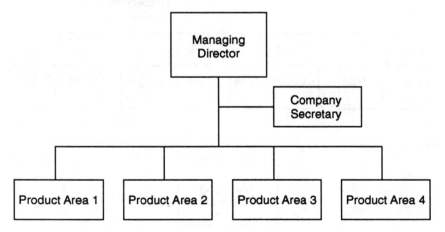

Figure 8.2: Product structure

8.4 Customer Organisation

Customer organisations are employed where the company caters for more than one sector of a market and special attention needs to be paid to that sector by organisational design. There may or may not be a production facility within the company producing for each customer grouping, but as far as selling into the customer groupings is concerned, the structure is typically like those shown in figure 8.4 and figure 8.5.

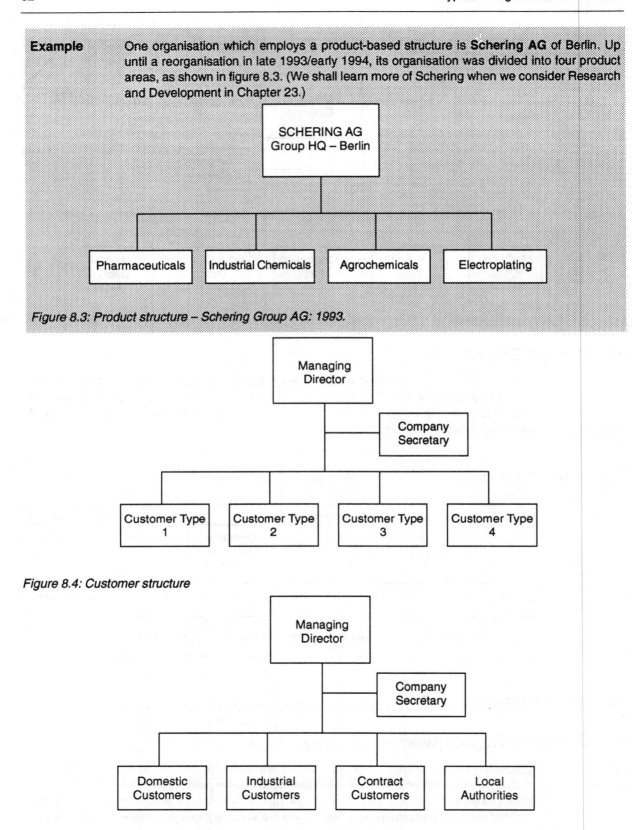

One organisation which employs a product-based structure is **Schering AG** of Berlin. Up until a reorganisation in late 1993/early 1994, its organisation was divided into four product areas, as shown in figure 8.3. (We shall learn more of Schering when we consider Research and Development in Chapter 23.)

Figure 8.3: Product structure – Schering Group AG: 1993.

Figure 8.4: Customer structure

Figure 8.5: An example of a customer structure

8.5 Geographic Structure

This structure is most suitably applied to large companies that operate across a number of different regions or even countries. They may have divisions or companies in separate regions which enable the organisation to gain the appropriate geographical coverage for the support of their business areas. This is a particularly common structure in very large multinational organisations. The example in figure 8.6 would be suitable for a very large company, but smaller UK companies may have separate divisions covering the regions of this country.

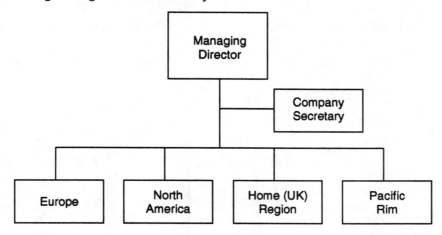

Figure 8.6: Geographic structure

8.6 Matrix Structure

The matrix structure is the most complex of the organisational forms we shall consider here. It is used in organisations where there is a great deal of interaction between departments or where staff are responsible to more than one manager, depending on which duty they are attending to.

In some large business organisations, work will be carried out along two avenues. Firstly, staff will work in their respective departments such as marketing, production or personnel. Secondly, staff from these departments will be assigned to projects or task forces, which will draw staff from across the divisions. This means that a member of the marketing staff may have responsibility to the Marketing Director and a Project Manager at the same time (see figure 8.7).

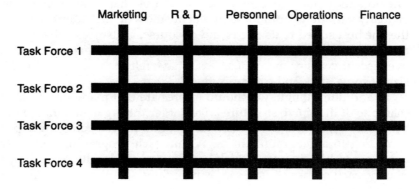

Figure 8.7: Matrix structure

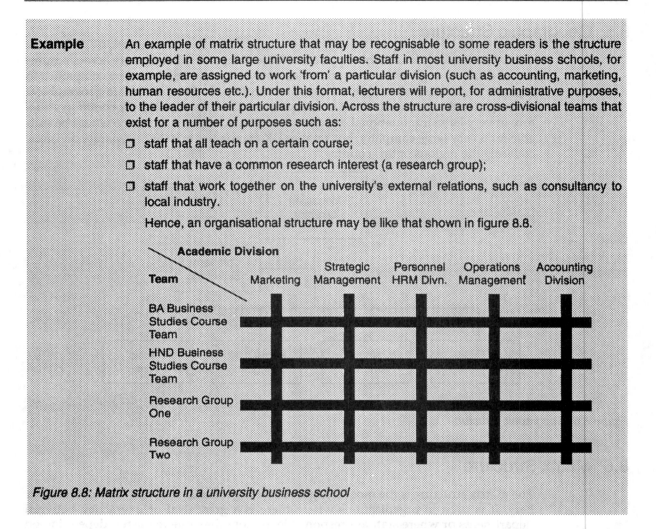

Example   An example of matrix structure that may be recognisable to some readers is the structure employed in some large university faculties. Staff in most university business schools, for example, are assigned to work 'from' a particular division (such as accounting, marketing, human resources etc.). Under this format, lecturers will report, for administrative purposes, to the leader of their particular division. Across the structure are cross-divisional teams that exist for a number of purposes such as:

☐ staff that all teach on a certain course;

☐ staff that have a common research interest (a research group);

☐ staff that work together on the university's external relations, such as consultancy to local industry.

Hence, an organisational structure may be like that shown in figure 8.8.

Figure 8.8: Matrix structure in a university business school

The matrix structure does work well when staff understand their positions in the matrix. They need to be more carefully managed than in other forms, and there are risks associated with it, such as staff being confused about whom they should report to first.

8.7 Combining Different Structures

The organisational structures described in this chapter are general types and there will be many variations from these in real business organisations. The company will adopt the one best suited to its needs and of course, as its needs change over time, so it may modify its internal structure. Restructuring has become a more common occurrence over recent years as many businesses have felt the need to rationalise and reduce the size of some parts of the organisation.

In addition though, we should appreciate that many organisations combine more than one of the above structures. The larger the organisation, the more likely this will be. It may be, for example, that a large multinational company is primarily structured according to a geographic form. Within each geographic region, the company then owns several businesses, which are divided up locally according to product types. Finally, each of these businesses is internally organised as a functional structure. This typical example is shown in figure 8.9 for a multinational chemical company.

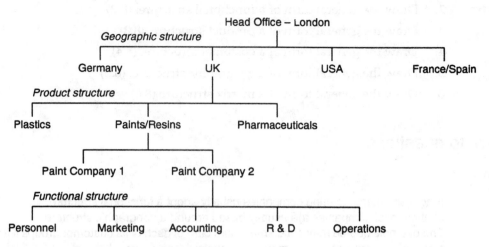

Figure 8.9: A typical multinational chemical company

Question 1 Which general type of structure will be most appropriate for the following types of organisation?

☐ A single site manufacturing company.

☐ A multinational motor manufacturer (such as Toyota which manufactures cars in 22 countries and sells them in 150).

☐ A company which sells cleaning services to many different customer groups.

Question 2 **Scottish and Newcastle Plc** is a large group engaged in brewing, leisure and retailing. Its group structure is as follows:

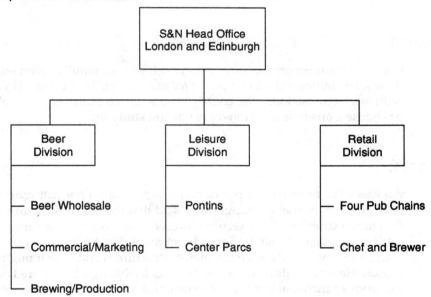

Figure 8.10: Group structure – Scottish and Newcastle Plc: Dec 1993

Which type of organisational structure does S&N most resemble? Explain your answer.

Review Questions

1. Summarise the factors that will affect the type of structure that an organisation adopts. (8.1)

2.   Draw the general form of a functional structure. (8.2)

3.   Draw the general form of a product structure. (8.3)

4.   Draw the general form of a customer structure. (8.4)

5.   Draw the general form of a geographic structure. (8.5)

6.   Draw the general form of a matrix structure (8.6)

Answers to questions

Question 1

Single site manufacturing companies usually adopt a functional structure.
Multinational companies are usually based around a geographic structure.
The example quoted may obtain maximum care of each of its customer groups if it were to divisionalise according to those groups – a customer structure.

Question 2

The structure of Scottish and Newcastle Plc shows us how hard it sometimes is to characterise a real life example according to simplified organisational structures. The three main divisions of the organisation, beer, leisure and retail do not fit neatly into any of the above. It is probably closest to a product structure in that the types of product supplied by each division is markedly different from the others. Others may argue that it is a customer structure, and this is also reasonable. Beneath the three divisions we are told insufficient information upon which to make any further observations.

Assignment 1

Choose a business organisation with which you are familiar. Find out *which structure(s)* it most resembles and *why it has adopted* that particular structure. If you are not familiar with any organisations, you could examine the structure of your college or university or choose a business local to where you are studying.

Assignment 2

An executive from a large public sector organisation has just returned from a conference at which he met a manager who said that the matrix structure is preferable to the functional structure. The executive is used to overseeing the functional structure and, until now, believed that it afforded him more direct control over his organisation. He wants to know exactly what the matrix structure is and how it might benefit an organisation. He also needs to know the drawbacks that may be suffered as a result of changing from a functional to a matrix structure. How would you answer his queries?

Further Reading

Cole G.A., *Management – Theory and Practice*, DP Publications (Fourth Edition, Chapter 21)
Mullins L.J., *Management and Organisational Behaviour*, Pitman Publishing (Third Edition, 1993, Chapter 10)

9 Structural and people issues in organisations

Objectives After studying this chapter, students should be able to:

- ❏ define and distinguish between *authority* and *responsibility*;
- ❏ explain what it means that these should be matched and why it is important;
- ❏ define *delegation* and explain the advantages and disadvantages of the practice;
- ❏ define *span of control* and describe some of the determinants of the span;
- ❏ explain what is meant be the *scalar principle* and describe how it is used in organisations;
- ❏ define and distinguish between *line* and *staff* employees;
- ❏ provide examples of where line and staff employees may be found in an organisation.

9.1 Authority and Responsibility

We have already seen how important it is that authority is taken up and respected. A concept closely allied to authority is *responsibility*. The two terms may be defined as follows:

> *Authority* is a person's *right* to make decisions, to allocate resources or to command others to carry out duties.

> *Responsibility* is a person's *obligation* to carry out certain tasks or activities. When a person is responsible for something, he will be held *accountable* for the outcome.

Within organisations, a certain amount of authority is necessary to ensure that all the tasks are carried out effectively. Those who have the authority for such tasks are also charged with the responsibility for them. This brings us to an important principle: that *authority and responsibility must be matched*.

The way this principle works is that if a manager is given the responsibility to oversee a project, a department or a task, he could not carry out the job unless also given the authority. The manager needs authority to organise and co-ordinate work in order to ensure that the area of his responsibility is fulfilled. A mismatch would give the manager in question a legitimate grievance against the relevant superior. It would also mean that the manager simply could not do what was expected of him.

In practice, to a greater or lesser extent, the principle often fails to be observed. This can be for a number of reasons, but the most common situations in which this principle is undermined are:

- ❏ When superiors 'interfere' in a subordinate manager's area of responsibility, for example by giving orders to junior staff under the authority of the subordinate. The subordinate still has the responsibility, but some of the authority is taken away by the superior.

❑ When the subordinate manager is held responsible for a happening which was not within his area of authority. The subordinate in this case does have authority, but not over the area for which he is being held responsible.

In practice, managers need to be given just the right amount of authority and responsibility to enable a task to be completed, and then left to 'get on with it'. Such an approach has the following benefits:

❑ If the person given the authority is successful in the task, then all the rewards will be due to that person. This serves to motivate and provide a degree of satisfaction in the task.

❑ If the task is poorly done or otherwise unsuccessfully completed, then there is no doubt as to who is to blame. Given that the person was given the authority, he also had the obligation to carry out the task. Hence, if rewards are given for success, then 'negative rewards' (e.g. punishments) or further development to improve the employee's performance will be the outcome of failure.

9.2 Delegation

Delegation is the method by which managers give work to other people. It should be understood though, that it involves more than just instructing a subordinate to undertake a certain task. In the delegation process, a manager who has responsibility (and authority) for a task, will appoint a subordinate to assume the responsibility and authority for the task in his place. The subordinate must execute the task in accordance with his superior's instructions and must not exceed his brief by stepping outside the small area of authority delegated to him. From the organisational perspective, the manager still holds the final responsibility for the task, even although it has been delegated. Therefore, the manager will ensure the delegate is performing the task (or has performed the task) to a successful conclusion.

The term *delegate* is often applied to a person who attends a conference or similar gathering on behalf of the organisation of which he is a part. In this context, the delegate is charged with representing the organisation with regard to a certain issue, and is instructed by the organisation on *how* to represent it. His responsibility does not allow him to act as he sees fit, but *only* as his organisation instructs.

Question 1   *When might passing work to a subordinate not be delegation as such, according to the discussion above?*

In the day-to-day working of organisations, delegation forms a regular part of normal functioning. It has, like most things, a number of advantages and disadvantages.

9.2.1 Advantages of delegation

❑ It relieves managers of some of their workload and gives them more time for important tasks like planning.

❑ It helps to develop subordinate staff. By giving a member of staff a little responsibility, he learns how to exercise it without the risks of taking on too much before he is ready.

❑ According to Herzberg, a major writer on motivation, responsibility is a motivating factor (See Chapter 28). It would follow that delegation helps to motivate staff.

9.2.2 Disadvantages of delegation

☐ In passing responsibility to a subordinate, the manager is introducing the possibility that the subordinate may not be up to the task. This would mean the task would not be successfully completed.

☐ A common failing of delegation is that the precise limits of responsibility and authority are not successfully communicated to the subordinate.

☐ Because he still holds ultimate responsibility, the manager may be reluctant to fully pass on the authority and responsibility for the task. This may result in an imbalance of the two.

9.3 Span of Control

The span of control (sometimes called the span of management) describes the number of people that report directly to a particular manager. If a manager has too large a span of control his effectiveness will be reduced as he will have to spend most of his time supervising staff. Conversely, a certain management function will require a certain span of control, and if insufficient staff are responsible to the manager, his effectiveness will also be reduced.

Conventional wisdom has it that a manager's span of control should be not more than twelve i.e. that not more than twelve people should report to any one manager. Ideally, it should be between four and six.

This approach though, is rather simplistic. In reality, there are a number of factors that will determine the ideal span of control for any management situation. These factors include:

☐ The complexity of the work.

The more complex the work, the lower the span of control.

☐ The variety of the work.

The more the variety, the lower the span.

☐ The quality of the management.

The better the management, the higher the possible span.

☐ The quality of the subordinates.

The more effective the subordinates, the more able they are to work with minimum supervision, hence the lower the span.

☐ The degree and type of technology involved.

Usually, the more complex the technology, the greater the individual supervision required, therefore the lower the span.

☐ The stability of the organisation.

In organisations where little change takes place and abrupt changes are not expected, there is an opportunity for a higher span.

☐ Health and safety considerations in the workplace.

The more hazardous the working conditions are, the greater will be the need for managerial oversight, hence the lower the span.

☐ Cost restraints.

Larger spans of control will result in fewer managers, which, because they get paid more than operatives, will result in a lower managerial salaries bill. This scenario often results from companies 'rationalising' in difficult economic conditions.

The implications as given above are meant to be indications only. There are always exceptions where a higher or lower span of control is necessary against the accepted wisdom.

9.4 Unity of Command

This is a very simple principle which states that any subordinate should report to only one 'boss' at any one time. Whilst this may seem an obvious requirement for the normal functioning of organisations, it is by no means always observed.

The purpose of this principle is to remove any potential ambiguity. Subordinates should know whom they report to and there may be a conflict of priorities if they are answerable to more than one supervisor.

Most organisational structures incorporate unity of command into each level of the business. The exception to this, as we saw in Chapter 8, is that of the matrix structure. Under this structure, staff may report to more than one 'boss' as part of fulfilling the objectives of the organisation.

Question 2   *What dangers might present themselves if unity of command is not observed? If an employee has two superiors, what negative effects may result?*

9.5 The Scalar Principle

9.5.1 What is the scalar principle?

The scalar principle states that a person referring to higher authority in the organisation proceeds through the chain of command one link (level) at a time. Its usage lies principally with grievances (complaints) but is applicable to a number of things in the workplace situation, such as gaining authorisation for a particular course of action.

The principle insists that individuals always contact their immediate superior first. If the subordinate fails to be satisfied by the meeting with his immediate superior, the procedure is to then go to his superior's superior, and so on up to the Chief Executive.

Many contracts of employment make reference to this principle under the 'grievances' section with a phrase which will typically read:

'All grievances should be taken up, in the first instance with your immediate superior ... The final authority in the matter of all grievances shall be the Managing Director'

Under this regime, a staff member is forbidden to make use of cross-functional lines of communication or informal networks (such as a particular rapport he may have with a senior manager).

9.5.2 The purposes of the scalar principle

There are several reasons why the scalar principle is observed.

❏ To give each level of management the right to make decisions about the subordinates over which it has authority.

❏ To ensure that senior management's time is not unnecessarily taken up with the concerns of junior employees.

❏ To reinforce the principle of hierarchy in the mind of the employee.

❐ To ensure that the subordinate's immediate manager is fully informed (in the first instance) as to the problems or requests of his subordinates.

❐ To weed out the trivial or valueless before it consumes expensive senior management time.

❐ To give the individual manager his 'right to manage' and to make decisions as he sees fit.

9.6 Line and Staff Employees

The demarcations 'line' and 'staff' are convenience terms, used to describe different categories of employees in organisations. They are not to be confused with other terms such as 'white collar' and 'blue collar' or 'factory' and 'office' employees.

9.6.1 Line employees

According to this distinction, *line employees* may be described as:

Those who have a *direct responsibility for fulfilling the organisations objectives*. In a manufacturing company, these will be those employees who have the direct responsibility for the flow of materials through the plant, from supplier to consumer.

Line employees will consequently be found in the following departments:

❐ production/operations;

❐ distribution;

❐ servicing;

❐ marketing/selling.

9.6.2 Staff employees

In contrast, *staff employees* are:

Those who have a *supporting or advisory role* to the line employees. They do not have any decision-making power over the flow of materials through the operation.

Again using the typical manufacturing company as an example, we can say that staff employees will be found in the following departments:

❐ personnel;

❐ research and development;

❐ work study;

❐ planning;

❐ secretarial, clerical and administrative;

❐ finance and accounts;

❐ maintenance and janitorial.

9.6.3 Line and staff employees in organisations

The terms line and staff do not indicate any particular level of management in the organisation. The line employees will include the factory operative, the Marketing Director and the Operations Director, and the staff employees will include the office junior, the Personnel Director and the Chief Accountant (see figure 9.1).

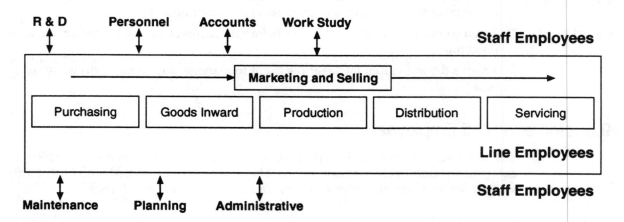

Figure 9.1 Line and staff employees

9.6.4 Significance of the line and staff distinction

In the example of the manufacturing company, line employees, because they are directly involved in the operations of the business, are the people who *add value* to stocks as they pass through the plant (see Chapter 19). This means that they take raw materials, and by making them into finished goods, make them saleable by the business at a price greater than the cost of the raw materials. Hence we may say that line employees *make money* for the business.

Staff employees, because they are involved in support and advisory activities (albeit very important and necessary ones), do not contribute directly to the value adding operations of the company. Put simply, staff employees *cost money*.

Personnel managers will monitor the ratio of line to staff employees in the business. The relative importance of each category will depend on the priorities of the organisation at any one time. It may be, for example, that when trading conditions are difficult, staff employees are considered to be relatively more dispensable than line. Other market conditions will reorientate the emphasis accordingly.

In some circumstances, staff responsibilities can be performed by people who are not part of the organisation. This is done in an arrangement called 'sub contracting'. Most commonly used with functions like cleaning and maintenance, it is also employed for more complex and confidential purposes like pay-rolls and recruitment. This has the benefit of reducing the number of staff employees.

Review Questions

1. Define and distinguish between *authority* and *responsibility*. (9.1)
2. Why must authority and responsibility be *matched*? (9.1)
3. What are the advantages and disadvantages of delegation? (9.2)
4. What is the span of control and why might it vary? (9.3)
5. Why is the unity of command important? (9.4)
6. What are the purposes of the scalar principle? (9.5)
7. What is a line employee? Give examples. (9.6.1)
8. What is a staff employee? Give examples. (9.6.2)

Answers to Questions

Question 1

Passing work to a subordinate is not delegation when the authority for the delegated activity is passed entirely to a subordinate and the organisational hierarchy recognises the fact. The subordinate is not responsible to the superior for the outcome of the activity.

Question 2

The principle of the unity of command says that an employee should have only one boss. In some organisations, an employee may have more than one boss, but this is usually for a particular purpose for a limited period of time (see Chapter 8 on matrix structure, for example). Whether such a situation results in negative effects will depend upon the employee and the particular situation. If the employee is self motivated and the two bosses are both aware of the employee's brief, then there need be no negative effect upon the employee's performance.

Problems may arise when the employee experiences a conflict of loyalties between the two bosses. This will inevitably result in him leaning towards pleasing one of his bosses which will result in the other boss being less than satisfied with the employee's performance. Perhaps most likely is the scenario where he makes efforts to please both bosses, but is actually unable to please either one fully.

For further thought

1. Examine the following scenarios. Do you think the span of control in the situations will be short, medium or long?

    The situations are oversight of:

    ☐ scientists in a cancer research team,

    ☐ line workers performing repetitive functions on a production line,

    ☐ monks in a monastery,

    ☐ academics in a university,

    ☐ spies working for the secret service,

2. What is the difference between a delegate and a representative?

3. Suggest reasons why some managers may be reluctant to delegate.

Further Reading

Cole G.A., *Management – Theory and Practice*, DP Publications (Fourth Edition: Chapter 22)

Mullins L.J., *Management and Organisational Behaviour*, Pitman Publishing (Third Edition, 1993: Chapters 3 and 16)

10 Culture, centralisation and growth in organisations

Objectives

After studying this chapter, students should be able to:

☐ give a definition of *corporate culture* and describe some of the factors that determine it;

☐ explain what is meant by *centralisation* and *decentralisation* with regard to organisations;

☐ describe the relative advantages of centralisation and decentralisation of organisations;

☐ describe the general mechanisms of organisational growth.

10.1 Internal 'Culture'

10.1.1 What is culture?

The culture of an organisation is a very hard term to define, but a very easy one to experience. It can be thought of as the sum total of the values, beliefs and personalities in the organisation. It is the 'feel' and 'morale' of the organisation and as such is experienced or observed. It cannot be seen from financial results or other corporate reports.

A useful way to look at it is as the *character* or *personality* of the organisation. Some organisations are characterised by a friendly atmosphere, some by an unpleasant one whilst others may be tense, individualistic or aggressive. One might expect a different atmosphere in an office of chartered accountants than in a shipyard or theatre company – they have different and unique cultures.

10.1.2 What determines the culture of an organisation?

Corporate culture can arise from many sources. but because it is so intangible, it is very hard to say how any particular organisation cultivates its culture. Typical determinants of culture include:

☐ philosophy of the founders of the organisation;

☐ nature and activities of the business;

☐ the employee relationships in the organisation;

☐ the degree of camaraderie and friendship that the employee enjoys;

☐ the quality of management-staff relationships;

☐ level of employee motivation;

☐ level of autonomy or control of employees;

☐ management style employed;

☐ nature and personalities of workforce;

☐ employees' perception of their job security.

Some organisations employ a very autocratic style of management, whereas others allow much more room for the personal expression of individuals. Whilst many of these differences can be explained by the type of organisation it is, many are due to seemingly intangible factors which are harder to define.

Determining corporate culture: British Telecommunications Plc

Some companies, in seeing the importance of corporate culture, try to determine it in advance by communicating the company's values to the employees in the hope that it will have a 'knock on' effect in the workplace.

BT has five 'values' that it encourages all employees to adopt. They appear on posters in working areas and the company recently introduced a scheme whereby staff can be nominated for small prizes for achievement of the values in their work. They are:

☐ We put our customers first;

☐ We are professional;

☐ We respect each other;

☐ We work as one team;

☐ We are committed to continuous improvement.

(Reproduced with the permission of British Telecommunications Plc: Jan 1994)

10.1.3 Why is culture important?

The importance of corporate culture is brought into focus when we consider the diversity of peoples' experience of working in organisations. Some organisations seem to inspire their employees to the point where they are proud to be associated with the employer, whereas employees in other businesses dread going to work and find the whole of their working day stressful and irksome.

The area of corporate culture is important as it can affect a number of the organisation's interests:

☐ employee motivation;

☐ staff turnover (the rate at which employees leave the organisation);

☐ the organisation's reputation as an employer in the community;

☐ the goodwill of existing employees and hence their willingness to 'go the extra mile' if so required;

☐ productivity;

☐ quality of work;

☐ absenteeism;

☐ industrial relations (management-union relationships).

So whilst the culture of an organisation is a rather difficult and inexact concept to articulate, it has a very real bearing on the way in which it operates.

Activity 1   *Try to find some phrases that describe the culture of your class at university or college. Do you think the culture is positive or negative regarding the achievement of success and teamwork in the group?*

10.2 Centralisation and Decentralisation

A key issue in *how an organisation is controlled* is the extent to which the organisation is decentralised. Let us define the terms:

In a **centralised organisation**, all decisions are made by one central control point ('the centre'). No decision making power is devolved to any other parts of the organisation.

In a fully **decentralised organisation**, some or all of the decisions are made by individual smaller centres. Whilst these centres still report to the central control, they enjoy autonomy, within limits, to allocate resources and generate money in the way they best see fit. A company in which most operating decisions are taken by individual centres is referred to as a *polycentric* ('many centred') organisation. The autonomous centres may take one of several forms:

❑ departments,

❑ divisions,

❑ separate companies (in the case of a holding company),

❑ cost centres (an arrangement in which a centre is made responsible for spending no more than a certain amount of money),

❑ profit centres (the centre is made responsible for generating a certain amount of profit from its activities).

The way in which an organisation is decentralised will depend on which type of structure it has adopted.

Between these two extremes are the varying degrees of decentralisation. The extent of decentralisation is highly important as it determines the nature of the control that the centre has over the organisation.

The following factors will have a bearing on the matter:

❑ the size of the organisation;
Usually, larger organisations will tend to be more decentralised than smaller ones.

❑ the nature and type of the organisation;
At opposite ends of the scale, sole traders will almost always be managed centrally, whereas the large Plc will usually be highly decentralised.

❑ the product or service that the organisation provides;
Some services can effectively be controlled from a single centre. Others require task-forces or autonomous divisions.

❑ the management style used in the organisation;
Some organisations have management that insist on making all key decisions from the centre. A philosophy growing in popularity is that of an 'enabling' or 'facilitating' management style. This encourages individuals and departments to assume the responsibility for decisions in their area.

❑ the application of the principle that 'authority and responsibility must be matched';
In this context, if a department or division has the responsibility over a certain area of the organisation, then it must also be given the amount of authority required to action accordingly. If the division has responsibility but the authority is exercised from the centre, then there is a mismatch under this principle.

As with all ideas in organisational theory, there are advantages and disadvantages associated with either option.

10.2.1 Advantages of centralisation

- ❑ Tight control can be exercised on all parts of the organisation. This means that the senior management who make the strategic decisions are also able to make operational decisions.
- ❑ Only the seasoned and experienced senior management make decisions. This reduces the risks associated with delegating authority to other sections.
- ❑ The company is, and appears to outsiders, to be unified and cohesive.
- ❑ Because decisions are taken close to the place where the orders are carried out, there is no need to introduce complex and expensive bureaucratic procedures. This cuts down on paperwork, meetings etc.
- ❑ There is no need to install expensive and complicated communications systems.

10.2.2 Advantages of decentralisation

- ❑ It relieves senior management of some of its burden of work, thus leaving more time for other activities. This advantage increases in importance in larger organisations.

- ❑ It is likely that divisional managers 'know best' how to act in their own local sphere of responsibility. Decentralisation enables them to make decisions as best fits the circumstances at the time.

- ❑ Divisional managers are made more aware of the financial implications of their actions, which will encourage them to be more cost conscious.

- ❑ It reduces the time taken for a decision to be made. This is because it is not necessary to make a request of the centre and wait for a reply. The decision can be made there and then by the divisional management.

- ❑ By devolving decision making to lower levels, staff are motivated and developed.

10.2.3 Examples of decentralised organisations

Common types of highly decentralised organisations include:

- ❑ multinational companies (MNCs);

  Under this format, the centre is in one country, but the different divisions of the company are in others.

- ❑ holding companies;
- ❑ Her Majesty's Government;
- ❑ government departments;
- ❑ some large private limited companies.

We can view the centralisation – decentralisation issue as a continuum (see figure 10.1).

Fully Centralised Operations		**Fully Decentralised Operations**
▬▬▬▬▬▬▬▬▬▬▬▬▬▬▬▬▬▬▬▬▬▬▬▬▬▬▬▬▬▬		
Single Site Business (e.g. Corner Shop)		Polycentric Businesses (e.g. Multinational Holding Company)

Figure 10.1: The centralisation – decentralisation continuum

Individual organisations can be situated at any point along the line, but the two extremes are *fully centralised* (e.g. a small single site operation) and *fully decentralised* (e.g. some very large multinational companies). Of course, most organisations will be somewhere in between.

10.3 Organisational Growth and Development

10.3.1 Two types of business growth

The growth of business has been a prominent feature of society over the past five decades. Whereas previously there were many small businesses, there has been an increasing trend towards fewer bigger companies. Broadly speaking, we can say that there are two general ways in which a business can expand. It can grow internally or externally.

Internal growth occurs when the organisation itself increases in size. This involves employing more people and increasing the volume of sales. Because of this, internal growth is sometimes termed *organic* growth.

External growth is the growth of a business through the *acquisition* (buying) of other companies, and through the merging of two businesses together. It is not at all uncommon for one business to buy another and this is done by buying a controlling shareholding in the acquired company. We saw how holding companies work in Chapter 6, and such businesses exist by growing externally (but this is not to say that the member companies of a holding group do not grow by internal means). Most of the worlds biggest businesses have made significant gains by external growth.

10.3.2 Ansoff's internal growth strategies

A major management theorist is **Igor Ansoff** from the United States. In an influential paper, he proposed that internal growth strategies can fall into four categories depending upon their use of products or markets to bring about the growth.

❑ **Market penetration** relies upon the increased use of the company's existing products in their existing markets. This strategy usually implies increased market share. Such a course of action requires some aggression towards competitors in order to take their market share. In some cases however, it can be achieved through the increase in the size of the market itself.

❑ **Product development** involves developing new products to sell to the company's existing markets. The products developed can either be completely new or be modified versions of those currently on the market (a 'mark 2' product). This strategy has the advantage that the company stays within the sector it already serves so the company's management will be able to use its knowledge of the markets to increase sales.

❑ **Market development** strategies are those where the company's existing products are placed in new markets. It is said that they develop the markets for their existing products. Markets differ both geographically (e.g. France is a different geographical market to the UK) and demographically. Markets are segmented according to age, sex, income etc. When a product is placed in a different segment, it is an example of market development. We shall learn more about this when we discuss marketing in Chapters 21 and 22.

❑ **Diversification** is when a company makes a significant change in direction. When a business diversifies, it launches new products into new markets. This is the highest risk of the internal growth strategies as it involves going into markets which the company may not be expert in, and by introducing products into those markets there is a significant chance of failure.

Igor Ansoff's product/market expansion grid, which shows his ideas visually, is shown in Figure 10.2.

	Existing Products	**New Products**
Existing Markets	Market Penetration	Product Development
New Markets	Market Development	Diversification

Figure 10.2: The product/market expansion grid

Internal growth: summary

Market Penetration	Same products, same markets
Product Development	Different products, same markets
Market Development	Same products, different markets
Diversification	Different products, different markets

10.3.3 External growth strategies

When a business grows by external acquisition, it buys another company. External growth strategies are categorised according to the type of company that is acquired. These strategies are divided into two types: *related acquisition* and *unrelated acquisition*.

Related acquisition is the purchase of a company that is in the same market sector as the acquiring company. The acquisition is given a different term according to the acquired company's relationship to the acquiring company. It is said that related acquisitions can be either vertical or horizontal where these terms rely on the reader imagining a schematic like that shown in Figure 10.3.

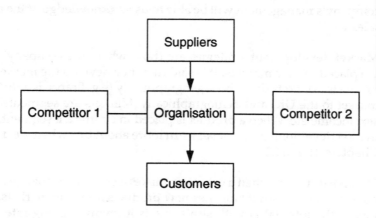

Figure 10.3: Related acquisitions

❏ **Horizontal acquisition** is when a business buys a competitor. This has two major advantages. Firstly, it automatically increases market share and the business becomes bigger in the specific market. Secondly, there is a probability that the acquisition will increase profitability. Not only is the company bigger and therefore more powerful as a buyer (being able to buy raw materials at lower cost) but as a supplier, increased market share means that the business has a more significant say over market prices.

❏ **Vertical acquisition** has two 'directions'. *Forward vertical integration* is the acquisition of a customer and *backward vertical integration*, the acquisition of a supplier. Buying a supplier should enable the company to be certain of continuous supply of the materials it needs for its processes as well as gaining a cost advantage over its competitors. By controlling the supplier, raw materials can be bought cheaper and at more convenient intervals. The reasons for buying a customer can include guaranteeing an outlet for products as well as gaining the profit margin that the customer charges on the products it sells.

Related acquisition: summary

Horizontal Integration	Buying a competitor
Forward Vertical Integration	Buying a customer
Backward Vertical Integration	Buying a supplier

Unrelated acquisition is the purchase of a company that is not within the product or market sector currently part of the company's portfolio. This too can be divided into two broad areas: *concentric acquisition* and *conglomerate acquisition*.

❏ **Concentric diversification** is said to have occurred when a business acquires another which, whilst not in the same product or market sector as itself, does have some other similarity. It may be that the business acquired uses similar technology, similar manufacturing processes or similar product marketing. An example of this might be a television manufacturer that acquires a micro-computer manufacturer. Both use micro-processors and involve electronics, so the company's existing expertise can be used with a little re-learning of product knowledge.

❏ **Conglomerate diversification** occurs when a business acquires another that has no obvious connection with itself. Accordingly, a conglomerate business is one made up of many different companies, each of which is involved in a different product offered in a different market sector.

Activity 2   In January 1994, the German motors group BMW acquired the British Rover Group from its previous owners, British Aerospace Plc. Describe this acquisition in terms of one of the acquisition strategies above.

Review Questions

1. What is 'culture' in an organisation? (10.1.1)
2. What are the determinants of an organisation's culture? (10.1.2)
3. Why is culture important in an organisation? (10.1.3)
4. What are the relative advantages of being centralised or decentralised as an organisation? (10.2.1 and 10.2.2)
5. Give three example of highly decentralised organisations. (10.2.3)
6. Define and distinguish between internal and external growth. (10.3.1)
7. Describe four generic internal growth strategies. (10.3.2)
8. Explain the various possible external growth strategies. (10.3.3)

Answer to Activity 2

Until the acquisition, Rover were a competitor to BMW. It follows therefore that this acquisition was *horizontal*.

Assignment

Prime Burger is a national chain of fast-food outlets which are located in busy shopping areas in town and city centres around the UK. The company's success over the past twenty years has been based on the provision of a restricted product range of consistent fast-food and beverage products in instantly recognisable surroundings. Its logo and restaurant design are also seen as important contributors to the well-known corporate image of the organisation.

The Prime Burger service philosophy is based around staff in uniforms, who can perform service tasks to an approximate script, from taking the customers order, entering it into the till/terminal and then giving the customer his purchased goods. Employees are discouraged from entering into any further dialogue with customers as a safeguard against distorting the image of efficiency and conformity the company wishes to portray to its customers. Service staff undergo a standard training programme when they join the company. This teaches them how to behave and what to say to a wide range of possible customer comments in addition to the scripts for taking orders and passing over food to the customer. One senior manager at Prime Burger describes the service policy as 'consistent service and consistent products – consistently'.

Tasks

1. Choose some appropriate adjectives to describe the corporate culture at Prime Burger.

2. Describe the strengths and weaknesses of such a culture.

A new Marketing Director has recently been appointed to the main Board of Prime Burger. After visiting a number of Prime Burger restaurants throughout the country, she has produced a discussion document which questions whether what she calls 'the straight-jacket approach' is the best way forward for Prime Burger. Her medium-term objective is to encourage more of a flexible culture where staff will be able to put more of themselves across to customers and to allow an upward flow of ideas from the shop-floor regarding possible improvements in the company.

3.   Outline the pros and cons of having a less regimented culture in Prime Burger restaurants.

4.   Describe some of the problems the Marketing Director may encounter in attempting to implement such a change in culture.

Further Reading

Buchanan, D.A. and Huczynski, A.A., *Organisational Behaviour – An Introductory Text*, Prentice Hall International (1985)

Richards, M., *Business Organisations*, NCC Blackwell Publications, Second Edition

Handy C., *Understanding Organisations*, Penguin Books, (Fourth Edition, 1992)

Pugh D S et al, *Organisation Theory*, Penguin Books (1990)

Mullins L.J., *Management and Organisational Behaviour*, Pitman Press (1993, Chapters 3, 9, 10 & 1)

Torrington D., Weightman J. & Johns K., *Effective Management – People and Organisations*, Prentice/Hall (1989, Chapter 9)

Luthans F., *Organisational Behaviour*, McGraw Hill (Sixth Edition 1992, Chapters 18 & 19)

Ansoff H.I., *Corporate Strategy: An Analytic Approach to Business Policy for Growth and Expansion*, McGraw Hill, New York (1965)

Quinn J.B., Mintzberg H. & James R.M., *The Strategy Process – concepts, contexts and cases*, Prentice-Hall International (1988 – The 1988 edition contains a condensed article by Igor Ansoff in Chapter 1, page 9)

For a more in-depth examination of the subject:
Morgan, Gareth, *Images of Organisation*, Sage Publications Inc. (1986)

Section 4

The Business Environment

So far we have dealt with businesses themselves. In this section businesses are put into the wider context of the various environments in which they operate, and their impact on the running of businesses.

Contents   **Page**

11 An overview of the business environment

Objectives   After studying this chapter, students should be able to:

- ❑ define and distinguish between external and internal environmental factors;
- ❑ describe the key areas of internal strengths and weaknesses in an organisation;
- ❑ describe the essential components of the external micro-environment;
- ❑ describe the essential components of the external macro-environment.

11.1 Introduction

The quotation 'no man is an island' refers to the belief that all people are, to an extent, interdependent. No single person is self sufficient. In the same way, no business exists in a vacuum. It depends for its success on a number of factors that exist in its environment, and therefore the people in the business should be aware of these factors.

We have seen already that all businesses need customers, employees and so on, but these groups form only part of the business environment. Many organisations and forces impact against the organisation, and for convenience, we can divide these into two main groups:

internal factors – those things that affect the business from within the organisation

external factors – those things that affect the business from outside the organisation.

External factors can further be divided into two: the external micro-environment and the external macro-environment. The business environment is shown diagramatically in figure 11.1 below.

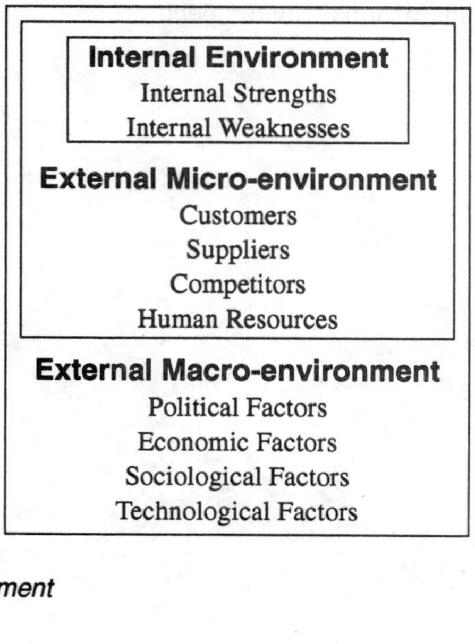

> **Internal Environment**
> Internal Strengths
> Internal Weaknesses
>
> **External Micro-environment**
> Customers
> Suppliers
> Competitors
> Human Resources
>
> **External Macro-environment**
> Political Factors
> Economic Factors
> Sociological Factors
> Technological Factors

Figure 11.1: The business environment

It is important to realise that the various components of the environment can affect the business in one of two ways. Firstly, they can pose a *threat* and secondly, they can offer an *opportunity*. One is a negative factor which can harm the business, and the other is positive and can benefit the enterprise. It is also possible that a change in the business environment will represent a threat to one organisation and an opportunity to another.

11.2 The Internal Environment

The success or otherwise of a business is greatly influenced by things inside the business itself, which can be considered as the internal *strengths and weaknesses* of the business. These can take many forms, but usually refer to one of the following areas. The things described below are, to a large extent, interdependent.

11.2.1 Quality of management.

The quality of management determines the success or failure of the business. Management decisions determine all aspects of the business's life. Poor decisions will work through into poor production, poor quality, poor products, poor marketing etc. In the same way, good decisions will lead to good results. The term quality, in reference to managers is a little hard to define. It can however be said to refer to such factors as:

❑ intelligence;

❑ leadership skills;

❑ interpersonal/communication skills;

❑ knowledge of the process, industry etc.;

❑ commitment and motivation;

❑ willingness/ability to change;

❑ resolve and perseverance ('staying power');

❑ initiative and 'flair'.

Two separate companies in an otherwise identical situation can prosper or fail as a result of the decisions of their respective management teams. This area is consequently of the utmost importance in any area of business or government.

Activity   *Make a list of the characteristics that a bad manager might have. How might each bad characteristic present a threat to the organisation?*

11.2.2 Financial position

The strength or weakness of a company's financial position can arise from a number of sources, not just how much 'money' it has. In extreme cases, a poor financial position can result in a company failing or 'going bust'. We can think of the financial position as a number of things, some of the most important being:

❑ ability to make good profits;

❑ ability to make more profits than competitors;

❑ cash in the bank;

❑ level of borrowing;

❑ amount of retained profit;

❑ cash flows;

❑ asset value (how much the business has invested in land, buildings etc.);

❑ ability to raise extra money;

❑ strength of the key accounting ratios;

❑ direction of the key accounting trends (sales, profits etc.).

(See Chapter 18 for a discussion of these features.)

Broadly speaking, a company with a strong financial position will have:

❑ high profitability (not necessarily high turnover);

❑ high retained profits (although this may be legitimately reduced by investment in the business);

❑ low borrowing, as loans must be paid back with interest;

❑ high cash flow, and little money tied up in stocks.

A company will have a weakness in this area if any of the above are reversed.

11.2.3 Competitive position

This refers to the ability of the company to compete in the market sector in which it operates and the characteristics of the market sector . Some companies occupy a strong competitive position, and this can result from one or more of a number of factors:

❑ high market share;

❑ high profitability;

❑ high retained profits (therefore more money for reinvestment);

❑ low production costs;

❑ modern and efficient manufacturing plant;

❑ unique or preferential access to raw materials;

❑ good products;

❑ good distribution networks;

❑ high year on year growth;

❑ strong brands;

❑ high customer loyalty;

❑ 'intellectual assets' – unique competencies the company has. These can take several forms:
  - formulations and recipes;
  - patents;
  - licenses;
  - uniquely qualified personnel.

11.3 The External Micro-Environment

The first level of the environment outside the organisation is what we may call the micro-environment. This is made up of the factors that impact upon the company from the immediate industry in which the company competes. This environment can be broken down into a number of components:

❑ suppliers of raw materials;

❑ customers and distributors;

❏ competitors;

❏ the availability of human resources;

❏ the availability of financial resources.

11.4 The External Macro-environment

Outside the immediate industry, other factors have a bearing on the organisation. These tend to be largely outside the control of the company and hence the business must learn to cope with them. They tend to be at the national or international level.

A commonly used acronym, which is helpful in breaking down this level of the environment, is **PEST**. This stands for:

❏ Political Factors

❏ Economic Factors

❏ Sociological Factors

❏ Technological Factors.

11.4.1 Political factors

These principally concern the laws that influence individual companies. In addition though, the way in which governments manage the national economy (referred to as their *policy*) can also affect businesses. There is also an increasing influence from the European Union (the EU, formerly the European Community) in the form of European regulations and directives.

11.4.2 Economic factors

These are influenced by Government, the performance of industry and by the cyclical movements in national and international economies. The main economic factors that affect businesses include rates of inflation, taxation and economic growth. Recessions are bad for business (low economic growth) whereas a buoyant economy is good, but it gets much more complicated when factors such as the budget deficit and the balance of payments position are taken into consideration. We shall look at these issues in some detail in Chapter 14.

11.4.3 Sociological factors

These concern those things that relate to large numbers of people. Businesses need people for a variety of purposes. The population and its movements can affect a business in several ways:

❏ trends, fashions and other factors that affect buyer behaviour;

❏ availability of appropriately skilled people to work for the business;

❏ population and the movements of population;

❏ concerns about the physical environment and the ethical aspects of business.

11.4.4 Technological factors

These have been an important part of the business environment since the industrial revolution in the late eighteenth century. During the course of the twentieth century, with the advent of the communications revolution, technology has assumed a greater importance in the life of business and of society in general. No business can ignore technological developments; if it does, it is at its peril. Since the middle of this century, every business has had a telephone and since the beginning of the nineteen eighties, microcomputers have been a commonplace adornment to accounts departments and factory management offices.

In the rest of Section 4 we will examine the various components of the external environment in a little more detail.

Review Questions

1. Explain the meaning of the terms *opportunity* and *threat* in the context of the business environment. (11.1)
2. What type of things should be considered when analysing the business internal environment? (11.2)
3. What are the components of the external business micro-environment? (11.3)
4. What are the components of the external business macro environment? (11.4)
5. What is the difference between the external business micro- and macro-environment? (11.3 and 11.4)

Answer to Activity

The question 'what makes a bad manager?' is a difficult one. It will depend in large part on the type of organisation the manager is in and the type of tasks that he is overseeing. As a broad generalisation, we may say that a bad manager may exhibit the following:

❑ poor communications skills;

❑ low intelligence;

❑ insensitivity to individuals needs;

❑ indecisiveness;

❑ no sense of direction;

❑ low ability to motivate;

❑ poor leadership qualities;

❑ disorganised and messy;

❑ poor technical knowledge of his speciality;

❑ lack of respect from his subordinates;

❑ poor level of education.

Assignment

In 11.3, we learned that the components of a business's immediate industry environment include its suppliers, customers, labour, financiers etc. Discuss the ways in which each of these factors can bear upon the company's ability to make profits. (Hint: this is to do with the strength of each group's influence upon the organisation).

Further reading on the business environment

Beardshaw J. & Palfreman D., *The Organisation in its Environment,* Pitman Press (Fourth Edition, 1992)

Palmer A. and Worthington I., *The Business and Marketing Environment,* McGraw Hill (1992)

Worthington I. & Britton C., *The Business Environment,* Pitman Press (1994)

Maitland I., *The Business Environment,* (*Made Simple* Series), Butterworth Heinemann (1994)

12 The political environment

Objectives   After studying this chapter, students should be able to:
- ❏ describe the structure and components of a state;
- ❏ explain the principal organs of state in the UK;
- ❏ describe the way in which the UK Government is funded;
- ❏ describe the way in which the Government is divided into departments;
- ❏ explain the distribution of Government spending in the UK;
- ❏ list the general objectives of the Government for the business sector;
- ❏ describe how Government can influence business through their departments, policies, and legislation;
- ❏ explain the principal areas of legislation that can affect businesses, including European legislation;
- ❏ describe some other political influences on businesses in addition to the UK Government.

12.1 The Structure of the UK Government

The United Kingdom, in common with all other advanced industrial economies in the world, is what is called a *mixed economy*. This means that there is a sizeable *private sector* (business organisations such as limited companies) and a *public sector*. The public sector includes central and local government and exists to provide those things that the private sector may not reliably supply, such as police, defence and education. The various organs of the public sector are also concerned with the regulation and monitoring of business organisations, to make sure they comply with the various laws that relate to them. In consequence, the Government is necessarily a very large body, employing, directly or indirectly, more than five million people, and handling finances to the order of hundreds of billions of pounds.

12.1.1 Government money – where does it come from?

The Government has many sources of income. Some money is raised for general expenditure and some is raised only for specific purposes. More than half of the Government's income comes from taxation. There are two forms of taxation.

- ❏ **Direct tax** is paid on income such as income tax and corporation tax (which is paid on company profits). Direct tax is charged as a percentage of income or profits.

- ❏ **Indirect tax** (sometimes called a *turnover tax*) is 'tagged onto' certain items we buy. These are called *duties* and the most common examples are VAT (value-added tax), and duties on tobacco, alcohol, petrol, solvents etc. The rate of indirect tax varies from item to item and it is revised from time to time. It is also charged as a percentage, but rather than as a percentage of income, it is calculated as a proportion of selling price.

Activity 1   *Find out the current standard rate of income tax, corporation tax and VAT.*

Other money comes from national insurance payments (linked to benefits in the Department of Social Security), rents on its property, land etc., dividends on shares it owns, and surpluses on trading operations (such as licences to extract oil from the North Sea).

In addition to these 'revenue' items, the Government also has *capital interests*. One important source of capital income in recent years has been the proceeds from selling off government companies to the private sector (privatisation – see Chapter 26). The sales of BP, BT and others has made significant contributions to government capital funds.

Figure 12.1 shows government income for the fiscal year 1992-93 (a fiscal year, or tax year, runs from April to April).

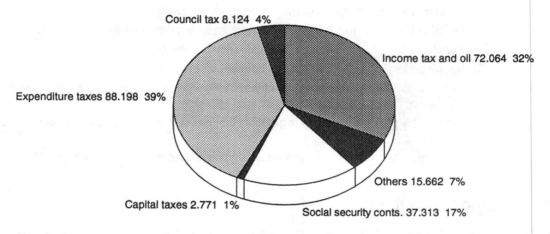

Figure 12.1: Government income for the fiscal year 1992-93 (all figures are in £ billions) (Source: Financial Statistics 1993, HMSO)

12.1.2 Components of 'the state'

A state is a self-governing geographic region. The UK, France and the USA are all examples of *nation states*, where the state is comprised of a nation of people with a common history (this is in contrast, for example, with *city states* – a feature of ancient Greece, where democracy was first practised). By definition, a state has the intrinsic right to raise taxes from its population and pass laws which the people must obey. All states are made up of four distinct components.

❐ **The executive**

The executive is what we commonly call 'the Government'. It is empowered to make the important decisions and to determine the policies that the state will implement. Because this is such an important job, in a democracy the people who will be affected by its decisions determine who will make up the executive. This is done by the voting in of a government usually every four to five years. The executive power rests in the hands of the senior politicians from the governing party – *the cabinet*. At the head of the cabinet is the *Prime Minister* and he or she chooses the members of the cabinet.

The office of Prime Minister (and *First Lord of the Treasury*) falls to the leader of the party which comprises the majority in the House of Commons after a general election. Within limits, the Prime Minister and cabinet colleagues can make decisions on their own initiative, but on most matters, they must gain the endorsement of Parliament.

☐ The legislature

This is the part of the state that is responsible for the drafting and passing of laws – sometimes called *legislation*. Again, in a democracy such as the UK, the individuals who make up the legislature are elected. The legislature in the UK is called *Parliament* (from the same origin as the French word *Parler* – to speak). There are two parts of Parliament, the *House of Commons* which is composed of elected members, and the *House of Lords*. The 'Lords' is composed of the *peers of the realm*, some of whom hold hereditary titles and of others who are awarded life peerages. Bishops in the established Church (The Church of England) and the so called 'Law Lords' are also members. The Head of State (the monarch) is also technically part of the legislature as the King or Queen must endorse Acts of Parliament before they become law.

The mechanisms by which legislation is drafted, debated and passed are particularly complicated, and much heated argument can occur between the political parties in both Houses of Parliament.

Definition **Democracy**

The word *democracy* is a conjunction of two words from the ancient Greek language. *Cratos* means 'rule by' and *demos* means 'the people'. Hence democracy implies a government ruling on a mandate from the people over whom it will rule. This is in contrast to *autocracy* (rule by the self) where a state is ruled entirely by a powerful individual with no reference to the wishes of the people, or *aristocracy* (*ariston* means 'the best'), where the most intelligent, the 'philosopher kings' impose their wills upon the state.

The earliest experiments in democracy were in the city states of Athens, Sparta and others in Ancient Greece where the men of the city were invited to express their opinions to the rulers in an open forum. The climate for the effective implementation of democracy evolved over the centuries with such things as the sixteenth century reformation in Europe and a number of other sociological changes. During the seventeenth and eighteenth centuries, philosophers in the West refined the theory of democracy into a more workable political format. Important names in this context were the British writers John Stuart Mill, and John Locke, whilst in Europe, Rousseau and others contributed to the intellectual debate.

Whilst a limited form of democracy was practised in several European countries, including the UK, 1776 saw it actually enshrined into a nation's constitution – the newly formed United States of America. As the nineteenth and twentieth centuries progressed, those given the right to vote for the Government increased with the inclusion of women as voters and the reduction of the voting age to 18. In advanced democracies, such as the UK, the people go to the polls to vote in a new government at least every five years, which is the maximum term any single government is allowed to serve. It must return to the people to receive a fresh mandate, and of course, if the people do not think the Government has done a very good job, it will be voted out and a new party voted in.

The philosophical architects of democracy stressed that democracy is a *social contract* between a government and the people, where each party agrees to act in a certain way. Equally important was that the political system should have 'checks and balances' built in, to prevent any single party gaining too much power. Hence, in the UK, we have a Government, and the job of *Her Majesty's Loyal Opposition* (the largest party in the Commons except for the Government) is to constantly oppose the Government. This way, the Government is forced to explain everything to the people and it is less likely that it will 'get away' with unfair policy, or a policy that acts against the interests of the people who elected it.

❏ **The secretariat or administration**

The administrative arm of the state is the largest and it serves whichever party is currently in power. It carries out the orders of the executive and legislature and ensures that the various laws are observed and that the country is generally kept running smoothly. The members of the administration are civil servants and other public sector employees, and they work for the various government departments.

❏ **The judiciary**

The judiciary is given the authority and responsibility by Parliament to enforce the laws that have been passed and the so called 'common law' (see section 12.7). The various components of this part of government ensure that the population adheres to the law by administering sanctions if it does not. Hence, the judiciary is made up of the courts, staffed by magistrates and judges who have varying degrees of authority to punish offenders or award damages.

12.2 Government Departments – Their Authority and Responsibility

Government departments are presided over by elected politicians who implement government policy in their respective departments. The departments which are seen as the most important are headed by a cabinet minister who is usually given the title Secretary of State. Beneath each Secretary of State is one or more Minister of State who is responsible for parts of the department's running. Figure 12.2 shows a typical department and the demarcation between executive and secretariat (in a simplified form).

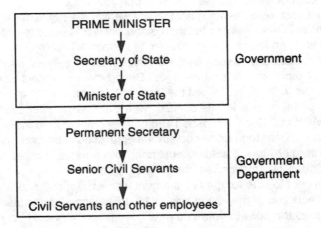

Figure 12.2: Authority structure in a typical Government department

Central government also oversees the activities of local authorities – what they are required or allowed to do. The Department of the Environment plays the major part in this, by helping to enforce the various pieces of legislation that apply to local authorities (such as the ways in which they may raise and use finance).

Each Government department is funded by the Treasury. The Treasury, in turn, receives most of its income from taxes, which are collected by the Inland Revenue (it supplements its income by borrowing). The head of the Treasury is the *Chancellor of the Exchequer*, who, along with the Foreign Secretary and Home Secretary occupies one of the three *great offices of state*. The amount of money allocated to each department is recommended to the cabinet by the Chief Secretary to the Treasury, another cabinet position.

12.2.1 Government spending through departments

The distribution of government (public sector) spending for the fiscal year 1992-93 is shown in figure 12.3.

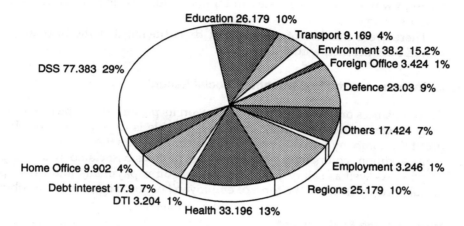

Figure 12.3: Government spending for the fiscal year 1992-93 (all figures are in £ billions)
(Source: Her Majesty's Treasury – report prepared specifically for the purposes of this text)

12.3 The Objectives of Government

Political parties disagree on many issues, and the stuff of politics is the arguing and debating of policy and ideas. Whilst they profoundly differ on the ways in which objectives should be achieved, there has historically been a high degree of concurrence between the main parties on those things that are desirable in relation to business and the economy. We shall look at these in some depth when we consider the economic environment, but to summarise, the principal objectives are:

- ❏ high growth rate in the economy (although environmental considerations may soon come to modify this objective);
- ❏ low unemployment;
- ❏ low inflation;
- ❏ the stimulation of exports;
- ❏ the encouragement of inward investment into the UK;
- ❏ low interest rates.

Favourable economic conditions make for a strong business sector which in turn can make the Government of the day more popular.

12.4 The Ways in Which the State can Affect Business

The state is highly influential to businesses. The influence arises from three sources. They are:

- ❏ direct influence through the actions of government departments;

❏ influence through economic policy;

❏ influence through legislation (laws).

We will examine each in turn.

12.5 Direct State Influence on Business

The first way in which the state can influence business is through its various government departments.

There are a number of government departments that the business organisation should be concerned with.

12.5.1 The Inland Revenue and the Department of Social Security

Every business organisation must pay tax on its profits. This type of tax is called company or corporation tax. The percentage payable is dependent upon the amount of profit the company makes. The Inland Revenue collects these taxes.

In addition, companies have a number of costs associated with the people they employ. As well as salary costs, the state requires payments into the Department of Social Security (DSS) in the form of employers' national insurance contributions.

12.5.2 The Department of the Environment

The legislation regarding local authority taxation is implemented in part by this department. It also has a role in administering legislation regarding pollution, industrial emissions regulations etc.

12.5.3 The Department of Trade and Industry (DTI)

The DTI and The Board of Trade have a wide influence upon businesses. They administer the wide range of grants and subsidies that are available. Some grants apply to small or developing businesses, and others are available for expansion and investment. The DTI tends to have two principle objectives: the reduction of unemployment and stimulating businesses to start up and grow. It is also responsible for the implementation of competition law in industry (see Chapter 25).

12.5.4 The Department of Employment (DoE)

This department administers the training and staff development grants that are payable to some businesses. It helps to enforce employment legislation and is principally concerned with increasing employment and improving the levels of training among the workforce.

12.5.5 The Department for Education (D for E)

We can consider the D for E as the government body which helps provide businesses with employees, as everybody is the product of education from either a school or university or both. Organisations also use the further and higher education sector as a source of continuing staff training and development.

12.5.6 Other departments

Other government departments act as important customers to some businesses. For example, departments such as Defence spend billions of pounds a year with the private sector, buying items such as electronics, planes and ships. Thousands of jobs depend on contracts to supply the Ministry of Defence.

12.5.7 QuANGOs

Another influence on some businesses are **QuANGOs** – (Quasi Autonomous Non Governmental Organisations). As the name suggests, these are not part of the Government as such, and they are usually created by specific legislation. They include some well known organisations such as the BBC, but others are charged with controlling or regulating certain sectors of the industrial environment. Among these are the Monopolies and Mergers Commissions which helps to regulate competition, and the various utilities regulatory authorities such as:

❏ OFTEL (Office of Telecommunications)

❏ OFFER (Office of Electricity Regulation)

❏ OFGAS (Office of Gas Regulation)

❏ OFWAT (Office of Water).

12.6 Government Economic Policy Influencing Business

The economic policies through which governments work can have profound effects on business. Usually when people talk about such policies, they mean one of two areas of policy: fiscal policy or monetary policy.

12.6.1 Fiscal policy

This describes the Government's regulation of the economy through taxation and public spending. Governments need taxation income (known as revenue) to fund the work of the government departments. However, whilst it may be good to invest money on public spending programmes, too high a tax rate is thought to stifle industrial growth. This is because corporation tax is paid out of profits. The more of its profit it must pay to the Government, then the less the business will have to reinvest to make it more competitive. Similarly, the more individuals pay in the form of tax (the higher the *rate of taxation*), then the less they will be able to spend on goods and services. Government policy tends to shift on fiscal policy as the economic climate changes, and there are differences of opinion in this area between political parties.

12.6.2 Monetary policy

Monetary policy refers to those policies that determine the *price and availability of money*. This area impacts upon such matters as interest rates (the price of borrowed money) and how much money is in circulation in the country at any one time. The knock on effects of monetary policy, as we shall see in Chapter 14, have a great influence on inflation, the company's cash flow and profits, and the value of the pound sterling against other world currencies. The Government is also concerned with the rate of growth in the money supply (the amount of money in circulation).

Activity 2   *Find out the current basic rate of interest (sometimes called the bank base rate).*

We will examine fiscal and monetary issues in more depth in Chapter 14.

12.7 Legislation Affecting Business

12.7.1 Introduction to law

In a democracy such as the UK, all activities, whether business or domestic, must be carried out within the framework of the law. Law can arise from one of two sources:

- ❐ **Statute law** (or legislation) is passed by the legislature, that is the elected House of Commons, the House of Lords, and then granted royal assent by the Queen. It is enforced by the courts, the police and prison services.

- ❐ **Common Law** consists of law that has arisen from the judgements of the courts in decided cases. It is sometimes called 'case law' as it arises from *judicial precedent* – the decided outcome of one case being an indication as to how a similar one should be resolved.

Activity 3	*We all agree that murder is a very serious crime. Do you think that murder is a matter of common law or statute law? Discuss your thoughts with colleagues.*

As a general rule, we can say that laws have three overall purposes, to *restrain* (or constrain), to *enforce* and to *permit*. Put more simply, there are things we must do, and things we may do, as prescribed under law. Whilst some sectors of society (including some business sectors) may complain that a certain law causes them some inconvenience or hardship, it should be remembered that the purpose of the law is to allow society as a whole to function in an orderly and predictable fashion. This allows people and businesses to make and implement plans unmolested by others. So whereas some may be penalised, the majority should benefit. Parliament, we have seen, is accountable to its electorate (you and me), and accordingly, it is assumed that laws passed by Parliament will have majority support from the population.

One of the duties of a company's agents (the directors) is to ensure that all parts of the law are kept by the business. In some organisations, this can be a very complicated concern, as a number of legal Acts may apply. We will consider some of the key areas where legislation affects business, but students are invited to refer to one of the texts mentioned at the end of this chapter for a more detailed look into this area.

Definition	**Act of Parliament**
	During the course of the passage of a piece of legislation through Parliament, a number of stages are observed. Legislation usually originates with a government department, but individual members of the Houses of Lords and Commons may also propose it. When it is passing through the various stages of discussion it is referred to as a *Bill*. Each Bill must receive three 'readings' in each House, and when it has completed all procedures, and assuming it has received majority support in both Houses, it goes to the Queen for *Royal Assent* and becomes an *Act of Parliament*.

There are several types of law that can affect business. Whilst law and business have many interfaces, we can say the most important legal areas fall into four broad categories.

- ❐ Company law,
- ❐ Contract law,

❏ Employment law,

❏ European Union law.

12.7.2 Company law

The laws which govern the ways in which companies must act go back well into the nineteenth century. Consequently, this area of law has evolved over time as conditions have changed and controls have needed to be introduced. **The Companies Act, 1985** served to draw together into a cohesive whole the many previous smaller Acts. Its purpose was to clarify the law and to a certain extent, bring it up to date. Companies legislation defines the various forms of business organisation (e.g., **The Companies Act, 1980**, section 1 defines a Plc) and also prescribes the documents that must be submitted upon incorporation (as seen in Chapter 6). One interesting development of the Companies Act 1985 was to change the *objects clause*. Whereas the memorandum of association previously required companies to state the exact businesses they intended to compete in, the 1985 Act allowed companies to state that they intended to 'carry on business as a commercial company'. This clause enabled companies to carry out any business – a convenient format for businesses intending to compete in more than one market. **The Companies Act, 1989**, made further changes in this area.

Legislation involving a company's financial liability to the Government can also be indirectly considered as company law. Money bills which are passed from time to time dictate the levels and types of taxation and impact on government spending and monetary policy.

12.7.3 Contract law

Contracts exist in business in a number of contexts. Common ones are contracts of sale, of supply and of employment. Put simply, a contract is *an agreement which the law will enforce*. In order for an agreement to be a contract, four conditions must apply.

❏ Parties in the contract must have *legal entity* (or capacity). This means that the contract exists between such as individuals, sole proprietors, limited companies etc. See Chapter 5 for a definition of legal entity.

❏ There must be an *offer*, and an *acceptance* of the offer. If goods are offered for sale at a certain price, no contract exists until somebody accepts the offer and agrees to pay the price. Similarly, a job offer with an agreed salary becomes a contract when the prospective employee accepts the offer.

❏ There must be a willingness to enter into a *legal relationship*. Both sides must be aware of their legal and binding responsibilities in respect of the contract and be willing to accept the implications of it.

❏ There must be *consideration*. Consideration is the legal word for payment, which is usually in the form of money, although exchanges of goods and services (swaps) can also come under contract. Hence, gifts and voluntary donations of time or money are not contracts in this sense.

There are several pieces of legislation that govern the general basis of contract law (the general form of contract is an area of common law). These can be considered as regulators of the general form of a contract agreement. As a collective group of Acts, these are usually considered as **Consumer Protection Law**. This is because they restrict and prescribe the commercial behaviour of a business towards its consumers.

❐ **The Sale of Goods Act 1979 (SoGA)**

This Act controls commercial contracts with regard to the quality of goods supplied and their description. For example, Section 13 of the Act refers to the insistence that the description exactly matches the goods sold – contravention of this renders the seller guilty of misrepresentation. Section 14 provides a condition that goods sold will be of merchantable quality and be 'fit for the purpose' for which they are intended or bought. This Act has implications for every commercial business organisation.

❐ **The Trade Descriptions Act 1968**

The Trade Description Act 1968 prohibits sellers from giving a false description of goods or services if the seller knows that such description is false. Because the Act is part of *criminal law*, those found guilty of contravention can be fined or imprisoned.

❐ **The Unfair Contract Terms Act 1977**

In summary, this Act prevents any attempt to negate or circumvent the terms of the **Sale of Goods Act 1979** or the **Trade Descriptions Act 1968**. It has particular relevance to those contracts made by businesses with consumers and has limited applicability to contracts made between businesses. In other words, the Act closes the loopholes that may allow businesses to sell products that are not of merchantable quality or 'fit for the purpose'. Put simply, it says that *no excuses will be tolerated*.

Definitions   **Civil and criminal law**

Laws vary in how seriously society views them. Some behaviour by individuals is viewed as so seriously wrong, that the state must act against the offender to protect the other members of society. This is the implementation of criminal law, and criminal offences include murder, burglary, assault and many other offences of this type. There is other behaviour however, that whilst not being as seriously wrong as criminal acts, are seen as being *unfair* to a certain member or members of society. In this case, the law sits not as executioner, but rather as umpire – to see that fair play takes place. This is civil law and can include anything from breaches of the common law of contract to accidentally throwing a snowball through somebody's window. In civil law cases, the 'offender' is not guilty of criminal wrongdoing, but rather of behaviour which merits some form of reprimand. The law is empowered to see that an offended party (the man with the broken window and a snowball on his lounge floor) is recompensed for the damage. The distinction between these is emphasised by the use of different legal terminology.

Criminal law	Civil law
The case is referred to as	The case is referred to as
The State (or 'R') v. Smith	**Smith** v. Jones
The **Crown** (State) initiates proceedings	The **plaintiff** (offended party) initiates proceedings
The Crown **prosecutes**	The plaintiff **sues**
The **accused** is prosecuted	The person sued is the **defendant**
The accused, if found **guilty**, is punished (e.g. by a fine or imprisonment)	The object of civil proceedings is to provide the plaintiff with a **remedy** (e.g. damages or compensation) if a defendant is found to be **liable**.

12.7.4 Employment Law

Employment law is a very large part of the business's legal environment and its complexity is due to the fact that it impacts upon so many areas. The weight of employment law is imposed by the state (and the EU) to ensure that employees are treated fairly and consistently by their employers and to legislate for good conditions of work. A list of the major areas of employment law will illustrate the breadth of its applicability.

❏ Employees' terms and conditions of service.

❏ Sexual and racial discrimination.

❏ Employment of ex-offenders.

❏ Employment of disabled workers.

❏ Maternity rights.

❏ Equal pay.

❏ Dismissal from employment.

❏ Redundancy.

❏ Health and safety laws and regulations.

❏ Sexual harassment at work.

There are several key pieces of legislation which govern the above and some Acts cover more than one area of employment law. A detailed discussion of this area is beyond the scope of this text, but readers are invited to refer to the further reading on this subject at the end of this chapter. Some of the principal areas of legislation are briefly described below.

❏ **The Employment Protection (Consolidation) Act, 1978** sets out the rules for the *terms and conditions of work* (sometimes called the contract of employment) and for the various scenarios that may surround an individual's leaving employment. According to this Act an employer must provide the employee with written terms and conditions of employment within two months of the beginning of employment. In practice, most contracts are issued in advance of the employee's starting date.

The contract must include details of, among other things, pay, hours to be worked, holidays allowable, sickness pay, who the new employee reports to, notice of termination (usually in days), job title, and the company's rules for disciplinary and grievance matters.

Unfair dismissal by an employer is protected against by section 54 of the Act, which states, *"every employee shall have the right not to be unfairly dismissed by his employer"*. This, however, does not apply to the forces (including police and armed forces) and normally only comes into effect when the employee has worked two years of continual service. Fixed term contracts are also excluded under these terms. Examples of grounds for unfair dismissal include trade union membership, pregnancy, sexual orientation, marital status, race or when the company is sold as a going concern. In addition, the employer must observe a dismissal procedure which may include warnings, appeals and the like.

Redundancy is covered by section 81 of the Act which says, *"every employee who is dismissed by reason of redundancy shall receive from his employer a redundancy payment"*. Redundancy occurs when the employer's need for a particular employee's labour stops or reduces. This can happen for one of several reasons, such as lack of product demand, strategic repositioning of the business etc. Again, the requirement to provide redundancy payment only comes into force when the employee has done two years of continuous work for the employer.

☐ **Discrimination**, which can be sexual or racial, is covered in at least six separate pieces of legislation. The **Sex Discrimination Act 1975, The Sex Discrimination Act 1986, The Race Relations Act 1976, The Employment Act 1989, The Equal Pay Act 1970** and **The Treaty of Rome 1957** all impact upon this area. Discrimination refers to the fair and equal treatment of all employees and prospective employees regardless of sex, race or anything else that may unfairly favour one group over another. It includes equal opportunities for employment, promotion, etc. and equal pay for equal jobs. Some secondary European legislation has also had a bearing on discrimination (see paragraph 12.7.4 of this chapter). An area linked to discrimination is that of sexual harassment, and this is covered, among other things, by a 1991 EU code of conduct on the subject. Sexual harassment can be directed at women or men.

☐ **The Rehabilitation of Offenders Act 1974** provides the legal framework for the employment of ex-offenders. In essence, this Act says that prison and other confinement sentences can become 'spent' as far as declaring them when applying for jobs is concerned. The length of time it takes to have a sentence spent depends upon the length of sentence – those over 30 months are never spent. This does not apply to certain important professionals such as doctors, teachers, accountants and nurses where sentences are never spent, however short they may have been.

☐ The responsibilities that employers have towards disabled individuals is covered by **The Disabled Persons Acts** of **1944** and **1958**, and more recently by the **Companies Regulations Act 1980**. Between them, these Acts say that companies that employ more than 20 employees must employ disabled workers at a rate of 3% of the workforce, and that larger companies (of more than 250 employees) must include a statement in their annual accounts regarding the way the company has acted towards disabled workers over the year.

☐ Maternity rights and maternity pay are described by two recent Acts, **The Trade Union Reform Act 1993** and the **Employment Rights Act 1993**. These cover the amount of time that women are allowed to take off work, their right to return to work and the monies payable during their absence.

❏ The final important area of employment law is health and safety issues. This is a large area of law in itself. The original **Health and Safety at Work Act (1974)** was introduced to restrict those employers who did not make adequate provision for employees in this regard. Some employers chose not to invest in personal protective equipment for their staff and this resulted in many serious and fatal injuries. With the advent of the **Control of Substances Hazardous to Health (CoSHH) Regulations 1989**, the responsibility for personal protection in the workplace was placed jointly on the employer *and* the employee. The employer is constrained to provide appropriate protective equipment and the employee is compelled to use it. Failure to use equipment provided by the employer could not only mean serious injury to employees, but could also attract a fine under CoSHH.

12.7.5 European Union law

When Britain joined the European Union in 1972, it automatically became subject to a whole new area of legislation in addition to the UK national law. The document that founded the EU in 1957, **The Treaty of Rome 1957**, is a legal document to which every member state must comply. This lays down the basics and underlying rules of Union activity and is referred to as the *primary* source of European legislation.

In addition to the primary legislation, the European Union also passes two areas of *secondary* laws. These are passed by the Council of Ministers and are consistent with the spirit of the framework of the Treaty of Rome. The two areas are:

❏ **European Regulations**

Regulations tend to be concerned with issues of European Union policy. The important feature of European regulations is that when they are passed by the Council of Ministers, they pass immediately into law in each member state – i.e., without passing through the legislatures of the various countries.

❏ **European Directives**

Directives, as the name suggests, are laws which are specifically directed at certain parties only (such as individual member states, some of the states or even all of the states). While the member state or states are required to implement a directive in full, they may choose when and how to do it (which is not the case with regulations). Directives that apply to the UK are usually implemented in the form of legislation in Parliament.

Case Study   **The introduction of tachographs in commercial vehicles**

EEC Regulation 1463/70 dictates that all commercial vehicles over a certain weight are to be fitted with a mechanical recording device called a tachograph. This instrument measures the speed of the lorry and the length of time that the driver has been in the cab driving. It was designed to prohibit lorries from exceeding their specific speed limits and to ensure that lorry drivers do not drive more than so many hours per day. It was believed that these measures helped to protect other road users from fatigued or reckless lorry drivers. As a regulation as opposed to a directive, this piece of legislation passed into law in all member states and it should have been implemented in full by the beginning of 1976. Three years later in February 1979, the UK was taken to the European Court of Justice for failure to implement Regulation 1463/70. In the case **EC Commission versus The United Kingdom**, the court held that the UK had violated the EC Treaty of Rome by refraining from introducing enforcement measures to apply the regulation.

The then new Conservative Government set about putting things right. Secretary of State for Transport Norman Fowler said that he planned to legislate this regulation into British law (even though it ought to have become law automatically) and by 1982 it was a statutory requirement of all lorries in the UK. This brought the UK in line with all other EU states and enabled it to comply with the EU Regulation.

12.8 Other Political Factors

As well as the influences of the UK Government on businesses, there are a number of other areas that ought to be considered. Some are international factors, but others are linked with the structures of the industrial and political environment. Some of these are discussed below.

12.8.1 The European Union

Since Britain joined the EU in 1972, the legislation from the Union has become increasingly important to the British business. Linked to this are the matters that relate to European integration, such as the pound in the *Exchange Rate Mechanism*, and the **Single European Act 1992** (Maastricht Agreement). Legislation and directives can affect a business on anything from pollution and chemical emissions to the insistence on the placing of an antiglare screen in front of a computer monitor.

12.8.2 Trade unions

Trade Unions attempt to represent the interests of their members in negotiations with their employers. Many of the things which unions wish to see, such as higher wages, safer working conditions and shorter hours, whilst being good in themselves, may have the effect of reducing company profits. At a national level, the larger unions lobby parliament and have strong links with the Labour Party. Hence, they may have an influence on a Labour Government's policy.

12.8.3 Foreign governments' policies

Because Britain trades extensively with the rest of the world, many companies rely heavily on business with overseas markets. In the same way that the UK Government can affect UK business, so the foreign governments can affect the domestic environment of foreign companies. For example, different countries impose different import tariffs which influence the price the imported goods sell for.

Definitions   **Tariffs and quotas**

These terms are applied to importing arrangements that exist in certain countries. They are designed to generate tax revenues and as a measure to protect, to a certain extent, the country's own producers.

A tariff is a certain amount of money that the importer must pay the host government in order to bring an item into the country. For example, cars imported from outside the EU attract a 10% tariff on purchase cost which the importer must pay when he imports the car. The proceeds from the tariff will go to the UK Government (if imported into the UK). The tariff will vary between different types of goods, and different arrangements exist between different countries and trading blocks.

> **A quota** is a maximum limit that is placed by a country on imports of a certain item. They might say, for example, that only so many Japanese cars may be imported in to the UK in any given year. Similar limits are placed on other goods, and again, these vary widely from country to country.

12.8.4 The role of international organisations

Some organisations exist to represent a particular interest at supranational level By obtaining international agreement on a certain course of action, such organisations can profoundly affect the exporting company. For example GATT (General Agreement on Tariffs and Trade) aims to abolish, or at least reduce, trading restrictions that exist between countries. Even the limited success of GATT has had some significant impact upon some industries.

Review Questions

1. List the four essential components of a state. (12.1.2)
2. Name the four principal organs of state in the UK. (12.1.2)
3. What are the essential objectives of Government as far as business is concerned? (12.3)
4. What are the three principal ways in which the state can influence business? (12.4)
5. Name the major government departments that businesses should be aware of. (12.2)
6. Define and distinguish between fiscal and monetary policy. (12.6)
7. What are the four broad types of legislation that can affect business? (12.7.1)
8. What are the major areas under the general heading of employment law? (12.7.4)
9. Apart from state influences, what other 'political' organisations can affect UK businesses? (12.8)

Assignment

Scirocco Plc is a large British company with manufacturing sites in the UK, Germany, Eastern Europe, North America, and the Middle East (Jordan). Its products fall into four broad areas: pharmaceuticals, plastics, tobacco and petrochemicals (oil and related products). It employs 112 000 people throughout its worldwide operation and it does business, either directly or through distributors in 76 countries.

There are many ways in which the political environment can influence Scirocco Plc. Outline the major areas of possible concern and support your answer.

Further Reading

Thomas G.P., *Government and the Economy Today*, Manchester University Press (1992)
Holland J.A. & Webb J.S., *Learning Legal Rules*, Blackstone Press Limited (1993) (a good introduction to legal reasoning)
Abbott K. & Pendlebury N., *Business Law*, DP Publications (Sixth Edition)
Curwen P. et al, *Understanding the UK Economy*, Macmillan Press (Second Edition, Chapter 1)
Beardshaw J. & Palfreman D., *The Organisation in its Environment*, Pitman Press (Fourth Edition, Chapters 17, 19, 20 and 21)

13 The economic environment 1
An introduction to the theories and demands of supply

Objectives   After studying this chapter, students should be able to:

- [ ] understand the general scope of the subject of economics;
- [ ] define and distinguish between *micro-* and *macro-* economics;
- [ ] describe the cycle in which money flows in a modern economy;
- [ ] define *demand* and explain the methods by which a demand curve can be used by managers;
- [ ] define *supply* and explain how the supply curve can be used by managers;
- [ ] describe how the supply and demand curves for a product can be used to calculate the market price;
- [ ] understand the term *elasticity* and its application with regard to predicting changes in demand and supply resulting from changes in price and income.

13.1 Introduction to Economics

We saw in Chapter 1 that business is all about trade involving money – making it, managing it and spending it. An underlying understanding of *how money works* is therefore essential to any study of business. The social science concerned with a society's commercial activity and the movements of money is **economics.** The broad theme of economics is then usually sub-divided further into two major areas – *micro-economics* and *macro-economics*.

13.1.1 Micro-economics

This is the study of the actions of individuals and companies. The Penguin Dictionary of Economics defines it as *'the way in which their [businesses] decisions interrelate to determine relative prices of goods ... and the quantities of these which will be bought and sold'*. It refers to such things as:

- [ ] the level of demand for particular products;
- [ ] the costs of production;
- [ ] the characteristics of the markets;
- [ ] the nature and behaviour of competitors and their products.

13.1.2 Macro-economics

This is the study of the actions of industries, companies and countries. Of particular concern to this area are:

- [ ] the rate of economic growth of the country as a whole;
- [ ] the ability of the private sector of the country to compete with those in other countries;

❏ the amount of money raised in taxes by the Government and the amount of money the Government spends (fiscal factors, see section 12.6);

❏ the 'price' of money, usually meaning the rate of interest charged on loans (monetary factors, see section 12.6);

❏ the value of the currency;

❏ other 'economic indicators' which are at the national level such as the strength of exports, the balance of payments, inflation, unemployment and the money supply.

13.1.3 The flow of money in an economy

Money circulates in the '*economy*' between individuals, companies and Government. A simple schematic illustration of this is given in figure 13.1.

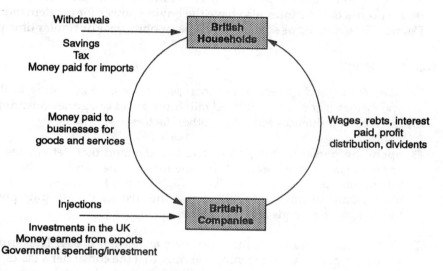

Figure 13.1: The money cycle – how money flows in an economy

Customers pay businesses for goods and services. Businesses then use this money to pay their own suppliers, their owners (shareholders) and their employees. These groups then use their earnings to spend money in other businesses. Hence we see the circulation of money in society. Money is taken out of this cycle when either businesses or individuals delay spending by saving (but even this money re-enters the cycle indirectly when banks use deposited money for loans).

The national circulation of money is also increased or decreased by dealings with other countries. When Britain exports, money from abroad flows *into* the national economy in exchange for goods and services. The converse is true of imports – money leaves the UK to pay foreign companies for imported products. All of these factors depend largely on the demand and supply of goods and services.

The amount of money in circulation, the ways in which it is spent by all three parties (individuals, businesses and Government) and the speed with which it moves depends upon a number of indicators or factors. It is also these indicators that determine much of the health or otherwise of the business sector. We shall look at these macro-economic indicators in Chapter 14.

13.2 Demand

13.2.1 What is demand?

The demand for a good or service can be defined as:

The *quantity* *demanded* of a certain good in a particular *time period* at a *certain price.*

We can see that demand has three components; *the quantity bought, the price that consumers are willing to pay* and a *time period over which the quantity is demanded.* Hence, what economists call *effective demand* is the desire to buy backed by the financial means to do so within the time period. There is little value in discussing how much people desire products, they must also have the buying power for the demand to be effective. Demand is measured as so many units per month, year or similar time period.

13.2.2 What causes demand?

Demand for a good or service can increase or decrease according to the influence of several factors. They can be divided into three broad categories: spending power influences, fashion influences and a few 'other' factors.

❑ **Spending power** is that part of effective demand that determines the customer's *ability to buy.* It is self-evident that the more money an individual has, the greater will be his spending power. Hence, high wages, low taxes, low interest rates and other factors of this kind will increase the customer's spending power and hence the demand for goods and services.

❑ **Fashion issues** influence the consumers *willingness to buy.* The term *fashion* is here to be seen in its widest meaning – simply that the consumer's tastes vary over time. Some fashions are very short-term, like pop music singles, whereas others are more long-term, such as popular motor car models (e.g. Vauxhall Cavalier). Willingness to buy can also be influenced by things like weather (in the case of ice cream), the extent to which the product is advertised, health concerns (e.g. tobacco), and changes in attitudes (e.g. in recent years consumers have become more concerned that goods are 'environmentally friendly').

❑ **Other factors** include the nature of the product itself. The demand for some products is related to the demand for other products. This introduces us to the concepts of *complementary* and *substitute* products.

    Complementary products are those which are related, in that increased demand for one product will also increase demand for its complement. If demand for cars increases, we can predict that the demand for petrol will also rise. This is because cars and petrol are complementary products – you cannot use one without the other. Hence, anything that causes more cars to be sold (such as a decrease in price of cars or increasing wealth) will mean that more petrol will also be demanded.

    For **substitute products**, an increase in demand for one product will result in a decrease in demand for its substitute. The nature of the products are such that you will use one or the other and you cannot use both at the same time. Increased demand for one will necessarily mean that you will have a lower requirement for the other. A good example of this is margarine and butter, in that you will use either margarine or butter on a slice of bread. It is unlikely that you would use both. Hence, an increase in the demand for butter is likely to lead to a decrease in demand for margarine. It follows that anything that causes more butter to be demanded (such as a fall in price), will signal a fall in sales of margarine.

Activity 1   *Think of six other pairs of products that are either substitutes or complementary – three of each.*

Changes in any of the above factors can cause an increase or decrease in demand. The patterns of such changes are described in the demand schedule.

13.2.3 Demand curve and demand schedule

The price of goods and their quantity demanded are related to each other by the *demand curve*. For most goods, all other things being equal, more will be demanded the lower the price. An increase in price, conversely, will result in a reduction in quantity sold. The simple form of the demand curve is shown in figure 13.2.

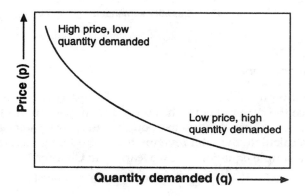

Figure 13.2: The general shape of the demand curve

The demand curve is the graphical representation of the *demand schedule*. This is the quantity that will be demanded at each price. A hypothetical example is shown below.

Price of product (each) £	Quantity demanded at the price
100	5
90	10
80	15
70	20
60	25
50	30

We can now express this schedule by plotting it as a graph, (figure 13.3).

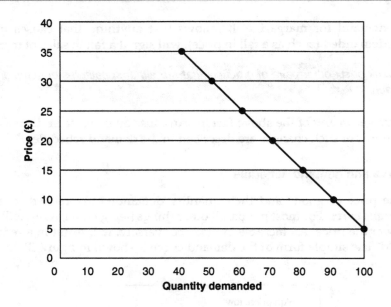

Figure 13.3

13.2.4 How to use the demand curve

❑ **Calculating revenue**

Once the demand curve has been drawn, we can use it for a number of helpful purposes. Because the two axes on the curve are *quantity* and *price*, it follows that we can calculate the total revenue that would be generated at any price. We make use of a simple equation that we learned in Chapter 1.

Revenue = price × quantity

Hence, on the demand curve we drew in figure 13.3, we can show the area of revenue if the price was set at £25. From the curve, we can see that this price would generate 60 sales in the unit time. Hence,

Revenue = £25 × 60 units = £1 500

The area under the demand curve always equals revenue. This is a useful tool as we can see how a change in price will affect revenue. For example, if the price was changed from £25 to £15, we would wish to know whether the change would generate more or less total revenue as a result. We can see from the shape of the curve that the change would mean we would sell a higher quantity, but would the price reduction mean more revenue or less?

Figure 13.4 shows the effect of the change – the demand schedule is the same as in figure 13.3.

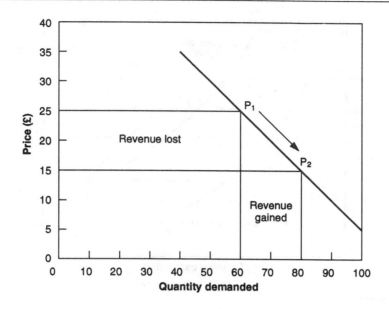

Figure 13.4

Figure 13.4

At £15 we would sell 80 units. This would represent a total revenue figure of £15 × 80 = £1200. We can alternatively examine the revenue lost and gained as a result of the change.

From the graph, we can see that by reducing the price from £25 to £15, we would lose:

$$(25-15) \times (60) = £600$$

The revenue we would gain, on the other hand would be:

$$(15) \times (80-60) = £300$$

Thus we can see that for the product with this demand curve, a cut in price from £25 to £15 has resulted in a decrease in total revenue of £300 (i.e. £600 – £300). Whether a price change results in more or less revenue depends on what is referred to as the *price elasticity* of demand. This is discussed in section 13.5.

❑ **Extension and contraction of demand**

We have seen that a change in price will mean a change in the quantity of a good demanded. If all other things remain the same, such a change will not affect the shape or position of the demand curve. When a price or quantity change moves the price *along* the demand curve *to the right*, it is said to be an *extension of demand*. An extension means that more goods will be demanded but a lower price will be payable. An alternative way to understand this is to consider that if demand is *extended*, the price must have been reduced.

The opposite of extension is a *contraction of demand*. This is when the price increases, forcing a move along the demand curve to the left. Such a change is inevitably accompanied by a lower quantity demanded (hence the term contraction).

❑ **Shift in demand**

A shift in demand is different from extension or contraction in that the curve *itself* moves. Hence, unlike an extension or contraction, a new relationship will exist between quantity and price.

A shift can either be a move to the left or the right. Figure 13.5 shows the scenario.

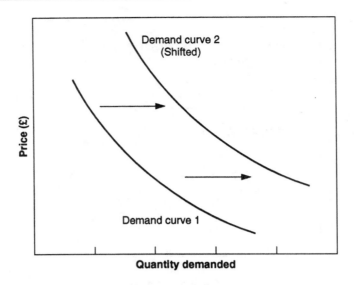

Figure 13.5: Shift in demand

Demand shift occurs when something happens that causes more or less of the good to be demanded *at every price*.

Let us construct a hypothetical example from the 'small car' market. Suppose that for various reasons the supply of the Ford Fiesta and the Peugeot 106 stops. At the same time, Volkswagen cannot produce the Polo for reasons of industrial dispute. In France, the production of the Citroen AX and Renault Clio cannot continue due to fires in their respective factories. In Italy, Fiat cars cannot be produced due to a long-term workers' strike. We would expect, under such circumstances, that the demand for the other 'small cars' to increase. The Vauxhall Corsa would be expected to be in great demand as a result causing more to be demanded whatever the price was set at. If Vauxhall kept its price the same, it would expect to sell a significantly higher quantity. If it decided to increase its price because of the increased demand, it could arrive at a price whereby it sold the same quantity of cars as previously but at the increased price. In this case, the demand curve for the Vauxhall Corsa would shift *up, and to the right.*

Activity 2	*Vino Français is a high quality French wine. Assume you are on a professional salary of £25 000 per year and that you enjoy wine. How many bottles would you buy in the course of a month if the price was:*

Price per bottle (£)	Number of bottles you would buy per month
0.25p	
0.50p	
1.00	
1.50	
2.00	
2.50	
3.00	
3.50	
4.00	
5.00	
6.00	
7.00	

Complete the above for yourself. If possible, get others (such as the members of your class) to also complete the table. Add the total demand together to get a demand schedule for the whole market (assume that your class is the total market). Plot the demand curve.

Answer the following questions.

1   How many bottles in total would be sold if the price was set at £3.75?

2   How many bottles would be sold at £2.10?

3   What would be the total revenue at £3.75 per bottle?

4   In what direction would the curve shift if all tax was removed from beer, thus making it much cheaper than it is now?

13.3 Supply

In the same way that demand responds to the prices at which goods are made available, the supply of goods also has a relationship to price. With supply, the curve slopes from the bottom left to the top right of a graph with the same axes as the demand curve (figure 13.6).

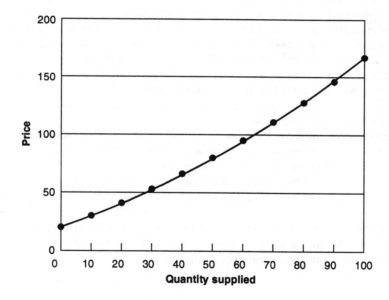

Figure 13.6: Supply curve

The supply curve, like the demand curve, is constructed from a schedule. The supply schedule for the hypothetical product in figure 13.6 is:

Price of product (each) £	Quantity demanded at the price
20	0
30	10
41	20
53	30
66	40
80	50
95	60
111	70
128	80
146	90
167	100

The supply side of the market relationship is relatively easy to intuitively understand. If the price of a commodity in the market goes up, suppliers will have an increased incentive to supply the good. This is because they will expect a higher return from the sale of their goods as the price rises. If the price falls, they will supply less of the good to the market in anticipation of lower financial rewards. Additionally, new suppliers will be attracted to supply a market if they believe that by doing so they will increase their earnings. This also increases total supply.

The supply curve in figure 13.6 shows another interesting feature of supply. At £20, the supply to the market equals zero. This means that the market must be prepared to pay in excess of this figure in order to be supplied with the good at all. £20 probably represents the point at which the suppliers begin to make a profit and it would not make economic sense to supply a market if, by doing so, they made a loss.

In the same way that we can get an extension, contraction and shift in demand, the same can happen to supply.

Extension and **contraction** occur when supply increases (extends) or decreases (contracts) resulting in a movement along the existing supply curve. All other things being equal, this will result in an adjustment in the market price of the good which will be determined by the existing position of the supply curve.

A **shift** in supply occurs when more or less of the good will be supplied into the market at *every price*. Suppose that in one year, the weather is exceptionally poor and the potato harvest is not as good as expected. This would result in an undersupply of potatoes causing a supply shift to the left (figure 13.7). Higher prices would be attracted for lower quantities of potatoes.

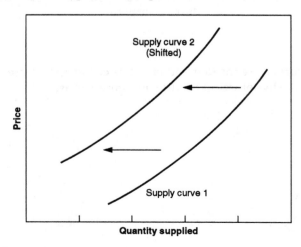

Figure 13.7: Shift in supply

Fewer potatoes are supplied, but because demand remains unchanged, prices rise. A shift in supply is different from extension or contraction because whereas these represent changes with price as the only consideration, shifts result from circumstances *other* than price movements. Shifts to the right can result from increases in supply for reasons of good harvest (in the case of, say, potatoes), or 'gluts' in the oil market. They mean that the supplier becomes more or less willing to supply as a result of factors (usually) outside of his control.

13.4 Equilibrium Point

Using the basic theories of demand and supply that we encountered above, we can turn our attention to using them to see how the actual market price is arrived at.

The demand curve describes the quantities that the total market would be prepared to buy at a range of possible prices. The supply curve, similarly, describes the quantities that suppliers would be prepared to supply at the same range of prices. Both of these graphs, when seen separately, express only intentions – the extent of the two groups' willingness to buy or supply. It is not possible to tell from either of these separately what the *actual* selling price of a commodity will be.

The *equilibrium point*, the point at which the demand and supply curves cross, expresses both the quantity and price at which both suppliers and buyers agree – where both groups are 'happy' with the price and quantity. Figure 13.8 shows this graphically.

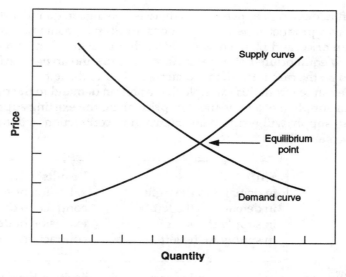

Figure 13.8: Equilibrium point

The term *equilibrium* is applied to this concept as the market will tend to fall back to this point after any disturbance to the status quo. For example, if suppliers attempt to sell at a price above the equilibrium point, the quantity sold will mean that the revenue gained would not be attractive to the seller so suppliers will be likely to return to the equilibrium. For the buyer, the equilibrium point acts as a *rationing* tool – the price tag of £23 000 for a BMW 5 series car may seem exorbitant, but it helps to ensure that those who want one need not queue for one nor go without.

It is important to appreciate that despite what we have said about prices returning to the equilibrium point, it is not 'cast in stone'. We know that in business, prices often change, so how can the equilibrium point be changed?

We have seen that the equilibrium point is where the demand and supply curves intersect. It follows therefore, that a change in equilibrium will occur when there is a **shift** in either curve. Figure 13.9 shows an example of how this can be brought about by a shift in the demand curve.

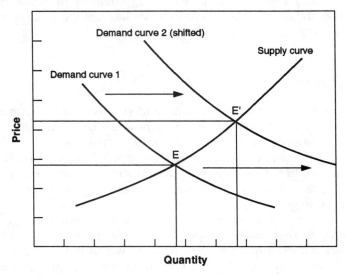

Figure 13.9: Change in equilibrium (by demand shift)

A shift in demand happens when there is a change in quantity demanded at *every price* (such as a product experiencing a boost or drop in fashion). E represents the old equilibrium price, and E', the new one. The shift in demand up and to the right means that the new equilibrium point is at an *increased price* and an *increased quantity*. The opposite would be the case if the demand curve shifted to the left.

We can see from this example that a shift in demand to the right results in an extension of supply (i.e. a movement of price along the existing supply curve). Similarly, a shift in supply will result in an extension or contraction of demand. This can be summarised as follows:

Shift	Results in ...
in demand to the right	extension of supply
in demand to the left	contraction of supply
in supply to the right	extension of demand
in supply to the left	contraction of demand

A shift in the supply curve will thus similarly reposition the equilibrium. Figure 13.10 shows the scenario for a rightward shift in supply. The new equilibrium (assuming of course, that demand remains unchanged) will be a lower price but a higher quantity.

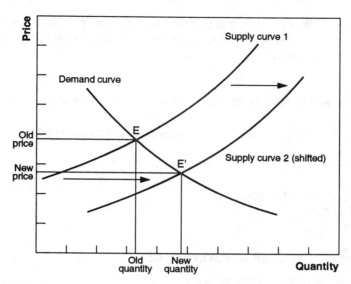

Figure 13.10: Change in equilibrium (by supply shift)

13.5 Price Elasticity of Demand

The theories of supply and demand offer several important uses to the businessperson. We have seen already that we can use it to establish the market price of a good or service by constructing the intersection point of the two curves.

In addition though, we can use the shape of the curve itself to examine how a price change would affect the total revenues that the business can achieve. This can be used by management to answer such questions as: 'If we were to reduce our prices, would we make more or less total revenue as a result?' This can be answered by analysing the **elasticity** of the demand and supply curves.

Example 1   Suppose the Sales Director of a company is contemplating reducing the price of a product by 2%. The accountant will wish to be assured that by doing so, the company will benefit from an increase in total revenue. In order for this to happen, the increase in quantity sold as a result of the reduction must more than make up for the revenue lost by the cut in price. Rather than relying on his 'gut feeling' to convince the accountant, the Sales Director can look at the product's demand curve, and from it, determine whether this will or will not be the case.

When we are considering this manoeuvre by examination of the demand curve, the relevant concept to look at is the *price elasticity of demand* (a number called the *coefficient of elasticity*, abbreviated as Ep). It can be expressed mathematically as:

$$\text{Coefficient of elasticity of demand (Ep)} = \frac{\Delta q/q}{\Delta p/p}$$

where;
Δq = change in quantity
q = original quantity (quantity demanded before the change)
Δp = change in price
p = original price (price before the change)

Example 2   If the Sales Manager of a company reduces the price of a good from £10 to £8 and the quantity of the goods demanded increases from 5000 units a month to 7000, the calculation above would work out as follows:

q = 5000
Δq = +2000 (i.e. 7000–5000. It is positive because it is an increase in quantity.)
p = 10
Δp = –2 (i.e. 10–8. It is negative because it is a decrease in price.)

Therefore,

Ep= (2000/5000)/(–2/10)
   = 0.4/–0.2
   = –2

The same equation can also be expressed as:

$$Ep = \frac{\text{percentage change in quantity}}{\text{percentage change in price}}$$

Where the change in quantity is that brought about as a result of price change.

Using this equation in either of its forms, we can say that:

- ☐ If Ep is greater than ±1, demand is *elastic* (a proportionately greater change in quantity than price).

- ☐ If Ep is less than ±1, demand is *inelastic* (a change in quantity exactly equivalent to a change in price).

- ☐ If Ep equals ±1, demand is said to be *unitary* (a proportionately lower change in quantity than in price).

Hence, using example 1 above, the Sales Director's intention to reduce the product price by 2%, demand would be elastic if the resulting change in quantity sold was greater than 2%. If, however, it caused a quantity increase of just 1%, demand would be inelastic and hence of doubtful commercial wisdom (you can imagine the accountant's response!).

Example 2 shows us elastic demand (because the coefficient is greater than 1). In this case, the reduction in price would seem to be economically justifiable.

One feature of elastic demand is that the increase in quantity which is in excess of the percentage drop in price also means that the business benefits from a net increase in revenue. Figure 13.11 shows this phenomenon.

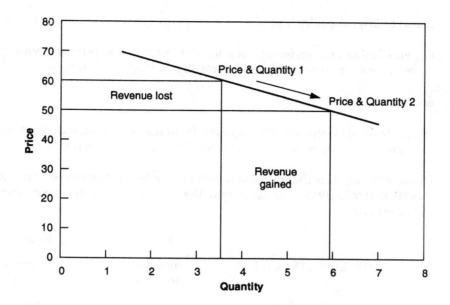

Figure 13.11: Elastic demand
Reduction in price = increase in revenue.

The revenue lost as a result of the reduction in price is less than that gained. Hence, we have a net increase. The converse can be said of inelastic demand (figure 13.12).

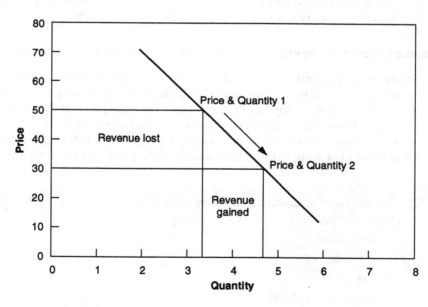

Figure 13.12: Inelastic demand.
Reduction in price = reduction in revenue.

It also follows logically that:

For **elastic demand**, an *increase in price* will result in a *decrease in revenue*, conversely, a *decrease in price* will result in an *increase in revenue*,

and,

For **inelastic demand**, an *increase in price* will result in an *increase in revenue*. conversely, a *decrease in price* will result in a *decrease in revenue*.

Unitary demand, as the equation shows us, is where the decrease or increase in price is exactly matched by the change in quantity. The revenue will remain unchanged whatever the price.

	Price	Revenue
Elastic Demand	increase	decrease
	decrease	increase
Inelastic Demand	increase	increase
	decrease	decrease

A product which has an elastic demand curve is said to be *responsive* to price changes because a small change in price brings about a proportionately greater change in quantity. Conversely, products for which demand is price inelastic are said to be *unresponsive* because quantity varies proportionately less than price.

13.5.1 Why do some products have elastic demand while others have inelastic demand?

The degree of elasticity will be largely determined by the nature of the product. Products for which demand is inelastic and which are therefore unresponsive, tend to be those which are relatively essential. We might say, for example, that demand for medicines is inelastic because they are needed. Products which show elastic response will tend to be those which are non-essentials or luxury goods. For example, we might expect the quantity sales of fillet steak to more than double if the price was reduced by half.

Activity 3

1   For the following products, say whether their demand is more likely to be elastic, inelastic or unitary.

  sports cars

  potatoes

  toilet rolls

  Nike training shoes

  drugs supplied to the NHS

2   Using the price elasticity of demand equation, say which type of elasticity the following price changes demonstrate.

  a) Price reduction 6%, quantity increase 4%

  b) Price reduction 4%, quantity increase 10%

  c) Price increase 2%, quantity decrease 1%

  d) Price increase 7.5%, quantity decrease 7.5%

13.6 Income Elasticity of Demand

The concept of elasticity can be extended to several other areas as well as just the price changes of a good or service. One of the most important of these is the *income elasticity of demand*. Suppose that you are on a salary of £20 000 a year, and then one happy day, your boss calls you in and tells you that he is pleased with your performance and intends to increase your salary to £30 000. The question is this: 'what difference would this make to your demand for certain goods and services?'.

In the same way that we learned how to calculate price elasticity above, we can express the coefficient of income elasticity of demand (Ei) as follows:

$$\text{Coefficient of income elasticity of demand (Ei)} = \frac{\Delta q/q}{\Delta y/y}$$

where,

Δq = change in quantity demanded,

q = original quantity demanded (before the change brought about as a result of the increase in income),

Δy = change in income,

y = original income (before the change).

Again, this can be similarly expressed as;

$$Ei = \frac{\text{percentage change in quantity demanded}}{\text{percentage change in income}}$$

The same product features exist for income elastic and inelastic products as for price elasticity. Luxuries tend to be have elastic income elasticity of demand, whereas essentials and basics tend to have inelastic income elasticity.

You have just received notification that you are to receive a salary increase to £30 000 per year. How many of the above items will you buy next year in total? (You can alter the list according to your taste.)

take away meals,
foreign holidays,
cans of lager,
toilet rolls,
pairs of jeans,
bottles of malt whisky
fillet steaks
cartons of fresh orange juice

Now calculate the income elasticity of demand for each of the above products according to your buying intentions next year against last year. For each product, state whether the coefficient of income elasticity points to the demand being elastic, inelastic or unitary.

Economists think of income elasticity in terms of *aggregate* income. This means that when the income of everybody in the country rises or falls, they use income elasticities to calculate how such changes will effect the demand for certain goods and services. Items that are considered as 'essentials' such as toilet rolls (in the question above), milk, and potatoes will usually be income inelastic, whereas those items that are 'luxuries' are elastic. These might include holidays, fillet steak, membership of health clubs etc.

Economics is a very complex subject when viewed as a whole. In this book we will look at the principal economic issues in relation to business. Please refer to one of the recommended texts at the end of this chapter and Chapter 14.

Review Questions

1. Define and distinguish between macro- and micro- economics. (13.1)

2. What is *effective demand?* (13.2.1)

3. Name the two general causes of demand? (13.2.2)

4. Draw the general shape of the demand curve, and label the axes. (13.2.3)

5. Define and distinguish between *extension* and *contraction* of demand. (13.2.4)

6. Under what circumstances would a shift in demand occur? (13.2.4)

7. What equation would you use to calculate the revenue for any given point on the demand curve? (13.2.4)

8. Draw the general shape of the supply curve and label the axes. (13.3)

9. During the Gulf war of 1991, the world supply of crude oil was reduced. The price consequently increased. Describe what happened to the supply curve. (13.3)

10. Explain, using a graph of demand and supply curves, how the equilibrium point is arrived at. (13.4)

11. What types of products would be expected to demonstrate inelastic demand? (13.5 and 13.6)

12. What type of elasticity of demand would result in an increase in revenue with a reduction in price? (13.5)

Answers to Activities

Activity 1

An important feature of substitute and complementary products is that some pairs are highly related and others are slightly related. This means that some products are direct substitutes (such as margarine and butter) whilst others may be substitutes under some circumstances (e.g. sugar and saccharin, gas and electricity). Complimentarity can also be total (petrol driven cars and petrol – you cannot use your petrol car without petrol) whereas others are less complimentary (e.g. beer and crisps). Examples follow but readers should be aware that the pairs vary in their relatedness.

Substitutes
petrol or diesel
coffee or tea
petrol or rail travel
trousers or skirts

Complimentary
video tapes and video recorders
strawberries and cream
curry sauce and rice
scarves and hats

Activity 3

1. Sports cars and Nike training shoes are usually seen as 'luxury' items and will consequently exhibit price elastic demand. Potatoes, toilet rolls and drugs are 'staples' or 'essentials' and so will have relatively inelastic demand.

2. This question uses the equation:

   $$\text{Coefficient of elasticity} = \frac{\text{percentage change in quantity}}{\text{percentage change in price}}$$

   a) 4%/–6% = **–0.66** = inelastic
   b) 10%/–4% = **–2.5** = elastic
   c) –1%/2% = **–0.5** = inelastic
   d) –7.5%/7.5% = **–1** = unitary

3. This question uses the equation:

   $$\text{Coefficient of elasticity} = \frac{\Delta q/q}{\Delta p/p}$$

   a) (200/2000)/(–1/5) = 0.1/–0.2 = **–0.5** = inelastic
   b) (2000/10000)/(–1/5) = 0.2/–0.2 = **–1** = unitary
   c) (10/500)/(–2/30) = 0.02/0.066 = **–0.3** = inelastic
   d) (12 000 000/28 000 000)/(–500/9000) = 0.316/–0.055 = **–5.69** = elastic

Assignment Questions

The following are multiple choice questions. There is only one correct answer to each question.

1. A typical supply curve runs from,
   A   top left to bottom right,
   B   top right to bottom left,
   C   vertically from top to bottom,
   D   horizontally from left to right
   E   none of these

2. The direction of a demand curve is usually:
    A   top right to bottom left,
    B   bottom left to top right,
    C   top left to bottom right,
    D   none of these,
    E   a vertical line.

3. The point at which the demand and the supply curve intersect is called the:
    A   elasticity of demand,
    B   equilibrium price,
    C   income elasticity,
    D   equilibrium point,
    E   supply equilibrium.

4. The demand for a product is said to be elastic when the coefficient of demand is:
    A   equal to 0,
    B   less than 1,
    C   equal to 1,
    D   more than 1,
    E   depends on other things.

5. If the supply curve shifts to the left, you get:
    A   a shift in demand,
    B   an extension of demand,
    C   no change in price,
    D   an extension of supply,
    E   a contraction of demand.

6. If the supply curve shifts to the right, and assuming the demand curve is a conventional shape, then:
    A   lower price and higher quantity,
    B   higher price and higher quantity,
    C   lower price and lower quantity,
    D   higher price and higher quantity,
    E   no change in either price or quantity.

Use the following possible answers to answer questions 7 to 12.
    A   no change in price regardless of quantity
    B   no change in quantity regardless of price
    C   less percentage change in quantity than in price
    D   more percentage change in quantity than in price
    E   same percentage change in quantity than in price

7. Describes the general principle of inelasticity.

8. Describes the general principle of elasticity.

9. Describes the demand for luxury yachts.

10. Describes the demand for cigarettes.

11. Describes unitary demand.

12. Describes the demand for toilet rolls.

13. A shift to the right in the demand curve for product M may be due to any of the following *except*:
    A   decrease in income,
    B   fall in the price of a complementary product,
    C   rise in the price of a substitute product,
    D   fall in the price of product M,
    E   change in consumer tastes.

In questions 14 to 16 the following terms refer to the price elasticity of demand for a given commodity:
    A   zero elasticity
    B   elasticity between 0 and 1
    C   elasticity equal to 1
    D   elasticity greater than 1

14. A 2% fall in price causes a 1% increase in quantity demanded.

15. A 3% fall in quantity demanded resulted from a 1% rise in price.

16. A 1% fall in quantity resulting when price rose by 1%.

17. A demand schedule for a product is constructed on the assumption that all of the following remain constant *except*:
    A   the price of the product,
    B   the price of other products,
    C   consumers' tastes,
    D   consumers' money income,
    E   the size of the population.

Questions 18 and 19 are based on the five states of price elasticity of demand:
    A   perfectly elastic demand
    B   elastic demand
    C   unitary elastic demand
    D   inelastic demand
    E   perfectly inelastic demand

Which of the above terms best describes each of the following situations? (Each term may apply once, more than once, or not at all.)

18. After a reduction in price, a greater quantity of the commodity is bought, but total expenditure on the commodity falls.

19. After an increase in price, a smaller quantity of the commodity is bought, but total expenditure on the commodity remains unchanged.

20. Products which are inelastic are generally
    A   luxury products,
    B   essentials or products which people need,
    C   poor quality,
    D   good quality,
    E   inexpensive products.

21. We would expect the demand for condoms in the UK to be:
    A   elastic,
    B   inelastic,
    C   unitary,
    D   unpredictable,
    E   seasonable.

22. If the demand for a product is price elastic you would increase total revenue by
    A   reducing the price,
    B   increasing the price,
    C   increasing income,
    D   changing the design,
    E   doing nothing.

The following data refers to questions 23 and 24.
    Original Price   5
    New Price   4
    Original Quantity   2
    New Quantity   2.2

23 The price elasticity of demand for the product is
    A   −0.5
    B   +0.5
    C   −2
    D   +2
    E   zero

24. The demand for this product is
    A   elastic,
    B   inelastic,
    C   unitary,
    D   perfectly inelastic,
    E   perfectly elastic.

25. Extension of demand is when
    A   the demand curve shifts to the right,
    B   the demand curve shifts to the left,
    C   demand moves along the demand curve to the right,
    D   demand moves along the demand curve to the left,
    E   none of these.

26. A decrease in price causes an increase in total revenue. The demand for this
    product is:
    A   elastic,
    B   inelastic,
    C   unitary,
    D   impossible to say,
    E   reliable.

27. A shift to the right of the demand curve means that there has been
    A   an increase in supply,
    B   an increase in demand,
    C   a decrease in demand,
    D   an decrease in supply,
    E   none of the above.

28. When we say that the demand curve for a commodity is downward sloping to the right, we mean:
    A   more of the commodity will be demanded as income rises,
    B   more of the commodity will be demanded as the price of a substitute good rises,
    C   more of the commodity will be demanded as its own price falls,
    D   more of the commodity will be bought as population increases.

29. A rightward shift in a supply curve indicates that:
    A   less will be supplied at each possible market price,
    B   the willingness of producers to supply the commodity has diminished,
    C   more will be supplied at each possible market price,
    D   none of the above answers is correct.

30. A rightward shift in the demand curve and a leftward shift in the supply curve will:
    A   increase price,
    B   decrease price,
    C   leave price unchanged,
    D   have an indeterminate effect on price.

Further Reading

Beardshaw J. and Palfreman D., *The Organisation in its Environment*, Pitman Press (Fourth Edition: Chapters 13–16)

Economics – First Year Study Guide, for first year degree students, BPP Publishing (Chapters 1, 2 and 3)

Lipsey R.G. & Harbury C., *First Principles of Economics*, Wiedenfeld and Nicolson (London), (Second Edition, 1992: Part 2)

Pappas J.L., Brigham E.F. & Shipley B., *Managerial Economics*, Holt Reinhart Winston Publishers (Chapter 5)

Samuelson P.A., *Economics*, McGraw Hill Kogakusha (Chapter 4)

Fuller N., *Basic Concepts in Micro-Economics*, Checkmate/Edward Arnold (1985)

14 The economic environment 2
The macro-economic indicators

Objectives   After studying this chapter, students should be able to:

❑ define the key elements of the macro-economic environment:

economic growth rates, inflation, unemployment, interest rates, balance of payments, value of currency, government spending and borrowing;

❑ and explain:

how each one is measured, how it is caused or brought about, how it affects the other macro-economic factors, and what effects each one has on a business organisation.

14.1 Introduction

We learned in Chapters 12 and 13 that the economic environment can be thought of as having two components, the micro- and macro-economic environments. The micro-economic environment is the immediate industry environment within which the business operates on a day-to-day basis. The macro-economic environment is composed of the influences arising from the condition of the economy as a whole. This latter category is very important as it determines the economic framework within which the organisation and its industry functions. Whereas to a certain extent, companies can manoeuvre in such a way as to influence their immediate (micro) environment, the elements of the macro-environment are largely outside the organisations control (although some very large organisations may have some minor influence). Because of this, each organisation must learn to cope with the features of the macro-economic environment. Those that understand it and can predict how it will change have an advantage over others.

You may have heard politicians or commentators on television and radio speak of the 'economic indicators'. These, as their names suggest, 'indicate' the state of the wider economy. By examining the elements of the macro-economy and by learning how they are tied together, we can gain an appreciation of the complexity of the factors that can affect the organisation from outside.

In this chapter, we shall consider the key areas of influence in the macro-economy and how each one is linked to the others. We will see that the management of the macro-economy – the job of the incumbent Government – is a very difficult task!

14.2 Economic Cycles, Growth and Recession

A feature of all advanced industrial economies is that there are periods of high economic activity and periods of low activity. These periods tend to be cyclical, but the duration of the gaps between 'booms' and 'slumps' are notoriously hard to predict. The reasons for these cycles are very complicated and, to a certain extent, unknown. Moreover, the booms and slumps can vary in intensity from very slight to severe. Figure 14.1 shows the growth in the economic outputs of the UK, the USA, Japan and

Germany over recent years. GDP is the *gross domestic product* – the total output of the domestic (UK based) economy. The GDP for the UK in 1992 was £595.2 billion.

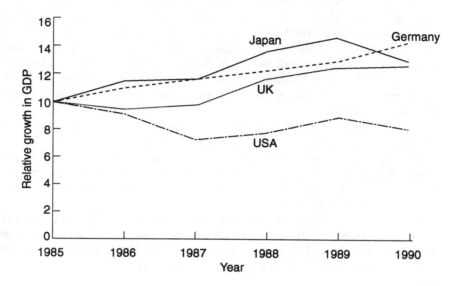

Figure 14.1: Growth in GDP (normalised units, 1985=10)
(Source: Eurostat, 19th Edition, 1992)

Notice that although there is a definite upward trend, the line is not straight – there are hills and valleys, peaks and troughs. This can be shown more clearly when viewed over the longer term, such as that for UK growth in figure 14.2.

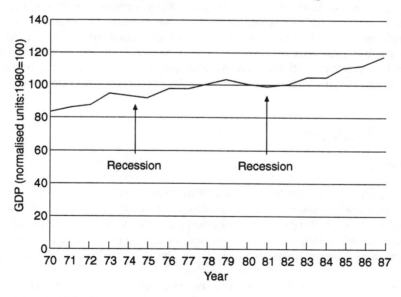

Figure 14.2: Growth in GDP in the UK
(Source: The Economic Review, Vol. 6, No 2)

Economic growth is the 'normal' state of western economies in that this year's total sales, across the whole country, are usually more than last year's. When the cycle turns down and output falls against the previous year, it is called 'negative growth' or, more bluntly, *recession* (the technical definition of *recession* is negative growth for two consecutive quarters, i.e., two three-month periods). This presents a lot of problems to businesses that have invested in their organisations and that rely on a certain profit level to pay back loans etc.

During the nineteen eighties and early nineteen nineties Britain had two recessions and one boom, all of which were characterised by some intensity. During the two recessions, unemployment increased, companies recorded losses (some became bankrupt), sales fell and millions of families suffered from the effects. In contrast, during the boom of the late eighties, all sectors of industry were optimistic and some outstanding profits were recorded. Unemployment, from its high of over three million in the middle of the decade, began to fall as companies took on more labour to support the increase in business.

It is important to point out that such swings are usually part of the international economic environment and are rarely restricted to one country only. The ways in which international economies are linked through thousands of trading relationships means that the economic conditions in one country quickly have knock-on effects in the economies of its neighbours. This is especially true in a closely-knit trading block such as exists in Europe.

The manner in which the Government deals with the differing economic conditions can have an effect on the extent to which economic cycles affect businesses. We shall see shortly that the key indicators such as inflation, interest rates, etc. can be influenced by governments to vary the impact of changing growth rates on companies in the private sector.

The individual business will usually be acutely aware of economic cycles. In times when the economy is buoyant, companies will generally perform well, increase their sales and profits, and have more money to invest to increase their size and improve their operation. In adverse economic conditions, sales will decrease and the business may have to contract in size in order to survive.

Management skill comes into its own when the business experiences differing trading conditions. In times of general growth, the company will want to make the most of the buoyancy by investing, increasing profit margins, retaining profits 'for a rainy day', and so on. In recession, it will want to reduce the impact of the negative growth on the business and keep sales as lively as possible. The fact that so many businesses fail in recessions indicates that they are often unforeseen or that management does not have the ability or resources to cope with the downturn in demand.

14.3 Inflation – Its Causes

14.3.1 What is inflation?

Inflation refers to the average rate of increase in prices across the economy *as a whole*. It is measured by comparing the price of a 'basket' of goods from one year to the next. The increase in the price of the basket over the course of a 12-month period is termed the 'rate' of inflation and is expressed as a percentage. The contents of the basket are chosen as being representative of those items typically used by the average consumer and in the same proportions. If the basket is priced at 10% more this year than at this time last year, then that is the rate of inflation of those goods. The most common way of measuring inflation is by use of the *retail prices index (RPI)*, which is based upon a 'basket' of purely retail items – i.e., it does not take into account industrial prices. Readers should be aware that other ways of measuring inflation do exist.

14.3.2 What causes inflation?

Inflation has two possible causes. The first is referred to as *cost-push* inflation and the second as *demand led* inflation.

Cost push inflation occurs when prices rise as a result of increased industrial costs. When companies are forced to increase their prices, it is usually because their own costs have gone up. These cost increases can arise from high wage rises demanded by powerful trade unions, increased costs of imported goods, higher energy costs and many other things.

Demand led inflation is caused by demand in excess of supply, or *'too much money chasing too few goods'*. Hence, demand led inflation can be caused by either or both of two features.

❑ **'Too much money'**

More properly, 'too much money' may be termed 'excess spending power'. This is where consumers have the means to spend a lot of money, a predicament which on the face of it may seem to be highly desirable, but it does have its drawbacks. Growth in spending power can arise in a number of ways. They all have the same effect – that once all essential bills have been paid, people have more money to spend on retail items. The causes may include:

❑ high or increasing salaries/wages;

❑ low or decreasing rates of taxation;

❑ low or falling interest rates (interest rates determine how much of people's incomes goes on servicing mortgage repayments and other loans, e.g. car);

❑ increase in the amount of money in circulation (*monetary supply*);

❑ increase in public spending.

❑ **'Too few goods'**

This side of the inflation 'formula' is concerned with the so-called *supply side* of the economy. If a situation arises where the supply of goods decreases, then a key fuelling component of inflation has been introduced. This can happen in the economy as whole when industrial output falls, or in segments of the market where supply of a product decreases.

This is well exemplified by the economic conditions in developing countries. It makes sense that if there is a shortage of goods, then each one will attract a higher price – the inclination of the seller is that he will take the highest price offered. Developing countries like modern-day Russia have a shortage of many consumer goods, and consequently more money must be paid per potato, piece of meat or tube of toothpaste. Western goods like electronic equipment and clothes attract particularly high prices. The effect is a direct increase in price to take advantage of the best price offered.

The 'too few goods' arguments are relative to the spending power of the consumer. Producers will tend to increase their prices if they believe that by doing so they will sell the same quantity as they would if they left the prices the same. So in a buoyant economy where consumers are prosperous, it may well be the case that demand outstrips supply – effectively too few goods to meet the demand.

Economists speak of changes in any of the above factors as being an 'inflationary' or a 'deflationary' pressure. Governments, for example, often attempt to influence employers to keep wage settlements down to just a few percent a year (a deflationary pressure). The reason for this, as we saw, is that high wages are an inflationary pressure in the economy as they mean that the consumer has more spending power. The same is true of interest rates – high interest rates are a deflationary pressure and low interest rates can be inflationary.

In some countries, inflationary pressures can build up to such an extent that the country's economy enters an unhappy state known as *hyper-inflation*. This involves pressure from both sides of the 'equation' – a weak currency (see section 14.9 of this chapter) *and* insufficient supply of goods. When currency loses its value, people hold lots of money which has lost its buying power. Because producers do not want worthless currency, they increase the price further. Hyper-inflation occurs in countries with weak economies and poor supply. The rates of inflation in such countries can rise to the order of 3000% per year.

Case Study   The UK Government and the ERM

In October 1990, Britain entered the European exchange rate mechanism (ERM). The purpose of the ERM was to maintain the values of the various European currencies within a few percent of each other as part of the process leading up to European monetary union (EMU). In order to maintain the value of sterling against other currencies, the UK was forced to maintain the bank base rates (see section 14.7 of this chapter) at a high levels in order to 'protect' sterling. Upon joining, the UK base rate was 12% and although this came down slowly over the next two years, it actually rose again to 12% in the events surrounding the UK departure from the ERM on 16 September 1992. Historically, such levels of base rate are very high for the UK. As well as helping to maintain the value of the currency (for a while) it also had the effect of depressing spending power and hence, reducing inflation. The rate of inflation fell from a high of 10.89% upon joining, to a figure of 3.57% when membership was suspended in September 1992.

This example shows the power of monetary pressure to influence inflation; monetary pressure (e.g. high interest rates) can exert a strong deflationary pressure.

Activity 1   *Find out the current rate of inflation as measured by the RPI. It is published monthly and is reported in the press and news – usually to a great deal of comment by politicians. How does the current figure compare with last month's figure and the figure of this month last year? Comment on the current trend in inflation.*

14.4 Inflation – Its Effects

It is the policy of every government to keep inflation as low as possible. This is because, unlike other aspects of macro-economics, inflation has no significant advantages, just disadvantages. The major economies in the world (the so called 'G5'), the USA, Japan, Germany, Great Britain and France have been successful in their attempts to maintain relatively low inflation over a sustained period of time. This has been both one of the principal causes of their prosperity and the result of it. Figure 14.3 shows how the UK inflation rate has varied over the nineteen seventies and eighties.

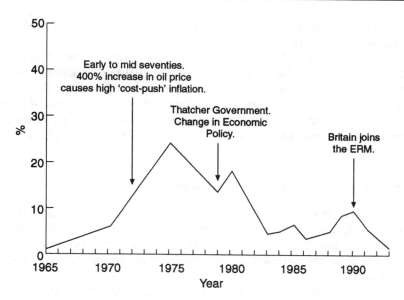

Figure 14.3: Inflation rate in the UK
(Source: Lloyds Bank Economic Profile of Great Britain, 1993 et al.)

Why is inflation such an 'evil' to an economy, and why do political leaders make tackling it such an issue?

14.4.1 It makes the British economy weaker compared to its international competitors

This aspect of inflation says that it is not the British inflation rate that is important in itself but its value compared to our main international competitors. A higher inflation rate will make British goods less competitive, which will mean that British companies lose business to foreign competitors thus reducing profits and possibly costing jobs.

A purely hypothetical example will show how this works. Suppose that both Britain and Germany sell cars to Spain. This year, the German car (say a BMW) costs the equivalent of £16 000 and the British car (say a Rover or a Toyota) costs exactly the same. The result is that, all other things being equal, the two cars cost the same and are theoretically equally attractive to the Spanish car buyer. However, over the course of next year, let us say for the sake of argument that British inflation is 6% and in Germany it is only 3%. In order for the British company to maintain its profit margin, it must sell its product for £16 000 plus 6%, which is £16 480. The German competitor will also have to increase his price, but only by 3%, i.e. to £16 240. The result is that the German car is more competitive than the British one in the international market. The likelihood is that as a result of the increased inflation in the UK, the British company will either have to decrease its profit margin to match the BMW price or accept a loss in market share – both equally undesirable outcomes.

If the UK has a higher inflation rate than its competitors over a sustained period of time, it will result in a general weakening of the economy as overseas companies take more and more business away from British businesses. For this reason, as well as being bad for competitiveness, inflation may also be symptomatic of weakness in an economy.

14.4.2 It puts pressure on company costs

Inflation can exert pressure on the costs of business in both direct and indirect ways. The direct mechanisms concern the rising costs of material inputs. If say, raw material prices rise due to an increase in the price of oil or the cost of imported goods rises because of a weak pound, then the individual business must find ways of attempting to absorb these increases.

Indirect effects include such things as pay rises. It is the usual practice of employee trade unions to ask for an annual pay rise equal to or greater than the current rate of inflation. This is understandable as a settlement less than the inflation rate would mean that the workers were worse off in real terms (i.e. once inflation has been taken into account). If the employer agrees to pay according to the rate of inflation, then he is increasing his costs by that amount – a thing he can often ill afford to do in times of high inflation.

14.4.3 It reduces the incentive to save, which can make inflation worse

When inflation rises, people rightly expect prices to rise and so decide to buy goods rather than save and risk not being able to afford them later (because prices have risen). This has the effect of increasing the demand for goods. We saw earlier that demand is inflationary and in this case, we see an example of inflation making inflation worse.

High inflation can also represent a disincentive for lending institutions (e.g. building societies and banks) to lend money. In one sense, inflation is a measure of how much value money has lost from one year to the next. If inflation is high, individuals will tend to spend now rather than save and risk their money losing value. Similarly, lending institutions will be less likely to lend if they perceive that the money will be worth less upon repayment than it was when it was lent.

14.4.4 It puts adverse pressure on the value of the pound and the balance of payments

Both the value of currency and the balance of payments (see Sections 14.9 and 14.8 of this chapter) are linked to the competitiveness of domestic industry. We shall see later in this chapter how these can influence inflation.

14.5 Unemployment – Its Causes

The unemployment figure in the UK is arrived at by recording the number of people who are *registered with the Government* as unemployed (i.e. unemployed and claiming benefit from the DSS). Some argue that this is not 'the true picture' as many people who are in work are in temporary jobs, unpaid or low-paid jobs etc. which some politicians contend is almost the same as being unemployed. Before someone can be registered as unemployed, they must be both eligible and willing to work.

Unemployment has, to a greater or lesser extent, been part of western society since the industrial revolution. It has increased in the twentieth century and this is partly as a result of population growth and partly because of changes in the economies of the countries themselves. The percentage unemployed figure itself varies significantly between countries and also shows variation over time. There are two underlying reasons why unemployment is a part of society: structural factors and cyclical factors.

14.5.1 Structural factors

There are three main structural factors.

☐ The fact is that in most countries, there are fewer jobs than there are people to fill them. This oversupply of labour necessarily means that there are not enough jobs to go round.

❑ Another element in this is that as industry has changed over the course of this century, it has become increasingly mechanised and automated. Whereas at one time, jobs in a factory or office were all done by people, many can now be done by machines of varying complexity. This has had the result of reducing company costs and increasing efficiency, but it also means that companies require fewer people than before. This is called *technological unemployment*.

❑ Many countries in Western Europe, including Britain, have experienced a reduction in their industrial base over recent years as the Far East has gained prominence in the world markets. This has particularly affected the traditional industries such as shipping, coal mining and other heavy industries, but others, such as electronics, have also been lost.

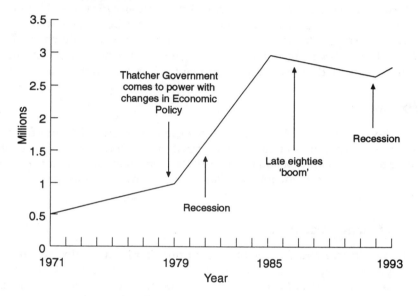

Figure 14.4: Numbers unemployed in the UK
(Graph is simplified to show general trends)

14.5.2 Cyclical factors

Figure 14.4 shows how unemployment in the UK has varied over the period 1970–1993. We learned in Section 14.2 that industrial economies experience cycles of varying economic growth. We can see how certain events and general economic conditions have had a profound effect on the numbers unemployed. There are a number of definite connections between the economic climate and unemployment. Generally, we can say that upward pressure on unemployment will result when the country experiences:

high inflation;

slowing growth or recession;

a weakening of international competitiveness;

high interest rates.

The fact that such factors tend to vary over time also means the same is true for unemployment.

14.6 Unemployment – Its Effects

There are several reasons why unemployment is a bad thing in a national economy. Among the most significant are:

14.6.1 High costs of state assistance

In developed countries such as the UK, the state provides financial help to the unemployed. This is paid for from contributions from income tax and national insurance. We saw earlier (Chapter 7) that the DSS is the biggest spender of government money, and it makes sense that if unemployment rises, then so does the DSS bill. At one or two points in recent British history, this has been a genuine problem for the Government. During a recession, because of weakening company profits and higher unemployment, less money is received in tax revenues. However, because of the increased unemployment, more people claim their benefits and so the DSS bill rises. Hence, in the short term, the Government must spend more money when less is coming in. Under such circumstances, the Government is forced to borrow – not a thing it likes to do.

14.6.2 Loss of tax revenues

We saw in Section 12.1 that the Government receives income from several taxation sources. One of the sources of direct taxation is income tax. This is taken from the earnings of those people who are in work. It is obvious that when fewer people are working, revenue from income tax falls, which in turn puts pressure on Government finance.

14.6.3 It is a waste of human resources

The wealth-creating power of any country is primarily tied up in its people. It is by people working that value is added and international competitiveness is strengthened. It is also the principal way in which the country gets its return on the investment it has made in education, training, health and so on. In the UK, which has a relatively skilled workforce compared to the rest of the world, unemployment also means that important skills are being lost as unemployment deprives individuals the opportunity to practice and cultivate their skills.

14.6.4 The misery and morale factor

The cost of unemployment for those involved is much harder to quantify than the financial aspects. As well as the boredom and restlessness that accompany unemployment, there is also a loss of self esteem, and over time, a growing sense of despair can develop. This, of course, is in addition to any financial hardships.

There is an additional 'knock-on' effect to those in work as well. When unemployment is rising and industry is having to contract and make redundancies, employees will have heightened fears for their own jobs. Such insecurity may result in lower job motivation and a reduction in productivity.

14.6.5 Other possible effects

There is some evidence to suggest that prolonged unemployment has adverse effects on health and can increase crime. Both of these effects, as well as causing individuals to suffer, can impose additional costs on Government finances and businesses.

It is a point of debate among politicians and economists whether 'full employment' is possible. Even in very prosperous times, there is, in most societies, a residual level of unemployment due to structural factors.

14.7 Interest Rates (The Price of Borrowed Money)

The way in which interest rates works is very complicated, involving Government, the banks and building societies and the other lending and borrowing institutions. Together with the money supply, interest rates form the *monetary* instruments of economic policy – the factors that affect the *price and availability* of money. The rate of interest is expressed as a percentage and in practice it represents the *minimum* that the banking and finance sector may charge on loans (called the *'base rate'*). Most banks will also base their interest paid on deposit accounts on the base rate. Bank loans, including those for domestic purposes (e.g. buying cars) are charged at an interest rate so many points above base, meaning that if the base rate shifts, so will the interest rate on the loan. The rate of interest on a loan is usually set to take account of the amount of risk associated with the loan. Hence, mortgage rates, secured against a house, are low, whereas credit cards (unsecured) charge high rates.

14.7.1 How is the base rate set?

In the UK, the base rate is set by the Chancellor of the Exchequer instructing the Bank of England. He will move it up or down in order to influence the various economic indicators. The direction of a move and its size will depend upon the current state of the economy and what he intends to achieve by the change. Some have argued that the control of interest rates should be taken away from the Chancellor and given to the Bank of England. It is believed by these politicians that the Chancellor may use interest rates to increase the popularity of the Government rather than to responsibly manage the economy.

14.7.2 What are the effects of a high interest rate?

The management of the base rate is one of the hardest parts of the Chancellor's job. This is because there are a number of advantages and disadvantages associated with both a high and a low base rate. At any one time, there will be a trade off, in that by moving the rate, one part of the economy will be advantaged whilst another will be disadvantaged. The Chancellor cannot possibly please everybody.

We will now consider the effects of high interest rates, but readers should appreciate that the opposite will be true when the base rate is low.

A high base rate will have the following effects:

❏ **It will exert a deflationary pressure**

This works by reducing the 'too much money' side of the inflation equation. On the domestic front, anybody with a mortgage or other loans will have to use more of their income to service the debt, leaving less to spend on other items. It also reduces spending and investment in business where most companies carry a hefty burden of debt. This may also feed through into lower wage settlements which will also have a deflationary effect.

❑ **It will reduce company profits**

Businesses pay interest on loans in the same way as consumers with mortgages. If more is required for this purpose, it follows that less will be left over for reinvestment or expansion. This is why a high base rate is very unpopular in business.

❑ **It will slow industrial growth**

Companies grow by reinvestment of profits, by buying new plant and equipment, employing new people and so on. When a high base rate is sustained over a period of time, the effect it has on industry is to reduce its ability to grow. In some situations, businesses have been known to shrink or go bust altogether as a result.

❑ **It will put upward pressure on unemployment**

A natural extension of the previous point.

❑ **It will increase the value of the pound against foreign currencies and therefore reduce the competitiveness of exports and encourage imports**

High interest rates act as an incentive for the international investment community to invest in British banks and other financial institutions. It also has an effect on the competitiveness of imports and exports. We will see how this inflates the value of the pound in Section 14.9, later in this chapter.

14.8 Balance of Payments

14.8.1 What is the balance of payments account?

The balance of payments account is a statement which measures all of the transactions make by UK individuals and institutions with the rest of the world. It is produced by the Government's statistical service annually, but updates are made available monthly, usually to a great deal of comment from politicians and business-people. Like a balance sheet in accountancy, it has two sides which always balance. The significance of the account can be studied by examining its various components.

14.8.2 Rules observed in constructing the account

In the UK, all figures in the statement are recorded in pounds sterling. Any entries that arise from other currencies are converted into pounds at the current exchange rates before they are entered into the account.

There are two important rules that determine whether items are a positive or negative entry in the account.

❑ Anything that causes money to flow into the UK is entered as a *positive item*. These include:
  - exports (because money from foreign companies *flows in* as payment for the goods exported);
  - investments in the UK (such as the acquisition of British companies by foreign ones or greenfield investments such as Nissan and Toyota);
  - deposits into UK banks by overseas companies and individuals.

❏ Anything that causes money to leave the UK is entered as a *negative item*. For example:

- imports (British companies paying foreign companies for goods);

- British companies investing abroad;

- overseas aid;

- tourists spending money abroad.

14.8.3 Components of the balance of payments account

There are two components of the account; the *'current account'* and the *'transactions in external assets and liabilities'*.

❏ **The current account** is the first part of the account and measures all of the money that flows in and out of the UK as a result of international business transactions (or trade). It has two parts.

The first part is termed the **visible trade** which is the import and export of physical (manufactured) products. The importation of Brazilian coffee, German cars and French wine will be entered as a negative number whereas the export of British electronics, chemicals and military tanks will be entered as a positive number. The total value of exports is entered as a positive figure (cash inflow) and the imports, the converse. The difference between visible imports and exports is called the *balance of trade*.

When the balance of trade figure is published monthly, it is invariably reported in the media and the figure is compared against both the previous month and the same month in the previous year. This is because the balance of visibles gives a good indication of the *competitiveness of the British manufacturing sector*. A deficit means that the UK has been a net importer of visible goods, the indication being that we have failed to make our home manufactured products sufficiently attractive to home and overseas buyers. This has unfortunately been the case for some years.

The second part of the current account is the **invisible trade**. This is the trade in intangibles such as services between the UK and overseas markets. When Lloyds of London insures a Greek ship or the University of Northumbria receives a foreign student onto a degree course, cash flows into the UK – a positive entry. Conversely, when British citizens fly to Zurich on Swissair funds leave the UK for Switzerland – a negative entry.

The **current account balance** is worked out by adding together the visibles (balance of trade) and the invisibles. This tells us the net (overall) inflow or outflow of cash as a result of trading activity over the year – from the trade in both physical goods and services. Whether the current account as a whole is in surplus or deficit is seen as an indicator of the UK commercial sector as a whole. In the same way as visibles give an indication of the health of the manufacturing sector, the invisibles show how competitive the services and transport sectors are. Historically, the invisibles are more likely to be in surplus than visibles in the UK.

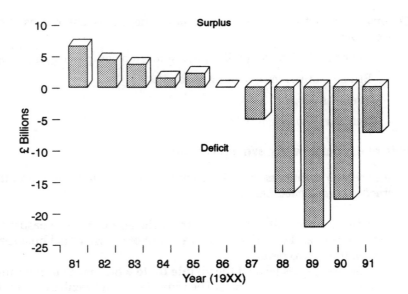

Figure 14.5: Current account balance in the UK
(Source: Annual Abstract of Statistics, HMSO, 1993)

❑ **The transactions in external assets and liabilities,** sometimes called the *capital account*, shows how capital (money) rather than trade has behaved between the UK and the overseas markets.

Money changes hands across international borders for many reasons other than as part of a trade transaction. As far as the UK is concerned, all of these cash movements involve changing funds to or from sterling. According to the balance of payments equation, this part of the account will more or less reflect the size of the current account position.

Britain is a significant player in international finance and the City of London, with its banking and equities sectors, deals with large quantities of foreign and UK capital. Included in this section are:

Foreign investment in the UK. When a foreign company buys a British one, or, in the case of say Toyota, builds a factory in the UK, money flows into the UK from overseas. This is a positive item in the account. The acquisition of Rover Group by the German BMW company in January 1994 is an example of a foreign company buying a British one.

UK investment overseas is a negative item as funds have left the UK to pay for overseas interests. For example, a British company like Hanson Plc that is active in North America, when buying a US company, 'exports' cash to pay for its investment. The same can be said for individuals who buy holiday homes abroad.

Currency transactions occur whenever one currency is exchanged for another. When an importer buys UK goods, he must buy sterling to pay the supplier. This means that the UK receives foreign currency (entered as a positive item converted into sterling value). Similarly, when overseas organisations deposit money in UK banks, the UK receives foreign currency. Outflows occur whenever UK organisations exchange money abroad.

Inward and outward bank deposits form a significant part of the capital account. Deposits in UK banks are obviously a cash inflow whilst UK deposits in foreign banks are an outflow.

Changes to the 'official reserves' refers to the Government's reserves of foreign currency. The official reserve is held by the Bank of England and is in the form of both sterling and foreign currency. It is exchanged by the Bank in order to influence the value of the currency and for other economic reasons.

❐ A third and much smaller part of the account is the **balancing item.** This is simply a device for making the balance of payments *balance*. The measurement of international money movements is very complicated and sometimes measurement and statistical errors occur. For example, 'black market' transactions in illegal arms, drugs and pornography do not go 'through the books' and these are accounted for in this item. The balancing item can be either positive or negative.

Activity 2

For the following items, say:

1. Where they would be entered in the balance of payments account, and

2. Whether they would be entered as a positive or negative item.

- *The 1986 Hanson (UK) acquisition of the US SCM Group.*
- *The Government of Oman's order for Challenger II Tanks from Vickers on Tyneside.*
- *The £900 million investment in the UK made by Nissan of Japan.*
- *The Renault car you are buying brand new when the new registration comes in on August 1 next year.*

The Balance of Payments Statement (1991)
(Simplified for easier understanding)

Current account	£ million	
Visible trade		
exports	103 413	
imports	(113 703)	
Visible balance	(10 290)	
Invisibles balance	3 969	
Current balance		**(6 321)**
Transactions in external assets and liabilities		
UK investment overseas	(41 169)	
Overseas investment in the UK	28 672	
Foreign currency transactions of UK banks	12 592	
Sterling transactions of UK banks	(4 382)	
UK dealings with foreign banks	(3 580)	
Net borrowings from banks abroad	12 918	
Other transactions	2 863	
Changes in official reserve	(2 662)	
Net transactions in assets and liabilities		**5 249**
Balancing item		**1 072**

(Source: Annual Abstract of Statistics 1993, HMSO)

14.8.4 The balance of payments equation

The term *balance* of payments is used because the account monitors every transaction and can account for how international funds are used by UK citizens and companies. It is not magic when it balances – it must, by definition, balance. The equation is simply:

$$\text{current account balance} = \frac{\text{net transactions in external}}{\text{assets and liabilities}} + \text{balancing item.}$$

In practice, the balancing item is added to the right hand side of the equation to account for minor errors in accounting and illegal (un-entered) transactions.

14.9 Value of Currency and Exchange Rates

The 'value' of the pound sterling refers to its exchange value against foreign currencies. Of particular interest are the key 'parities' of sterling against the other three major investor's currencies: the German *Deutsche mark*, the Japanese *yen* and the American *dollar*. However, the pound at any one time, has a value against all currencies and the exchange rate of concern to a company will depend upon the country it does business with.

All business done with other countries involves changing money. If a foreign company buys goods from a British business, then the seller will want to be paid in pounds sterling (in the same way, when we go to France on holiday, we take French francs with us). This will necessitate the foreign buyer changing his domestic currency into sterling in order to carry out the transaction. Similarly, a German company will want to be paid in Deutsche marks, a French company in francs and so on. As a result of this large volume of international business, huge amounts of money are changed from one currency into another every day. The value at which one currency is exchanged for another is termed the *exchange rate*.

Activity 3	*Find out the current exchange rate of the pound against the Deutsche mark, the dollar, the yen and the French franc. Hint: try the broadsheet newspapers.*

International business becomes much more complicated when the fact that exchange rates can be highly variable is taken into consideration. On 16 September 1992 ('black Wednesday'), the value of sterling against the Deutsche mark fell from DM 2.95 to one pound to DM 2.45, a fall of 17%. Such a devaluation can have profound effects on import and export prices. There are two rules of thumb:

❑ An increase in the value of sterling against other currencies increases the price of exports and decreases the price of imports (not because the price has risen in sterling, but because more of the foreign currency is needed to pay the sterling price).

❑ A fall in the value of sterling causes exports to be cheaper and imports to be more expensive. Such a change may have a beneficial effect on the visible balance of trade by encouraging exports and by making imports more expensive.

14.9.1 Pros and cons of a high exchange rate

Like most economic indicators, exchange rates can 'work both ways'. It cannot be said that a high exchange rate is good or bad – it all depends on how one looks at it.

Let us look at the 'knock on' effects of a high value of sterling, and again we may assume that a low value will have the opposite effects.

❑ **Expensive exports**

When the pound has a high value, resulting from a high demand for British goods, more Deutsche marks (or whatever currency is relevant) will be required to buy the currency. This makes British goods and services less price-competitive abroad which can adversely affect exporters in the UK.

❑ **Deflationary pressure**

Traditionally, a high exchange rate is accompanied by factors that support the high rate, most particularly, high interest rates. We saw previously that high interest rates attract investment money into the UK which increases the demand and hence the value of sterling. The reverse of this is that high interest rates also reduce spending power – a deflationary pressure.

14.9.2 What determines the exchange rate?

The exchange rate is determined by a number of factors. Like other products and commodities, the value of money is governed by the forces of demand and supply. These forces dictate that a high demand for a commodity will increase the price and a low demand will force it down. Hence, anything that increases the demand for sterling will increase its value against other currencies (it might help to visualise the shape of the supply curve when thinking about this issue). The question thus becomes: *what factors affect the demand for sterling*?

❑ **Interest rates**

We saw earlier that the base rate (interest rates) determines the price of borrowed money. Because the bank rates are based on the base rate as set by the Government, the return that investors will receive will attract or discourage bank deposits depending on the rate.

High interest rates – increased bank deposits

Low interest rates – reduced bank deposits

Put simply, if the interest rates are high in the UK compared with other countries, then those who are responsible for investing money will realise that they can get a higher return in the UK. However, in order to make deposits in UK banks (and other interest bearing assets) to get their return, they will have to buy sterling with their own currency. This will increase the demand for sterling and hence its value. Interest rate rises tend to produce an inflow of money, and the converse is true of interest rate reductions.

❑ **Increased Exports/Industrial Productivity**

Industrial productivity is the ability of industry to produce goods at competitive prices. Productive businesses can produce higher quality products at cheaper prices. This results from maintaining low costs (e.g. salaries, raw materials etc.) whilst keeping quality up. On the international markets as with any other markets, such products will be more attractive than poorer products or more expensive ones. In the case of increased productivity in British industry, the results will be twofold.

❑ British buyers will buy British products rather than imported ones. This will serve to reduce imports, meaning that there will be less demand for foreign currency in the UK.

❑ Foreign buyers will buy British goods (exported from the UK) rather than goods produced in their own country. Increased demand for British goods abroad will mean that there will be an increased demand for sterling to pay for the goods. This will have an upward pressure on the value of sterling, particularly when one considers that in buying a British product, they are not buying a similar product from a foreign country.

We see here how important the 'health' of domestic industry is in determining the exchange rate of the currency. On a long-term basis, this is an essential factor if a high exchange value is to be maintained.

14.10 Government Spending and Borrowing

Each year, the state receives money from its various sources of finance. It must also spend money in the Government departments in order to maintain the normal functioning of the state. These two 'sides' may not match up.

There are two possible situations that can result. If, in any given year,

the Government receives more than it spends, the difference is called a *budget surplus*.

the Government spends more than it receives, the difference is called a *budget deficit*.

This principle is very easy to understand. Suppose that in the course of a year you earn £25 000 in income and your outgoings are £30 000 because you buy a new car and have an unexpected series of expenses on your house. You will have to find £5 000 to fund the deficit and this is most commonly done by approaching your bank manager for an overdraft or extended loan. The principle is exactly the same for governments, but obviously on a much larger scale.

Like most financial decisions, a government cannot have it both ways. If it wishes to have a high spending programme, it must find ways of funding the spending. This presents governments with a dilemma.

High spending may increase the Government's popularity by injecting cash into the politically sensitive departments such as Health, Education and Trade. However, because the money must come from somewhere, an increase in taxation may need to be introduced. This makes the Government unpopular. The 'tax and spend' approach has become unfashionable in recent years in the UK.

The favoured approach has been to reduce taxation and then attempt to keep public spending within tighter limits. This ideal has not always been possible.

When a budget deficit occurs, the books are made to balance by borrowing in the same way that you or I may take out an overdraft. The amount of debt is simply the difference between what the Government has spent and what it has raised. It is referred to as the *public sector borrowing requirement* (PSBR). Like all loans, it must be serviced by repayments, including interest, and eventually be repaid.

We can consider the effects of high public spending and, as before, assume that low spending will have the opposite effect. One important feature of high spending, as we shall see, is that some of the effects cancel out others.

14.10.1 Government spending exerts a downward pressure on unemployment.

Government spending can reduce unemployment through two mechanisms. The *first* is the direct result of increased employment in Government functions. Increased spending on Health, Education and so on will necessitate higher numbers working in the relevant departments, in hospitals, schools etc. *Secondly*, where Government spending involves sub-contracting work out to the private sector (e.g. roadbuilding, new schools etc.) then private sector jobs are also generated.

14.10.2 Government spending has beneficial short-term effects on economic activity.

The effects on economic activity can be either direct or indirect. Direct stimulation of economic activity can be achieved by such things as giving out grants to industry, offering work to tender and so on. Most of the range of grants that the Department of Trade and Industry issues are for small businesses that are growing or that wish to set up in areas of high unemployment. The cash injections from the DTI enable the recipient businesses to grow and take on more labour as a result.

Indirectly, the Government can use fiscal policies, which are costly to government funds, to reduce the costs of industry. Fiscal adjustment in this context would be the reduction of taxes. The UK saw a significant stimulation of economic growth in the late '80s when the then Chancellor, Nigel Lawson, reduced the standard rate of tax from 27% to 25%. This measure was a major contributory factor in the short economic boom that the UK enjoyed at that time.

14.10.3 Government spending helps to 'invest in the future'.

There is no doubt that some government spending is used to invest in the future of the country and its people. Education and Health ensure the continuity of a supply of skilled and healthy labour to industry and commerce. Investment in infrastructure like roads and railways allows business to have improved channels of distribution over the longer term. Defence spending, as well as providing thousands of jobs, is the source of our national security. Successive governments have agreed that all of these things are essential.

14.10.4 Government spending may necessitate higher taxation, which is bad for business.

If a high public spending programme is to be maintained, then it must be paid for, and as long-term debt is a highly unattractive prospect, increased taxes are often the answer. Corporation tax is paid by companies out of their profits and so increased taxation reduces the profit retained. This means that less is available for reinvestment and growth. Increased taxation can also adversely affect the demand for a company's products because customers are likely to have less disposable income.

14.10.5 Government spending can exert inflationary pressures.

When public spending is increased, it means that with more people in work a higher aggregate (total) spending power results. This intensifies pressure on the 'too much money' element in inflation.

14.10.6 Government spending increases the PSBR

A high PSBR eventually catches up with you! Debt is not considered to be a sound long-term financial strategy, and when the time comes to reduce it the Government is forced to make the unpleasant decision between reducing public spending or increasing taxation (or both).

Case Study: The United States Federal Budget Deficit

During the mid to late 1980s Presidents Reagan (until 1989) and Bush (1989-1993) pursued a policy of imposing low taxation throughout most sectors of personal and corporate taxation. This necessarily led to an increasingly competitive business sector as profits were made that enabled reinvestment and expansion.

Unfortunately, they failed to keep public spending levels down to amounts comparable to the national revenues. The result was a steadily increasing public sector (budget) deficit. Figure 14.6 shows how this grew over the years in question.

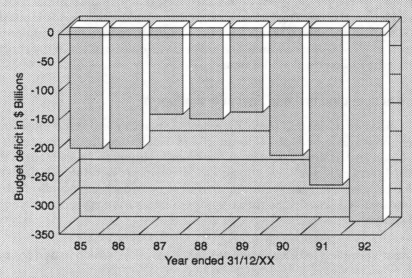

Figure 14.6: The US budget deficit (Source: Datastream)

When President Clinton assumed office in January 1993, the deficit stood at over $330 billion ($3.3 trillion). This is a huge debt by any standards, requiring large interest payments to be made on it as well as payments to reduce the capital amount. It was obvious to all observers that it had to be cut. There were two ways of doing this: to reduce public spending or increase taxes (or both) – neither of which is politically popular.

One interesting feature of the turn of events around that time was that the deficit was brought about during the administrations of the two Republican Presidents, Reagan and Bush. Bill Clinton, a Democrat, inherited the debt and it therefore fell to him to 'clear up the mess', but this meant that he, and not the Republicans, would have to make the politically unpopular decisions to reduce the deficit.

President Clinton's policies reflected the need to reduce the deficit. He introduced a number of tax increases and attempted to stimulate further economic growth in the hope that higher profits could be made by companies meaning that higher corporation tax revenues would be received. Projections published in 1992 suggested that by the end of President Clinton's term in office, the deficit will be cut to $181 billion. (Source, IMF Survey, Feb. 17, 1992)

14.11 The Economic Environment – A Summary

The state of the UK economy and the main indicators as discussed above are all of vital importance to business. Senior business managers make it their habit to keep an eye on each indicator, knowing the effects that each one can exert on their businesses. Because it is so complex, and the fact that each indicator affects the others, there tends to be a broad range of opinions as to how the Government should manage the economy at any point in time. The following table shows the complexity of outcomes for any change in economic policy.

Direct Effect of Policy on Economic Indicator				
Policy	Inflation	Unemployment	Economic Growth	Value of Sterling
FISCAL MEASURES				
Increase in Income Tax	Downward pressure	Upward pressure	Downward pressure	Downward pressure
More Spending	Upward pressure	Downward pressure	Upward pressure	Upward pressure
Decrease in Tax	Upward pressure	Downward pressure	Upward pressure	Upward pressure
Cut in spending	Downward pressure	Upward pressure	Downward pressure	Downward pressure
MONETARY MEASURES				
High Interest Rates	Downward pressure	Upward pressure	Downward pressure	Upward pressure
High Monetary Growth	Upward pressure	Short-term upward pressure		Downward pressure
Low Interest Rates	Upward pressure	Downward pressure	Upward pressure	Downward pressure
Low Monetary Growth	Downward pressure	Short-term downward pressure		Upward pressure

In an ideal Great Britain, there would be consistently low inflation, low interest rates, low tax, high spending and booming exports. The fact of the matter is that it isn't that simple. The Chancellor of the Exchequer who must manage the whole economy is rarely popular and any action will benefit one section of society and disadvantage another. Managing the economic environment is one of the most important functions of government and we have seen that much of it is a case of balancing one indicator against the others.

Individual businesses usually have to accept the conditions of the macro-economic environment. The skill comes in predicting and anticipating how the economic environment will change and managing the business to best cope in varying economic conditions.

Review Questions

1. List the major 'economic indicators'. (14.1-14.10)

2. Describe why the rate of economic growth is important to a business. (14.2)

3. What is the more common name for *negative growth*? (14.2)

4. Describe what inflation is in terms that the 'ordinary person' can understand. (14.3)

5. What two factors cause demand-led inflation? (14.3.2)

6. Summarise the disadvantages associated with a high rate of inflation. (14.4)

7. How does the government measure the unemployment figure? (14.5)

8. What are the principal causes of unemployment? (14.5.1 and 14.5.2)

9. What are the general disadvantages of unemployment? (14.6)

10. Are interest rates a monetary or a fiscal measure? (14.7)

11. Who sets the bank base rate in the UK? (14.7.1)

12. What are the effects of a high interest rate? (14.7.2)

14. What are the two main components of the balance of payments statement?(14.8.3)

15. What is the significance of a growing current account deficit? (14.8.3)

16. What determines the exchange rate of sterling against other currencies? (14.9.2)

17. Describe the pros and cons of a high value of sterling. (14.9.1)

18. What is it called when Government spending exceeds Government revenue and vice versa? (14.10)

19. What are the advantages of high Government spending? (14.10)

Answer to Activity 2

Hanson acquisition of SCM.
negative item (money is leaving the UK to buy the SCM shares),
capital account – UK investment overseas.

The Government of Oman's tank order.
positive item (money is coming into the UK in payment for the tanks),
current account – visible trade,

Nissan's investment in the UK.
positive item,
capital account – overseas investment in the UK.

Buying a Renault car in the UK.
negative item (Renault is a French car therefore it has to be imported),
current account – visible trade.

Assignment

Warren (Electronics) Limited is a British manufacturer of high-tech electronic systems for industrial monitoring and control applications. It supplies other manufacturing companies with systems that represent major capital investment for the customer, as the systems in question are very expensive. At a recent Board meeting, the MD, Simon Warren said "I hate uncertainty in the national economy. It makes my job so much harder, and adds uncertainty to our profit projections".

Warren Ltd sources many of its incoming parts (mainly electronic components and integrated circuits) from abroad, principally from the US, Japan and Germany. It sells its finished products to six European countries, the US, Canada and to the Far East via a distributor in Tokyo. The directors are hoping to soon sell to manufacturers in South America.

The capital value of the company is £30 million, and at any one time, it has long-term bank loans of about £8 million – a figure considered to be quite high by industry analysts. Employing about 2000 people, the company has suffered from declining profitability over recent years as a result of increasing costs of materials bought from abroad.

Tasks

Discuss the ways in which the following macro-economic factors can affect the profitability of Warren Limited. You should state the changes that would be brought about in Warren Ltd by movements of the factors in either direction.

❑ economic growth;

☐ interest rates;

☐ value of sterling;

☐ inflation.

Complete the task in less than 2000 words.

Further Reading

Lipsey R.G. & Harbury C., *First Principles of Economics*, Wiedenfeld and Nicolson (London) (Second Edition, 1992: Parts 4 and 5)

Curwen P. et al, *Understanding the UK Economy*, Macmillan Press (Second Edition, 1992)

Thomas G.P., *Government and the Economy Today*, Manchester University Press (1992).

Economics – First Year Study Guide, for first year degree students, BPP Publishing (Chapters 10–15 and 17)

Abel A.B. & Bernanke B.S., *Macroeconomics*, Addison Wesley Publishing Company

Powell R., *Economics for Professional and Business Studies*, DP Publications

15 The sociological environment

Objectives   After studying this chapter, students should be able to:

❑ describe the sources of 'people' influence upon an organisation and say how some of these can directly affect the organisation;

❑ define *demography* and describe how the various demographic variables can influence a business;

❑ define and distinguish between *fashions* and *trends* and describe how they can influence business;

❑ describe the nature of the threat to the physical environment;

❑ describe the components of the environmental concern and how they can affect business;

❑ describe the nature of the ethical debate in business and outline the key issues involved.

15.1 Components of the Sociological Environment

The sociological environment is all about **people**. People are necessarily strategic to any organisation and there are many ways in which they can influence a business, both favourably and unfavourably. Figure 15.1 shows the various sources of 'people' influence.

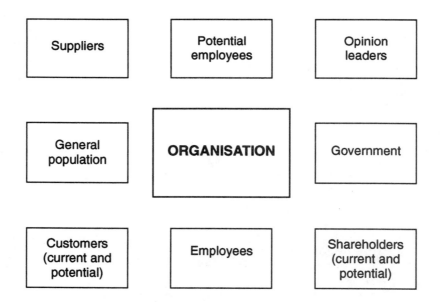

Figure 15.1: 'People' influences on an organisation

Many interesting cases exist of businesses that have prospered, suffered or changed their direction as a result of people. Influence can arise from inside the organisation (employees) or from any number of sources outside.

To a large extent, most of the sociological environment is outside the control of the business. In this respect, it is similar to the macro-economic environment. The population is constantly changing, both in size and in its opinions. The successful business is thus one that can anticipate such changes and accommodate them as becomes necessary.

In order to more fully appreciate the components of the sociological environment, we will examine the principal ones.

15.1.1 Customers

Business makes its money from customers. It follows that the strength of the *customer base* is of vital importance to the business.

The customer base relates both to the number of customers and to their ability or willingness to buy. This can be affected by demographic factors (see paragraph 15.2) or by fashions and trends. For some products there is a declining customer base (e.g. vinyl record players since the advent of CD's) and for others, the customer base is increasing (e.g. personal computers). Businesses should always be aware of trends in buying behaviour.

15.1.2 Employees

The business relies on its employees and the business is only as good as the quality of its employees. There are two key features of the population that the business requires in relation to employment. The first is the size of the pool of potential employees and the second is the quality of the people. Employee 'quality' can result from a number of factors:

☐ level of education;

☐ availability of key personnel (e.g. scientists to a chemical company);

☐ skills – type and degree of competence;

☐ motivation.

15.1.3 Opinion leaders

Opinion leaders are those individuals and groups who are able to influence public opinion. This may be important to a business, as good or bad opinion could significantly affect its sales or its employees (or potential employees).

Such groups include the pressure groups and lobbyists who campaign for an increased profile for certain issues. Others are politicians and other prominent people who, whilst espousing a particular cause, may swing opinion with regard to a business. 'Experts' of all kinds can have a remarkable effect on opinion and there are a number of instances where medical opinion, for example, has stifled or stimulated sales for a business.

Opinion leaders are also responsible in part for fashions in consumption. Obviously, items sell when they are in fashion and do not sell well when they have gone out of fashion. It is notable that what an influential person wears can quickly 'catch on' with admirers of that person. Companies make use of this willingness to emulate people by using celebrities to advertise their products or by sponsorship, e.g. sponsoring sports personalities to wear their particular brand of clothing.

Case Study   **Public opinion – The mines closure programme (1992)**

In the autumn of 1992, British Coal announced a significant reduction in the number of coal pits to be operated. This, the Government said, was because of a reduction in the demand for coal by the main power generators that had increased their use of gas as a fuel for generating electricity. At the time, the supply of coal outstripped demand by around a million tonnes a month and many pits were simply uneconomical to run.

British Coal proposed the closure of 31 pits, leaving Britain with a core of around 20 pits which would supply industry's needs for the foreseeable future. They could not have anticipated the outcry that resulted from the announcement!

The opposition parties rounded solidly against British Coal and the Government. A few 'Tory rebels' joined their cause. Needless to say, the mining communities affected made their feelings known vociferously and opinion polls in national newspapers indicated that there was a sizeable body of opinion against the closure programme. This all forced the Government to think again.

Michael Heseltine, the President of the Board of Trade, returned to the House of Commons with a compromise. Taking into account the unpopularity of the initial proposals, he offered to close a smaller number of pits and to put others on a 'care and maintenance' footing. In addition there would be a three month 'consultation period' during which the Government would more fully investigate the grievances of opponents to the plan.

15.2 Demographics

Demographics is the study of the population, particularly with regard to how it is made up and how it moves – both over time and geographically. It can affect the business in many ways as all of the groups of people that make up the organisation's interests can eventually be considered as part of the total population.

Population growth has been a prominent feature of modern times. Over the course of the last 1000 years, the world population has grown at a striking pace. Since the industrial revolution in the late eighteenth century population growth has accelerated, and the rate of growth has been such that the term 'population explosion' has been coined.

The world population is estimated to have been around 300 million in AD 1000 and this grew relatively slowly to 728 million in 1750. By 1962, however, it had expanded to 3000 million (3 billion) and projections suggest that by the year 2000 it will have reached the order of 6 billion. World population is projected to reach 8.5 billion by 2025.

One key feature hidden within these figures is that the principal areas of growth have been the developing countries rather than in the West. Compared to the increases in the third world, Western Europe and the United States have shown relatively low growth. Some countries actually have a slowly declining population (e.g. Belgium and Denmark).

The causes of population growth are the disparities between the *birth rate* and the *death rate*. It follows that if, in any given year, these two figure are equal, then population will remain stable. In reality, both of these tend to be cyclical.

The causes of varying birth rates tend to be largely unknown. After the war, up until the mid sixties, Britain experienced a 'baby boom', but births dropped off significantly in the late nineteen seventies. In countries where there is an effective 'welfare state' families do not procreate as an insurance against the parents' old age (commonly the experience in the third world). This has been a cause of the stability of the population in the UK.

Death rates increase rapidly in times of war and in protracted health crises. With improvements in medical technology, people in the West are living longer and in consequence, the numbers of elderly people have increased over recent years. The crude death rate, which does not take account of age structure in the country, shows the following trend:

Year	Deaths per thousand
1900	17.1
1921	12.4
1992	11.2

(Source: Social Trends (1993), HMSO)

The shift away from traditional ('heavy') industries towards 'safer' occupations may also have contributed to this trend.

Figure 15.2 shows the changes in UK population as a whole.

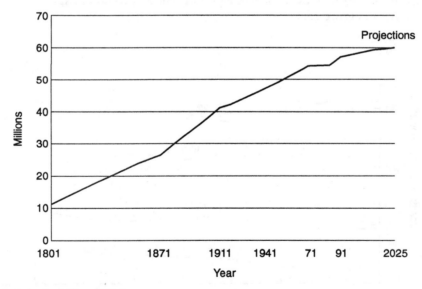

Figure 15.2: Growth in the UK population
(Source: Annual Abstract of Statistics 1993 (HMSO) and Social Trends 1993, (HMSO)).

As well as the size of the population, demographics also takes into account the distribution. There are a number of distribution features of the population that are relevant. Businesses will be concerned about population distribution in relation to both the supply of labour and materials and the demand for its products or services. It may have a bearing on their staffing, their marketing (the target markets) and even on where they set up the business in the first place. Government will also make it their business to carefully monitor these population features as they can influence the shape and character of society as a whole.

15.2.1 Population Density

This is defined as the number of people that live in the country, county or city divided by its area. The figure is consequently expressed in *individuals per square kilometre*. In the UK, the density over the whole country is around 230, but this figure conceals the two extremes of population. In some parts of the country (Northern Scotland, North Wales etc.) the density is very low, whereas the major conurbations have figures far higher than the average.

It is not surprising that most business is located where the people are. The major centres of population attract a much higher concentration of business and industry in order to take advantage of the supply of labour and ready supply of customers that such concentration affords. Business location is discussed in Chapter 3.

Population density varies, in addition to the disparity between births and deaths, by population migration. This is the movement of individuals from one region to another. For example, recent trends show a net migration away from London, and in the early nineteen nineties there was a net migration *into* Northern Ireland.

15.2.2 Age Distribution

As longer life has become a feature of UK demography, and birth rate has dropped off in certain periods, the age distribution map has become increasingly 'lumpy'. As a nation, Britain is getting older. The percentage of the population aged over 65 has increased from 9.5% in 1951 to 12% in 1992. Those over 80 years old have increased from 1.4% to 3.7% over the same period. The key trends in age structure in the UK are shown in Figure 15.3.

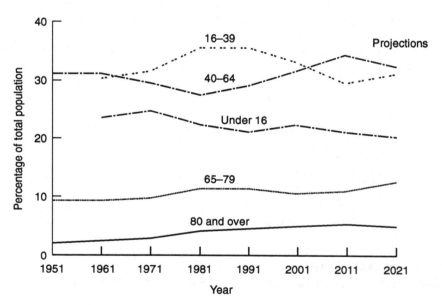

Figure 15.3: Age structure of the UK population.
(Source: Social Trends, 1993, HMSO)

Such trends have many implications, not only for business but also for the Government. The increased numbers of elderly people will necessarily mean increased claimants on the DSS pensions department and reduced numbers of income tax payers. It may also affect housing and other social provisions. For business, like many changes, the increase in the number of elderly people offers both an opportunity and a threat. The opportunities include an expanding market among the elderly, many of whom will have significant spending power. The threats, in addition to the possibility of increased taxation to pay for the elderly, includes a drop in the supply of labour in the key age bands (the income tax payers).

15.3 Fashions and Trends in the Sociological Environment

As well as the demographic issues that are vital to business, there are a number of other areas of this environment which can affect businesses.

15.3.1 Fashions

The first, and perhaps the most obvious issue, is that of fashions. We need look no further than the clothes we wear to see that in some sectors of business this is of immense importance. It should be realised though, that the idea of fashion extends beyond the clothes market.

Not only is it the case that some products are not fashionable whilst others are, but it is also true that fashions change. Products which were not fashionable last year are fashionable this year. This can apply to food products, colours of motor car, toys, furniture and many other products.

Because fashions are predominantly a feature of the 'demand side' of the economy, it falls to the marketing department to predict changes and cater for them accordingly. In exceptional circumstances, adroit marketing can actually cause a change in fashion which the business can then exploit.

Businesses that rely for their sales on products which are subject to fashion changes tend to be seen as risky by investors. They necessarily exist in a less stable environment than other companies – one in which the opportunities and threats presented by the changes can be more intense than in other sectors.

Activity 1   *Make a list of products that are currently in fashion. It may help to think of products that you expect will go out of fashion before too long.*

15.3.2 Trends

If fashions can be understood in terms of their short-term effects, then trends are usually taken to mean changes over the longer term. We have already seen the impact that demographic trends have (potentially) on business and government (such as the increase in older people). Longer term trends give businesses more time to respond, but are nevertheless a threat which must be taken account of.

The examples of trends in population and consumer behaviour which have brought about changes in business practice are numerous. Good examples might be:

☐ the development of out-of-town retail outlets which exploit the trend in increasing car ownership (it will not have escaped your notice that they all have enormous car parks);

☐ the many double glazing companies that have sprung up as a result of increased home ownership. The increased home ownership is primarily as a result of the sale of council houses to tenants in the nineteen eighties;

☐ the introduction of numerous 'eco-friendly' consumer products as a result of the trends in environmental consciousness;

☐ ethical investment funds, operated by most financial institutions. These are funds which invest only in companies which are seen as ethical companies in that they do not mistreat employees, make or sell weapons, exploit the third world etc. This is again in response to consumer trends in this area.

15.4 Environmental Issues

One of the striking issues that has been in the ascendant since the late nineteen seventies has been the concern for the physical environment. Such has been the effect of this issue that it has redirected government policy and many business strategies. The changes have been brought about because (it is perceived), the population as a whole considers it an important issue.

We are all aware of the well used phrases that have been used to describe the various environmental threats. The nature of the environmental threat is complex, but in general, all of the areas of concern are either concerned with **pollution** or with **resources**.

15.4.1 Pollution issues

Pollution describes anything that contaminates the physical environment. It can arise from such things as chemical agents or from radiation. The main threats under this heading include the following.

❑ **Acid rain**

Acid rain, as the name suggests is rain that has been made acidic. The chemical agent that causes it is a gas called sulphur dioxide (SO_2). SO_2 is a product of burning some fossil fuels, particularly coal. The gas rises into the atmosphere and drifts with winds and other weather systems. Eventually, it reacts with water in clouds and together they form the chemical product sulphurous acid (H_2SO_3). When this rain falls, it increases the acidity of the affected land or water, and this has a detrimental effect on plants, fish and other animals that rely on these as food.

❑ **The 'greenhouse effect'**

The greenhouse effect is a popular way of describing the broader theme of *global warming*. This phenomenon is one that involves the average temperatures of all parts of the earth rising. For the equatorial regions, this would mean an increase in the areas of desert and, because it would involve parts of the polar ice-caps melting, some islands and low-lying land would disappear under sea water. It would also affect agriculture and the habitats of many animals and plants. It is caused, as the colloquial name suggests, by the atmosphere acting in the same way as a greenhouse. The sun's rays in the form of radiation heat the earth. Whereas they would normally 'leak' back into space, under the greenhouse, gases in the atmosphere reduce the leakage by reflecting rays back onto the earth. This means that the earth under the atmosphere warms up.

'Greenhouse gases' include CFCs (see later) and most particularly, carbon dioxide (CO_2). Carbon dioxide is the product of the burning of all fossil fuels and their derivatives. It arises from oil, gas and coal burning including those fuels used in cars, power stations, and domestic homes. The more fossil fuels are burned, the more 'greenhouse gases' are produced.

❑ **Holes in the ozone layer**

Ozone is like oxygen except that whereas the oxygen molecule is two oxygen atoms 'stuck' together (O_2), ozone is three (O_3). High in the atmosphere, there is a layer of ozone which encompasses the earth. Its purpose is to deflect some of the suns most harmful rays (called *ultra violet* radiation – UV) away from the earth's surface.

When UV reaches the earth's surface, it not only adds to the global warming effects, but is thought also to increase the incidence of skin cancers.

During the late nineteen eighties, satellite imaging identified 'holes' in the ozone layer over the North and South poles. Scientists working on the problem suggested that one of the principal causes of the holes was the use of chloro-fluoro carbon (CFC) compounds. CFCs were traditionally used in three product areas: as a propellant in aerosols (e.g. paint cans and deodorants), as a coolant in refrigeration systems and as the chemical used to 'blow' polystyrene from a flat, brittle plastic into the commonly used packaging material. Most advanced industrialised countries have taken action to reduce or eliminate the use of CFCs in these products and this is expected to go a long way in reducing this particular environmental threat. The chemical manufacturers who have traditionally produced CFCs, including the British company ICI Plc, have announced plans to run down their production in the short term and cease altogether in the medium term.

❑ Disposal of rubbish and waste

As population has increased and products have used increased amounts of packaging as part of their marketing, so the amount of waste has increased markedly over recent years. The increased use of 'disposable' and convenience products have added to the problem. Both domestic and industrial waste present a potential problem in the environment. The threat arises from two sources; firstly there is the sheer volume of rubbish, and secondly there are the hazards associated with its storage and disposal.

❑ Nuclear waste

Whilst the generation of energy from fossil fuels produces gaseous by-products like carbon dioxide and sulphur dioxide, nuclear power is 'clean' in this regard. Energy is produced by the actions of radioactive metal elements, particularly uranium and plutonium.

However, whilst the process itself does not generate any chemical pollutants, the problem arises when the fuel is to be disposed of. 'Spent' uranium emits harmful radiation, even when it is of no further use for the generation of energy, and will continue to be radioactive for in excess of 10 000 years (some radioactive materials can remain so for over 20 000 years). In addition to the nuclear materials from the energy generation process, recent developments have shown that there are also certain amounts of nuclear waste from old nuclear weapons.

Other 'heavy' metals, particularly lead, have a shielding effect on radiation, and when it is disposed of, spent uranium is wrapped in lead and cast in concrete. Some nuclear waste can be re-processed and used again, but most is either dumped in the sea or in specially created subterranean chambers. The objections raised regarding nuclear waste focus on the length of time that the waste remains harmful. Future generations will have to avoid the areas where nuclear waste is dumped, and this has caused some dissension.

❑ Agro-chemicals

Chemicals used in agriculture have a number of purposes. Most are used to kill or deter insects and fungi that can have a detrimental effect on the crops. Agricultural efficiency growth over recent years has been due in large part to the use of such chemicals, usually sprayed over the crops. The very nature of agrochemical use means that they must have a degree of toxicity (ability to poison) in order for them to fulfil their biocidal (life-killing) expectations.

Concerns about agro-chemicals stem from three sources, all of which centre around their toxicity. *Firstly*, there is concern that the chemicals may leak into rivers, streams and drinking water supplies. *Secondly*, it is believed that continual use of some agro-chemicals contributes to the exhaustion of land. The toxicity will build up in the soil meaning that production of food crops in the soil becomes less likely in the longer term. *Thirdly*, the use of mild toxins on food crops has raised suspicions about the safety of such products as food.

The response to these concerns has been for the chemical manufacturers to pay attention to the toxicity of their products, especially with regard to human consumption, and for some farmers to switch entirely to the use of 'organic' fertilisers. Organic fertilisers are those which are produced naturally, such as horse manure.

Case Study   Agro-chemical spillage into the River Eden, Cumbria

At 8 am on 27 March 1993, a farmer in a field adjacent to the River Eden at Little Musgrave near Appleby in Cumbria, accidentally allowed 8000 litres of the agricultural fertiliser ammonium hydroxide to spill into the river. When this chemical meets water, it generates ammonia, which, as well as its characteristically unpleasant odour, also makes the water alkaline.

This chemical change in the river Eden killed all of the fish life for a sixteen mile stretch. The problem was made worse by the National Rivers Authorities' two day delay in treating the spill (they eventually added hydrochloric acid to the river to neutralise the alkalinity). The managers of the fishing and gaming beats along the river were naturally angry. They predicted it would take 3 to 4 years for the fish stocks to fully recover to their former levels.

In addition, businesses that relied on the angling business such as local hotels, shops, pubs and fishing equipment retailers anticipated a significant loss of sales as fishermen would not visit the river while the fish stocks were so low.

❑ **Chemical emissions**

Many industries, as well as producing waste that is 'taken away', produce emissions that are discharged directly into the environment. Some of these are allowed under existing legislative guidelines, whilst others are not and are discharged by mistake. It was mentioned earlier that sulphur dioxide is produced as a result of burning coal, but as well as gaseous emissions, some companies also discharge their liquid waste products into rivers. As a result of such discharges over protracted periods of time, rivers have lost their populations of indigenous fish as well as representing an increasing health risk.

Case Study   Union Carbide in Bhopal, India

Union Carbide Corporation (UCar) is a US based multi-national chemicals group and one of the world's largest chemical companies. Like many of its competitors, UCar has plants and distribution outlets throughout the world. The UCar plant in Bhopal, northern India is just one of its foreign interests.

Union Carbide India Limited, among other things, produced a pesticide called *Sevin*. A highly poisonous chemical called *methyl isocyanate* (MIC) was one of the intermediates that went to make up Sevin, and this was stored on the Bhopal site. On 3 December 1984, water contamination in the MIC storage area caused a cloud of MIC gas to be leaked from the plant. As there were light winds over the plant at the time, the gas drifted over the town of Bhopal. The cloud of gas killed 2 600 local people within a few hours and left an estimated 300 000 others with long term health problems. A report in 1991 reported that Bhopal residents were still dying at the rate of 1 a day as a direct result of the MIC leakage.

Initial claims by local residents against UCar amounted to $15 billion. Whilst the company admitted liability for the tragedy, they actually paid an amount significantly less than the claimed figure. The news of the incident caused great suspicion of UCar throughout the world and the company were forced to abandon plans for investments in Scotland and the USA. They launched a public relations campaign called *'Excellence in the Environment'* in an attempt to restore some public confidence in the corporation.

15.4.2 Resource issues

Consumption of resources is an implicit part of industrial activity. Manufacturing processes use inputs which are composed of raw materials. Put simply, the materials must come from somewhere and physical resources are essential industrial inputs. As consumption has increased, so has the use of resources. Increased industrialisation over the course of the twentieth century has meant that a genuine concern has arisen about the earth's finite resources. The resources issue is centred around three main concerns.

❑ **Energy resources**

We have already seen that energy is generated, among other methods, by burning fossil fuels. The principal fossil fuels are coal, natural gas and oil. Oil is also used, through chemical processing, to generate petrol, diesel, solvents, pitch, bitumen and a wide range of plastics. As the number of cars has grown, so has the consumption of oil. Because of the high dependence that the developed countries have for energy resources, a good deal of attention has been focused on the existing reserves.

As at 1993, public relations literature from Sellafield nuclear reprocessing centre in Cumbria (operated by British Nuclear Fuels Ltd) made the following predictions regarding existing energy at current rates of consumption and price.

Fuel	Years left (world)
Oil	50
Gas	50
Coal	220
Uranium	1000

These figures are shown in figure 15.4.

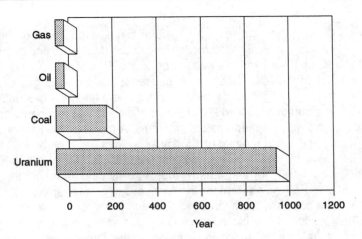

Figure 15.4: Projected energy reserves at current usage.
(Source: British Nuclear Fuels, 1993)

It is predicted that attention will increasingly be focused on the energy resource concerns as the resources dry up. It is important to appreciate that further resources will become available after these dates if the consumer is prepared to pay a higher price. Old oil fields can be re-excavated to extract fuels that are uneconomical at today's prices.

❑ **Mineral resources**

As well as the concerns over energy requirements, concern also exists about other components of the earth's natural resources. Industry uses metals such as copper, iron, zinc etc. The reserves of these vary from mineral to mineral. The one thing they all have in common is that they are all finite – i.e. there is so much and no more in the earth. The large British mining company RTZ Corporation Plc estimate the following reserves of some of the most important minerals.

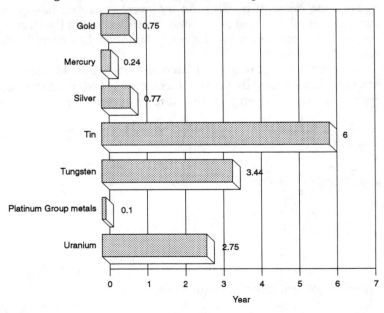

Figure 15.5: Estimated total world resources in millions of tonnes – rarer minerals
(Source: Minerals Handbook 1992-93, Phillip Crowson, Chief Economist,
The RTZ Corporation Plc – with kind permission)

In contrast to these relatively rare metals, others are in comparative abundance. RTZ Corporation estimates that world reserves of iron ore amount to 151 billion tonnes, lead has 120 million tonnes, magnesium, 3400 million tonnes and talc (an important industrial material), 1.12 billion tonnes.

☐ Extinction and over-fishing

We have already seen the growth that has occurred in populations all over the world. These changes have necessarily meant that more food is needed to feed the increased numbers of people. For those animals that cannot be farmed, reliance must be placed upon the existing supplies of the species. For some species, their over-harvesting has meant that stocks have been drastically reduced. This has placed pressure on the stocks and in some examples, doubt has been cast over their continuing existence. The most commonly cited example of this problem is fish stocks in the sea.

Over-fishing means taking more fish out of the sea than can be replaced by the existing fish breeding to replace them. When this happens, stocks inevitably fall. Falling stocks not only threaten the supply of fish for human food, but also the lives of other animals, including birds, that feed off the fish.

In recent years, this problem has begun to be addressed by governments. The European Union imposes strict fishing limits (called *quotas*) upon its member states. This means that the UK is only allowed to catch so many tonnes of fish a year.

Ecologists and environmental pressure groups have indicated that there are significant over-fishing problems within European waters. The most over-fished sea region in European waters is the Baltic Sea and scientists have advised that fishing should stop completely for many years if fish stocks are not to be completely eliminated. In the North Sea, fish stocks are also a cause for concern. The same groups say that stocks have become depleted to the point that it will soon become commercially unviable to put to sea to fish in the North Sea. In other parts of the world, the problem is no less pressing. The Atlantic Tuna is fished by the Japanese as a key ingredient for their local delicacies sushi and sashimi. Stocks of the Atlantic Tuna have become so low in Japanese waters that it is thought to be in danger of extinction.

Fish stocks in The North Sea

Tonnes of breeding stock

	1970/71	1990/91
Cod	263 000	64 000
Haddock	403 000	64 000

In 1977, fishing for **Herring** in the North Sea was banned for five years. Over this time, stocks recovered from 300 000 breeding tonnes to 1.2 million tonnes. (Source: *The Guardian*, 18 August, 1992)

In recent years there has been a move to encourage consumption of fish species which have not previously been considered as food. Such species include the Grenadier, the Rat-tail and others which are equally unknown to the average fish consumer. It is hoped that by changing away from the main food species, their stocks will be preserved.

15.5 Ethical Issues in the Sociological Environment

In addition to the many concerns about the physical environment, pollution and resources, another issue of increasing importance has been that concerning the ethical standards that businesses have adopted.

It could be said that traditionally, businesses have been so concerned about the financial returns and making profits, that they have largely ignored the moral and ethical implications of their actions. As customers have become increasingly concerned about a range of ethical issues, businesses have been presented with both opportunities (if they respond to the trend in opinion) and threats (if they do not). Such concerns arise from a large number of possible consumer convictions. We will consider some of the most influential issues.

15.5.1 Third World issues

We saw earlier in this chapter that there are enormous disparities between the developed countries (North America, Western Europe and the Pacific Rim) and the third world. The third world consists of Africa, Southern Asia, and some parts of South and Central America. Such regions are characterised by lack of industrial development, poverty, over-population, chronic shortages of food and a lack of meaningful jobs. Due to the nature of these countries, they are based on what is called a *primitive economy*. This is one based on agriculture, and objectives tend to be concerned with subsistence and survival rather than wealth and economic growth.

The principal ethical concerns about business and the third world centre around the so-called *fair trade* issues. The developed countries, such as the UK, buy many of their imports from the third world. Because Western companies tend to be powerful buyers (owing to the quantities in which they buy and their use of 'hard' currencies), they are able to offer low prices for goods.

The offering of low prices to third world producers has been criticised as exploitative. Moreover, the fact that these countries do not enjoy the same employment protection laws that the developed countries do, can also mean that the suppliers are being encouraged in their use of exploitative labour (e.g. low-paid and child labour). Fair trade purchasers are those that reportedly vet their suppliers for ethical employment practices and then pay them a fair price for their produce.

15.5.2 'Animal cruelty' issues

This issue has two parts. The first is the keeping of animals for food in cramped and otherwise uncomfortable conditions, and the second is the use of animals for the testing of chemical substances such as cosmetics.

Like all ethical issues, there are a wide range of opinions about this matter. Some people have reacted to the first issue by becoming vegetarians whilst others have insisted on eating only meat that has not caused 'distress' to the animals concerned. Chickens kept in batteries and pigs chained in small pens have been of particular interest, and this has encouraged sales of such products as free range eggs and similarly raised chicken and pigs.

On the animal testing issue, some activist groups have advocated the boycotting of the products of companies that engage in such testing. Companies like Body Shop Plc have made a successful business out of claims of 'cruelty-free' cosmetics.

15.5.3 Employment practices issues

The ways in which an organisation treats its employees has increasingly become an issue in the ethical debate. Whilst most employment practices are now legislated under law, there is necessarily some room for interpretation of these laws. There are several areas of concern in this regard.

Equal opportunities practices are often measured by the relatively simple method of seeing how many women and individuals from ethnic minorities the company has in senior management. This can easily be seen from the annual accounts, where companies must declare the members of the Board of Directors.

Health and safety policies may also be called into question if the organisation is perceived to have suffered higher poor health rates among its employees (or former employees). Working hours may be an issue if employees are forced to work longer than they would choose. Allied to this is the organisation's management style. Some forms of management that rely on intimidation or undue pressure might be deemed unethical. This concern is of especial significance in foreign or third world suppliers where EU employment legislation is not applicable.

15.5.4 Pollution issues

As public opinion has intensified about the environmental debate generally, some individuals have begun to view companies favourably or unfavourably on the grounds of how much they contribute to pollution. This area is on the border between the environmental and ethical concerns. Some chemical and energy companies have come under condemnation from pressure groups.

Organisations that are seen as guilty of pollution are not necessarily condemned by public opinion. History has shown that the company's responses to pollution incidents can swiftly repair public confidence in the organisation.

Case Study **The Exxon Valdez Oil Spill**

Exxon Corporation is one of the worlds largest companies whose interests include a number of major petrochemicals companies (in the UK, its petrol is sold under the Esso brand). Like all major oil companies, it transports huge quantities of oil in large shipping tankers.

In March 1989, one of its large vessels, the Exxon Valdez ran aground in Prince William Sound – a waterway in Alaska, USA. Eleven million gallons of crude oil spilled from the tanker causing havoc to the animal and plant life in the area over a total of 1 100 miles of coastline. It has been estimated that among the fatalities of the spill were over 5 500 sea otters and around half a million birds, as well as the cost in fish and plant life. Ecologists who studied the scene considered it one of the greatest environmental catastrophes ever.

A great deal of criticism was levelled at Exxon Corporation because of the way it responded to the spill. The company paid $125 million in criminal compensation, $1 billion in civil lawsuits and it contributed $100 million towards the massive clean up operation. Despite the payment of these large sums, some economists and ecologists rounded against the company for being irresponsible. These groups estimated that the real cost of the spill – the *social cost* – including loss of livelihoods, tourism etc., amounted to between $3-5 billion. This is clearly well in excess of the amounts actually paid.

Activity 2 *What would your response to the Exxon payments for the Valdez 'disaster' be if you were:*

☐ *an Exxon employee,*

☐ *an Exxon shareholder,*

☐ *a fisherman who fished Prince William Sound in Alaska,*

☐ *a local Alaska hotelier.*

15.5.5 Donations issues

An issue of lesser importance in the ethical debate is the use to which a company puts its profits. According to the rules on financial reporting, a company must publicly declare any donations it has made to charitable or political organisations over the financial reporting year. It is in the area of political donations that most controversy has been raised.

Some companies consider it to be in their interest that a particular political party is in government. In order to assist the party in its campaigns, the company may make donations to party funds. Customers who do not have the same political convictions as the Board of the company may disagree with such donations and this may have a bearing on the willingness of such customers to do business with the company.

15.6 Responses to the Environmental and Ethical Issues

The environmental and ethical debates have reached all levels and areas of society in the developed countries. A general feeling has emerged that *something must be done*. Both individuals and businesses have made changes in their behaviour as a result of the issues raised in the debates. As well as presenting a threat to the ongoing way of life we have come to enjoy, environmental concern has offered business many opportunities. Many companies have been keen to project an animal or environmentally-friendly image, and some new products launched with these concerns in mind have proven to be most lucrative. Some of the responses to the concerns are as follows:

15.6.1 Buyer behaviour

Most consumers have made *some* changes to their buying habits as a result of the environmental and ethical concerns. Growth in sales of such items as free range chickens and recycled toilet paper illustrate this point. More concerned consumers have made gestures by boycotting suppliers they see as 'guilty' of ethical or environmental misdemeanours whilst others have become vegetarians. Changes in buyer behaviour result from changes in life-styles. Individuals vary in the degree to which they have modified their life-styles to account for their environmental and ethical concerns.

15.6.2 Recycling

Whereas at one time society saw no need to recycle used products, recent trends have shown an increased willingness to save some household and industrial refuse items for recycling purposes. The most common materials which are recycled include paper, glass and a range of metals such as aluminium. Most local authorities and many supermarkets have 'recycling points' where consumers may deposit their selected rubbish. Closely allied to this response has been concern over the amount and type of packaging used in the presentation of products. This has presented marketers with something of a dilemma as packaging attracts buyers to their products but excessive packaging will attract criticism.

15.6.3 Efficiency

One conviction which has grown over recent years is that we must get more from less, i.e. resources must be used more responsibly because that they are finite and that waste of all sorts must be reduced. This response has spread into many areas of life and business. There has, for example been increased interest in economical motor cars: use of 'lean burn' engines and catalytic converters has grown enormously and the latter are now required for all new cars sold in the European Union. In the home there has been growth in double glazing, cavity wall insulation and loft lagging. Efficiency factors have the joint benefit that as well as preserving resources, they also save money!

Review Questions

1. What are the sources of the various 'people' influences on an organisation? (15.1.1–15.1.3)

2. What is demography? (15.2)

3. Describe some of the ways that demography can influence an organisation. (15.2.1 and 15.2.2)

4. Define and distinguish between fashions and trends. (15.3.1 and 15.3.2)

5. Describe the nature of the components of the environmental debate. (15.4.1 and 15.4.2)

6. What are the major issues in the ethical debate as it affects business? (15.5.1 and 15.5.2)

7. What responses have there been to the environmental and ethical issues in business? (15.6.1–15.6.3)

Assignment

A friend of yours who is a company director says to you, '*I don't need to bother with any of this environmental or ethical stuff. Business is all about money and looking after number one!*'. Do you agree with him and if not, advise him as to the reasons that he should heed the environmental and ethical issues of business.

Further Reading

Simms C., *The Green Business (the impact of environmental issues on strategic management)*, Horton Publishers (1991)

Welford R. & Gouldson A., *Environmental Management and Business Strategy*, Pitman Press (1993)

Drummond J. & Rain B., *Managing Business Ethics*, Butterworth Heinnemann (1993)

Hoffman M.W. & Moore J.M., *Business Ethics*, McGraw Hill (1990)

Clutterbuck D., Dearlove D. & Snow D., *Actions Speak Louder*, Kogan Page Publishers Ltd (1992)

Davis J., *Greening Business (Managing for Sustainable Development)*, Blackwell Ltd (1991)

Simpson S., *The Times Guide to the Environment*, Times Books (1990)

Peattie K., *Green Marketing, M&E Business Handbooks*, Longman Group UK (1992)

Social Trends (followed by name of year), HMSO (Social Trends is published annually and contains the vital statistics of population, spending trends etc.)

16 The technological environment

Objectives   After studying this chapter, students should be able to:

- ❑ describe the main areas in which technology is used in business;
- ❑ outline the advantages of technology to business;
- ❑ describe some possible disadvantages that technology can cause;
- ❑ define *information* and *data*;
- ❑ describe the developments and applications in information technology;
- ❑ explain how a business uses IT and describe the benefits that can be gained from its use;
- ❑ understand how business gains from the use of computers and telecommunications;
- ❑ describe some ways in which technology is used in manufacturing and design.

16.1 Key Areas of Technology

Technological innovation has been one of the characterising features of the twentieth century. Since the turn of the century, much of what we now consider as the normal features of our society have been invented, discovered or developed. Modern technology did not just happen. Each area has seen an evolution wherein one development has led to another. This has meant that technology has grown enormously in complexity, power and in usage by society.

Each area of technology arose from an initial breakthrough or a series of discoveries or inventions. These are the key innovations upon which subsequent developments were made. Some of the most significant developments of the century include:

- ❑ flight;
- ❑ anaesthetics;
- ❑ antibiotics;
- ❑ electromagnetic transmission (TV, radio, radar, satellites etc.);
- ❑ semiconductor technology;
- ❑ nuclear fission (used in power generation and in weaponry).

It is not an exaggeration to say that the effects of these innovations have shaped society. If we consider the implications of one of these discoveries (the electronic semiconductor), we may illustrate the 'knock-on' effects that such innovations can produce.

16.1.1 Electronic semiconductors

Since the early silicon transistors replaced the old valve 'tubes', a number of further developments became possible. Several key areas of technology rely on **semiconductors** and their introduction allowed great advances to be made in many other areas.

Semiconductors are used in electronics to accurately control electrical signals and they are capable of 'switching' signals on and off very rapidly.

Applications of semiconductor technology

- ☐ telecommunications
- ☐ computers
- ☐ robots
- ☐ television and radio
- ☐ control and monitoring systems (e.g., airlines and space flight)
- ☐ medical diagnosis and technology

Developments in transistors have meant that circuitry has become smaller in size and increasingly powerful. What would have filled a large room twenty years ago can now fit onto just one part of a microchip. The 'silicon chip' – the basis of modern electronics – contains many electronic components in microscopic form.

Activity 1   *Make a list of all of the technologies you have used so far today.*

16.2 Benefits of Technology to Business

Technological development has benefited business in many ways.

Firstly, it can **reduce costs** as tasks which were previously performed manually are replaced by automated procedures. Some industries, particularly in the manufacturing sector, were previously characterised by their use of entire 'armies' of semi-skilled workers performing repetitive tasks. Much of the work of the typical factory 'line worker' can now be performed by automated machines such as robots. As well as saving on labour cost, this also has the advantage that machines can work in conditions that would be unacceptable to humans, such as low temperatures in winter and working continuously around the clock. Machines do not require tea breaks and are not subject to boredom.

Technology offers the opportunity for **the reduction of errors** as the 'human factor' is reduced. Most errors are introduced into procedures by human fatigue, negligence, carelessness or even deliberate malice. Automation of such activities can mean that inconsistency is reduced or eliminated. **Quality can be increased** as machines can make items with greater conformance to specification, and greater consistency can be achieved. It should of course be remembered that the performance of a machine is only as good as the humans who designed or made it.

Efficiency improvements are gained as more work can be produced at lower cost. Efficiency is simply the expression of how much output is achieved for a given level of work input. An inefficient system will cost a lot in terms of effort, time and money, and produce an output lower or less than desired. Because automation can often increase output for the same cost (or less), efficiency gains are common long term benefits of technology.

Operations are greatly **speeded up**. Information can be transmitted much more rapidly by using electronic methods (such as telecommunications) than could be achieved by manual means. Similarly, reports and management information can be generated much more rapidly when computers are employed.

Technology can be used by businesses in many areas of **communication**. It can be used to communicate marketing messages to the appropriate buyer groups or as part of control and monitoring systems. Communications technology is discussed in more detail in section 16.6.

16.3 Possible Disadvantages of Technology

It is generally accepted that technological innovation has had a beneficial effect on society. Since the Luddite rebellion of the nineteenth century, few have seriously questioned the advantages of technology. It should be pointed out though, that great as the advantages might be, certain negative aspects can arise.

The most obvious disadvantage is that it has contributed to the increased levels of unemployment (referred to as *technological unemployment*). Whereas at one time, all tasks in a production process were done by hand, many have now been replaced with automated procedures and robots. Similarly, in areas like accounting, the introduction of comprehensive computer based packages has replaced human operators in data entry functions and the production of reports.

Some have argued that the introduction of data management systems (such as computers) have provided a false sense of accuracy. According to this argument, individuals irrationally trust computer information simply *because* it is information from a computer (the implication being that it *must* be right). The fact is that any computer programme or the data input to it is only as good as its human programmer or data entry personnel. Human errors in inputs can produce errors in the information provided. This over-reliance on computer data may result in poor or incorrect information upon which to make important decisions.

The increase in usage of IT systems in business has meant that personal contact between individuals has been replaced by electronic linkages. This has become more of an issue since the introduction of electronic mail (EMail). Such isolation may have detrimental effects upon the culture of an organisation which may rely heavily upon camaraderie which arises from the personal contact between employees.

16.4 Information Technology (IT)

16.4.1 What is information?

Information has become an extremely important part of life in the modern industrialised economies. The demand for it supports entire sectors of industry both in the manufacture of equipment and in the dissemination of information itself.

In its most fundamental form, information can be considered as

the **signals** and the **form of those signals** that represent meaningful communication to the recipients.

Information is usually considered to be a separate concept to that of *data*. According to this distinction, data is information in its raw state. Data needs to be further processed to make it into meaningful information. Information, in contrast to data, is in a form which can readily be received by its intended recipient without further processing. This demarcation is not always helpful as many forms of communication can be considered as both data and information.

It is important to realise that the senders and recipients of information are not always humans. Machines can send and receive information as electrical impulses, as indeed the various parts of the human body send information to each other to facilitate normal functioning. One part of the body or one machine *informs* the other so that appropriate action can be taken by the receiving unit. In the body, information is passed electrically along nerve fibres and chemically in the bloodstream.

16.4.2 The need for information

Information has many important functions. Communication in the form of information is the essential 'bloodstream' that provides cohesion to society or any sub-sector of society. We can consider the following as the principal functions.

❑ It enables effective **control**. Control systems rely on the accurate and timely flow of information in order to ensure that all activities are co-ordinated. Similarly information can be 'fed back' to a process so that outputs more accurately meet expectations. The flow of information in a control system is shown in figure 16.1. The mode by which control information is carried will depend on the nature of the system. Some, like central heating thermostats use electrical information to drive boilers and regulators. Others, such as the control involved in running a department in business will often use face to face verbal communication.

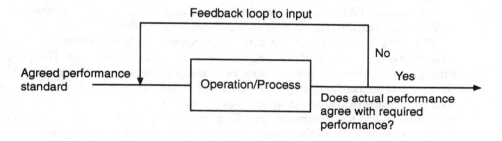

Figure 16.1: A simple control system

❑ Information is used to cause **actions**. Such communication can either be instructive or restrictive. Instructive information describes the correct course of action by which a task must be carried out. Restrictive information defines what must not be done or places limits on the course of action.

❑ Information is essential in business if managers are to **make intelligent decisions**. Most organisations employ formal methods of information communication to senior managers in order that decisions made are based on the most accurate information available. Such information can be about the organisation's internal or external environment and changes in strengths and weaknesses. Information is also used to **inform**. This is the use of information to communicate news and developments that may be relevant to the intended recipients.

❑ A key function of information is to **educate** and **entertain**. This book is an example of educational information and television and radio use information mainly to entertain but also to educate. Both of these form an important part in the normal functioning of society.

Activity 2   *What ill effects might an organisation suffer if it has an insufficient flow of information?*

16.4.3 Information technology in business

The communication of meaningful information is vital in all sectors of business. All organisations rely on correct information handling and failures in this area can have catastrophic effects. There are two key areas of IT which are particularly relevant to business:

❑ computers;

❑ telecommunications.

Both of these areas arose as a result of the development of the semiconductor but as the technology of this has developed into the silicon micro-chip, enormous strides forward have been made. Such has been the change in this technology and in society as a result, that the term 'communications revolution' has been coined. It is said that the world has 'become smaller' as information can now be passed around the world almost instantaneously. Whereas at one time the fastest method of communication was the galloping horse, the combined effects of computers and telecommunications means that information can now be communicated literally 'around the world' in less than a second.

16.5 Computers

Nowhere is the inexorable innovation in technology better exemplified than in the area of computers. They form an essential part of almost every business and are now increasingly finding uses in homes and other areas of life.

The early innovators in the computing sphere included Herman Hollerith in the United States (1890's) and the English inventor, Charles Babbage. Their designs were mechanical devices for the purpose of managing large volumes of data. Throughout the ensuing years, the rate of innovation has been extraordinarily fast. Alongside massive reductions in the physical size of computer systems have come developments in data storage and the enormous speeding up of computer operations. This is in addition to the improvements in the programmes used to control the computers.

Computing has its own 'jargon'. The most important terms in computing jargon are *hardware* and *software*.

❑ **Hardware** refers to the physical computer itself. It includes the circuitry, the data storage facilities, output devices, memory and processor.

❑ **Software** is the name given to the programmes used to run the hardware. Software is 'written' by computer programmers to make the hardware perform the tasks required by the users of the computer. It includes operating systems, applications, tools and compilers.

Both hardware and software are necessary in order to make a computer work.

The central part of a computer is referred to as the *processor* (sometimes also called the *central processing unit (CPU)* or, in some computer systems, *microprocessor*). Processors are used in a wide variety of applications in addition to desk-top or mainframe computers. Examples of their wider usage include control systems in aircraft and cars, and in a whole host of domestic appliances from microwave ovens to burglar alarms. When a processor is included in such a device, it is referred to as a *dedicated* processor; so called because it is dedicated to perform one function only and cannot be reprogrammed for other purposes. We shall see later that some manufacturing technologies utilise this type of processor.

The most common usage for processors is in a computer *system*. A system comprises a number of components as figure 16.2 shows. The size and complexity of the various components will depend on the type of computer system. The CPU receives data from the input devices which it then works on according to the programme that has been fed in. The data that the CPU uses frequently in any given programme is stored in the *Random Access Memory* (RAM), which has a much faster access time than going back to the disk drive to retrieve data. The CPU cannot write to the *Read Only Memory* (ROM). This is part of the computer, installed when it was manufactured which forms part of the control system of the machine as a whole. The computer show the results of its workings through an output device. This is usually a VDU (visual display unit) monitor, but printers are used for 'dumping' out documents such as letters. In addition to these, information can also be output to other computers and storage devices.

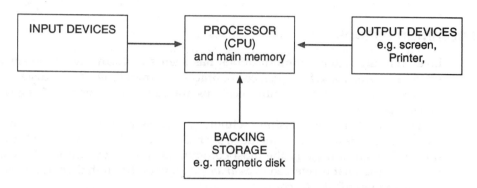

Figure 16.2: A computer system

The **mainframe system** has a very large and powerful CPU, a large RAM and many input and output devices. It can support many users at any one time, sometimes many hundreds. Such systems are used by large organisations that need to process a lot of information rapidly. The users are located at terminals which are each connected to the CPU. Terminals can be located all over a building or even in other parts of the world (connection in this case would be via a telecommunications link-up). The complexity of mainframe systems demands that they be kept in special air conditioned rooms and a team of specialist staff are responsible for the various parts of their functioning. Data and programmes are stored centrally rather than at the terminal and users 'log on' to use the mainframe and 'log off' when finished.

Mini computers are rather deceptively named. Whilst they are mini compared to a mainframe, they can still be very large and powerful in their own right. The principles by which they work are similar to the mainframe in that there is a central CPU, but they have fewer terminals. Mini computers are used by organisations that have fewer data handling requirements than mainframe users but more than those that utilise microcomputers.

The **micro computer** is the main growth sector in the computer world. They are 'stand alone' machines that employ a microprocessor as a CPU and are only capable of being used by one user at a time. The power afforded to microcomputer users and their relative ease of use, have made them increasingly popular such that they are beginning to take over many of the functions previously performed by much larger machines. Each microcomputer has its own CPU, data storage device (usually a hard disk drive and a floppy disk drive), output devices (e.g. printer) and VDU (visual display unit or 'monitor'). The autonomy that the microcomputer user enjoys, and the many recent developments that have aided their use have meant that their attraction has increased.

Networks are a common way of linking (usually) microcomputers in an organisation. Networking means that users can retain their autonomy but still have some of the advantages of a mainframe. Resources and information can be pooled by the users of the network. More correctly called *local area networks* (LAN's), they work by providing a number of services to network users on micro-computers from a central point. Software is stored in such a central point and is sent to users when they request it. The use of *file servers* in this way reduces the amount of software that the individual user needs to store and it also means that any updates can be loaded at the file server rather than having to go round to each machine to load it separately. Some networks also support electronic mail (EMail) facilities. This enables microcomputer users to send messages to each other without the need to consume large quantities of paper.

Business uses computers for a wide range of purposes. All of them concern managing information. We shall look at a range of common IT applications later in this chapter.

16.6 Telecommunications

Like computers, telecommunications has seen significant development over recent years. The word itself implies communications travelling over a distance. There are two media by which telecommunications are transmitted; signals using *physical cables* or *wires* and *radio waves*.

The **physical transmission** technology centres around the traditional telephone sector but increasingly also includes such things as cable television. Historically, electrical cables (traditionally the most common means of transmission) are carried over land and use what is referred to as *analogue* signals although there has been an increasing move towards *digital* communications.

Definitions – analogue and digital

Traditionally, information has been recorded and transmitted in an analogue form but this has increasingly been superseded by digital technology.

Analogue technology uses physical objects or quantities to measure or represent other quantities. For example, the hand of a traditional watch indicates the time by its position on the dial – it is a physical quantity (the amount the hand has moved) which represents the quantity of time which has passed. Another example of analogue technology is the vinyl record which uses a groove to represent sound. The shape of the groove is proportional to the sound which it represents, so the needle moves further if the sound is louder. In essence the representation is an analogy – hence the word analogue.

Digital technology uses numbers to measure or represent quantities. A digital watch indicates the amount of time passed using numbers only. In all modern digital systems, the numbers are transmitted and stored in base 2, or 'binary'. This has only two possible digits – 1 and 0, and this enables the information to be easily processed and stored by computers. In a digital compact disc, for example, the sound is stored in binary. Some parts of the disk reflect light whilst others do not and this is used to represent a 1 and a 0. The sound may be reconstituted by other circuitry in the compact disc player from the information supplied by the numbers.

Digital systems are less prone to distortion and noise than analogue systems and, due to their compatibility with computers, are rapidly gaining ground over analogue systems.

Radio waves technology (electromagnetic technology) has been the major area of innovation in recent years. Since the early satellites permitted signals to be transmitted over long distances, the underlying technology has been further developed and applied to more areas of life. The key applications that rely on this type of technology include:

❑ radio and television;

❑ teletext;

❑ satellite broadcasting;

❑ some international telephone linkages;

❏ mobile telephones;

❏ bleepers and other non verbal signalling devices.

In addition to the above two communications technologies, two others are worthy of mention. These are newer than the above, but recent growth in their use has shown that they offer many advantages.

❏ **Fibre-optics** are special cables along which digital information can be passed in the form of digital laser light bursts in place of the analogue systems of copper wires. Not only do these cables permit many times the number of calls to be transmitted than was possible along a single copper wire, but fibre-optic communications literally move at the speed of light (186 000 miles per second). British Telecommunications' lines are already employing this technology and it has also enjoyed increased usage in Europe as a whole.

❏ **Infra-red systems** are low in power but allow the use of remote control units. This is the basis of the much used remote control television hand sets and new applications are being found for this technology.

16.7 The Applications of Information Technology

Business has hundreds of uses for the various forms of IT. Many applications combine both computers and remote communications. Inter-office communications of this nature are expected to increase further.

We can consider the uses of IT in business to fall into three main areas, although it should be understood that such divisions are rather artificial. Most applications will cross into other areas and impact upon them accordingly.

16.7.1 IT and business administration

The first area is in **business administration** and in the context of the office. The traditional office filled with administrative clerks each with several filing cabinets has been replaced with much fewer staff with computers. The most common office computer is the micro, and the most usual office applications are as follows:

❏ **Word processing** (WP). WP's have replaced the conventional typewriter as the essential office 'writing' instrument (although word processors are more than a *replacement* as such – they do far more than a typewriter). A word processor is a computer programme designed to act as a page upon which text is entered on a keyboard. Whereas on a typewriter errors had to be corrected using erasers or correction fluid, the WP allows for simple correction on the screen. Once a document has been written, it can be printed out like a typewritten page or it can be stored in electronic form as a data-file. Such files can then be retrieved, changed, added to or sent electronically to another user. The versatility that WP's afford and their increasing 'user-friendliness' have caused them to become a standard software item on almost every office micro-computer. The text of this book was written on a word processing package using a micro-computer.

❏ **Spreadsheets**. These are software applications that enable very large amounts of numerical information to be worked on. The traditional role of the spreadsheet is as a 'number-crunching' tool and as such is commonly used by staff who work with figures like scientists, engineers, statisticians and accountants. They are ideal for performing 'what if?' calculations and for constructing scenarios and future projections. The screen on a spreadsheet is divided up into many small 'cells' into which a number or formula can be entered. Cells can then be linked, added to each other, multiplied up or whatever. The software itself is usually loaded with several complicated mathematical abilities so that, say, statistical analyses can be performed on data entered onto it. Spreadsheets, along with the calculator have replaced the pencil and paper as the most significant numerical computation tool.

❑ **Databases**. As the name suggests, a database is a programme used for handling large volumes of data, and was initially designed to replace the 'form' which was commonly 'filled in' in some parts of office work. The 'forms' may contain anything from customers names and addresses to employee information, suppliers and materials bought etc.(databases have been called *electronic filing cabinets*). The usefulness of a database arises from its ability to sort these forms and to accept enquiries. For example, it would enable a user to find out all employees over 45 years old, the customers who bought more than a certain amount etc. Before an enquiry can be carried out the data in question must first be entered on the individual forms (such as employees age).

   In some organisations, the database represents one of their major strategic assets. It might contain all of the company's information on its customers, its suppliers or its competitors and the same database can be consulted for different information by different managers. For example, the marketing manager might enquire who has bought a certain product in the last month whereas the accountant may wish to know who has spent more than £10 000 in the current financial year. A database application has its own 'query language' which enables a wide range of enquiries to be made of the data stored in the system.

❑ **Accounting applications**. Before the introduction of software applications for accountancy purposes, all of the figures for the plethora of accounting functions were laboriously done by hand. Computerisation has reduced the amount of work in accounts significantly. Figures are 'plugged in' to the programme and the various computations are performed automatically. Proprietary software packages also have the ability to generate special management information for specific purposes.

16.7.2 IT and telecommunications

The second area of significance to business is, as we saw earlier, **telecommunications**. Whilst the telephone itself has contributed in huge measure to the expansion and globalisation of business, of increasing significance is the combination of computers and telecommunications. The distinctive feature of such communications is that it is generally in digital form.

❑ **Telephones** and **telephone exchanges** are gradually being changed over to digital in order to enjoy its benefits. It is predicted that eventually, opto-electronic infrastructure will completely replace copper wires. As well as gaining speed and cost reduction such a changeover will also mean that digital communications (say between computers) generally will be much easier.

❑ A second example of telecommunications is the **facsimile** or **fax**. The fax has the ability to read a page of writing, a drawing or similar, break it down to its composite digital data and sending it to another fax – anywhere in the world. The receiving fax decodes the digital signal and reprints the page. The growth of the fax largely replaced the telex which could send and receive written information only. As well as greatly speeding up the conveying of literature between businesses, the fax has, to a small extent, also replaced the conventional postal system.

❑ **Mobile telephones** use a combination of radio signals, electrical wires and fibre-optics. Common users of mobile phones are business people who are out of 'the office' for much of their time. They can be placed into cars or carried in the hand. The signal from a mobile phone, in the first instance, is transmitted to a land based receiving pylon. From here, the signal is carried to its recipient. If the recipient is another mobile phone, the signal is carried to another land based pylon where it is transmitted to the appropriate telephone. This technology has meant that individuals can spend more of their time either *contactable* or with the *ability to contact* when necessary.

❑ A fourth key technology in the area of telecommunications is the variety of **on-line information sources**. Such technology is the accessing of information at one point where the source of the information is at another site via a telecommunications link. The receiving unit for on-line sources can be a television (such as teletext) or a computer (in the case of the many databases that can be sourced). Common on-line applications include constantly updated share prices and a variety of academic literature databases. The high storage capacity of CD ROM's (see definition later) have meant that some formerly on-line data can now be accessed locally. One key opportunity for on-line sources is the accessing of data which changes frequently (such as share prices).

Definition: CD ROM (Compact Disc Read Only memory)

The Compact Disc, as well as causing a stir in the audio hi-fi sector has found an important use in storing computer information. Whereas a typical floppy disk can store up to 1.44 megabytes of data, a CD-ROM can store up to 700 megabytes. Because it is a ROM (Read Only Memory), users cannot store their own data on CD, only read what has previously been stored. It has found uses due to its high capacity – the Encyclopaedia Britannica, usually bound into several volumes, can easily fit onto one CD.

❑ The ongoing process of digitisation of telecommunications has resulted in virtually all developed countries telephone networks being internally digitised (very much the case in the UK). The **Integrated Services Digital Network (ISDN)** – an international telecommunications standard – is increasingly being used to exploit this technological development. ISDN facilitates a number of public switched voice and data services, allowing the simultaneous transmission of media such as sound, data, video, and graphics. The technology provides a 'seamless end-to-end' high-volume digital transmission medium, with the capacity to connect to any digital communications device (such as a computer). The ISDN is currently under the process of upgrade to 'broadband ISDN', a development that will see the introduction of very high-speed, high-capacity transmission. Although this change is several years away it has quite profound implications for the practical transmission of the on-line multimedia services that are beginning to emerge in both the business and leisure areas (such as video signals sent through a domestic telephone line).

❑ **The InterNet**, a special example of an on-line information source, was once a cloistered secret confined to academics, government scientists, and researchers. Increased computer ownership has meant that the InterNet has finally entered into the public domain. Essentially the InterNet is a world-wide network that links computer networks and mainframes in research establishments, universities, and increasingly, businesses. Through the InterNet it is possible to access over two million separate databases, and to transfer their contents to your personal computer. Access is simple, all that is required is a personal computer or access to a linked mainframe, a modem (a device for enabling a computer to 'speak' to a telephone line), and a simple piece of communications software. The main drawback of the InterNet is that as it is not a regulated profit making on-line service, it can be hard for novice users to find their way around the system. There are, however, an increasing number of guides to the InterNet appearing which should make life a lot easier for the user who wishes to navigate their way through the virtual world of the so called 'cyberspace'.

16.7.3 IT and operations

The third area where businesses use IT is in the factory or in the **automation of operations**. We are not here describing the relatively simple automation that performs repetitive tasks, but the use of flexible production aids that use a micro-processor.

☐ Like the 'electronic office', factories are increasingly using **software on computer systems** to increase efficiency and speed things up. Common applications include stock control and ordering software, product costing systems, work measurement and other calculation functions. Work can also be scheduled on computer to optimise the resources of the operations department. In most companies, these types of applications will be capable of being run on a micro-computer.

☐ A second application of IT in factories is the incorporation of **micro-processors in machinery**. The computer numerically controlled (CNC) machine tool has been established for some time where the machine, for example a lathe, can be programmed to produce parts consistently the same and to very tight tolerances. 'Robots' are gaining increasing attention as their designs become more sophisticated. There are several other technologies that fall within the computer-aided manufacturing (CAM) area.

Technology in the Factory – Nissan Motor Manufacturing (UK) Limited.

Nissan's investment in the UK is centred around its £900 million fully integrated car and component manufacturing plants in Sunderland, Tyne and Wear. The 'greenfield' development offered Nissan the opportunity to build a plant incorporating many modern technological developments in automotive manufacture. This, coupled with the introduction of a unique company philosophy combining the best of British, Continental and Japanese working practices has meant that Nissan's Sunderland plant can produce cars more efficiently than most other European car manufacturers. Indeed, the plant is widely recognised as Europe's most productive and efficient car manufacturer – building cars with an enviable reputation for quality.

On 10 August, 1992, Nissan in Sunderland produced its first example of the new Micra supermini. The launch of its second model, built alongside the larger Nissan Primera involved the company investing an extra £500 million. 1,600 new employees were taken on as a direct result of the introduction of the new Micra.

Supply logistics at Sunderland are highly advanced. The just-in-time low stock system of component delivery has been superseded in some areas by en even more rapid 'synchronous supply' arrangement with 7 key local manufacturers of high-cost and bulky items such as seats. Here, the suppliers are connected to Nissan's own Central Control Room. They do not receive an order to make a component until the car for which it is intended has begun its journey in one of the two Final Assembly plants. Small batches of parts are delivered directly to the production lines four times per hour by the component maker.

The introduction of the Micra was an opportunity for Nissan to introduce a more complex production environment. The joint objectives of high quality and cost reduction were coupled with a desire to make the product as 'environmentally friendly' as possible. Environmentally friendly water-based painting techniques, which are in advance of future requirements governing solvent emissions, have been introduced. A family of more than 200 robots provides an automation level in excess of 80%. Six high-speed tri-axis transfer presses – one 5 000 tonne, two 3 200 tonne and three 2 700 tonne machines – mean the Sunderland plant has the highest concentration of these advanced presses in Europe. Both the Micra and Primera use five layer, blow moulded plastic fuel tanks made from a sandwich material of polyethylene and nylon. Engineers at Sunderland have developed new recycling technology enabling excess material to be recovered, processed and fed back into the system. Fuel tank production uses around 30% recycled and 70% virgin material.

Metal castings for engine production are also made at Sunderland. The machine plant has high volume automated lines for making inlet manifolds, cylinder heads and camshafts. Quality is assured by the use of a computer controlled technique called Statistical Process Control which constantly monitors the accuracy of the processes.

(Source: Nissan – with kind permission)

Technology in retailing – The technological supermarket

Most of us will have noticed the changes at the supermarket checkouts as manual price entry has been replaced with bar-coded information. This is only one of the innovations that are gradually being introduced in your local supermarket.

Video Trolleys have a screen on the handle which receives electronic messages as you push it round the shop. When you reach any given aisle, it shows you messages sent from a transmitter in that aisle about discounts, promotions etc. on products in that part of the shop.

Aromatics are distinctive aromas circulated throughout the shop to whet customers appetites and encourage certain sales. Such aromas may include fresh coffee, chocolate, pizza, savoury cooked meats etc. The aromas are produced synthetically and circulated via pipework installations.

Talkback is an innovation whereby a voice appears when you pick up a leaflet or promotional brochure from a pile of leaflets. An infra red beam 'sees' your hand reaching for the leaflet and triggers the box to speak to you. The voice will reinforce the sales message and inform you of the benefits of the product being promoted.

Checkout Savers are money off vouchers automatically generated when the bar code reader records that you have bought a certain product. These are paid for by the shops suppliers rather than the store itself. For example, if you buy a six pack of one brand of cola, a money off voucher for a six pack of another may appear, encouraging you to switch brands next time. This is highly targeted promotion – more cost effective than 'blanket' promotion.

Pedestrian Monitors record the numbers of people who enter the shop. An infra red beam is aimed across the entrance and every time the beam is broken, it means that someone has come into the shop. This can be used to signal more or less checkouts to be open as well as monitoring the success of advertising campaigns.

(Condensed from The Sunday Times, Lloyd and Skipworth, 24 October, 1993)

16.8 Technology in Design

As well as the growth in information technology, there is also the area of technology that is increasingly being employed in the products that businesses sell. One need look no further than the motor car to see how new technological discoveries have improved their design over the years. Engine design has made significant strides in increasing efficiency, reliability and longevity, and the bodywork designers have reduced wind resistance etc.

As new discoveries emerge from the research departments, either in businesses or in universities, development people quickly find ways of using them in product designs. This pathway to new products applies to all types of products; those that use electronics, chemicals, engineering materials to name but three. The whole area of IT itself arises from the technology that is incorporated in the electronics that makes them work.

Design Technology at Nissan

Nissan is a multinational motor manufacturer based in Japan. Its product design takes place literally all over the world. Its motor design for European markets is carried out by the *Nissan European Technology Centre* (NETC). In the UK NETC has two design facilities, one at Cranfield just north of London on the Technology Park of the Cranfield Institute of Technology, one of the country's leading centres of academic applied research. The other is adjacent to Nissan's manufacturing site near Sunderland in the North East. Cranfield is a purpose built site and it focuses on body, chassis, electrical, engine and trim design. NETC at Sunderland is concerned with the testing of engines, whole cars and the development of cars already in production.

> *'The brief for our [design] engineers is straightforward yet wide ranging'* says Nissan, *'to create vehicles that are environmentally friendly and suited to the needs of European society; to instil driving pleasure, comfort and a refined sense of design into every vehicle to give our customers products they are proud to own.'*

We need look no further than the way that the appearance of Nissan cars (and other makes for that matter) have changed over the years to see the impact of design technology. Developments have been made to enhance appearance (which is arguably a matter of fashion), increase efficiency, achieve higher fuel economy, reduce toxic emissions, increase reliability and longevity. Engineers use a wide range of technologies in design. Computers are used to simulate airflow over cars, the effect of changes in body shape, engine performance characteristics and these can all be 'modelled' on special computer programmes. In addition, quality is designed into new and existing products by arriving at the most reliable design for a car and then working out how new designs can be successfully turned into a new model of car.

(Source: Nissan – with kind permission)

Review Questions

1. Name some of the key technological developments of the twentieth century. (16.1)

2. Summarise the general benefits of technology to a business. (16.2)

3. Are there any potential drawbacks of technology? What are they? (16.3)

4. Define and distinguish between information and data. (16.4.1)

5. What are the general functions of information? (16.4.2)

6. Define and distinguish between the following:

   Hardware and software (16.5)

   Mainframe, mini and microcomputers (16.5)

7. What is a *local area network* and what features have caused their increased popularity? (16.5)

8. What are the two principal methods of telecommunication? Give examples of the uses of each. (16.6)

9. Distinguish between analogue and digital forms of communication. (16.6)

10. Describe the major areas where technology is employed in business. (16.7.1, 16.7.2, and 16.7.3)

Answers to activities

Activity 1

Today, you may have used technology in one or more of the following. There may be others that you have identified which are not on this list.

- Foods and milk,
- Water purification,
- Heating systems to heat your house and water,
- Plastics from which many things including some of your clothes are made (e.g. acrylics),
- Electronics in your TV, hi-fi, computer, etc.,
- Your telephone,
- Books and magazines you read are printed in automated and computerised printing plants,
- Transport makes use of internal combustion engines (cars, buses etc.) or rocket and turbo technology (aircraft).
- Drugs and medicines you take,
- Cash machines and recording systems in banks,
- Bar-coding at supermarket check-outs,
- Materials in your house (e.g. kitchen top laminates, metals for tools, utensils etc.),
- Soap, shampoo, washing up liquid etc. are examples of detergents (metal stearates, sulphonates etc.),

Activity 2

If an organisation does not have an adequate information flow then:

- instructions do not 'get through';
- feedback on activities does not get communicated to senior managers;
- cross-functional communications do not happen.

This will eventually lead to:

- lack of cohesion;
- lack of co-ordination;
- an individualistic type of culture;
- sub-optimal decision making (managers do not have all necessary information on which to base decisions);
- morale suffers and rumours intensify;

and other similarly undesirable effects.

Assignment

Discuss the ways in which business has used computers and micro-electronic technology and summarise the advantages and disadvantages that have arisen from their employment.

Further Reading

Lucey T, *Management Information Systems*, DP Publications (Sixth Edition)

Evans C, *The Mighty Micro*, Gollancz Publishers (1979)

Strassmann P A, *The Information Payoff*, Free Press (1985)

Laudon K.C. & Laudon J.P., *Management Information Systems – a contemporary perspective*, Macmillan (Second Edition, 1991)

Laudon K.C. & Laudon J.P., *Business Information Systems – a problem solving approach*, Dryden Press (Second Edition, 1993)

Tapscott A, *Paradigm Shift – The new promise of Information Technology*, McGraw Hill (1992)

17 The international environment

Objectives   After studying this chapter, students should be able to:

- ❏ explain the factors that have created the conditions to encourage businesses to expand internationally;
- ❏ describe the competitive pressures that force businesses to internationalise;
- ❏ describe the entry strategies open to a business and the essential features of each;
- ❏ describe the structure of the European Union;
- ❏ explain what influences the EU exerts to help businesses to trade in Europe.

17.1 The Globalisation of Business

There have been two important features of business since the end of the Second World War. Firstly, there has been a growth in the size of businesses, and secondly there has a been a marked geographical expansion of business. The traditional one-site company is now the domain of the small and medium sized business. Larger companies are almost invariably located at more than one site, and in many cases this extends to locations in more than one country.

17.1.1 Factors that have contributed to the globalisation of business

There are a number of factors that have contributed to the overseas expansion of business.

- ❏ The **communications revolution**, as we saw in the last chapter, has enormously speeded up the transfer of information and this has been developed into the many international communications links.

- ❏ The increasing use of airlines and the improvements in **transport infrastructure** have also hastened the circulation of goods, services and personnel. Whereas at one time driving from Glasgow to London would have taken almost a full day, with the necessity of going through the numerous towns, the construction of the M74, the M6 and the M1 now means the journey can be made by car in around six hours. In Europe, the Euroroutes, Autobahns and the high speed toll roads have similarly reduced journey times. The construction of the Channel Tunnel, designed to take special trains only, also has beneficial effects in this regard. Frequent internal and external flights are available from hundreds of airports throughout the developed world, and in many countries there are high-speed rail links.

- ❏ The **relative stability of exchange rates** between the major first world currencies has reduced the uncertainty of trading with overseas markets. There have been several attempts at managing exchange rates since the end of the Second World War, and their successes have been variable. The most recent attempt at providing a framework for maintaining parities, the European ERM (Exchange Rate Mechanism), appeared to work for a period, but later developments caused several countries to withdraw their currencies from it. It should be pointed out though, that variable though the major currencies may be within a few percentage points of each other, they demonstrate nothing like the large variations between currencies in developing counties.

☐ The development of several **political institutions** has also intensified the trend towards internationalisation. A number of international bodies have been set up which have made international trade much more straightforward. The most obvious example for the UK is the European Union (EU), but in North America, the North American Free Trade Agreement (NAFTA) has afforded similar expansion opportunities. The United Nations (UN), based in New York has increased the trust between member countries and it should not be forgotten that Britain still enjoys good relations with most former members of the British Commonwealth.

☐ **Competitive pressures** which have become increasingly intense over the past few decades have contributed significantly to international expansion. The fact is that if an organisations competitors grow by international acquisition, then the organisation must make similar manoeuvres if it is to avoid falling behind.

17.1.2 Sources of pressure to internationalise

In addition to those factors mentioned above, there are three highly important strategic pressures behind the globalisation of business:

☐ **Market push pressures**

Market push factors are those features of the domestic market which represent a limitation to the business. They *force* a business to expand into other markets because it cannot meet its expectations by serving just its home market. Examples of such factors are:
- ☐ declining market;
- ☐ low profitability;
- ☐ market oversupply;
- ☐ restrictive legislation;
- ☐ poorly skilled/motivated labour market;
- ☐ excessively high labour costs;
- ☐ high corporate taxation;
- ☐ governmental instability;
- ☐ other destabilising influences, e.g. civil war.

☐ **Market pull pressures**

These factors, predictably, are the opposite of push factors. They are features of foreign markets that *attract* businesses into them. Examples include:
- ☐ stable or growing market;
- ☐ high profitability;
- ☐ market undersupply;
- ☐ permissive or loose legislative frameworks;
- ☐ highly skilled and motivated workforce;
- ☐ cheap labour costs;

❑ low corporate taxation;

❑ stable democratic government;

Market push and pull

A simple way to remember the meanings of these two terms is to consider the following.

Push implies *repelling* something from yourself. Hence, Push pressures are *repulsive* in their nature. They repel businesses from their domestic markets.

Pull implies *attraction*. Something which pulls you also attracts you to itself. Hence, pull pressures are *attractive* forces.

Push = Repulsive; Pull = Attractive.

❑ **Portfolio management**

In a business context the word 'portfolio' is used to describe the range of products, services or regions that an organisation is involved in. Investors in the stock market speak of their portfolio of stocks to describe the range of companies or sectors in which they hold shares. Similarly, individual companies often have a portfolio of interests which may include the ownership of several different subsidiary companies.

The reason for holding a portfolio of business interests is to avoid having 'all your eggs in one basket'. If, for example, a company is selling just one product, then when something threatens demand for that product the business is immediately vulnerable. The same argument can be applied to regional concentration of business activities. By spreading activities across several market sectors and more than one country the company reduces its vulnerability. The other interests in buoyant markets will ensure that the company as a whole remains viable. Portfolio management enables an organisation to spread its opportunity and risk.

International markets can vary in profitability and growth rates. By pursuing activity in several countries, the business is best poised to cope with a downturn in one. It also means that it will be able to quickly capitalise on countries that may generate a particularly high demand for the company's products.

17.2 Choices in Internationalisation (Entry Strategies)

When a business becomes convinced of its need to explore foreign markets, it has a number of options open to it. The outcome of its choices will depend on such factors as:

❑ the company's reasons for seeking international markets;

❑ the resources available, particularly financial;

❑ any longer term strategic objectives towards which internationalisation may form part of the means;

❑ the types of products and markets the company is engaged in.

In should be pointed out that many companies have 'internationalised' without becoming a 'multinational' company. Many of the choices do not involve the company actually investing in a foreign country (this would make it a multinational company). The common internationalisation strategies are:

❑ exporting;

❑ international franchising;

❑ international licensing;

❏ international (strategic) alliances;

❏ foreign direct investment;

all of which are discussed in detail below.

17.3 Exporting

Most companies begin by exporting, mainly because it is usually the cheapest and most straightforward entry strategy. Put simply, exporting from Britain means sending British goods to foreign buyers and receiving payment, in pounds sterling, from those customers.

The competitiveness of exports relies heavily upon the value of sterling against other currencies. A weak pound, whilst having many drawbacks in other areas of the economy, greatly benefits exporters as it makes British goods comparatively cheap against other countries' products. The devaluation of the pound from 2.95 Deutsche marks to 2.45 in September 1992 made UK goods cheaper by 17% in one day to buyers in Germany. Increases in the value of the pound cause the opposite effect.

Whilst historically, Britain's major export markets have been the former commonwealth countries, the increased cohesion of the European Union has meant that around half of total exports now go to EU countries (1987, 49%). Because of, among other things, the favourable effect that exporting has on visible balance of trade, the government tries to encourage it. The **Export Credit Guarantee Department** (ECGD) is a government backed organisation that offers services for some exporting organisations. Exporting necessarily carries with it an element of *risk* and the ECGD attempts to minimise this by offering *insurance* and *guarantees* to the exporter. The insurance service covers the creditworthiness of the importer (foreign customer) and political and economic risks associated with the importing country. The guarantee service concerns those exporters who sell on credit. Exporters usually use a bank to bridge the loan until payment arrives. The ECGD guarantee underwrites the loan so that the exporting company can gain the bridging finance at lower rates of interest than would have otherwise been possible.

17.3.1 Export contracts

Exporting usually involves the carriage of goods over long distances and this also adds to the risks. A number of **export contracts** exist which offer suppliers and customers a choice of points at which ownership of the goods changes hands. The responsibility for loss or damage also changes from supplier to customer at this point. The price of the goods will obviously be influenced by the type of contract employed.

❏ **Ex-works**

An ex-works contract involves the supplier having the goods available for collection by the customer or his appointed carrier. The buyer assumes responsibility for the goods as soon as they leave the suppliers premises. The seller must assist the buyer in meeting the collection deadline and in the preparation of necessary documents such as the export licence.

❏ **FOR (free on rail)**

Under a FOR contract, the seller must package the goods and deliver them to the nearest rail goods depot. Responsibility for the goods changes hands when delivery to the rail depot has been successfully undertaken. The customer must make the necessary arrangements to have the shipment moved from there to the required destination.

❏ **FAS (free alongside ship)**

FAS contracts go one stage further than FOR. The sellers responsibility is to deliver the goods to a shipping port and leave it there. Responsibility passes to the buyer at the dock.

❏ **FOB (free on board)**

The seller not only packs and transports the goods to the ship, but he also places the goods on board the ship before responsibility passes to the customer.

❏ **Ex-ship**

Transport by ship not only incurs shipping costs, but also attracts additional insurance premiums. Under an ex-ship contract the seller must pay all costs for the goods until they arrive at the port in the importers country.

❏ **CIF (cost, insurance, freight)**

A CIF contract is formed when the exporter agrees to pay all costs to the destination as specified by the customer. Responsibility for the shipment remains with the seller (and his insurer) until the importer personally takes possession of the goods. If the goods are being imported by a customer in Bahrain, the contract will be defined as CIF Bahrain.

Arrangements for the distribution of exported products can take several forms. UK companies can establish a subsidiary company in the host country or appoint an agent to perform the same function. Others do export 'cold' to foreign buyers, but the risks of doing so usually constrain the business to establish some form of distributor or make some similar special arrangement.

17.3.2 Disadvantages of exporting

Exporting has several potential drawbacks:

❏ the transport of goods over long distances necessarily incurs high carriage costs and this can also increase the risks of damage, breakage or loss of goods in transit;

❏ dealing with companies from certain parts of the world can result in complications in payment for goods – monies owed might be disputed or arrive late. Care is often taken in arranging an agreement with banks in the country in question to organise payment in the event of default;

❏ the imposition of import tariffs and quotas can impede business expansion in foreign countries. If the country of destination imposes or increases an import duty (extra money payable on imported goods) then export prices would become less competitive;

❏ the fact that the business is involved in foreign markets means that it must be prepared for economic and political changes in that country as well as its own. Such changes can be anything from an increase in local interest rates to war.

17.4 International Franchising

Franchising offers businesses the opportunity to gain revenue from foreign markets without making any direct financial investment. A business in another country (the host country) will buy the right to use the brand, logo or product in that country.

Definition   **Franchising**

Franchising is the arrangement whereby the owner of a successful and established brand or business idea (the franchisor) allows another (the franchisee) to use it. In exchange for the right of use, the franchisee gains an increased chance of business success. The franchisor will usually require the payment of an initial 'signing on' fee and then a percentage of annual turnover or profits. Advice on location, marketing or other areas of strategic interest will be provided by the franchisor in order to make the franchise outlet a success, and the franchisee will be bound to abide by the usual business practices of the franchisor.

The franchisor gains the substantial benefit from the arrangement of receiving income from the franchisee for no investment. Because the franchisee is a separate business entity to the franchisor, business failure means the loss of income but will incur no further liabilities.

Summary of benefits for the franchisor
Revenue for little or no work
No financial risk or liability

Summary of benefits for the franchisee
Established brand or business idea
Free or cheap business advice

Brands or businesses that have a proven track record of success in the domestic market will, it is assumed, be attractive to potential franchisees abroad. Several British franchise operations have successfully operated franchises abroad. Examples include:

❑ Burger King (part of Grand Metropolitan Plc. As at 1992, Burger King had over 6000 outlets in almost 40 different countries);

❑ Avis Rent-a-Car;

❑ Body Shop;

❑ Holiday Inn International Hotels;

❑ Tie Rack.

17.5 Licensing Arrangements

In some senses, licensing is like franchising in that it involves a foreign company paying the UK based company for the use of part of its business. The licence in question is usually a 'permit' agreement to manufacture or market (or both) a brand or product in the foreign country. The foreign company will pay the licenser a royalty for the privilege of use in exchange for the sole rights to market the brand in the foreign country.

The licenser gains the advantage of exposure of its brand in foreign markets and the income from royalties for no direct investment. The Licensee has the advantage of the use of an established product or brand, and the probability of increased business success.

Licensing is used in several sectors, for example some of the more well known beers whose brands are owned by foreign companies are made under license in the UK.

17.6 International Alliances/Joint Ventures

Alliances are usually referred to as *strategic* because they are entered into for specific purposes, often as part of a longer term strategy. Their purpose is usually to enable both of the partners in the alliance to further their individual objectives by acting together rather than by competing. Such an arrangement borrows a term from biology – *symbiosis*.

A symbiotic relationship is one which benefits both parties. This is in contrast to parasitism wherein one party acts against the interests of the other.

A successful alliance will also result in synergy. This arises as a result of the co-operation of the two businesses and both will gain more from the relationship than they could have done by acting in competition.

In an international strategic alliance, both companies retain their independence – it is not a merger. Alliances can be entered into either as a short-term or long-term measure. Like all business relationships, they enjoy varying degrees of success. Because it is likely that the two partners will be in the same industry, there may be an underlying sense of mutual suspicion and this can undermine the alliance.

An alliance can help each party gain a foothold in the other's national markets, or there can be a 'borrowing' of each others expertise. One of the most commonly cited international alliances is that of Honda Rover (Honda are Japanese, Rover Group, previously part of the UK British Aerospace Group, are now part of the German BMW Group).

Case Study	Honda Rover – A successful ISA?

The history of the Honda Rover joint venture goes back to 1979. The constraints and conditions of the automotive industry at the time meant that many manufacturers were seeking market penetration in foreign markets by means of partnering up with overseas car companies. Such relationships involved both partners retaining their independence whilst co-operating on design and manufacturing.

The first fruit of the alliance under discussion was the **Triumph Acclaim** – the result of a deal signed between Rover and Honda on December 27, 1979. This included technology and parts from both companies and proved to be successful, selling more than 130 000 units across Europe until it was replaced in 1984 by the **Rover 200**. The Honda version of the Rover 200, the **Honda Ballade**, was made for the European market at the Rover plant in Longbridge. The launch of the executive **Rover 800** and the **Honda Legend** in 1981 marked the next stage in the relationship. Whilst the two cars looked visually different, they shared the same body 'platform' and many other components.

Hondas investment in the UK included a £200 million plant in Swindon, Wiltshire. When the **Rover 200** and the **Honda Accord** were launched, the panels for both cars were produced at Rover's panel pressing plant and both cars comprised common parts produced at other Rover plants in other parts of the UK.

In addition, Honda, a Japanese company, began to distribute some of Rover's British-built vehicles in the Far East. For example, the **Land Rover Discovery** was sold through Honda's dealer network in Japan, 'badged' as a Honda.

In April 1990, the alliance was strengthened by the exchange of a mutual 20% shareholding (i.e. Rover bought 20% of Honda UK's shares and vice versa). This was expected to be the basis of a long-term alliance which would work to the benefit of both companies.

Advantages of the alliance included the following:

☐ Honda gained access to the European market,

☐ Rover gained access to the Far Eastern markets,

☐ Designs improved as expertise was shared,

☐ Economies of scale were gained as the joint companies had greater buying power, used common parts etc.

Similar joint ventures have occurred between other major motor manufacturers in other parts of the world.

Everything seemed to be going favourably for both partners until British Aerospace Plc, the owners of Rover Group, sold their financial stake in the company. The sale of Rover Group Motors to the German BMW Group on 31 January 1994, put a severe strain on what was previously a strong alliance between the two companies to the point that Honda announced the sale of their 20% interest in Rover Group on 21 February 1994. The £800 million sale of the Rover Group was done with the explicit displeasure of Honda. Some commentators at the time of the sale said that Rover had 'turned their backs' on Honda, who had done so much good for Rover during the period of their strategic alliance.

(Source: 'History of Rover Joint Ventures with Honda' – Rover Group Motors – with kind permission, and press reports on 1 February and 22 February 1994)

Activity 2   *Honda-Rover is just one example of a joint venture in the world automative industry. Can you think of any others (either past or present). Find out who they were between and the countries to which the parties belonged.*

17.7 Foreign 'Direct' Investment (FDI)

As the name suggests, investment abroad means that the company commits financial resources to the foreign country in order to gain a presence in its market. This is in contrast to franchising and licensing where no investment as such occurs.

Investment abroad can take one of two forms:

☐ **Acquisition**

This is when the company buys an existing business (or part of one) in a foreign country. Such business activity is common among those companies that are active in international markets. Multinational corporations frequently buy and sell foreign subsidiaries (see the example of the Hanson acquisition of SCM mentioned in Chapter 6).

☐ **'Greenfield' development**

A greenfield development is one in which a company buys land abroad and builds a plant on the land using the existing identity of the company rather than of a subsidiary it may have acquired in the host country. Because such developments are expensive, it is likely that this option will only be used when the 'acquisition' route has been explored and eliminated. Businesses that develop a greenfield site will have the advantage of planning it to meet precisely their requirements with new equipment etc. This can work out more cost-effective than acquisition in the longer term.

17.7.1 Reasons for direct investment

Businesses that directly invest abroad find that the costs of such ventures are very high, and as they are 'moving in' to a foreign country, they expose themselves to several potential risks. If conditions change in the foreign country, the company risks massive losses, both of business sales and of their investment itself. It therefore follows that they must have very good reasons for adopting this strategy.

Firstly, direct investment can result as a natural extension of exporting. Most companies use exporting as their initial entry strategy, but when the volume they export increases, it may become more economical to invest directly. The establishment of a plant in the foreign country will enormously reduce transport costs and it will also mean that import tariffs will no longer be payable.

Secondly, linked to the previous point is the use of direct investment strategies to circumvent import restrictions. If a UK citizen wishes to import a motor vehicle from outside the EU (say Japan), he must pay a percentage of the foreign purchase price as an import tariff to the UK government. Alongside this is the fact that the UK government imposes an import quota on Japanese cars to a maximum of 12% of new car sales in any year. Such factors restrict the expansion of the Japanese car business in the UK. Two manufacturers have circumvented these restrictions by directly investing in the UK. Once established, Toyota and Nissan can legitimately be called EU or UK manufacturers. Because they are circulating cars from within the UK, they are free to sell as many cars as they can in the UK and no export restrictions apply to the rest of the EU.

Thirdly, some large organisations invest abroad simply to broaden their business portfolio. We have encountered this principle earlier in the chapter. Linked to this are a number of specific strategic reasons for such actions, such as gaining access to raw materials, buying competitors to increase market share or buying customers to increase their presence in their chosen end markets.

Greenfield FDI in the UK: Toyota

The Japanese Toyota Motors Corporation is Japans largest motor manufacturer and the third largest in the world (by volume). In 1991, the worldwide production of Toyota vehicles amounted to 4.75 million units with a turnover of over £30 billion. Their operations extend to 29 manufacturing plants in 22 countries and they sell their products in 150 countries through more than 7 000 dealers. The total group workforce exceeds 100 000 people.

The first Toyota vehicles in Europe arrived in the early 1960s when the company began importing cars into Denmark. Since then, their European activity has grown significantly and this has been backed up by inward investment to the EU of almost £1 billion. By 1992, they were selling their cars through more than 3 500 distribution outlets in 22 European countries.

As a result of the growth of sales in Europe, Toyota announced in 1989 its plans to build its first manufacturing plants in the EU. They chose two sites in the UK, one in Deesside, North wales and one in Burnaston, Derbyshire. Their investment in these two plants amounted to £840 million. Building began in 1990 and the first cars left the factories in December 1992. In addition to the two UK plants, the company built a European Parts Centre in Diest, Belgium with an investment of around £26 million.

The Deesside plant is dedicated to the production of engines and the Burnaston plant, to the construction of passenger cars, using the Deesside produced engines.

(Source: Toyota – 1993)

Activity 3   *Suggest reasons why Toyota would invest directly in Europe in the way they have.*

Summary of internationalisation strategies

Strategy	Financial commitment	Financial risk	Potential return
Exporting	medium	medium	medium
Franchising	very low	very low	low to medium
Licensing	very low	very low	low to medium
Alliance	medium to high	medium to high	medium to high
Direct Investment	high	high	high

17.8 The European Business Environment

Europe has assumed increasing significance for UK businesses over recent years. Whereas previously, Britain's major export markets were the former commonwealth countries, over half now go to countries which are members of the European Union. Whilst this can be partly explained by the fact that they are nearby (and therefore high transport costs are avoided), the political events of the last fifty years have been the principal forces behind the trend.

The history of Europe is heavily influenced by the two world wars. It is estimated that the numbers killed on all sides in the two wars (1914-18 and 1939-45) amounted to around 58 million. It was not surprising then that after the Second World War, political leaders made attempts to bring nations together in formal organisations. Two of the most significant of these are the United Nations, based in New York and the European Union, based mainly in Brussels and Strasbourg. After the initial objectives had clearly been met of guarding against a future world war, the members of (particularly) the European Union, turned their attention to the advancement of business interests and a number of social issues.

17.8.1 The European Union

The **Treaty of Rome** in 1957 established the European Economic Community (now referred to as the *European Union*). It arose from the success of the *European Coal and Steel Community (ECSC)* which sought to promote co-operation between Coal and Steel companies in Europe. This programme succeeded in reducing tariffs and quotas in the coal and steel markets between the participating countries.

Following the Treaty of Rome, the EU became a reality on January 1, 1958. The founder members of the EU were France, West Germany, Italy and the Benelux countries (Belgium, Netherlands and Luxembourg). It remained in this form until Britain, Ireland and Denmark joined in 1972. The Union was extended further by the admission of Greece in 1981 and then Spain and Portugal in 1986.

The objectives of the EU have changed over the years. Initially, the aims were to abolish all internal quotas and tariffs and to impose a common external tariff on countries outside the Union. These measures meant that as far as imports and exports went, the Union acted as one country.

17.8.2 Components of the European Union

The parallel of the Union acting as a single nation now extends beyond the preliminary objectives. The components of the EU correspond to the organs of state we encountered in Chapter 12. It has its own executive, legislature, secretariat and judiciary.

❑ The **executive** of the EU is made up of **The Council of Ministers**. This is composed of elected politicians from each of the member countries. Hence, when the Council of Ministers is considering finance matters, it will be made up of all of the Finance Ministers (in the UK, this is the Chancellor of the Exchequer). The Heads of State meet as the Council of Ministers when particularly important items are under consideration. The Presidency of the Council rotates between the twelve members of the Union every six months. Under this system, the head of state of the country which holds the presidency also assumes the title *President of the Council of Ministers of the European Union*. Hence, when the UK held the presidency in the first six months of 1993, Prime Minister Major also held the office of President of the Council of Ministers of the European Union. As in the case of the domestic executive, the Council of Ministers is the highest authority in the EU. It must endorse and authorise EU policy and any applications for membership or significant change.

❑ The **secretariat** or Administration is based in Brussels and is called the **European Commission**. Unlike the Council of Ministers, the employees of the Commission are not elected – they are the European equivalent of civil servants. As well as administering the various arms of the European 'state', the Commission is also responsible for drafting and proposing legislation for the Council of Ministers to vote on and approve, amend or reject. The Commission is controlled by a President and a number of Commissioners. The larger countries send two Commissioners to Brussels and the smaller ones, just one.

Activity 4

1. Which country currently holds the presidency of the EU?

2. What is the name of the current President of the European Commission?

3. What is the name of your local MEP and what party does he/she belong to?

4. In which European capital is the European Bank for Reconstruction and Development (EBRD) located?

❑ The **legislature** is in Strasbourg, France and is called the **European Parliament**. This is composed of over 500 elected *Members of the European Parliament* (MEPs). Like in the UK, MEPs sit in the Parliament according to their political leanings rather than nationality. Because the EU is not a state as such, the Parliament does not assume the same degree of power that a national Parliament does. The number of MEPs from each member country depends upon its size. The UK, Germany, France and Italy each send over 80 MEPs to Strasbourg, whereas Luxembourg sends just 6. Because the Parliament has little authority over the affairs of the EU (it does not control the finance budget or key policy areas), its role has been criticised. Critics say that it is expensive to run and superfluous to requirements as the EU stands in its present form. However, the longer term plans for the EU include closer links between the member countries and this will involve a more prominent role for Strasbourg.

❑ The European **judiciary** is the **European Court of Justice**. It is presided over by 13 judges (at least one from each country) and an overall President, elected from among the judges.

Review Questions

1. Describe the principal developments that have contributed to the internationalisation of business. (17.1.1)

2. Define *market pull* and *market push* factors and give two examples of each. (17.1.2)

3. List the principal methods of internationalisation available to a business. (17.2)

4. Why is it important that both sides of an export contract (exporter and foreign importer) both clearly understand the terms of the contract? (17.3.1)

5. Define and distinguish between a franchising and licensing agreement. (17.4 and 17.5)

6. Describe the advantages of franchising to the franchisee and the franchisor. (17.4)

7. Why might two companies enter into an international strategic alliance? (17.6)

8. Describe two types of direct investment in foreign countries and give an example of each from the motor car industry. (17.7)

9. What are the advantages to be gained by investing directly in a country rather than exporting or employing any of the other entry strategies? (17.7.1)

10. When and why was the EU founded? (17.8 and 17.8.1)

11. What is the name given to the EU institutions fulfilling the following 'state' roles: (17.8.2)

   executive,

   legislature,

   secretariat,

   judiciary?

Answers to Activities

Activity 1

The liability for the lost cargo will depend on the nature of the contract under which the goods were sold to the Gothenburg importer. If, for example, the import contract was a FOB contract, liability would fall to the importer (although it would actually be his insurer that pays for the loss).

Activity 2

There are many examples you could select. Well known recent examples include joint ventures between the French Renault company and the Swedish Volvo, and the US based General Motors and Swedish Saab.

Activity 3

We can speculate that the strategic reasons behind this investment were threefold. *Firstly*, to reduce import costs; transport costs from Japan are high, and because the EU imposes import tariffs on non EU imports, production within the EU eliminates this cost. *Secondly*, cars produced in the EU are not subject to the import quotas. *Thirdly*, there is a large market pull factor when one considers that Europe is the single largest car market in the world – sales of passenger cars reached 13.53 million units in 1991.

Activity 4

For questions 1 to 3, look them up. The presidency of the EU changes every six months. The EBRD is located in London.

Assignment

Niff (Sportswear) Limited

Niff Limited are a manufacturer of sportswear and related products, based in North London. The NIFF brand has gained a large following over the years through powerful marketing efforts, involving advertising and sponsorship of sports personalities. They occupy a niche market among serious sports buyers who are prepared to pay a premium for a better quality of product. Their Marketing Director, Mike Smith is currently considering the various strategies open to him which would allow Niff to exploit the European markets. At a recent Board meeting, whilst reporting on his thoughts so far, he explained that the developments of the early 1990s involving the abolition of quotas and tariffs between EU countries offered a significant opportunity for the company. He said, "The political developments in the EU can work both ways. The single market will almost certainly mean that some of our European competitors will penetrate the UK market threatening our current market share. We will have to protect our markets in the UK and reciprocate by entering their markets. We cannot afford to just stand still".

The Financial Director, Jeff Wren interjected, "This sounds expensive, Mike. I know that we are successful in the UK and have built up a good name in this country, but however you decide to expand abroad, I smell a large investment in the offing – I hate spending money".

"Let me try to put your mind at rest Jeff," replied Mike, "a decision of this nature is a major strategic issue for the company and I can assure you that I will take all pros and cons of each option into account. When I finally come to you to authorise investment, it will be the right choice for the company".

Tasks

1. Identify the market push and market pull factors that encourage Mike Smith to consider internationalisation.

2. Advise Mike Smith of the options open to Niff Limited for his move into the European market. Inform him of the pros and cons of each option, paying special attention of the investment issues raised by Jeff Wren.

3. Recommend an internationalisation strategy to Mike (from your options in Question 1), giving good reasons for your choice.

Complete the above in less than 1500 words.

Further Reading

Palmer A., Worthington I. et al, *The Business and Marketing Environment*, McGraw Hill (First Edition, Chapter 7)
Blake D., *A Short Course in Economics*, McGraw Hill (1993)
Beardshaw J and Palfreman D, *The Organisation in its Environment*, Pitman Press (Fourth Edition, Part 4 – Chapters 20 and 21)
Terpstra V., *International Marketing*, Dryden Press
Perry K., *Business and the European Community*, Butterworth Heinemann (1993)
Lipsey R.G. & Harbury C., *First Principles of Economics*, Wiedenfeld and Nicolson (London, Second Edition, 1992, Chapter 20)

Newspaper article:
Hutton W., "The European train we must not miss", The Guardian, p13, 1 November
1993
(Most university libraries will have a newspaper archive – possibly on CD-ROM)

Section 5

Functions in a Business Organisation

It has been found that the functioning of organisations is optimised when the whole is divided up into smaller units. In most organisations such sub units are referred to as departments, functions or division. The departmentalisation of an organisation will depend largely on its size, but in this section we consider some of the more common functions found in larger organisations.

Contents

18 The accounting function

Objectives   After studying this chapter, students should be able to:

- ❐ understand the role and structure of the accounting function in a business organisation;
- ❐ describe the administrative roles of the accounting function;
- ❐ explain the role and purpose of the Financial Accountant;
- ❐ explain the role and purpose of the Management Accountant;
- ❐ understand the structure and components of the three financial reporting statements;
- ❐ analyse published accounts and use them to evaluate the financial state of a limited company.

Featured Organisations: British Telecommunications Plc and **British Aerospace Plc.**

18.1 Introduction

The accounting department is that part of the organisation which is concerned with the financial resources of the organisation. It addresses how money is allocated and spent, and how much money comes in and from where. Its *raison d'être* is to record all of the financial transactions in an organisation and from this, provide information to enable individual managers to make well-informed decisions. The information is also processed in order that the company may comply with the legal requirements regarding the submission of annual accounts.

18.1.1 Structure of the accounting department

The department is staffed by various personnel, but is usually headed by the Financial Director (FD). As his job title suggests, the FD has a seat on the Board of Directors and therefore is a key decision maker in the company. A typical organisational chart would show the accounting function as in figure 18.1, but it should be borne in mind that other internal structures do exist.

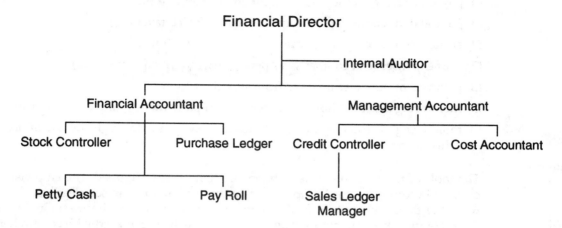

Figure 18.1: Structure of a typical accounting department

18.1.2 People in the accounting department

The senior personnel in the department including the FD are usually all qualified *accountants*. An accountant is a person who has successfully completed a course of study enabling him to gain membership to one of the chartered bodies that set and uphold accounting standards among accounting professionals.

Accountancy qualifying bodies
(Brackets indicate designatory letters of holders)

Institute of Chartered Accountants in England and Wales (ACA)

Institute of Chartered Accountants in Ireland (ACA)

Institute of Chartered Accountants in Scotland (CA)

Chartered Association of Certified Accountants (ACCA)

Chartered Institute of Management Accountants (ACMA)

Chartered Institute of Public Finance and Accountancy (IPFA)

In addition to the professional accounting bodies, the *Association of Accounting Technicians* (AAT) is a body that qualifies people to work closely with accountants and to assist them in managing the accounting function. Accounting technicians form an important part of the administration in many accounting departments.

Owing to the diversity of the jobs that need to be done in the department, there are also likely to be several junior and administrative staff. These will work either with the accountant or accounting technician to assist them in the more clerical areas of their jobs.

18.1.3 The administrative role of the accounting department

Although we shall go on in the next two parts of this chapter to look at two particular areas of the work of the department, it should be borne in mind that the accounting function carries out a range of administrative tasks within the company. These are the jobs that need to be done just to keep things working on a day-to-day basis. In most companies, these will include:

❏ payroll (paying employees the right amount and on time);

❏ payroll deductions (e.g. national insurance, PAYE taxation);

❏ administering company pension scheme contributions;

❏ staff expenses (e.g. company car petrol costs, conference costs etc.);

❏ payment of purchase invoices from suppliers;

❏ monitoring debtors (those who owe the company money) and credit control;

❏ monitoring all receipts and payments as they occur (through the use of accounts called *ledgers*).

The tools of the accounting department are 'books' and 'figures'. The emphasis is on clear and thorough record keeping so that the accountants can see clearly and quickly what the financial position is at any point in time. Much of the traditional work of accountants in keeping books, ledgers etc. has now been replaced with comprehensive computing packages that manage the information and allow reports on the figures to be generated as they are needed. It has been said that accounting is all about *managing financial information* and this is a good simplification of the department's role in the business.

The role of the department within an organisation is primarily concerned with two key areas. Both of these are concerned with managing the flow of financial resources through the organisation. These two functions are *financial accounting* and *management accounting*.

18.2 The Financial Accounting Function

Financial accounting is concerned with a broad range of accounting practices which fall into two main areas:

❏ the on-going provision of cash for the business (called *'financing'*);

❏ the preparation of year end accounts, summarising the financial activities over the course of the past year (called *'financial reporting'*).

We will examine each of these two functions in turn.

18.2.1 Financing

We have already seen that businesses need cash for a number of reasons. Raising it can be a complicated and involved process. The amount of financing needed at any given time will depend upon the needs identified in the *cash-flow forecast* – a projection of the company's income and expenditure over the coming year.

The cash-flow forecast

Planning the finances of a business for the forthcoming year relies upon a number of projections. The Financial Accountant needs to know approximately how much cash will flow into the company each month and how much cash will need to flow out in same period. By subtracting outflows from inflows, he generates a monthly cash surplus or deficit figure.

If the company cannot meet its outflows in the short term it will seek to gain finance from outside the business. It may be that finance is needed for just a few months, in which case it will incur a *short term liability*, or, for longer term shortfalls, a longer term arrangement must be found. The general form of a cash flow forecast is as follows.

	Jan. £000's	Feb. £000's	March £000's	April £000's	May £000's	June £000's	July £000's	Aug £000's
Opening balance	50	(10)	(20)	(10)	(20)	(20)	80	200
Sales	350	370	390	410	350	450	470	400
Costs	(410)	(380)	(380)	(420)	(350)	(350)	(350)	(360)
Cash surplus/ (deficit) on month (This is carried forward)	(10)	(20)	(10)	(20)	(20)	80	200	240

We can see from this forecast that the company has cash short-falls for the first five months of the year. These will need to be funded from somewhere and it is the financial accountant's job to identify the sources of finance and make the necessary arrangements.

A business uses finance for several purposes. These are the items 'hidden' in the *costs* category of the cash-flow forecast, and are listed below.

❑ To invest in plant, machinery and other equipment and buildings,

❑ To fund the normal workings of the business:

to buy stock to turn into products.

to pay the running costs of the business whilst it is waiting for debts to be collected;

to pay bills and invoices;

to pay overheads such as rent, rates and electricity;

to pay expenses such as trips, car costs etc.;

for sundry items (stationary, lightbulbs etc.).

❑ To invest in other companies (by buying shares).

❑ To pay interest on loans.

❑ To pay dividends to shareholders.

The Financial Accountant is concerned with how money is raised and how it is used by the business. Money that the company uses can come from a number of sources:

❑ retained profits – profits kept back from previous years;

❑ borrowings, including long term loans and overdrafts;

❑ share capital (money supplied to the company by shareholders);

❑ government grants and money from similar investment bodies;

❑ debentures (specific loans from individuals for a fixed term);

❑ rights issues (the issuing of new shares to the existing shareholders);

❑ proceeds from the sale of companies that the company owned (divestments);

❑ proceeds from the sale of assets (such as land and buildings);

❑ working capital surpluses (see box);

❑ rent charged on properties or land let out;

❑ interest and dividends received.

Key concept   Working capital

Working capital is the money the company uses to fund the day to day workings of the business. It is different from other forms of capital that might be tied up in machinery, building, or in other fixed assets (fixed assets have a certain degree of permanence and can be physically seen and touched). It is made up of a number of components:

money tied up in stock;

money that the business is owed (debtors);

cash in the bank;

cash in the company ('petty cash');

money the business owes to suppliers (creditors).

The accountant's objective in managing working capital is to minimise it. This has traditionally meant that he tries to pay invoices as late as possible and to get money from debtors as early as possible. Similarly, he tries to buy stocks as late as possible and to turn them into cash again at the earliest opportunity (and of course to reduce overall stockholding). By carefully managing the working capital he can improve the company's cash flow – an important element in good financial management.

The way in which the financial accountant actually funds the business from day to day will depend upon the economic conditions of the moment and, to a certain extent, his particular inclinations. For example, there are good reasons why he may wish to buy new machinery using borrowed money rather use up the company's retained profits (interest rates might be low). Retained profits are monies made in previous years that are kept for future investment in the business.

18.2.2 Financial reporting

At the end of each financial year, every private limited company and Plc must submit their financial statement (annual accounts) to Companies House and to the shareholders.

The annual accounts prepared by the financial accounting function are composed of three separate accounts which, as we saw in Chapter 6, are:

❏ profit and loss account (P&L);

❏ balance sheet;

❏ cash flow statement.

The year end accounts are prepared in accordance with various accounting standards including the *financial reporting standards* (FRS), the *statements of standard accounting practice* (SSAP) and the legislation contained in the Companies Acts. These are observed throughout industry, commerce and government and they detail how each stage of the accounts should be drawn up. The purpose of these standards is to ensure that the accounts of different companies are comparable so that comparisons can be made on a like for like basis. For example, we know that when companies report a certain sales value or assets figure in their accounts, that they are measuring on the same basis and that they mean the same thing. The accounts that appear later in this chapter are the actual accounts of two major British companies. We know that we can place them side by side for the purposes of comparison because both companies will have fully observed the relevant accounting standards in their construction. Hence, we know that **British Telecommunications Plc** are a larger company than **British Aero-**

space Plc because BT sales amounted to over £13 billion in 1992, and BAe sales amounted to just under £10 billion.

The actual task of preparing financial statements is performed by drawing together figures from a number of smaller accounts upon which are entered the details of each transaction the business has made. These are the various ledgers and other 'books'. It is very important that all relevant data is entered into these books and that all entries are accurate. The staff who perform the data-entry functions need to be able to work neatly and with a high degree of accuracy.

18.2.3 The audit

Before it is sent to Companies House, the corporate report must be *audited*. The audit must be carried out by an independent firm of chartered or certified accountants and its purpose is to *check* that the accounts do represent a *'true and fair view'* of the affairs of the company at the given date. The external auditors check the books from which the main accounts are constructed and the other points that are mentioned in the statements, such as stock levels. This is also legally required because there are powerful incentives for companies to report figures that might falsely represent the state of the company.

The contents of the corporate report are very important in understanding business. We will examine each in turn later in this chapter.

18.3 The Management Accounting Function

Management accounting is concerned with providing the management of the business with timely and appropriate information in order to allow them to make intelligent decisions. Because the management accountant is in possession of important financial information about the affairs of the company, the job also carries with it an important supporting role in the decision making of the business. Advice and recommendations will be sought on a regular basis. For example, the Production Director will consult with the Management Accountant before he invests in new plant or machinery for the factory, and the Sales Manager might go to him to take advice on the costing of a new product.

18.3.1 The Management Accountant's job

Included in this area are the following important functions:

☐ planning the finances of the business for the future, usually the coming year. This is called *budgeting*;

☐ setting budgets for the individual departments of the company;

☐ comparing actual performance against budget;

☐ preparing detailed monthly accounts as an important source of information to management (the 'management accounts');

☐ compiling other reports on aspects of company finance as may be required from time to time by individual managers;

☐ calculating product costs to assist pricing decisions.

The preparation of budgets and the use of these as a means of controlling the business is clearly one of the major roles of this part of the accounting function.

A day in the life of a Financial Director – Sue Turton BA(Hons), ACA, MBA.

Sue Turton is 29 years old and is the Financial Director of a medium sized textile company in West Yorkshire. She controls a department including a financial accountant, a management accountant and five clerks. Sue spends a few weeks of the year in the preparation of the year end accounts, but she says that for most of her time she is concerned with management accounting issues.

Her day typically begins at 8 am. On the day the author visited, she spent the first hour completing a report evaluating the purchase options for a new piece of equipment which had been requested by the Chief Executive. When the accounting staff came in at 9 am, Sue was ready to give out the work for the day. At an early meeting with the Credit Controller, she asked specifically about the status of the debt from one customer for whom a large despatch was planned for later in the week.

At 9.30 am, Sue attended a directors' meeting lasting most of the morning. During the meeting, she had the opportunity to highlight and explain to fellow directors, items of concern identified in the last monthly management accounts. Immediately after the meeting, she reviewed and amended a report made by the management accountant which sought to show the causes of fixed cost spending in excess of budget. She continued this analysis over lunch, (with a sandwich from the canteen) using a spreadsheet package on a personal computer to see how these overspends would affect the business if they continued throughout the rest of the year and had to be shown on the annual accounts.

In the afternoon, Sue held a series of meetings with salesmen and sales administrators in order to get them to help construct a forecast of sales for the forthcoming half year. She insisted on the sales personnel coming up with predictions of likely sales by month and by product type. From these discussions, she compiled a spreadsheet to calculate the profits that would arise and other conclusions that could be drawn from the data. Sue drew comparisons of these figures with the sales budget for the year (drawn up three months previously) and calculated the variances that would arise if the salesmen's forecasts turned out to be accurate.

This forecast, and the report that arose from it, was completed by 7.00 p.m. Before clearing her desk for the night, Sue reviewed the day's payments raised by the purchase ledger clerk. She signed a number of purchase cheques but withheld approval on two cheques on the grounds that payment could be delayed until the following week. Finally, she filled in her ongoing *'jobs to do'* sheet, deleting *'half year sales forecast'* and adding two other items arising from the earlier Board meeting. She added *'evaluation of costs and benefits associated with weekend working on the shop floor''* to her list – a job for tomorrow. At 7.30 p.m., Sue finally got into her car and drove home.

Activity 1   *Sue recently took a 'phone call from a distraught shareholder who was complaining about the company's most recent financial results. The shareholder seemed to hold Sue responsible for the poor results as it was she who 'did the accounts'. Is this a fair criticism and what would be your reply to the shareholder?*

18.3.2 Budgeting

The budgetary procedure begins when the accountant plans the business for the year in advance. He will construct a budget for the business from what he knows about last year's figures and how he thinks it will and ought to go next year. An annual budget for the total business will then be set including forecasts for sales, all costs and profits. This is then broken down so that it makes sense to each department. The sales and marketing department will be given sales and profit targets (the *sales budget*) which it will be required to meet or exceed. This in turn is then usually broken down in order to give each sales representative or sales outlet its individual budget. On the costs side, spending departments such as operations, will be told how much they are allowed to spend in the year, and again this will be broken down into sub-departments and also into time units, typically months or quarters (a quarter is three months).

The Management Accountant will constantly monitor *actual* performance against *budget*, and keep a check on the *variances* – the differences, be they above or below budget. Naturally enough, the accountant will be pleased if sales and profits are above budget and if spending is below budget.

Companies differ on how much autonomy is given to each department when they are given their budget and how much say the department has in the setting of its budget. One way that large companies tend to operate is to make each department into a *'cost centre'* or a *'profit centre'* whichever is appropriate. Under this system, the department will be constrained to meet the budget, but the centre (the finance department) will allow a certain degree of autonomy to the department until the year end when individual assessments will be made. The Management Accountant will obviously monitor each department's progress despite the autonomy they enjoy. The theory behind this approach is that it passes the authority and responsibility entirely over to the departmental manager. An important feature in the implementation of this type of system is that the individual in charge of the cost centre is held responsible *only* for those costs over which he has control. It would be unfair to penalise or reward a manager on the basis of somebody else's spending habits.

18.4 The Accounting Reporting Statements

18.4.1 The profit and loss account

The profit and loss account, sometimes called the *income statement*, is a summary of the company's trading performance over the past year. It gives details of the company's total sales and how much money has been spent over the year in order to generate the sales figure. The 'year end' in accounting does not necessarily mean the calendar year end (i.e. December 31st). It can be any date in the year provided that the account covers one year. Some companies find it convenient to work near to the fiscal year and make their year end March 31st, whilst others organise it so that the year end is that time of the year that business is at its slackest. To demonstrate the contents of the profit and loss account, we will consider two major UK companies. **British Telecommunications Plc (BT)** has its year end at 31 March, whereas for **British Aerospace Plc (BAe)** it is 31 December.

The construction of the account is as follows:

	BT	BAe
	31 March 1992	31 December 1992
	£ millions	£ millions
Sales	13 337	9 977
Cost of sales (operating costs)	(9 922)	(10 052)
Profit (loss) before interest and tax (sometimes called *operating profit*)	**3 415**	**(75)**
Other costs and extraordinary Items	(38)	(1 000)
Interest payable	(304)	(126)
Tax payable	(999)	272 (i.e. a rebate)
Profit after interest and tax (Sometimes called *net profit* or *earnings*)	**2 074**	**(929)**

*(**Sources:** 1992 published accounts for British Telecommunications Plc and British Aerospace Plc. The accounts are simplified for the purposes of this example. Reproduced with the permission of British Telecommunications Plc and British Aerospace Plc.)*

The figures in brackets mean that the figure is negative. Hence, the interest payable on loans is *paid out* and is consequently negative.

BT and BAe compete in very different markets. We are all aware that BT have a powerful presence in the telecommunications sector. BAe manufacture a wide range of civilian and military aircraft and similar electronically based products.

We can see from these accounts that the two companies have very different **results**. Whilst both are very large concerns, with sales well into the billions, BT made a *profit* after interest and tax of over £2 billion in 1992 whereas BAe made a *loss* of almost £1 billion.

Let us look briefly at the components of the profit and loss account.

❑ **Sales** is the total value of sales for the year. This includes *only* income from trading activities and *not* other sources of finance that the company might have benefited from (such as those shown on the balance sheet). For BT, this means the total of all telephone bills, fax bills, standing charges and the other areas of its business. For BAe, it will be the total of its worldwide sales of aircraft and related products.

❑ **Cost of sales** is the total cost of producing and distributing the products. It includes the raw materials and the direct labour costs (see accounting concept box on next page), salary costs and the money the companies have paid out to have their products installed or distributed. In some profit and loss accounts, this section is split up to show the separate areas in which the costs have been incurred.

❑ **The profit before interest and tax** (PBIT) is sometimes called *operating profit* and represents the excess of income over expenditure. The company must pay tax to the Inland Revenue from this figure and the interest on any loans it has from its banks (in the same way that interest is charged on overdrafts, mortgages etc.). If the company has deposits with the bank rather than debts, the interest earned will be added in at this stage. In the example above, BAe are in the unhappy condition of making a loss at this stage of £75 million.

❑ **Profit after interest and tax** is the excess income when everything has been paid for. If a loss is made at this stage, the shortfall must be found from somewhere (if the company has not got money saved from previous years, it must be borrowed from the bank). The company has three possible uses for profits:

it can be retained by the business to fund future investment and expansion;

it can go towards off-setting losses incurred in previous or future years; or,

a proportion of the net profit can be paid as *dividends* to shareholders.

Accounting concept Direct and indirect employees

Accountants use a distinction to enable them to identify the sources of employee costs. This is not to be confused with what we have previously identified as line and staff. **Direct employees** are those who work in production and who are responsible for adding value to products as they are being made. The cost of this labour is included in the cost of sales figure in the P & L. **Indirect employees** are those who do not add value and are in supporting, administrative or advisory capacities. For example, the accountant is an indirect employee whereas the factory line operator is a direct employee.

18.4.2 The balance sheet

The balance sheet is different from the P & L in that it does not describe the financial movements of the financial year, but rather it describes the financial state of the business on the day that is the company's year end. It has been called a 'snapshot' of the financial state of the company on that day. The content of the balance sheet does not describe revenue items or illustrate the performance of the company (that is the domain of the P & L account). Rather it is concerned with how the business is funded, i.e. its capital.

Put simply, the balance sheet asks 'how much capital has the company got, where did it all come from, and how has it been used?' In order to do this clearly, it is broken down into a number of separate sections. The format is as follows (using the same examples as previously):

	BT at 31/3/92 £ millions	BAe at 31/12/92 £ millions
Fixed assets		
Tangible assets	15 785	3 257
Investments	660	431
	16 445	3 688
Current assets		
Stock	201	3 448
Debtors	2 615	2 109
Investments	2 046	1 255
Cash at bank and in hand	175	382
Total current assets	5 037	7 194
Less current liabilities		
Loans	(958)	(342)
Other creditors	(4 229)	(4 051)
Total creditors falling due within one year	(5 187)	(4 393)
Net current assets (liabilities)	(150)	2 801
Total assets less current liabilities	**16 295**	**6 489**
Less creditors: amounts falling due after more than one year (Loans and other borrowings)	(3 768)	(3 089)
Provisions for liabilities and other charges	(665)	(1382)
Net total assets	**11 862**	**2 018**
Funded by ...		
Called up share capital	1 540	105
Profit and loss account	9 193	407
Other reserves	1 021	1 268
Shareholders funds	11 754	1 780
Minority interests	108	238
Total capital	**11 862**	**2 018**

(Source: published accounts, British Telecommunications and British Aerospace Plc at above dates – simplified. Reproduced with the permission of British Telecommunications Plc and British Aerospace Plc).

It is called a balance sheet because the two sides must always balance, or equal each other. The *net total assets* side says what the capital has been spent on or invested in and the *funded by (capital)* side describes where the invested capital has come from.

Because the balance sheet takes all sources and uses of company money into account, the two side always balance. This can be expressed as an equation.

total net assets = sources of funds

Let us look at the items in the account.

18.4.3 The assets side of the balance sheet

❑ **Fixed assets** include plant, machinery, buildings, motor vehicles, and land. They have a certain degree of permanence and can be physically seen and touched. A business invests in fixed assets when it wishes to increase its space or capacity. A new warehouse for storage, new equipment for the factory or even a new factory are all examples of fixed assets.

❑ **Current assets** are those things in which the business has capital tied up that enable business to be carried out in the relatively short term. Current assets are divided here into three items. **Stocks** are the physical resources the business uses to generate its products. In the case of BT, we can see that it has a relatively small amount of stock compared to the size of the business. This is because it is not a manufacturing company – stock at BT will be spare telephones, parts for repairs, and stocks to sell in BT shops. BAe, being a manufacturing company, carries much more stock. This will be a huge range of parts including electronic components, sheet metal, finished aeroplanes etc. The company has paid for stock and hence has money in it, money which will be realised again (turned back into cash) when the finished products are sold. **Debtors** are other businesses or individuals that owe money for goods and services which have been supplied. Cash will be realised from debtors when they pay. BT, at any time, has thousands of people who owe the company money for their phone bills. BAe similarly sell a product one month and payment will not fall due for another month or so. **Cash** is money in the bank or in cash form in the business (e.g. 'petty cash').

❑ **Current liabilities** – These are items that are amounts owed by the business that it must consequently pay for. In the same way that debtors (in current assets) is money owed by customers for goods supplied, **creditors** is money the business owes to its suppliers for the stock it uses in its processes. Both debtors and creditors accounts should be settled within an agreed credit period – usually between 30 and 90 days. Because creditors must be paid, the company considers it on the balance sheet as money it has not got. It is due to be paid out, hence it is a liability.

18.4.4 The 'funded by' side of the balance sheet

This side describes how the capital has been raised that the company has in use. It usually comes from share capital (usually used to buy the initial fixed and current assets) and retained profits, money the business has saved from previous successful years. New capital resulting from the issue of new shares (a *rights issue*) is also included in this section.

18.4.5 Cash-flow statement (CFS)

This statement shows how the movements in the balance sheet from the previous year to the present one have been brought about. All the movements in cash and the movements in fixed and current assets and liabilities are shown. It can be said that the cash-flow statement 'ties together' two consecutive year end balance sheets, so a lot can be learned about a business by examining two balance sheets and the CFS together.

In order to allow the reader quickly to see the flow of funds over the year, the statement is broken down into six main areas. In its basic format, it will be as follows:

	£
Cash generated from operating activities	xxx
Returns on investments and servicing of finance	xxx
Taxation paid	xxx
Cash generated from investing activities	xxx
Net cash inflow/outflow before financing	xxx
Payments to the sources of finance	xxx
Net cash flow for the year	**XXX**

For **British Telecommunications Plc**, the cash-flow statement for the year ended 31 March 1992 was as follows.

Cash-flow statement – **British Telecommunications Plc**, 31 March 1992

	£ millions
Operating activities (cash inflow)	5 710
Returns on investment and servicing of finance (outflow)	(1 210)
Taxation (outflow)	(897)
Investing activities (outflow)	(2 938)
Net cash inflow before financing	665
Financing (outflow)	(116)
Net cash flow (increase in cash)	**549**

(Source: British Telecommunications Plc Corporate Report, 31 March 1992, simplified. Reproduced with the permission of British Telecommunications Plc.)

❏ **Operating activities** show cash movements resulting from the trading activities of the business. There is more than one way of showing this, but it will usually be simply the cash injections from profits. It will be hoped that this part of the account will show a net cash inflow, indicating that the organisation is richer rather than poorer after the year as a result of its trading activities. This is important as it focuses on the trading activities of the business. We can see that 1992 was a good year for BT.

❏ **Returns on investments and servicing of finance** show the cash movements as a result of interest paid and received by the business. It will receive interest on investments it has made (such as in the bank) and will similarly pay interest on loans. This category also includes dividends paid to investors from last year's profits. The net difference between inflows and outflows will be shown in the account.

❏ **Taxation** paid on profits, interest received and other sources will be entered here. Any rebates received will be taken off the 'paid' figure before it is entered into the account. One might imagine that Her Majesty's Treasury will be pleased with the £897 million paid into it from BT during the year.

❏ **Investing activities** shows cash movements resulting from asset purchase or disposal. Investments in other companies (by buying shares) will also be included.

❏ **Financing** refers to the long-term provision of cash to the business and represents such items as:

new long-term loans;

loan repayment (not interest paid on loans);

proceeds from the sale of new shares (share issues).

When the statement has been completed, it shows the net change in the cash position over the year. This is the net inflow or outflow as a result of all activities of the company over the year.

18.5 How to Read and Analyse Accounts

The question has often been asked of accounting statements 'that's very good, but what does it all mean?'. In order to make sense of accounts and to extract meaningful information from them, we must learn a few guide-lines. A turnover figure on a P & L account will simply tell us how much the business has sold over one year's trading, but from that alone we can't say, for example, whether the business is a good company in which to invest. Similarly, the net profit figure, in itself, is just a number. In order to make sense of it, we need to know a little more. Hence, accounts must be analysed, and there a number of useful approaches to their analysis.

There are three main tools which business people and accountants use for this purpose: *trends analysis, ratio analysis* and *comparisons*.

18.5.1 Trends analysis

Trends are used to show the movements of important figures in the accounts over time. This way, someone who wants to know about the company can see if it is doing well or badly. Some corporate reports show five year trends, although they do not have to. To construct a trend analysis, we must have access to as many years' accounts of the company as we want to see the trend over. The most common items used in this way are turnover and profits, although stockbrokers will also use it to show their clients trends in share price and dividends.

The figure chosen to be represented as a trend will depend on what we want to find out about the company. As well as the three main financial statements, the corporate report also details a number of other things such as directors' earnings (called *emoluments*) and the number of employees. These may be of interest to some shareholders.

Common methods of expressing the data are as a simple list or a bar chart. Line graphs are also suitable, but it should be remembered that as a trend is an example of continuous data, it must never be shown as a pie chart or similar. Figures 18.2 and 18.3 show a number of trends from the year end results of BT for the years 1988 to 1992.

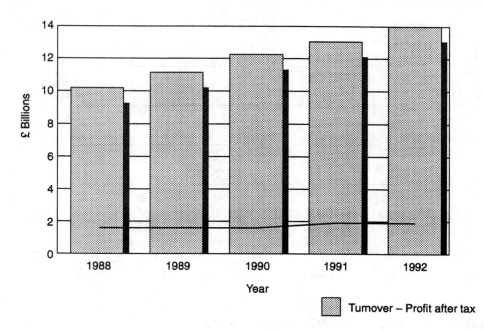

Figure 18.2: British Telecommunications Plc – trends in turnover and profits. (Source: FAME)

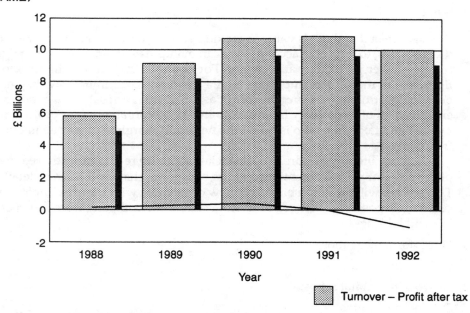

Figure 18.3: British Aerospace Plc – trends in turnover and profits. (Source: FAME)

As well as expressing financial results as trends over time, it is sometimes helpful to show other aspects in the same way. Figure 18.4 shows the changes in numbers employed by BT over the years 1988 to 1992. By plotting the figures as a line graph, we can see at a glance that their numbers rose in the late eighties to a peak in 1990. Since then, numbers have been falling (note, incidentally, how sales and profits have continued to rise despite the decrease in workforce).

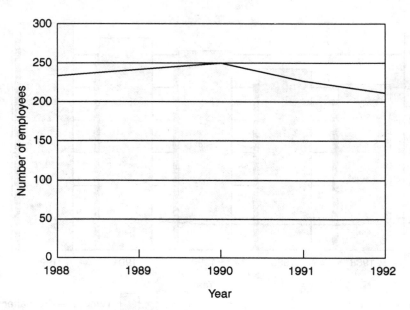

Figure 18.4 – number of employees, British Telecommunications Plc (Source: FAME)

18.5.2 Ratio analysis

We have seen that there is value in looking at how figures vary over time. To add further meaning to figures in accounts, we can manipulate them to see how a figure might compare when divided by another one. For example, the turnover figure and the profit figure are in themselves important, and a trend will determine how they have grown or fallen over time. However, net profit as a percentage of sales is a good gauge of the effectiveness of a company in its aim to increase profitability (net profit is profit after interest and tax). This ratio is called the net profit margin and is used in business very frequently.

There are literally hundreds of financial ratios and readers are advised to access one of the accounting texts mentioned at the end of the chapter if further detail is sought. This section will provide a brief overview of this area with a few examples and, for our current purposes, we can use ratios to examine the company from four perspectives. We will look at:

❒ performance ratios;

❒ liquidity ratios;

❒ working capital ratios;

❒ efficiency ratios.

❒ Performance Ratios

Performance ratios, as the name suggests, test how a company has performed. This is done by taking the profit the company has made in the year and seeing how it compares with either the total sales for the year or the capital employed by the business.

Net profit margin, or *return on sales* is the profit after interest and tax for the year, divided by the sales. As well as giving an indication of the magnitude of a company's costs, it shows how much of the sales figure is left over for re-investment and development. It is expressed as a percentage.

$$\frac{\text{net profit}}{\text{turnover}}$$

Return on capital employed (ROCE) is often seen as the most important ratio in business. It tells how much return a business has made compared with the money used to run the company. It can be compared with the current interest rate to see if the business is making more than could be made by investing the capital in a building society instead (not that this is an option for the company). The financial return on capital is a critical indicator, and a good business will make a good return, certainly above the interest rate.

$$\frac{\text{net profit}}{\text{total assets}} \text{ (i.e. – one side of the balance sheet)}$$

☐ Liquidity Ratios

Liquidity refers to the current cash situation of a business. Liquid cash is cash that is in money or 'near money' form, i.e. that which can be realised (turned into cash) immediately or quickly. It is important when managing cash flow to ensure that the company has sufficient liquid cash to manage a business on a day-to-day basis, without having to borrow to increase working capital or dispose of assets to make good a cash shortfall.

Current ratio. This ratio tells the analyst whether a company is owed more than it owes or vice versa, and this in turn gives an indication of the cash flow position. If it is more than 1, it is a positive cash position, if it is less than 1, it is a negative cash position.

$$\frac{\text{current assets}}{\text{current liabilities}}$$

Remember that current assets are items that are either cash or can easily be turned into cash (e.g. stock and debtors), and that current liabilities are items that the company must use cash for.

Liquidity ratio is sometimes called the 'acid test' or quick ratio, because it is seen as the essential indicator of the company's liquidity position. It is the same as the current ratio except that stock is excluded. This is because stock is regarded as slower to convert to cash than debtors and cash. The significance of this ratio is to find out, if company failed to produce for any reason, if it could it meet its short term cash debts. A result of less than 1 is taken to mean that the answer is no. This would be of interest to parties owed money by the business (such as suppliers).

$$\frac{\text{current assets – stock}}{\text{current liabilities}}$$

☐ Working capital ratios

There are a number of ratios that can be employed to determine how well or badly a company uses its working capital. Let us remind ourselves that the components of working capital are *stocks*, *debtors*, *creditors* and *cash*.

Debtor days ratio tells us how long, on average, a business allows its debtors to settle accounts. Because debtors are a current asset, it is in the company's interest to have low debtor days. This is consequently an indication of the credit control efficiency of the business.

$$\frac{\text{total debtors}}{\text{turnover}} \times 365$$

(Turnover from P & L. debtors from balance sheet.)

Creditor days. In the same way that debtor days measures how good the company is at calling in debts, creditors days says how many days on average the company takes to pay its debts. High creditors days will aid cash flow, especially if the business can also sustain low debtors days.

$$\frac{\text{total creditors}}{\text{turnover}} \times 365$$

(Turnover from P & L, creditors from balance sheet).

Stock turnover expresses how many times, in accounting (money) terms the business has 'turned over' its stock in order to generate the turnover it has. Again, it can only reflect an average and this will conceal many fast moving stock items and some lines which may have lain unused for years. The ratio is important as it is a good indication of the company's ability to turn stocks into sales and its rate of stock usage. It is to the advantage of the business if a high stock turnover can be achieved.

$$\frac{\text{turnover}}{\text{stocks}}$$

This means that if a company has a turnover of £1 million and average stocks of £200 000, then stock turnover is:

$$\frac{1\ 000\ 000}{200\ 000} = 5 \text{ times}$$

❏ Efficiency ratios

It could be argued that some of the ratios already mentioned, such as stock turnover, can be used as indicators of efficiency. There are others, though, that are used primarily for this purpose.

Sales per employee ratio answers the question: How much turnover was each employee responsible for?

$$\frac{\text{turnover}}{\text{number of employees}}$$

The number of employees is not mentioned in the accounting statements themselves, but is usually detailed as an average for the year in the *notes to the accounts* towards the back of a Corporate Report.

Profit per employee, like the previous ratio, gives an indication of how well the business utilises its workforce in money making activities. An efficient business in this regard will have a higher profit per employee than an inefficient one.

$$\frac{\text{net profit}}{\text{number of employees}}$$

Activity 2   **Accounting ratios**

For the British Telecommunications Plc accounts shown earlier in this chapter, calculate the following ratios for the year ended 1992.

☐ Return on sales

☐ Return on capital employed

☐ Stock turn

☐ Debtor days

Calculate the same for British Aerospace and compare the two. What can you surmise from your calculations. (return = profit after interest and tax).

It is often helpful to express ratios as trends. This can show how, say, efficiency or return on capital has changed over time – often more meaningful than simply a trend in turnover. Again looking at the results of BT, figure 18.5 shows the trends in return on capital employed and return on turnover (net margin, which is profit after interest and tax divided by sales) over the same period as we saw before.

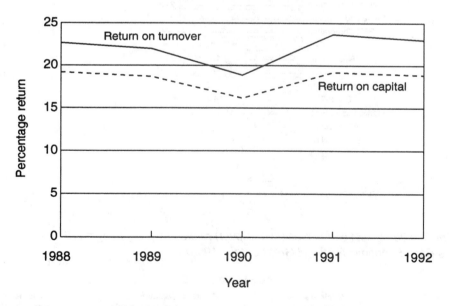

Figure 18.5: British Telecommunications Plc – trends in return on capital and turnover.

The **Chairman's Report** in the annual financial statement will often outline the year on year changes in the key ratios. The Chairman is particularly keen to report upward trends in the performance ratios in order to convince potential shareholders that the company's shares represents a good investment. The same is true for the efficiency and profitability ratios. These are among the most meaningful analytical tools used in scrutinising company performance through published accounts.

18.5.3 Comparisons between companies and sectors

So far we have looked at examining accounts for trends and ratios, but in order to assess if these figures are good or bad, they must be seen in the context of their competitors and the wider economic environment. For example, the company might make 15% net margin, and whilst the management might be happy with it, if competitors are making 20%, it means that the company is a relatively poor performer in its sector. Similarly, in examining growth figures, if the business has grown at 5% a year for the past 5 years, but competitors have shown 7% growth over the same period, then we can conclude that the business is 'losing ground' to the more successful companies.

If we examine the two companies we have been considering in this chapter, we can readily see that BT have had a much more successful run than BAe. The trends in sales for BT have been consistently upwards. For BAe, 1992 saw a distinct downturn in turnover accompanied by a loss on Sales of over 12%, compared to the 1992 BT result of 20% profit. These figures enable us to predict that in the economic climate of 1992, telecommunications represented a more profitable investment than defence and civilian aircraft.

A more detailed analysis of these inter-sector variations can be made by looking at the net profit margins of some of Britain's biggest companies. Figure 18.6 shows the UK's 20 biggest companies, ranked by profit margin.

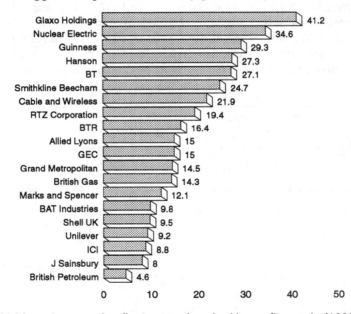

Figure 18.6: Britain's 20 biggest companies (by turnover) ranked by profit margin (1992). (Source: Lloyds Bank Economic Profile of Great Britain, 1993)

Key to figure 18.6

Position	Company	Business Sector
1	Glaxo Holdings	pharmaceuticals
2	Nuclear Electric	power generation
3	Guinness	brewing
4	Hanson	tobacco, mining, industrials
5	British Telecommunications Plc	telecommunications
6	SmithKline Beecham	pharmaceuticals
7	Cable and Wireless	telecommunications
8	RTZ Corporation	mining
9	BTR	construction, energy etc.
10	Allied Lyons	brewers, hotels etc.
11	GEC	electronics, defence equipment etc.
12	Grand Metropolitan	brewing, retailing, hotels etc.
13	British Gas	gas supply
14	Marks and Spencer	general retailers
15	BAT	tobacco, financial services
16	Shell UK	petrochemicals
17	Unilever	food, detergents, consumer products.
18	ICI	chemicals, paints, pharmaceuticals, etc.
19	J Sainsbury	general retailers
20	British Petroleum	petrochemicals

From an analysis of these figures we can see that the UK's biggest businesses have performed very differently. Although British Petroleum is Britain's biggest company by turnover, its profit margin is relatively low compared to the rest of 'the big 20'. From the figures, we might also conclude the following:

❏ telecommunications, pharmaceuticals and brewing tend to return high profit margins.

❏ petrochemicals and general retailing tend to return *relatively* low margins.

By a careful study of some other companies' accounts, we can learn that some sectors are renowned for either their exceptionally high or low profitability *as a sector*. The textiles industry, for example, will usually produce low profits and electronics will often return relatively high profits.

As well as comparing different sectors (e.g. telecommunications and aircraft),this type of analysis can also be used to assess the strong and weak players who compete in the same market. Two of the companies shown in figure 18.6, Glaxo Holdings and SmithKline Beecham, compete in essentially the same market – pharmaceuticals. We can see from the graph that in 1992, Glaxo made a profit margin of 42.1% and that SmithKline Beecham made 24.7%. This shows us the variations that can exist between companies competing in the same sector.

Review Questions

1. Summarise the role of the accounting function in a business organisation. (18.1)
2. What are the major administrative duties of the accounting function? (18.1.3)
3. Describe the elements of the Financial Accountant's job. (18.2)
4. What are the sources of finance open to the Financial Accountant? (18.2.1)
5. What are the components of working capital? (18.2.1)
6. Name the three accounting statements in an annual report. (18.2.2)
7. Distinguish between the work of the Financial and the Management Accountant. (18.2 and 18.3)
8. What is budgeting? (18.3.2)
9. What does the profit and loss account record, and what are its components? (18.4.1)
10. What does the balance sheet record, and what are its components? (18.4.2)
11. What does the cash flow statement record and what are its components? (18.4.6)
12. What are the three major analytical tools for analysing accounts? (18.5.1, 18.5.2 and 18.5.3)

Answers to Activities

Activity 1

The shareholder complaining about poor financial results is complaining to the wrong person. The accountant's job is largely to report what is actually happening and to give financial advice to managers as appropriate. Sue's job does not directly affect the company's financial results, although her advice, if inadequate, may result in overspending or similar financial misjudgements. We learned in this chapter that the accountant is an information manager, not an operational manager. The shareholder would be better talking to the Chief Executive who is responsible for the entire business.

Activity 2

	BT	**BAe**
Return on sales	$\dfrac{2074}{13\,337} = \mathbf{15.55\%}$	$\dfrac{929}{9\,977} = \mathbf{(9.3)\%}$
Return on capital employed	$\dfrac{2074}{11\,862} = \mathbf{17.48\%}$	$\dfrac{929}{2\,018} = \mathbf{(46)\%}$
Stock turnover	$\dfrac{13\,337}{201} = \mathbf{66\ times}$	$\dfrac{929}{2\,109} = \mathbf{4.7\ times}$
Days debtors	$\dfrac{2\,615}{13\,337} \times 365 = \mathbf{71.56\ days}$	$\dfrac{2\,109}{9\,977} \times 365 = \mathbf{77.15\ days}$

Comments

In the year 1992, BT was highly profit-making; BAe made a large trading loss. BT's return on capital was highly attractive to investors whereas BAe's loss on capital shows it had a bad year. BT's high and BAe's low stock turnover principally show the different trading activities of the two companies. BT, being primarily a service organisation, is a low stock user. BAe, as a manufacturing business is obviously a high user of stock, hence the lower turnover. On average, BT's customers took 71.5 days to pay their bills and BAe's industrial customers took slightly longer at 77 days.

Assignment

Obtain the most recent year end financial report from one of the 'top 20' companies mentioned in figure 18.6 above. You could try your university or college library, a computerised facility like FAME or EXTEL, or you could write directly to the company (address your enquiry to the registrar's department).

1. If the report has details of previous years' financial results (such as a table of the last five years), plot the following on appropriately scaled and labelled graphs.

❑ Turnover and profit before interest and tax (on the same graph).

❑ Sales per employees (calculate this by dividing the number of employees in the year into the year's turnover).

❑ Days debtors.

2. For the year over which the accounts report, calculate the net margin, the return on capital employed, the profit per employee and the increase in profits and turnover over last years results. Express the change in turnover and profit as a percentage.

$$[\text{Note: percentage change} = \frac{\text{change in figure/last years figure}}{\text{last years figure}}]$$

Further Reading

Walton P. & Bond M., *Corporate Reports – Their Interpretation and Use in Business*, Hutchinson Management Series

Bendrey M., Hussey R. & West C., *Accounting and Finance for Business Students*, DP Publications

Berry A. & Jarvis R., *Accounting in a Business Context*, Chapman & Hall Publishers

Wood F., *Business Accounting 1*, Pitman Publishing

Dyson J.R., *Accounting for Non-Accounting Students*, Pitman Publishing

Cox D., *Business Accounts*, Osbourne Books

19 The operations function 1 Purchasing and production

Objectives   After studying this chapter, students should be able to:

- ☐ explain what the operations function is;
- ☐ define the scope of the operations function;
- ☐ describe how operations can contribute to the strategic success of an organisation;
- ☐ outline the processes involved in a simple manufacturing process;
- ☐ understand the function of and processes in purchasing;
- ☐ explain the significance of the goods inward department and its functions;
- ☐ define and distinguish between the five general types of production: project, job, batch, line and continuous;
- ☐ explain the important features of each type of production.

Featured organisation: **Thorn Lighting Limited**

19.1 What is the Operation Function?

The term operations function is often thought to be the same as the manufacturing or production function – it can be, but it isn't necessarily. Production is only part of operations. Let us begin with a good working definition of the function.

operations is that function which is directly responsible for achieving the organisation's' objectives.

Examples of operations functions

Organisation	Operations function
Manufacturing company	production/factory
Restaurant	kitchen
Police Force	commissioned officers
National Health Service	wards and operating theatres
Tottenham Hotspur Football Club	Tottenham Hotspur football team
Price Waterhouse management consultants	the consultants themselves

We can see a distinction between operations and all other functions. Accounting, personnel and the other functions exist to *support* the primary purpose of the organisation. If the organisation is a product manufacturing company, then the part of the company which manufactures the products is the operations function. If the business is a service organisation then whichever part actually delivers the service is operations.

It is in the area of manufacturing that the principles of operations are best illustrated and exemplified. In a manufacturing company, operations is concerned with all of the activities associated with the conversion of 'raw' materials or purchased parts into finished goods. Any procedure that manages any stage in this process is part of the operations function.

In summary, the function involves those stages as shown in figure 19.1.

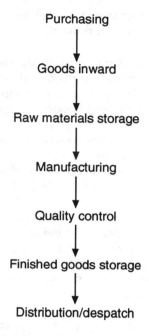

Figure 19.1: The flow of materials in an operations functions.

Operations   **An everyday example**

Suppose that you decide to make a lasagne. Your first step is to go to your kitchen and see if you have all the ingredients. Unless your fridge is particularly well stocked, it is likely that you will need to go and buy in some of the components at the supermarket. This is the **purchasing** stage. You return to your kitchen and as you unpack the carrier bags and prepare the ingredients, you visually inspect the mince, the tomatoes, garlic and the other components to make sure they are of the quality you require. This is the **goods inward and inspection** stage. If you are not going to make your lasagne straight away, you will store your ingredients in the fridge, and this is the **materials storage** stage.

Eventually, you get round to preparing the food. All of the stages from getting the lasagne dish from the cupboard to taking the fully cooked dish out of the oven are part of the **production** or **manufacturing** stage. As you take it from the oven, it is likely that you will examine your creation for quality. You may smell it, examine it visually, and stick a fork in to make sure it is cooked all the way through. You will also probably taste a small part of it. All of this is your **quality control**. It may be that after an initial examination, you decide it needs a little longer in the oven, so you put it back in and then repeat the quality control procedure a little later.

When you have satisfied yourself that the lasagne is up to your usual excellent standard, you will either put it aside to be microwaved later (**finished goods storage**), or you will serve it up there and then. We might say that the stages involving serving the lasagne onto plates and delivering it to the waiting table in the dining room are the **despatch and distribution** stages.

19.2 Operations and Competitive Advantage

A good operations department can be the making of a business and conversely, problems in the operations department can cause a company's downfall. Its strategic significance can be summarised by considering the following:

❏ **Materials used** – A key determinant of the utility of the product will be the materials used to make it. Purchasing the right materials for the process from reliable suppliers is consequently very important.

❏ **Quality** – The product, as produced by operations, is the principal important point of contact with the customer. Customer perceptions of the business and its goods will be formed by their experience of product quality. Getting the product 'right first time, every time' will lead to satisfied customers and repeat orders.

❏ **Lead Times** – Often, orders can be won or lost on the basis of when the order can be completed. The business that can 'turn round' an order quickly, i.e. completing the order soon after it is placed, will have an advantage over a slower one. Shorter lead times on orders as a whole will benefit the business.

❏ **Distribution** – All products must leave the factory and arrive at the customer. The method by which this is done and the reliability of promised delivery times can be vital in securing future orders from that customer. In industry, it is often of the essence that a promised order is delivered at a certain day and time, and that failure to do so will result in the customers process being stopped until the order arrives. This can be costly for the customer.

❏ **Packing and Packaging** – Most products need to be packed in some way in order to be transported. The packing must be sufficient to ensure that the product doesn't break in transit. It must be robust enough to contain the product in all foreseeable eventualities (e.g. being dropped) and with some products, must still be attractive in order to encourage customers to buy the product.

❏ **Costs** – In most manufacturing businesses, operations will be by far the largest department and therefore will represent the largest 'spender' of company money. Costs will be incurred in a number of areas:

❏ raw materials/purchased parts;

❏ wages and salaries;

❏ 'fixed costs' (rent, rates etc.);

❏ energy costs;

❏ costs of investment in new equipment;

❏ packaging and distribution costs;

❏ maintenance.

In addition to the above, the operations department can also incur 'invisible costs', examples of which are the 'hidden' costs of poor quality products, such as having to scrap items, rework them, or pay claims to customers whose goods fail while still under warranty. The lesson to be drawn from this is that the company that can minimise its costs of production will generate higher profits that those that can't. This is a key source of advantage to a business.

Case Study   **Operations at Thorn Lighting Limited – an introduction**

Thorn Lighting is one of the world's largest lightings fittings manufacturers. It is acknowledged as a leader in technology in lighting for a wide range of industrial and construction applications. The company has manufacturing sites in eight countries and has established activities in a total of twenty two. Its manufacturing activities in the UK are centred around a new development in Spennymoor, County Durham where it employs 1100 people and produces in excess of 2 million fluorescent light fittings a year.

The company has been active in the lighting industry for more than 60 years. Among its more high profile projects have been the lighting of the Sydney Opera House and the Tower of London. Spennymoor has enjoyed a great deal of investment in recent years. Since 1990, it has been transformed into one of the most modern factories in Europe for the design and manufacture of lighting fittings and the control gear that accompanies them. The site has computerised systems that help in both the design and manufacture of the products. It has been successful in gaining registration under BS 5750 Part 1 (ISO 9001) – a quality standard which includes assurance of quality in both design and production.

In 1992, the new Technology Centre was opened at Spennymoor to provide advanced product design using the latest electronic developments. Its aim is to *'maintain leadership in lighting technology into the 21st century and to enable it to offer the highest levels of customer support in the competitive new international markets'*.

Thorn Lighting has a great sense of mission when it comes to quality and excellence in its manufacturing processes. This is shown in its stated objective to involve 'all employees in exceeding our customers expectations' and in providing 'the highest quality of products, services and delivery at a competitive price'. It employs a Just In Time operational philosophy, together with a programme of continual improvement, Statistical Process Control (SPC) and Total Quality Control (TQC). Some of these terms are explained later in this chapter and in Chapter 20.

Now let us turn to the procedures in the operations function. We will look at each in turn.

19.3 Purchasing

19.3.1 What is purchasing?

Purchasing, sometimes called *procurement* or *buying*, is concerned with:

buying the right material

of the right *quality*;

in the right *quantity*;

at the right *price*;

from the right *supplier*;

with the right *delivery arrangements*;

with the right *delivery time*;

with the right *payment terms*.

The Purchasing Manager is an extremely important position in the company because he is the one who spends most of the company's money. In a typical British manufacturing company, the materials purchase bill will amount to around 65% of the total turnover of the company. Hence, for a company with annual sales of £10 million, the purchaser will spend £6.5 million of that.

19.3.2 What does purchasing involve?

The Purchasing Manager's job can include a number of activities:

❑ administering the purchasing of raw materials and other physical inputs;

❑ keeping abreast of developments in the markets that supply the company, such as new products, changes in the state of supplier companies, etc.;

❑ visiting suppliers to check on their quality procedures and ability to supply as required (although this is increasingly being taken over by a Quality Assurance Manager);

❑ negotiating supply contracts;

❑ 'shopping around' for cheaper prices for equivalent products, whilst taking due regard to total cost in the longer term rather than just the price of one order;

❑ seeing suppliers representatives, finding out about their new products, prices, changes in delivery etc.;

❑ examining supplier's pricing structures to find the most economical quantity to buy;

❑ calculating the most economic quantity of material to order;

❑ cultivating good relationships with suppliers – essential when the company needs a 'favour' such as an immediate delivery of materials or a small delivery in order to fulfil an order;

❑ acting as a 'window on the world'. Because it is the purchaser who will be the main person to see representatives, it will be he who is the first to receive intelligence on what is happening in the wider industrial environment. Travelling representatives go from company to company rather like the blood stream in a body. They are often an invaluable source of information and news.

The administrative part of the purchaser's job can be rather repetitive, but is nevertheless an essential part. In a large company, parts of it may be delegated to a more junior member of the purchasing department. The process starts when an ordering signal is received for a particular material. This signal is computerised in some companies – a development which removes one of the routine tasks from the Production Managers remit.

1. Ordering signal is generated (see later).

2. Factory raises a 'purchase requisition', which contains the information:

   name of material or part required;

   grade/quality required;

   requested supplier;

   quantity required;

delivery date;

form of delivery (cartons, boxes, bulk etc.).

3. Purchaser receives purchase requisition and authorises and issues a purchase order. He will add on further information to that supplied in the purchase requisition, including:

    order number and customer reference;

    agreed price;

    payment terms (number of days credit);

    any credit notes that may be applicable;

    terms and conditions of supply;

    The purchase order will be sent or faxed to the supplier.

4. Upon delivery of the goods at the 'goods inward' store, the materials will be inspected to ensure they match the order. Goods inward then issue a 'goods received note (GRN)' to the purchaser.

5. When the GRN is received in purchasing, the purchaser may also check the actual delivery against the order. On this basis, he will authorise payment with finance, but this will not take place until the invoice is received from the supplier.

Case Study   **The purchasing process at Thorn Lighting**

Thorn Lighting employs an operational philosophy called Just In Time (see description in Chapter 20). This is currently being implemented in a number of key cells within the business and will eventually be introduced throughout the company by liaison with suppliers who provide the incoming materials (a *cell* is a small group of workers who work as a team on the assembly of a particular product line). The internal stores and materials (stock) control people also play an important role in the implementation of JIT. Materials arrive *just in time* to begin their passage through the factory – there is no incoming materials inspection or storage within the cells which employ JIT.

When Thorn Lighting places a purchase order, it is based upon forecast annual budget volumes and is called-off (ordered) from suppliers on the basis of production schedule documents. These documents plan production either weekly, fortnightly or monthly and they specify the volume and frequency of orders which will be required to be ready for the production line within a short delivery lead time – sometimes just a few hours.

Thorn Lighting is able to adopt this purchasing supply chain methodology particularly because it is a large company with high purchasing power. In addition though, it has developed close relationships with a number of its key suppliers in which both parties are committed to providing the Thorn Lighting customer with products *on time, every time*. Thorn Lighting recognises that it is not in its interests to exploit suppliers and so it stresses a 'partnership' or 'co-operative' relationship with its most important suppliers. Prices are negotiated annually and are fixed for a 12-month fiscal year. In return for Just In Time supply and the annually negotiated price structure, Thorn Lighting is prepared to offer ongoing and regular business for the supplier (i.e. it doesn't 'shop around' for the cheapest price on a day-to-day basis). Thorn Lighting pays a market price for its materials and in return, it expects suppliers to continually review their own internal costs and make every effort to reduce and eliminate waste. As at 1994, plans were in hand for suppliers to be linked by computer direct to the Thorn Lighting purchasing office. This should not only speed up the purchasing process, but also avoid unnecessary paperwork and provide a two-way communications process where information can be exchanged which may affect the ability to supply or buy.

Activity 2   *What would be the implications for Thorn Lighting if, having no raw materials stock, it places an urgent order with a supplier to find that the supplier cannot deliver within the time specified by Thorn Lighting? What might be the implications for the relationship between the two companies of such a failure?*

19.4 Goods Inward, Inspection and Storage

Goods Inward is the department within operations which acts as the reception point for all incoming raw materials and purchased parts. We have already seen that part of its purpose is to inspect deliveries to see if they are the same as that which was ordered. Other responsibilities of this department are:

❒ to design the most appropriate method of storage of raw materials, using shelving, floor space etc. This will involve taking into consideration such factors as frequency of usage, reaction with other raw materials, conditions of storage such as moisture or light, and health and safety implications;

❒ to store the stocks in a logical and tidy fashion and to keep accurate records of where each material is and how much of it remains;

❒ to issue materials to the production unit as they are needed and in the form required. Records must then be amended to show the depletion of stocks as a result of the issue;

❒ to monitor stock levels and condition, and to instruct purchasing when the re-order level (or other ordering signal as appropriate) has been reached for a given raw material;

❒ to inform the production manager of any slow moving stocks so that they can be used up (or 'worked off') if possible.

It follows that if this department is poorly organised or managed then the production processes could not run smoothly. Possible problems arising from poor raw materials management are wrong materials issued to the factory, wrong materials ordered, materials deteriorating in storage, or the minimum stock level being ignored – a 'stock out'.

19.5 Production

This part of operations is variously called *the factory, production* or *manufacturing.* It would be more accurate to call it 'conversion' or 'processing', as it is here that the raw materials and purchased parts are transformed, assembled, reacted, mixed, or undergo similar working, to convert them into the final product. Some production units are very simple, with only a minimal conversion taking place, whereas others take sheet metal and electronic components and turn out space shuttles or defence aircraft. Factories vary from a 'one man band' working in a small industrial unit, to massive plants employing thousands, such as shipyards and motor car manufacturers.

Key concept | **Added value**

Production has as its overall objective, to 'add value' to materials as they pass through the plant. At every stage in the process, as the product comes nearer and nearer to its finished form, more investment has been made by the company in it. More importantly, at every stage, the value of the item has increased. Let us consider a simple costing of a production item.

Item: Widget	£
Raw materials in widget	1
Labour costs	1
Energy costs (electricity)	0.15
Total variable cost	2.15
Selling price	5
Therefore, value added as a result of the process	2.85

It is important to understand that value is only being added to the widget when it is being worked on. If, for any reason the materials are not being converted, then value is not being added and the company is foregoing money it could be making – time is of the essence in production!

19.6 Types of Production

Production processes are commonly divided into five categories:

❐ projects;

❐ job manufacture;

❐ batch manufacture;

❐ line manufacture;

❐ continuous manufacture.

Whilst these are simplifications, they do help us to understand the essentials of each type.

19.6.1 Projects

Project production is that which involves the making of a 'one off'. When a business is engaged on a project, all of the operations function is given over to that one piece of work. Project jobs are usually large or very large construction tasks where the producer makes the product to the exact specifications of the customer. Hence, when the producer is tendering for the job, it is 'selling' its capabilities and its track record rather than individual off-the-shelf products.

The products of project manufacturing are usually characterised by the fact that once built, they are big in size, and often so big that they cannot be moved. They are performed on site rather than in a factory and are overseen by a project manager rather than a production manager (although this distinction can be confusing on some projects).

Common examples of project production are:

- ☐ civil engineering projects
  buildings (e.g. Canary Wharf);
  road building (e.g. the M40);
  railways (e.g. the Docklands extension);
  special projects (e.g. The Channel Tunnel);
- ☐ building modifications and refurbishments;
- ☐ off-shore equipment (e.g. oil-rigs, platforms etc.).

> **Activity 3**   *Identify three project manufacturing processes currently going on in the region in which you are studying. They may be construction projects, either buildings or roads. Try to find one example that does not fall within the building or roads category.*

19.6.2 Job manufacture

'Jobbing', like project manufacture, is about 'one off' products which are made one at a time, and like project manufacture the product made is to the customers specification, and the company's image as a competent manufacturer is important in winning a job. Jobs are, by definition, non standard products where each order won by the company will be different from the last. However, it differs from project production in that jobbing usually implies a smaller scale, factory based operation. Operatives in a job shop will usually be relatively highly skilled either in a craft or trade.

Job manufacturing examples are those things which cannot be obtained as a standardised product, such as:

- ☐ engineering workshops (e.g. prototypes etc.);
- ☐ artists, sculptors etc;
- ☐ tooling manufacturers (including machine parts);
- ☐ customising operations (e.g. specialist motor vehicle workshops).

19.6.3 Common features of project and job manufacture

These forms of manufacture have a number of unique features, some of which could be seen as disadvantages and some as advantages.

Firstly, many projects or jobs require highly skilled operatives with multiple skills. This is because the project will have many variable stages, and in order to keep all workers busy, they may be required to perform more than one function.

Secondly, it is likely that the project or job, as it passes through the processes of construction, will use any one machine only once or twice. This results in low machine utilisation. On construction projects, this disadvantage is overcome by hiring plant and equipment as it is needed on site.

Thirdly, the very nature of projects and jobbing means that the business must achieve a relatively constant flow of orders. A project operation will result in an 'all or nothing' situation. So whilst employees will be fully engaged when a project is active, they will be totally inactive if there is a period with no work. This obviously requires careful management.

Finally, because all employees are working on the one product, value is added quickly. There is no waiting or 'queuing' between stages as might be the case with other forms of manufacture (see batch and flow in the next two sections of this chapter).

19.6.4 Batch manufacture

Batch production is the predominant form of manufacture in modern economies. As the name suggests, under this format, products are made in batches, or lots. It fits the type of business for whose products there is a steady or predictable demand, but not a constant one. It is also used in businesses that make a range of standard products or a number of modified versions of a core of standard products.

Batch operations have a number of features which demarcate them from other forms of manufacturing.

❏ It can deal with much higher volumes than job or project operations.

❏ The manufacturing programme is split into a number of distinct stages, often based at certain locations or work stations. This means that value is only being added when the batch is being worked on. Queuing often occurs between processes (see figure 19.2).

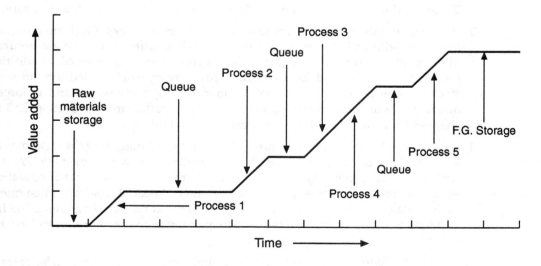

Figure 19.2: Progress of added value in batch production.

❑ The equipment and plant is set-up to run the batch through each of the stages in the production process. At the end of the batch, equipment is *tooled-down* (or washed down) before being re-set to run another. The terms tooling-up and tooling-down refer to the preparations necessary to run a batch and then to change machinery after the batch in order to run the next one. It may be, for example, that a die needs to be set-up on a milling machine or a programme fed into a CNC (computer numerically controlled) lathe. This all takes time.

❑ The focus of the organisation is on the products rather than on the production process. The company 'sells' itself on its products rather than on its competence as a manufacturer (as is the case on project and jobbing).

❑ The batch based factory will usually be expensive to fit out. The emphasis will often be on maintaining high plant throughput and in keeping the machines busy.

As a mode of production, it has a number of pros and cons.

Favourable features of batch manufacture

❑ Allows for fluctuations in demand as batch sizes can be varied.

❑ Gives high plant utilisation compared to project manufacture.

❑ Allows for the specialisation of operative skills. This means that a worker will spend most of his time at one stage in the process, allowing him to become proficient in just the one area, rather than having to learn lots of different procedures. This can also be a disadvantage (see below).

❑ Allows the business to offer a wide range of standard products.

Unfavourable features of batch manufacture

❑ It can be very difficult and complicated to organise. Batch scheduling and planning is a task which is becoming increasingly handled by computer in order to optimise the progress of jobs through the factory.

❑ Gives low plant utilisation compared to flow and continuous manufacture. This is due in part to the need to set up and tool-down machinery between batches, but also because plant can sit idle unless there is a continuous flow of batches through the factory.

❑ The increased specialisation of operatives can mean that staff flexibility is reduced. There is value to be gained if operatives can do more than one job in a factory.

❑ It usually involves holding a relatively high level of stocks. Batch manufacture is often sporadic and the usage of raw materials is difficult to forecast accurately. Many stocks need to be kept 'just in case' a certain order is received. In addition to raw materials, a second kind of stocks result from batch, called *work-in-progress* stocks. These occur when the batch moves through the works and is forced to queue at a work station for the next stage of manufacture. See Section 20.3 (next chapter) for further details on the drawbacks of holding stocks.

❑ It can result in longer manufacturing lead times, meaning that the customer must wait for the order to be completed. This results from two problematic areas. The first is that, as previously mentioned, it is hard to schedule a batch operation as some batches are necessarily made before others. Secondly, batches must queue at various stages in the process, including of course, at the very beginning. See figure 19.3 for a working example of how much queuing is involved in a typical industrial process.

Examples of products made by batch manufacture are pharmaceuticals, cosmetics, most food products and paints (see figure 19.3).

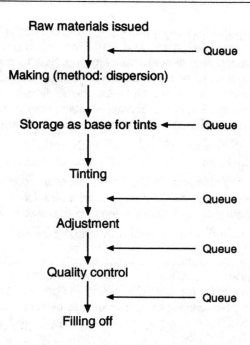

Figure 19.3: Stages in the batch manufacture of paint

19.6.5 Line manufacture

Line production, sometimes referred to as flow manufacture, is employed by (usually large) businesses that make an assembly based product and have a relatively predictable demand. Technically, flow manufacture occurs when queuing, as discussed in the previous section, is eliminated. The product, as it is being produced, goes directly from one process to the next.

Features of line systems are:

☐ large investment in plant;

☐ high volume production;

☐ processes (lines) are dedicated to making one product only. It is not possible to tool down to make a different product like batch operations;

☐ usually, line operations make only a small product range;

☐ operator skills can be very specialised, with tasks tending to be repetitive;

☐ setting up production lines requires much preparation and accurate forecasting of volumes to be made.

Common applications of flow systems are:

☐ automobiles;

☐ electronic consumer goods e.g. video's, hi-fi's etc;

☐ consumer kitchen appliances e.g. cookers, washing machines, fridges.

Case Study   **Flow production at Thorn Lighting**

The manufacturing operation at Thorn Lighting, Spennymoor is centred around two distinctive product areas. Firstly, it produces light fittings – an operation involving the cutting and shaping of metal sheets. Secondly, it makes the electronic circuits that control lighting systems for industrial and construction applications. Hence we see two quite separate production areas on the same site: metal fabrication and electronic circuit construction. Both are closely controlled by computerised systems.

Lighting fittings

Thorn lighting fittings hold fluorescent tubes in position. Spennymoor is the 'home' of Popular Pack – the world's best selling fluorescent lighting fitting with some 60 million units sold. Several other fittings products are also manufactured at the Spennymoor site. Sheet metal is cut using a number of flexible CNC (computer numerically controlled) machines. Assembly then occurs in production cells, each designated with a family of products and consisting of a small number of people working as a team. This is an arrangement in contrast to a large impersonal line where individuals sit side by side and work on separate operations. The cell sits in a circle and assembly is passed around. It is thought that this layout enables employees to enjoy more of a team spirit when they relate to each other as they are doing their work. Cell members rotate between jobs which means not only that their jobs are more interesting but also that each member becomes proficient in each of the assembly tasks within the cell's area of responsibility. Because assemble workers are based in a small team, members feel a sense of belonging and this encourages a more responsible approach to work. Thorn representatives report that since the introduction of cell manufacture, production lead times for standard products have been cut from 30 days to 5-10 days; order backlogs reduced from 5 days to zero and scrap (off-specification material which cannot be sold) reduced by two thirds. Thorn management say that, 'teamworking and a personal commitment to quality and efficiency is the essence of cell working'.

Electronic control gear

The Spennymoor operation combines many areas of electronic expertise in the design and manufacture of the lighting control systems. As in lighting fitting production, this area of the operation is also centred around a cellular structure which has reduced the floor space required for assembly by 28%. Technology is, not surprisingly, of greater importance on this side of Thorn's operation. Equipment is employed that can place 13 000 electronic components per hour on a printed circuit board, and on one system, the Fluoropulse electronic starter, the 14 different components are automatically inserted onto the circuit board in just 5 seconds. The combination of cell working and the use of new technology have had the added advantages of cutting work-in-progress stocks by half and of reducing scrap by a similar amount. Changeover time from one product to another has been cut from 45 minutes to 10 minutes which speeds up production and reduces manufacturing lead time.

19.6.6 Continuous manufacturing

The most distinctive features of continuous processes are that they are geared up for very large volume production and they are enormously capital intensive. Investment in plant can run into hundreds of millions of pounds. Because of the high setting up costs, the plant must make its return on investment by running constantly – usually all day, every day. Costs are incurred if the machinery has to be shut down for any reason and just starting the process up again can be a major cost to the company.

The materials processed in this type of operation are those that lend themselves to mass production, such as chemicals, fluids and gases. Operators in continuous manufacture are predominantly engaged in monitoring and checking rather than actually working on the line.

The end products of this type of operation are usually 'commodities' or similar products which are sold at relatively cheap unit prices. Work in progress stocks are very low but large finished goods stocks can often result.

Common examples are:

❑ steel;

❑ petrochemicals;

❑ energy (particularly electricity generation);

❑ some chemical intermediates (e.g. ammonia).

19.6.7 Hybrid processes

Some operations processes do not fit neatly into just one of the types detailed above. Companies will plan production according to the format which best suits the product and the market conditions. In addition, organisations sometimes change their production methods over time, such as moving from batch to line as volumes increase.

Example 1   Job Batch Production: **Philips Communication and Security Systems – Cambridge.**

This division of the Dutch Philips Group produce closed circuit television systems. It employs a hybrid system of production using elements of jobbing and batch. Each contract it wins is different from the last as it must conform to specific requirements as determined by the customer. The circuitry is different from job to job. However, each 'job' involves making a number (not a 'one off') of camera assemblies, monitors etc., necessitating the plant to be set up as a batch, for the particular job run in hand – effectively a batch.

Example 2   Batch Continuous Production: **Schering Agrochemicals – Hauxton, Cambridge**

Schering Agrochemicals makes pesticides and insecticides for agricultural use. There is a constant flow of materials through the reactor vessels, pointing to a continuous type of process. However, the reactions themselves take place in individual vessels before passing on to the next via a pipework connection. After a vessel is emptied, it is immediately refilled with more unreacted materials. It is possible to trace the contents of a vessel through the process from start to finish as one would with a batch process. Each vesselful can legitimately be referred to as a discreet batch in its own right. We might therefore say that production is by a continuous batch method.

Review Questions

1. How can the operations function contribute to the competitive position of the business of which it is a part? (19.2)

2. What are the stages involved in a typical manufacturing process? (19.1)

3. Describe the essential features of good purchasing. (19.3)

4. Outline the processes from order point to delivery of incoming stock. (19.3.2)

5. What does the goods inward department do? (19.4)

6. What are the five general types of production? (19.5)

7. Give examples of what types of products made by each type of production. (19.6)

8. Summarise the different types of personnel required for each method of production. In particular, draw the contrasts between personnel in project manufacture and those in line processes. (19.6)

9. Thorn Lighting Ltd employ a cellular structure as part of their line manufacture. What are the benefits of this arrangement?

Answers to Activities

Activity 1

1. Sales increase by 10%

    Sales rise from £10 million to £11 million,

    Purchasing spend therefore rises pro rata from £6.5 million to £7.15 million – a rise of 10%,

    Gross Profit rises from £3.5 million to (£11m – £7.15m) £3.85 million.

    Therefore, a 10% increase in turnover results in a 10% increase in gross profit.

2. Purchasing spend reduced by 10%

    Turnover remains unchanged at £10 million,

    Purchasing spend is cut by 10% from £6.5 million to £5.85 million,

    Gross Profit rises from £3.5 million to (£10m – £5.85m) £4.15 million.

    Therefore, a 10% cut in purchasing spend results in a 18.57% increase in gross profit.

Activity 2

Because Thorn Lighting operate a JIT system, failure to supply incoming raw materials on time will result in the production line being stopped. This would mean that delivery time of the finished goods would have to be postponed, thus making Thorn Lighting unpopular with their customers. The relationship between Thorn Lighting and its supplier may be damaged as the supplier would have shown itself to be unreliable in its ability to supply to a JIT schedule.

Assignment

Engonics (Engineering) Limited

Dr David Paige is the Operations Director of Engonics. He oversees a staff of 450 in the production department, including a purchasing manager called Duncan Ben. The factory, which manufactures a wide range of general engineering products, employs a batch system, which, according to Dr Paige, gives the company maximum flexibility to respond to fluctuations in demand for its products.

Recently, Duncan approached Dr Paige regarding his salary and conditions of work. Duncan began the meeting by complaining that Dr Paige didn't realise half of what went on in the purchasing office. "I tell you, Doctor," began Duncan, "I sit in that office all day, everyday and you don't seem to be very concerned about the purchasing function". David replied to Duncan in an attempt to reassure, "On the contrary, Duncan. I know full well how important you are, and I think you are doing a sterling job. It's just that I believe that purchasing is only one part of operations, and is less important than managing stocks, getting people to work and getting finished goods out the door. Don't rise above your station, Duncan. Your job is routine, and is largely just clerical procedure stuff. You get on with your job and that will mean that I can get on with the real operational work – I couldn't do it without those stocks you order so well."

Duncan became incensed. "Last year, I spent £13 million of the company's money," he retorted, "and you seem to think my job is routine. You give me a poky office and you treat me like an office boy. I tell you, Doctor, purchasing is central to the company's success or failure. You ought to take a more active interest in it, give me more support, an assistant and a pay-rise". The meeting ended with Dr Paige staring into his morning coffee with a few things to think about.

Tasks

1. Take a side. Who do you agree with and why?
2. Assume you are Duncan. Write a report to Dr Paige describing the following:
   - ❏ the role of purchasing in a business;
   - ❏ why it should be given prominence by the Operations Director:
   - ❏ how it can affect or influence those things that Dr Paige is concerned about (managing stocks and getting 'finished goods out the door');

Further Reading

Lockyer K., Muhlemenn A. & Oakland J., *Production and Operations Management*, Pitman Press (Sixth Edition)

Galloway R.L., *Principles of Operations Management*, Routledge

Ruch W.A., Fearon H.E. & Wieters C.D., *Fundamentals of Production/Operations Management*, West Publishing Company (Fifth Edition)

Hayes R. & Wheelwright S.C., *Restoring our competitive edge. Competing through Manufacturing*, John Wiley & Sons

20 The operations function 2
Quality, Stocks, JIT and TQM

Objectives   After studying this chapter, students should be able to:

❏ describe the common approaches to quality control and the various destinations of finished goods stock;

❏ name the four types of stock used in manufacturing and explain the uses of each;

❏ describe the various approaches to re-stocking of raw materials;

❏ understand the essentials of two of the most influential operations management philosophies: Just In Time, and Total Quality Management.

Featured organisation: **Thorn Lighting Limited**

20.1 Quality Control (QC)

After the product has been made, it must pass through the quality control stage where it is tested for quality. Quality in this context is not to be confused with the common usage of the word. In business, quality means *'conformance to specification'*. This means that what may be considered as a 'low quality' product may meet the specification and hence be 'quality' as far as conformance is concerned.

The product, on arriving at QC is tested against the internal quality standards of the company for that particular product. These refer to the properties of the product such as dimensions, performance, appearance, weight, and tolerances. When arriving at the standards against which products will be tested, the business considers both technical factors and economic factors.

❏ **Technical factors** are those which the product must meet if it is to function properly. They can be considered as the minimum standards, such as minimum measurements, minimum performance or minimum safety levels.

❏ **Economic factors** are those which ask the question: are the standards tight enough to meet the technical standards but not so tight that the product is better than it needs to be? Badly designed quality standards may overspecify and this will make the risk of failure at QC unnecessarily high as well as asking more of the production process than is necessary. Overspecification incurs costs over and above those which are necessary.

The actual process of QC involves the *enforcement* and *verification* of the quality standards that have been previously agreed from the point of view of technical and economic considerations. Because it involves the testing of products made by production, the responsibility for QC usually rests with a manager who is not responsible to the Operations Director – often it is part of the Technical Department. This is to prevent any compromise that might occur if the Quality Manager reported to Operations – meaning that there might be pressure to pass borderline materials rather than fail them as would be required according to the strict technical criteria.

Testing can take a number of forms. The precise QC procedures will depend upon the type of process, the product and the degree of control that is required.

20.1.1 Testing every product

This type of control has the advantage that the company can be sure that every product that leaves the plant meets the QC specification as laid down. Whilst this sounds like the ideal, for some products, this is simply impracticable or uneconomical. It is possible when:

☐ the product is very big, such as a project (e.g. a ship, a civil engineering project);

☐ the product is the output of a job process, where the number of products made is small and it is economical to test each output;

☐ the company is a batch producer and the batches are homogeneous. This would apply to chemical compositions such as beer, powders and gases and any part of the batch would be exactly the same as every other part.

20.1.2 Product sampling

With many types of product, a gauge of overall conformance is gained by taking a representative sample of the batch and making the assumption that the success or otherwise of the sample in QC is sufficient to base a decision about the batch on. This type of testing is appropriate for products which are numerous or difficult to test. Examples would be:

☐ ball-bearings;

☐ nuts and bolts;

☐ small confectionery items;

☐ razor blades.

The methods of sampling and the statistical arguments behind this method of control are complicated and beyond the scope of this text.

QC at Thorn Lighting

Thorn at Spennymoor employs a quasi-Japanese approach to quality control. It does not replace the traditional approaches; rather it adds to it. It is called *Total Quality Control* (TQC).

The aim of TQC is defect-free production. Rather than testing products at the end of the production process, emphasis is placed upon 'getting it right first time'. The responsibility for quality rests not upon a separate Quality Control Department, but rather upon the production operatives themselves. Thorn operate a system called FIAT (Fault Inspection and Test) where operatives are trained to keep an eye on the process for faults in products as they work on them. Cells are awarded a system of Bronze, Silver and Gold for four, eight and twelve weeks' defect free production respectively. After the first nine months of FIAT, the production performance rose to 99.6% 'right first time'.

Activity 1   *What do you think are the advantages and disadvantages of the two quality control regimes described above (testing every product and sampling)?*

20.2 Finished Goods and Distribution

Finished goods are the stocks that result from materials passing through the manufacturing process that have subsequently been cleared by QC. Of course some materials will fail QC, and companies have procedures for dealing with such stock which will depend upon the nature of the product (see figure 20.1)

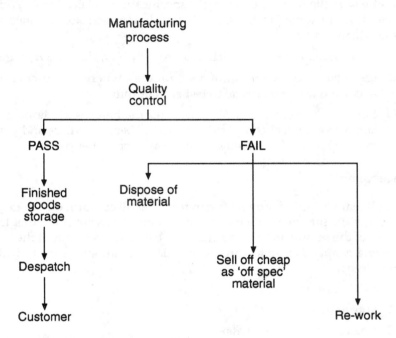

Figure 20.1: Possible destinations of completed stocks

20.2.1 Product Passes Quality Control

When a product passes the quality standards in QC, it will be identified as such and be made available for sale. It passes through two more stages in the company before it arrives at the customer.

❑ *Finished goods storage,* as the name suggests is the area given over to retaining finished goods stocks until they leave the site. The amount of finished goods stock and the length of time the stock remains will depend upon the industry and the nature of the operation. Some industries, such as coal mining will generate large amounts of finished goods owing to the low and variable sales of their products. Others will generate products which sell very quickly, either because there is a high demand for them or because the product is perishable. Examples of the latter are products made to order, fresh foods, or some 'elitist' and under-supplied sports cars (for which there may be a waiting list).

❑ *Distribution* is the procedure by which products leave the point of manufacture and arrive at the customer. Again the nature and complexity of this stage will vary greatly from the complex global systems of a petrochemical company to the simple distribution of a sole proprietor selling hot dogs on a street corner. Many companies, particularly transportation businesses, make their living by distributing products for companies. Whatever the method chosen and the complexity of it, a good distribution system will satisfy the following criteria:

❏ it will ensure that the product arrives at the point of consumption on time – that is, within the time scale as determined by the customer;

❏ the product will not be damaged in transit;

❏ it will be cost effective, meaning that the cost of distribution does not make the selling of it uneconomical at normal market prices.

20.2.2 Product fails Quality Control

If a product fails to attain the minimum quality standards, the company has a number of potential choices of what it can do with the stock. The actual course of action will depend largely on the type of product.

❏ **The materials can be disposed of**

This choice is open to the company whose 'off spec.' products cannot be dealt with in any other way or whose raw material content is such that it is more economical to dispose of it rather than rework it. It also implies that the 'off spec.' product is useless to the end user and couldn't be sold off cheaply. Examples of products in this category are:

❏ food products;

❏ beer (batches of beer can be as much as 340 600 pints – an expensive failure!);

❏ items where there is a minimum safety requirement such as tyres, timing belts etc.

❏ **The materials can be sold off**

When 'off spec.' materials are sold off, they cannot be sold at normal market prices, and so the company seeks to cover the investment made in the materials by selling them as 'reject stock', 'seconds' or simply 'off spec.'. The thinking behind this is that some consumers, for whatever reason, do not need to have fully approved products and can use such materials profitably. Products that lend themselves to this type of disposal are:

❏ clothes;

❏ food products (e.g. misshapen chocolates);

❏ industrial products such as 'off colour' paints etc.;

❏ furniture (e.g. with marks or minor scratches).

Of course, the saleability of off spec. materials will depend just how far off spec. they are and in what parts of the quality standards they have failed.

❏ **The materials can be re-worked**

Re-working is the usage of completed goods as raw materials or as work in progress stocks (see part 20.3 of this chapter). This has the advantage that less of such stocks will have to be used up to generate the same quantity of finished goods. It is usually more economical to sell off failed goods than to re-work them, and the types of product that this can be used on is limited. It is usual in re-working that the failed material forms only a part of the total stock of the 'new batch' so that the effect of the defective stock is reduced or 'diluted'. Examples are:

❏ some plastic items that can be re-granulated and used again;

❏ metal items that can be melted down or re-machined;

❏ some chemicals where health and safety would not be risked by such a process.

For assembly based products (e.g. cars) re-working might involve something as simple as replacing a part or even tightening a screw. Such products, after re-working, would be expected to be as good as 'right first time' goods. Re-working does not necessarily mean a compromise of quality.

20.3 Stock Management

20.3.1 Types of stock

Stocks or *inventory* are essential to any manufacturing company. They are the materials that the business is processing in the different stages of production. For convenience, we can divide stocks into three types and one 'other'.

❏ **Raw materials/purchased parts**

Stocks as they are bought in from suppliers. These are the materials waiting to begin the manufacturing process.

❏ **Work-in-progress**

Stocks actually going through the factory. These can either be those materials being worked on, or queuing in production between procedures.

❏ **Finished goods**

Stocks that have completed the production procedure that are waiting to go out to the customer.

❏ **Service parts**

This category is usually tiny in comparison to the main three. It includes machine parts, and consumables such as paper, stationary and food in the canteen.

The relative quantities of the three main types of stock will depend greatly upon the type of production and the nature of the manufacturing process. Batch processes will tend to have higher overall stock levels than job processes and line manufacturing can be higher or lower depending upon the company's 'philosophy'. It is traditional in the automotive industry, for example, to hold relatively high levels of finished goods stocks in order to respond rapidly to changes in demand.

20.3.2 Costs of stock

It should be borne in mind that essential as stocks are, they do, for a number of reasons, cost money. Costs can be incurred both from keeping stocks for too long and for not having enough.

Let us examine how the cost of stock can be made up.

❏ Purchase cost:
   the price paid to the supplier.

❏ Direct holding cost:
   floor space must be paid for in initial purchase (or rent) and local authority tax;
   operatives must be paid to look after and manage the stock.

❏ Financial holding cost:
   cash is tied up in the stock that could otherwise be earning interest;

unless the stock is actually in process, value is not being added;
insurance of stock and buildings must be paid for.

☐ Other costs
obsolescence – stock 'going off' or becoming otherwise useless;
theft of stock.

Of course it is equally undesirable to have too little stock. The effects of under stocking include stockouts whereby,

☐ products cannot be made, therefore orders are lost,

☐ the business loses revenue it could otherwise have made.

Example	A Personal Story
	The author worked for a while as Operations Manager for a chemical company. Towards the financial year end he was invited to take a walk around the factory by his Managing Director. The purpose of the 'walk' was to draw the author's attention to the levels of slow-moving finished goods stock in the hope that he could reduce them by means of rework. The Managing Director pointed out the quantities of stock and said 'You see David, when I look around this store, I don't see products lying on the shelves, I see ten pound notes – get rid of them!'. The point was well received.

The purpose of all stocks is to turn them into cash as soon as possible. In this way, businesses can make stocks work for them without paying excessively for their use.

Activity 2	Accountants always monitor stock levels. From what we learned about working capital in Chapter 18 of this book, explain why accountants are particularly keen to see stock levels kept as low as possible.

20.3.3 Stocking tendencies

The policy that a company has with regard to holding stocks is by no means straightforward. Different departments in the company have different motivations for holding stock. These can often lead to conflict and the business must ensure that policies are agreed with all interested parties. The tendencies are as follows.

☐ **Marketing Manager**
Tendency: High finished goods stockholding.
Reason : Fast response to customer demand. High finished goods stocks will mean that products will be available immediately and will not need to be made.

☐ **Accountant**
Tendency: Low overall stockholding.
Reason: Stock is expensive and reduces cash flow.

☐ **Operations Manager**
Tendency: High raw materials stockholding.
Reason: Enables a swift response when orders come in. No need to order materials before a job can begin.

☐ **Technical and Personnel**
No particular tendencies.

❏ **Managing Director**
Must balance all tendencies for the good of the company.

20.3.4 Elements of restocking

There are a number of ways in which stocks (particularly raw materials) are replenished. The method chosen will of course, depend upon the nature of the material, the habits of the company and the pricing structures of the materials.

There are two general 'ordering signals' that can signal the need to order raw materials. They are order point generation and stock point generation.

❏ **Order point generation**

Under this system, raw materials are ordered when an order comes in for finished products which use the raw materials in question. Hence, the company will not hold high raw materials stocks, but will only order them when specifically needed. The name means that orders for raw materials are generated when a product order comes in. This has one obvious advantage and one equally obvious disadvantage.

Advantage: low raw material stockholding so cash is not being tied up.
Disadvantage: as orders cannot be supplied from finished goods stocks, longer lead times may result.

❏ **Stock point generation**

Under this system stocks are replenished as a result of the levels of the stock, rather than as a result of the finished goods requirements. This is, of course, much simpler and 'safer' than order point generation, and is the predominant replenishment method used in batch manufacturing companies.

There are a number of common methods of replenishment under this system.

Minimum stock level

Figure 20.2 shows graphically how this works. There is a minimum level of 'safe' stock which, when reached, signals when new raw materials should be ordered. It is likely that an order will be placed when it is expected that the next factory 'call off' (order) of the material will take it below the minimum stock level and into the safety stock. Under this system, orders will be placed at irregular intervals, depending upon when stock reaches the re-order level. Figure 20.3 shows a typical schedule.

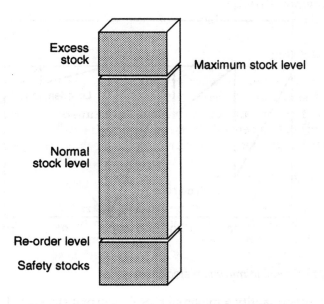

Figure 20.2

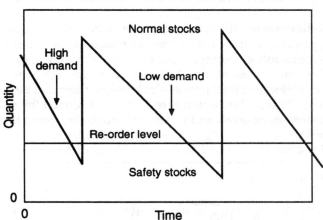

Figure 20.3: Minimum stock replenishment

Cyclical (regular) replenishment

Cyclical replenishment is a very simple method of ordering. The company orders raw materials at regular intervals regardless of the existing stock levels. Within this system however, there are two subdivisions which refer to the amount of stock that is actually ordered at the point when a stock order is due.

Cyclical Replenishment *to maximum stock level* is rather like filling a petrol tank, in that most people 'fill up the tank' when they buy it, regardless of the present quantity of petrol in the tank. Hence, a company may determine that the maximum stock level for cardboard boxes is 10 000 units. When the stock order is due, they will see how many they have and order the difference. See figure 20.4.

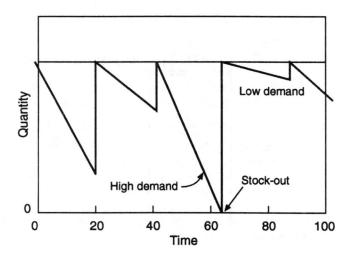

Figure 20.4: Cyclical replenishment to maximum stock level

Order quantity = maximum level – current stock level

Cyclical replenishment *by fixed amount* is the simplest method of ordering. Regardless of stock usage, the same quantity is ordered at he regular intervals, be it monthly or quarterly. An everyday example of this is milk deliveries where a household may receive 2 pints a day regardless of how much is leftover in the fridge. Because this ignores stock levels, there can be a wide variation in stock levels. This is shown in figure 20.5 (more refined 'by fixed amount' systems do observe stock levels and orders will not be triggered if stock is above minimum level).

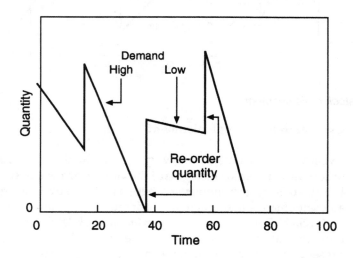

Figure 20.5: Cyclical replenishment by fixed amount.

20.4 Operations Management Philosophies

We have already seen that the operations function is often the largest part of a company, particularly when it is a manufacturing company. Because of this, the amount of money used by it can be critical to the wider success of the company. Similarly, great gain can be achieved if costs can be reduced in operations. A number of 'philosophies' are used in industry which have the overall objectives of:

☐ reduction of costs;

☐ increase in quality;

☐ reduction of lead times;

☐ increased flexibility to respond to customer demands.

Because they are philosophies and not just procedures, businesses who operate them pay great attention to the cultural aspects and in maintaining commitment throughout the business and at all employee levels. There are several widely used philosophies, which are usually abbreviated to initials. Some, such as Manufacturing Resource Planning (MRP 2 – an order point stock generation control system) rely on powerful computer systems whilst others can be operated manually. In this section, we will consider two of the most common operational philosophies: *Just In Time* and *Total Quality Management*.

20.5 Just In Time

Just In Time (JIT) production is sometimes called 'stockless production', and whilst this is a good description, it only tells part of the story. In summary, JIT can be described as an operational philosophy dedicated to the elimination of waste in all its forms.

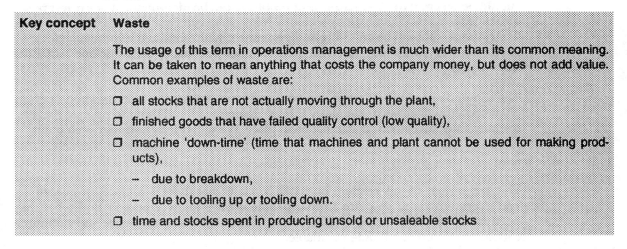

Key concept   Waste

The usage of this term in operations management is much wider than its common meaning. It can be taken to mean anything that costs the company money, but does not add value. Common examples of waste are:

☐ all stocks that are not actually moving through the plant,

☐ finished goods that have failed quality control (low quality),

☐ machine 'down-time' (time that machines and plant cannot be used for making products),

　　– due to breakdown,

　　– due to tooling up or tooling down.

☐ time and stocks spent in producing unsold or unsaleable stocks

Given that it sets out to eliminate waste, JIT has a number of core themes, and attached to these, a number of operational practices that are strictly observed. The JIT cycle is shown in figure 20.6 below.

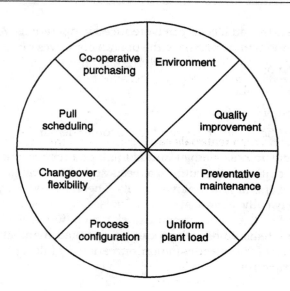

Figure 20.6: The JIT cycle

The most important features of JIT are that all parts of the operations department should observe:

Simplicity – keeping all procedures as simple as possible.
Visibility – refers to systems and the physical environment, requiring that everything should be where it can be seen, so that problems can be identified at the earliest possible stage.
Continuous – should be on-going and permanent with continual improvement.
Involvement – everybody must be involved, not just management or one particular department.

The components of the JIT cycle as set out in Figure 20.6 are the 'nuts and bolts' of how JIT works. It will be seen that many things are involved in JIT and to operate this philosophy fully, all components must be in place. We will briefly consider each point.

20.5.1 Environment

The importance of this element of the JIT cycle is that there is a place for everything and everything is in its place so that people always know where to find what they need. Similarly, all activities will be more streamlined if all paperwork and communications are orderly and understandable.

20.5.2 Quality

Under JIT, everybody is responsible for quality, not just the quality control. It implies that attention should be paid to detail at every stage and that causes of poor quality should be corrected at their source. Quality standards should be consistent and consistently high. JIT recognises that poor quality is costly and that prevention is better than cure.

20.5.3 Preventative Maintenance

This element recognises that poor quality is expensive and that products should be right first time. Under JIT, in addition to the observance of regular maintenance schedules, each operator in the plant is a 'quality inspector' so that faults are detected at the earliest possible point. This principle also applies to plant and equipment. Instead of machine maintenance being the responsibility of a separate part of operations, each machine operator will immediately report all irregularities in machine performance. This will prevent the line stopping because of the machine needing a major repair.

20.5.4 Uniform Plant Load

JIT works best when materials can be scheduled through the plant at a consistent rate. This prevents excess demand (queuing) and under demand (underutilisation of human and physical resources), both of which cost money.

20.5.5 Process Configuration

Factory layout should be planned as 'product based' rather than 'process based'. This means that the factory and where things go can be easily and quickly identified. Simplicity is the key and a product based layout means that the progress of any product manufacture is visible. This approach also means that with one line dedicated to one product, tooling up and down is minimised and progress through the plant is hastened. Under a batch production configuration, the emphasis is placed on increased flexibility within the constraints that a batch process tends to impose.

20.5.6 Changeover Flexibility

Setting machinery up (or tooling up) and down for a job is a waste in that it does not add value. In the same way that a motor racing support team can change a wheel in just a few seconds, this can also be the case in business if the team wants to win! Machines should be as uniform as possible within the limits of the processes so that changing tools can be as streamlined as possible.

20.5.7 Pull Scheduling

JIT is an example of 'order point generation' in that materials are not ordered until an order is received. However, under JIT, the procedures are much more involved. JIT uses a system called KANBAN. A KANBAN (Japanese for 'card') is a signal from one work station to the preceding work station that stock is needed. The KANBAN principle works right back through the process from the distribution of finished goods to purchasing. No finished goods stock is built up and no raw materials stocks are held. Everything starts to move when an order comes in and if no orders come in, then (theoretically) nothing is made.

How KANBAN Works

1. An order is received.

2. Despatch signals (KANBANs) the final stage of production to supply the order.

3. The final stage of production KANBANs the second last stage of production to supply it with the volume of the order in the appropriate level of assembly.

This continues backwards through the process until the first stage of assembly signals that it needs the raw materials stocks to begin the order. The supplier is notified and is expected to supply exactly the volume of stock needed to fulfil that order.

20.5.8 Co-operative Purchasing

JIT requires that raw materials are ordered at very short notice and in highly variable quantities. This is because of the KANBAN principle. The philosophy states that suppliers are few and that the business develops a special relationship with them. They demand much of suppliers and so purchasing is seen as a partnership rather than the usual buyer-supplier arrangement. The company will remain faithful to the one supplier in order to gain the level of service required. Hence, contractual arrangements are discouraged and co-operative and amicable relationships are encouraged.

20.6 Total Quality Management (TQM)

TQM has been one of the growth philosophies among companies over recent years. Many of the emphases of TQM are similar to those under JIT, but the overarching theme of TQM is **quality** rather than waste. The systems under TQM rest upon what are referred to as the *Four Absolutes of Quality* (as described by quality 'guru' Philip Crosby in his important book *Quality is Free*):

1. **Quality is defined as conformance to specification (or requirement)**

    This reinforces the JIT quality message, that quality does not hinge upon the absolute quality (in the popular meaning of the word) of a product, but in how well it conforms to the quality standards determined for it. Hence, it is perfectly consistent to operate TQM for products which are not 'high quality' and may occupy a 'budget' position in the marketplace.

2. **The systems for causing quality are based upon prevention rather than appraisal or control**

    This stresses the reliance on process operatives and in product design to assure quality rather than the detection of poor quality at the quality control stage.

3. **The performance standard is Zero Defects**

    Zero defects (ZD) means that every product conforms to specification every time. This means there will be no costs incurred as a result of completed stocks failing to meet quality standards. The 'that's good enough' approach is not part of the TQM philosophy.

4. **The measure of quality is the financial cost of non-conformance**

    It should not be overlooked that organisations that operate TQM do so in the belief that it saves money rather than costs money. The cost of products failing to meet standards can be high and in TQM companies, a financial value is put upon it in order to encourage the necessary tightening of systems to prevent its repetition.

There are many reasons for implementing TQM in a company, and it does seem to amount to a convincing argument. *Firstly*, as we have already seen there are the financial considerations. The cost of failure can be high, both in terms of the costs of the stock, and possibly more importantly, in the loss of confidence from customers. In some markets, it doesn't take much to put a customer off buying a company's products and to encourage him to look elsewhere. *Secondly*, there is a more intangible reason for

TQM in that it may be a source of increasing the market's confidence in the company and its products. This will result in the organisation gaining a competitive advantage over competitors if a good reputation can be achieved in this area. *Thirdly,* in some markets, a consistently high quality conformance is required as a condition of market entry or in order to conform to regulatory standards. Examples of these are some government defence suppliers, pharmaceuticals etc. TQM is an established vehicle for achieving such ends and so is not uncommon in these industries.

The success of TQM in the workplace relies upon the strict observance of seven 'principles' of TQM.

1. Get it right first time

Eliminate the risk of QC failure at source. Build quality into the design.

2. Make quality easy to see

This encourages the visibility factors we mentioned in JIT. Keep a clean and organised environment. Keep designs such that faults can be detected at the earliest possible stage.

3. Insistence upon compliance

All employees must be convinced that TQM is a good idea. Each must have a quality consciousness and in the same way that the company insists that all employees comply with the philosophy, so each employee must ensure that each part of the product complies with specification.

4. Line stop authority

In keeping with the desire to correct faults at the earliest stage in the manufacturing process, each operator on the line has the authority to stop production if he detects non-conformance in a product when it arrives at his work station. This has the effect of devolving the responsibility for quality to everybody and of taking it away from quality control.

5. Correct your own mistakes

This principle states that each employee should make good any poor workmanship before it leaves his workstation. It means that rather than leaving faults to be corrected later they should be put right as soon as they occur.

6. 100% checks

Every part of the product should be checked and not just a few tests as might be the case under the traditional quality control system. Because this would not be possible when the product is finished, it must occur as the product is passing through production.

7. Continuous improvement

Emphasis is placed upon improving the product or the process as often as is necessary in order to increase quality. Again, the responsibility for this is placed upon everybody, and in some companies groups are set up so that employees can discuss possible improvements in a conducive environment ('quality circles').

There has been a marked increase in the observance of quality issues in business over recent years. Companies have seen the advantages of lower costs and more satisfied customers. Whilst few companies have fully implemented TQM, many have qualified for BS 5750 and others have used parts of the TQM philosophy selectively.

The changing assumptions about quality can be summarised as follows:

From	To
Reactive management	Proactive/forward planning
Inspection (QC)	Prevention (QA)
'Acceptable' quality	Zero defects ('right first time, every time')
Placing the blame	Solving the problem
Cost *or* quality	Cost *and* quality
Quality costs more	Quality actually costs less!

Review Questions

1. Discuss the various approaches to quality control. Draw a clear distinction between final inspection quality control systems and in-process monitoring. (20.1)

2. Describe the four types of stock that a manufacturing process will use. (20.3.1)

3. Explain the sources of cost which are attached to stock. (20.3.2)

4. Define and distinguish between stock point and order point generation of stock orders. (20.3.4)

5. Describe the various approaches to stock point generation of raw materials. (20.3.4)

6. What are the perceived benefits to an organisation of Just In Time production? (20.5)

7. Describe the essentials of JIT as illustrated by the JIT cycle. (20.5)

8. What are the perceived benefits of employing TQM in an organisation? (20.6)

9. Summarise the features of TQM. (20.6)

Answers to Activities

Activity 1

The choice between a quality control regime involving sampling or testing every product will invariably be made upon the nature of the product and the volumes in which it is being produced. Put simply though, the pros and cons can be stated as follows:

Testing every product
Advantage: Tightest possible QC regime – a fault, theoretically, cannot be missed.
Disadvantage: Can be costly, especially if the products are numerous, small etc.

Product sampling
Advantage: Usually cost effective, especially if a statistically meaningful sampling method is employed.
Disadvantage: It is always possible for errors to be missed.

Activity 2

Accountants are concerned to keep stocks as low as possible because they are one of the three components of working capital (along with debtors and creditors). When the company has money tied up in stocks, the money cannot be used for any other purpose by the company. This has the effect of reducing the cash available to the accountant at any one time (his cash flow). He will consequently seek to:

❑ reduce the overall stockholding of all kinds of stock;

❑ postpone raw material purchases until the last possible moment;

❑ discourage queuing, both of raw materials and of work in progress;

❑ sell finished goods as soon as they are made;

❑ sell off (often cheaply) any off-specification stocks;

❑ work-off any stocks of any kind that have proven to be unsaleable.

Remember this: accountants hate stocks and love cash!

Assignment

Engonics (Engineering) Limited

At a recent Board meeting of Engonics (Engineering) Limited, the Financial Director, Ken Lowe found himself in the position of identifying the reasons for yet another quarter's poor financial results. "The same old story, I'm afraid." he began, "Profits have declined again this three month period for two reasons. Firstly, we have had a number of key customers switch suppliers because of what they describe as unreliable delivery and poor quality. Secondly, the operations department has had a massive overspend against budget. I don't know how they do it. They cost us a fortune and produce rubbish!" The Operations Director, Dr Paige, became increasingly uncomfortable as Ken continued, "I have noticed with some alarm, our increased stockholding. Raw materials stocks up 5% on this time last year and finished goods up by an inexplicable 12%".

The Managing Director, Alan Dix, tried to calm things down and turned to Dr Paige for his interpretation of the situation. "It's not easy, Alan." began David, "I am aware that stocks cost money, but Ken would be the first to complain if we didn't have enough stocks to complete an important order. Moreover, I try to get the purchaser to order in the most economical quantities, and this occasionally results in relatively high raw materials levels." Before Alan could reply to David Paige, Ken interrupted, "But what about the poor quality Dave? We can't afford to lose customers at any time, and it's nothing to be proud of when they come on the phone and say that they feel our production output is variable and that orders are frequently late."

Alan approached the problem constructively. He asked David Paige what he knew about what he referred to as the "new ideas" of Just in Time and Total Quality Management. David replied that he learned about these philosophies at Business School, but felt unable to implement them at Engonics due to the traditional culture of the workforce. Alan retorted that they had better come up with something to reverse the downward trend in profits and that he (Alan) would fully back David in his efforts to implement JIT and TQM at Engonics. Ken agreed and confirmed that financial resources would be made available to pay for a consultant to advise David on the first steps in this ambitious project.

You are the consultant.

Tasks

At a preliminary meeting, Dr Paige asks you to explain, as simply as possible the following:

1. What the essentials objectives are of JIT and TQM,

2. The features of the two systems as operational philosophies.

3. David is particularly keen to know the ways in which JIT and TQM can help him to reduce his production costs and increase his quality. With reference to the situation in Engonics Ltd, apply the benefits of the two philosophies to the problems in the company.

Complete the assignment in less than 2000 words.

Further Reading

Evans J.R., *Applied Production and Operations Management*, West Publishing Company (Fourth Edition, 1993, Chapter 13 on JIT)
Vonderembse M.A & White G.P., *Operations Management – Concepts, Methods and Strategies*, West Publishing Company (Second Edition, 1991, Chapter 12 on JIT, Chapter 17 on Quality)
Oakland J.S., *Total Quality Management*, Butterworth Heinemann (Second Edition)
Crosby P.B, *Quality is Free*, McGraw Hill

(In addition, there is an excellent booklet available from your local DTI office called 'The Quality Gurus'. It summarises the work of the major writers on quality throughout the world, and is written in a very readable fashion. Best of all, like quality, it is free!)

21 The marketing function 1

Objectives After studying this chapter, students should be able to:

- ❑ define *marketing orientation*;
- ❑ outline the emphases of the marketing philosophy;
- ❑ describe the scope of marketing within an organisation;
- ❑ describe the components of the *marketing mix*;
- ❑ explain the general nature of the product and the ways in which products are sub-divided;
- ❑ analyse a company's product range according to two analytical 'tools'.

Featured Organisation: **Nestlé UK Limited**

21.1 The Marketing Philosophy

21.1.1 The organisational context

Let us begin this discussion by considering two companies. **British Coal** is the UK's major extractor and distributor of coal. **Nestlé UK Limited** is the UK operation of the Swiss based multinational Nestlé SA Group, which has a worldwide turnover of the order of £25 billion. Whereas British Coal is based around the various collieries ('pits') where the coal is extracted, Nestlé UK Limited operates from its head office in Croydon and a number of manufacturing sites around the country, including plants in York and Newcastle upon Tyne.

Nestlé UK Ltd is focused primarily on the food and beverage markets and sells such household brands as Nescafé, Branston, Findus, Kit Kat, Chambourcy, Carnation, Crosse and Blackwell, Buitoni and Friskies Petcare products. The Nestlé SA Group has also diversified into cosmetics with a minority shareholding in L'Oréal and into ophthalmics with the acquisition of Alcon Laboratories.

The two businesses, British Coal and Nestlé UK, obviously differ in many respects. The key difference that we shall consider in this chapter is what we can refer to as their respective philosophies or emphases. Certainly we might expect the two organisations to have quite different cultures (see part 10.1) but the very nature of their trading activities introduces us to a new and important distinction. This is usually referred to as the corporate *emphasis*.

Different companies have different corporate emphases. Some companies are geared up primarily for production, some for service and some for selling. It will depend in large part upon the type of organisation, the nature of the industry and the intensity of competition that exists in their markets. The markets for coal are well established and the level of demand is predictable – the power generators use coal in some power stations and a small percentage of homes have 'solid fuel' heating systems. Nestlé, on the other hand, operates in much more complicated markets. Its various food products appeal to many different types of people and in each of its markets (frozen foods, coffee, petfoods etc.) there are several other powerful competitors. As a result of their respective situations, British Coal can be considered as a *production ori-*

ented organisation and Nestlé as a company which emphasises *marketing*. Both are equally appropriate within their respective contexts.

Production orientation is fundamentally concerned with improving productivity in the organisation's operational areas. This will focus on reducing production costs, increasing output, reducing lead times and other important indicators that we encountered in Chapters 19 and 20. Marketing orientation does not mean that production is unimportant, but that production *follows* rather than *leads* – marketing takes prominence. Implicit within the marketing philosophy is a knowledge of what the customer wants. This involves finding out about a number of aspects of consumers' demand and this is the domain of the marketing research area.

Marketing research

In order for organisations to produce the right product at the right price, they must first research the market and find out the details of the demand. Marketing researchers employ a range of techniques to gather meaningful data. Most of us will have been interviewed on the street by market research people, but this approach forms only a part of the research process as a whole.

Market research is about establishing the size of a market for a product and the characteristics of a product that buyers would find appealing. *Product research* involves testing new concepts upon potential buyers and then testing the actual product before it is launched. The *pricing* of the product is also examined. Marketing researchers will find out how much potential buyers will be prepared to pay for the product. The process also extends to deciding how to *promote* the product and the effectiveness of previous promotional campaigns. Finally, marketing research examines how and where to *sell* or *distribute* the product.

Marketing organisations take marketing research seriously. It is important that products are designed, priced, advertised and distributed correctly and a failure to gather good research data can be very expensive.

Case Study   Marketing research at Nestlé UK Ltd

Nestlé operates a wide range of marketing research activities. Among the most important of these is market research – a continuous analysis and monitoring of the size of its market groupings and the changes in those groups with regard to product preferences. The cost of launching a new product is very high, and this, combined with a reliable estimation that fewer than 1 in 20 new products actually succeeds, emphasises the need for market research to find out what customers are actually demanding.

Nestlé UK employs a number of research channels and techniques to provide the best and most reliable information about their markets. Within the frozen foods markets (where Nestlé markets the Findus brand), market research comprises a constant monitoring of two broad areas: *consumer trends* and *market trends*.

Consumer trends

This is research into the changing preferences of the consumer. There are three areas of particular importance to the Findus marketing people.

Health awareness trends concern how well consumers understand the links between eating and health. The issues surrounding eating to lose weight will be included in this area. *Eating* trends monitor the growth in such things as vegetarian consumption and attitudes to meat. Thirdly, *Lifestyle* trends examine such things as the changing eating patterns away from formal and towards informal ('TV') dinners and the growth of snack and light meal consumption. Also included in the lifestyle trends area are the increasing concerns over environmental issues and changing taste preferences, i.e. the growth or decline in the popularity of ethnic, international and traditional flavours.

From time to time, Nestlé commissions a study of consumer attitudes to new or proposed product changes. This research is often conducted using organised sessions where 6-8 consumers at a time attend for a couple of hours to express their personal views on a range of issues. This format has proved useful in examining consumer opinions on packaging types and designs, new product ideas, advertising etc. In addition to these sessions, Nestlé periodically commissions 'in home' product placement tests. A sample of around 400 homes is selected, and they are supplied with an existing Findus dish together with a dish containing a proposed change to the product. The consumers then supply Nestlé with their honest opinions of the change and the results are used to endorse or reject the proposed change, depending upon the consumers' preferences.

Market trends

Of equal importance to monitoring the changes in consumer tastes is the examination of the changes in the size of the frozen food market as a whole, the activities of competitors and the opportunities and threats offered by Nestlé's primary customers – the large retail companies.

Included in market trends research are such things as:

☐ the size and growth patterns of existing and developing market segments, such as 'recipe dishes' (ready meals like Findus Lean Cuisine), burgers, fish, vegetables etc.;

☐ the number of households in the UK that are likely to consume Findus foods;

☐ the amount of frozen food purchased by different age groups and different socio-demographic groups;

☐ the market shares of the main retailers and their relative growth or decline of market share;

☐ the examination of Findus's major competitors.

Those businesses that produce with specific demand in mind are those which best characterise the marketing philosophy. It does not rely on selling products that nobody wants, but is a business philosophy with one overall objective in mind – to meet the needs and wants of the customer. The obvious success of Nestlé in the UK demonstrates that they are in the latter of the two categories.

21.1.2 What is marketing?

A common misconception of marketing is that it is concerned primarily with the promotion and advertising of a product. Marketing does include this, but it is much more than this.

The British **Chartered Institute of Marketing** defines Marketing as a whole.

Marketing is the management process which identifies, anticipates and supplies customer requirements efficiently and profitably.

We see here a distinct preoccupation with the *customer*. The philosophy is further underlined by prominent management thinker **Peter F Drucker** who said that:

Marketing is not only much broader than selling ...It encompasses the entire business. It is the whole business seen from the point of view of its final result, that is, from the customers' point of view.

(Drucker, The Practice of Management, 1954)

Given Drucker's view on marketing, it seems inappropriate to speak of marketing as a department. In the context of most organisation's actual operation however, the interface with the customer is done primarily through such a department.

21.2 Departmental Structure

Marketing will probably have several sub-divisions within the Marketing department, with different managers responsible for different areas of the marketing function. An example of the typical structure of a Marketing department is shown in figure 21.1.

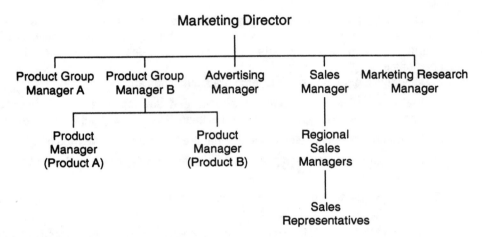

Figure 21.1: Typical marketing department structure

21.3 Introduction to The Marketing Mix

In order to ensure that all aspects of meeting the customer needs 'efficiently and profitably', a simple formula is followed called the *marketing mix*. How organisations emphasise the different components of the mix will depend upon their individual circumstances and the nature of the competition in their sector.

The marketing mix can be seen as the process undertaken when a company introduces a product to a market. It also forms the framework for planning new products and services and how they are going to be marketed. It comprises four essential components – the **four 'Ps'** of marketing.

❑ Product

❑ Place

❑ Price

❑ Promotion

We will consider each in turn.

21.4 The First P – Product

Starting point in marketing is necessarily to ask: *What does the customer want or need to buy?* i.e. what product should be produced. There is an illustrious history of 'white elephants' – products that were developed and launched which proved to have little or no demand (one remembers the infamous Sinclair C5 electric car and the BetaMax video format). More subtle failures are those products for which there is a demand but not in the form in which it is supplied. Perhaps the detail of the product differs in some way from that required by the market rendering it a marketing failure. It is consequently of paramount importance that the product is right.

We have already seen that the concept of 'product' is much wider than tangible 'things'. A service such as dry cleaning is also a product in that it is the output of an enterprise. The principles of product management in the marketing mix are equally applicable to physical products and services.

Product management is concerned with a number of features including size, shape, specification, appearance and performance. Some businesses will also place a great deal of emphasis on packaging and presentation, and this, too is part of the product.

21.4.1 Two dimensions of a product

Marketers see at least two dimensions to the concept of 'product'. **Firstly**, there is the *basic* product. This is the basic car, the washing powder, the tea-bag. The basic product will meet the basic customer need, but marketers add a **second** dimension – product *'augmentation'*. This is the basic product but with something else that serves to *differentiate* it from other competitors. It could be simply a brand name or it might be an innovation, a different packaging concept or a different shape of tea-bag. The purpose is essentially to create a distinctive impression of the product in the mind of the customer. Much of the marketing input into product design is the augmentation of the product in an attempt to introduce a *unique selling point*, or *proposition* (USP) for the product. Generalised examples of augmentation in the consumer goods sector include:

❑ claims of increased performance over competitors. (washing powder, bathroom cleaners);

❑ image of high quality (some retail chains);

❑ strong brand identity (most confectionery and retail food items);

❑ distinctive packaging (chocolates, perfumes, pens);

❑ claims of reliability or longevity (some cars and consumer durables like washing machines);

❑ claims of increased environmental hygiene (cars, cleaning materials);

❑ convenience to use/prepare or simplicity of use;

❑ an image associated with the use of the product (e.g. youth, excitement etc.).

Case Study	**Product/brand properties: Findus Lean Cuisine**

The Nestlé brand, Findus Lean Cuisine was launched in 1985 and pioneered the first low fat/low calorie sector of the frozen recipe dish market in the UK. The brand benefits to the consumer can be categorised into core and augmented (sometimes referred to as generic and premium) features. Consumers perceive a number of core benefits that would be expected from this category of product which include convenience, portion size, the expectation of a complete meal (i.e. no need to add anything else) and similar benefits.

Lean Cuisine commands a higher price than some brands in this sector because of a series of premium benefits. These benefits are threefold; quality, nutrition and image. The quality is achieved by a combination of using the best quality ingredients and culinary expertise in recipe development. The nutritional characteristics are achieved without compromising taste and reflect international guidelines on healthy eating and dietary requirements. The image has been created by the use of aspirational advertising (making advertisements show an image of what consumers would like to be or look like and to then associate this image with the Findus Lean Cuisine brand).

Activity 1   *Can you identify the augmentation features associated with the following types of consumer products?*

Example   Premium or augmentation features of *washing powder* include:

- ❑ 'washing whiter',
- ❑ 'shifting' blood, oil and other 'stubborn stains' from fabrics,
- ❑ environmentally friendly,
- ❑ endorsements from major washing machine manufacturers,
- ❑ concentrated powder means less powder is needed.

Now try these:

- ❑ fabric conditioner,
- ❑ margarine,
- ❑ double glazing,
- ❑ banks and building societies,
- ❑ breakfast cereals,
- ❑ package holidays.

21.4.2 Categories of product

The nature of the product, or output, of a business, will depend on the nature of the organisation. There are two generic types of product:

❑ **Consumer goods**

These are products that are bought by the final user. Once bought, they undergo no further processing – they are 'consumed'. The consumer is not necessarily an individual member of the public, it can be an organisation. The two broad categories of consumer goods are **fast moving consumer goods** (FMCGs) and **consumer durables**. As the names suggest, FMCGs tend to be bought quickly from shops and are consumed relatively quickly. They are bought frequently and will tend to be of low to medium price, such as foods, cleaning materials, magazines etc. Durables are items which are bought infrequently and last longer than FMCGs. Examples of consumer durables are electrical goods such as washing machines, cookers, hi-fi and television systems.

❑ **Industrial goods**

Industrial goods are those products that are used to go into, or support, an operations function. They are used in industrial processes and are usually processed further in order to produce a consumer good.

Each of these types of product can be further subdivided.

Industrial products are rather numerous as industry requires a wide range of products depending on the specific needs of a business. Common examples are:

- ❑ raw materials;
- ❑ parts, spares and accessories;

❑ machines and installations;

❑ consumables;

❑ industrial services.

Figure 21.2 shows how consumer goods are organised.

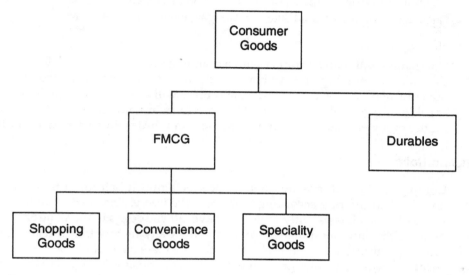

Figure 21.2: Types of consumer goods

Example	Consumer brands at Nestlé

Nestlé markets many well-known brands in the FMCG foods sector. The brand identity of each one is strong and serves to differentiate itself from other products within the market sector in which it operates. Some of the best known are:

Nescafé	Gold Blend	Perrier	Kit Kat	Rolo
Smarties	Polo	Quality Street	Black Magic	Aero
Milky Bar	Lean Cuisine	Findus	Chambourcy	Rowntree's
Coffee Mate	Libby's	Carnation	Go Cat	Friskies
Sarsons	Yorkie	Buitoni	Crosse & Blackwell	Branston
Gales	Waistline	Sun Pat	Nesquick	Alta Rica

21.5 Strategic Issues in Product Management

21.5.1 Product positioning

Product positioning refers to the placing of the product at a certain point in the market. Some products are commodities and are relatively uniform wherever they are sold, but some can be differentiated in an attempt to increase market share among a certain group of customers.

Key concept: differentiation

Product differentiation is the procedure by which a product or service is made different from others in an attempt to attract buyers. It can be achieved in a number of ways. A standard product can be modified, or a new product can be developed specifically for the purpose. It is said that a differentiated product occupies a *niche* market, i.e. one that is a small but productive part of the larger market. Because of the perceived difference that has been generated, a price premium can usually be charged and higher profits made.

Companies will plan a product with a market in mind. We will see later in this section that there are number of ways in which the market can be 'segmented'. Some products are launched into the mass market, and these will tend to be competitively priced and capable of use by the majority. Other products are aimed at smaller markets, either higher or lower quality than the 'standard', and these will be priced accordingly.

21.5.2 Product portfolio

Companies that sell a wide range of products find it helpful in product planning to analyse their offering according to the *portfolio theory*. The wisdom of this theory rests in the idea that it is patently unwise to have 'all your eggs in the same basket'. If a business makes only one range of products, then any factors that threaten sales of that range will threaten the profitability of the business as a whole (and possibly its very survival). Similarly, sales grow in some sectors of business and companies that already have a presence in that sector are already placed to gain from increased sales when they arise. Hence, portfolio is all about spreading the company's opportunity and risk.

At its simplest, this theory suggests that companies that wish to take advantage of increased opportunity and reduced risk should offer several different products into several different markets.

A more formal and detailed model exists that enables businesses to place each product area into a category according to its market share and the growth of the market in question. The Boston Consulting Group portfolio matrix identifies four types of product area. These are as follows:

❑ **Stars**

Products with a high market share in a high growth market. These products, as the name suggests are the ideal for every business. They will generate higher profits with the prospect of increasing profits as the market grows.

❑ **Cash cows**

Products with a high market share in a low growth market. Cash cows are products which have a large amount of investment in them but have little need for continuing investment. They tend to generate reliable and ongoing profit which can be used in other parts of the business (they can be *milked*).

❑ **Question marks (problem children)**

Products in a high growth market but with low market share. Question marks are often relatively new products which have failed to take off. Such products can go either way – with investment, they could grow into stars, but many amount to nothing.

❑ **Dogs**

Products with low market share in a low growth market. Dogs offer little or no prospect of reasonable profit.

The matrix representing the BCG theory is as follows.

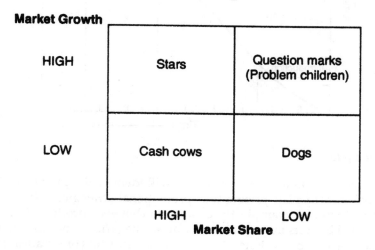

Figure 21.3: The BCG portfolio matrix.

Once a company has identified its products with regard to the BCG matrix, it has can employ a more intelligent approach to product management. The profits from cash cows can be used to invest in the stars and question marks. Question marks tend to be spilt into those worthy of investment and those that should be discontinued. Once a dog has been identified, it is usually divested (sold off).

Strategically, according to the Boston Consulting Group matrix, a company may well try to achieve a balanced portfolio of products across more than one market sector and with varying opportunity and risks associated with each. A 'balanced' portfolio will have a cash cow which can be used as a source of profits, stars which generate high profits and increasing sales, and new products – the question marks.

21.5.3 Product life cycle

When planning product strategies, use is often made of the *product life cycle (PLC)*. The PLC is a good tool for examining where a product is in its 'life-span', and from this, planning decisions can be intelligently made. Figure 21.4 shows the general format of the PLC.

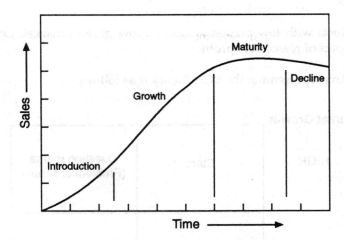

Figure 21.4: Product life cycle

A company making several products will identify the phases for its products. These can be used to plan pricing and promotional strategies. When a product is in the mature phase, for example, the competition between products from different manufacturers will be at its most intense. For most categories of product, the mature phase will be the phase it spends longest in – this might be years or decades. These products tend to be the most heavily advertised and they are sometimes differentiated in an attempt to stimulate a growth spurt in sales. A 'mark 2' product is a common feature of some categories of products, good examples being washing powders and convenience food products (see figure 21.5).

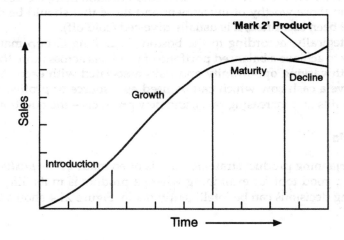

Figure 21.5: Product life cycle, mark 2 product introduction.

| **Activity 2** | *Think of any products that have been relaunched as a 'mark 2' type, and decide if you think that this was a successful marketing strategy.* |

Case Study — Strategic product management at Nestlé

Nestlé operates in many different sectors of the total food and beverage market. Each sector has its own characteristics of growth, maturity etc. and the Nestlé products in those sectors have widely differing market shares.

Whilst these market segments are very different in their individual consumer profiles, the strength and appeal of the various Nestlé brands means that the same brand may participate successfully in more than one part of the market. A good example of this is Milky Bar.

Traditionally, Milky Bar, the white chocolate brand, was found in the confectionery market. However, it has now been launched as a 180 ml white chocolate drink in the RTD (ready to drink) soft drinks market. The same brand has also been successfully launched as an individual white chocolate dessert within the chilled dessert market. Each of these introductions remains faithful to the core brand properties of the parent Milky Bar confectionery product (i.e. taste profile, packaging design and the signals the brand communicates to consumers).

The use of one brand in more than one market sector is referred to by marketers as *brand stretching*. The brand stretching of Milky Bar has enabled Nestlé to capitalise on the consumer appeal of the brand by enabling consumers to enjoy the brand benefits in a variety of forms and for the satisfaction of different needs. For Nestlé, it represents a more cost effective investment compared to the alternative, which is to introduce a completely new brand.

Review Questions

1. What is marketing research? (21.1)
2. Briefly distinguish between a *production oriented* and a *marketing oriented* organisation. (21.1)
3. List the components of the marketing mix. (21.3)
4. Define the terms *core product* and *augmented product*. (21.4.1)
5. What is a USP? (21.4.1)
6. What are the two broad categories of product? (21.4.2)
7. What is product positioning? (21.5.1)
8. What are the reasons for companies holding a portfolio of products? (21.5.2)
9. What are the components of the BCG matrix and what does each one mean? (21.5.2)
10. Why is it important to project a product's life cycle? (21.5.3)

Assignment

Choose an organisation with which you are familiar or into which you can gain access. Report on the following:

1. The nature of the product or service the organisation provides;

2. The way in which the organisation divides up its total offering into groups (if appropriate).

3. The relative growths of the markets in its various product areas.

4.   The market shares of its key products.

Then:

5.   Identify the relevant stage on the PLC for each of the organisation's products (or product areas).

6.   Attempt to construct a BCG portfolio for the organisation's products.

If you have difficulty finding an appropriate organisation you could base your study on the university or college where you are studying. Its products might include standard courses, consultancy services, providing short courses to industry etc.

Further Reading

Lancaster, G. & Massingham, L., *Essentials of Marketing*, McGraw Hill Publishers.
Cannon T., *Basic Marketing (Principles and Practice)*, Cassell Publishers (Third Edition)
Oliver G., *Marketing Today*, Prentice Hall (Third Edition, 1992)
Morden A.R., *Elements of Marketing*, DP Publications
Kotler, P., *Marketing Management*, Prentice Hall (Eighth Edition, 1994)
Articles in Journals:
Levitt T., '*Marketing Myopia*', Harvard Business Review, 18(1), July 1960.
Levitt T., '*Exploit the product life cycle*', Harvard Business Review, Nov – Dec 1965

22 The marketing function 2 Place, price and promotion

Objectives After studying this chapter, students should be able to:

- ❏ explain the purpose and uses of pricing, and the marketers approach to it;
- ❏ understand how markets are segmented and how the business uses market segmentation;
- ❏ explain the components of the business's marketing communications tools and outline the value and place of each.

Featured Organisation: **Nestlé UK Limited**

22.1 The Second P – Place

The 'place' component of the marketing mix refers to the target market for the product. The very philosophy of modern marketing says that the business must find out what the customer requires before it designs the product. It follows from this that it will also have a good idea of the customer type that the product will be aimed at. The word used by marketers to describe a part of the total market with a certain type of customer is a *segment*. The use of the term *place* in no way implies that the business will sell its product in a particular physical location.

22.1.1 Market segmentation

The extent and nature of market segmentation varies widely across the business sector. Some organisations exist only to supply one small market segment and others, particularly the large industrial conglomerates will supply hundreds of different segments. It is generally true that any one product will have a specific target market at which it will be aimed, and the *scope* of the segment can very enormously.

Case Studies **Marketing scope**

Some organisations have a very wide marketing scope whilst others are extremely narrow. Let us look at the two extremes.

General Motors is a US based company and is the largest motor manufacturer in the world. It makes a huge range of vehicles including a leading model in each of the car segments as well as a full range of commercial and freight carrying motors. It owns subsidiaries or has a powerful presence in every country in the developed world and many others beside. In the UK, its cars are called Vauxhall; in Europe, Opel and other countries have their own GM 'brand'. Its marketing scope extends not just in its very wide product offering, but also to the enormous geographical area over which it operates.

Linton Street is a terraced residential street in Carlisle in the far north-west corner of England. One of the houses has been converted into a traditional **fish and chip shop**. The shop offers the usual range of hot food products of a chip shop – i.e. a narrow product scope. In addition to the narrow product offering, its geographical coverage is literally just a few streets in the Linton Street area of Carlisle.

Both are business organisations, but with very different marketing scopes.

There are any number of ways that the total market can be segmented. Put simply, a segment is a part of the market which contains individuals with particular buying characteristics. Examples are best demonstrated by considering the consumer products market.

22.1.2 Bases for segmentation

Decisions about which market segment to aim a product are often bases are based upon demographic variables – features of a segment resulting from people's individual circumstances or characteristics. The most commonly used variables are discussed below.

❑ **Age**

Many products are aimed at a certain age group. Obviously toys are aimed at children and products like magazines are clearly designed for people of specific ages (compare the different markets for *Home and Garden* and *Viz*). It is most common to combine age with another segmentation base such as special interest or socio-economic group (see below).

❑ **Sex**

Obvious examples of sex segmented products are clothes, shavers, after shave, hygiene products and magazines. Others are less obvious such as drinks and tobacco brands, which are sometimes seen as products predominantly used by one sex.

Activity 1   *List five products that are predominantly aimed at men and five at women. The products should not be obvious ones like after shave and feminine hygiene products. Here are two examples to start you off.*

Men: Bitter Beer and Real Ale (e.g. John Smith's Bitter)
Women: Fabric Washing Powder (e.g. Daz)

❑ **Family circumstances**

Products for the home, cars, food products etc. are often segmented either by family size or the stage of family life cycle. It is self-evident that young married couples will have different buying inclinations to a those of retired couple, who in turn will have different needs to middle aged married couples with three young children. It might be assumed, for example, that young married couples without children, who both work, will have more disposable income for leisure pursuits that the large family with one income. A married couple with no children might decide to spend their holiday at a hotel skiing in Switzerland, whereas the family with three young children might be more inclined to hire a caravan in Dorset.

❑ **Socio-economic groups (income groups)**

This method of segmentation divides up the population according to the type of job they hold. The assumption made by this division is that the separate segments will have, generally speaking, comparable interests and disposable incomes. It is also used by political parties as, it is assumed, each group will have roughly similar voting patterns.

Socio-economic groupings

A   senior managerial, senior administrative, 'true' professionals (accountants, lawyers, doctors), inheritors of wealth.

B   intermediate (mid) management and administrative, other professionals.

C1 supervisory, junior managerial, clerical, some professionals.

C2 skilled manual workers (electricians, plumbers and other tradesmen)

D   unskilled and semi skilled manual workers (factory operatives, labourers).

E   unemployed, state pensioners, low grade workers, casual workers.

❏ **Type of residence/neighbourhood**

According to this line of segmentation it is argued that much can be said about buying inclinations from looking at the type of neighbourhood consumers live in. At the two extremes, one might say that the 'landed gentry' will have different buying practices to those of residents in an inner city high rise council block. The accepted way of segmenting according to this basis is known as ACORN (*A Classification of Residential Neighbourhoods*). The most established ACORN classifications are shown below.

ACORN classification groups

A   Agricultural areas

B   Modern family housing, higher income

C   Older housing of intermediate status

D   Poor quality older terraced housing

E   Better-off council estates

F   Less well-off council estates

G   Poorest council estates

H   Multi racial areas

I   High status non-family areas

J   Affluent suburban housing

K   Better-off retirement areas

❏ **Education**

The formal education that individuals have undergone will often have a bearing on their tastes in purchasing. Perhaps the most common example is the daily newspaper. The 'broadsheets' are principally aimed at the educated and the 'informed', and the tabloids, predominantly the popular reader. This is reflected in the editorial style and the usage of grammar in the papers. The same idea also extends to types of music, books and other products that may require some prior understanding if they are to be fully utilised.

22.1.3 Using market segmentation

Companies will use the various bases in a variety of ways. It would make sense, for example for a supermarket aimed at the C2/D/E to locate in an area predominantly populated by such groups. Combining the bases to arrive at a more precise definition of the company's segment is also common. Some magazines, for example, are aimed at Female A/B over 50 years, whilst others products might be aimed at young mothers A/B/C1. Such targeting has implications for the way in which products are advertised and also where and when the adverts appear. We shall look at this in more depth when we consider marketing communications later in this chapter.

Case Study	Market segmentation of Nestlé products
	A great deal of thought goes into how markets are segmented for Nestlé products. The use of a segmentation technique (for example the use of demographic variables) is valuable if it enables the company to identify the motivating factors that drive a 'set' of customers to buy.
	For Lean Cuisine, Nestlé has identified a customer profile of female ABC1, 25 to 45 years old. In addition, the product is appropriate for anybody who is on a diet, and with up to 40% of the UK population on a diet at any one time, the potential market is substantial.
	A more complicated segmentation occurs in Nestlé's approach to the marketing of pet-foods. In this sector, the segment boundaries can be identified according to the degree of emotional attachment that the purchaser has to the animal (in the case of Nestlé, to the cat). The emotional attachment can range from the cat being treated like a child and a member of the family, to the other extreme where the cat is merely tolerated with a fixed financial value placed upon its welfare. The purchaser's attitude towards the pet cat will determine the price and quality of the catfood that is purchased. As a result of this, the market can be segmented along five distinct product types: economy, mid-range, sub-premium, premium and super-premium. The marketing people at Nestlé use this method of segmentation method to place their Friskies catfood brand.

In addition to using demographic features as a basis for where and to whom to sell the product, a company will consider some wider issues. Some markets, including geographical areas will grow at different rates to others, and will have different levels of demand. Allied to this is the markets' ability to buy and the prices that can be achieved in those markets. These are strategic issues and one can apply the market push/market pull arguments here that we encountered in Chapter 17.

Activity 2	Which market segments do you think the following products/shops are aimed at?
	Mothercare
	Marks and Spencer
	Netto (cash only budget supermarkets)
	The Ford Escort
	Ariel Ultra Dishwasher powder
	Alta Rica instant coffee
	Barbi dolls
	The Sun newspaper

22.2 The Third P – Price

The price set for a product will depend upon several considerations. It is highly dependent on and interlinked with the nature of the product specification and the target market at which it is aimed.

22.2.1 The purpose of the price

We can recall from our consideration of turnover (or revenue) in Chapter 18 that it is the sum of all the prices charged over the course of a financial year. As the company has many costs associated with making, distributing and selling a product, it follows that the recovery of these costs must be the primary function of the price. In addition though, 'for profit' organisations will also seek to charge a price in excess of the costs in order to generate a profit (profit = revenue – costs).

Price has other purposes in addition to this. Among the most significant is that price gives a signal as to the quality of the product and will consequently attract the buyers identified in the 'place' considerations of the marketing mix. The 'cash only' supermarkets for example, have low prices due to their cost structure, but the low prices also serve to attract their target market. Similarly, a 'high class' restaurant will attract customers' attention in the first instance simply by being expensive.

22.2.2 Pricing decisions

In order to arrive at the price to charge for a product, the business will consider a number of factors. Accountants, economists and marketers have differing ideas of how prices should be arrived at.

The simplest pricing model is *cost plus*. This is where (usually) the accountant will calculate the total cost the product has incurred, including its share of overheads, and then add on a profit figure. This has the advantage that the business can know throughout the financial period the profit amounts it is generating. The disadvantages include the fact that it effectively ignores market conditions and it is quite possible that by using a fixed mark-up on goods, the company will either *under* or *over* price its products. This will have the effect of the company failing to optimise its profits. Many businesses still use this model, but many have turned to a more market oriented pricing formula.

The marketing philosophy sees the cost plus model as inadequate. Instead it asks questions like:

☐ what is the maximum price that the market will bear for this product?

☐ at what price will we maximise our total profits through the sale of this product (often over the longer term)?

☐ what price will generate the maximum *long-term* profits?

☐ what price would be competitive in the marketplace? (what do competitors charge for comparable products?)

Whilst this approach seems eminently sensible, it becomes quickly apparent that much research is needed to gather the information on the market. This is part of the domain of the Marketing Research Manager. There are many pricing strategies that a company can adopt within the market oriented approach, for example to provide introductory offers on new products.

In retailing, a common pricing manoeuvre is the **loss leader**. This is when a particular good is advertised at what will be perceived by the market as cheap (or good value). Arriving at this price may mean that the shop will have to sell it at a loss, hence the term loss leader. The success of this approach relies upon the belief that once in the shop, customers will be tempted to buy other goods at increased profit margins, which will recover the losses incurred in the loss leader.

The two extremes of product pricing are the upper and lower limits that can be charged for the product. Usually, the lower limit will be the cost of the product (except in the case of a loss leader). The upper limit will be the maximum price a customer will pay for it. It is likely that in order to ensure a continuous flow of sales, the actual price will be below the upper limit (see figure 22.1).

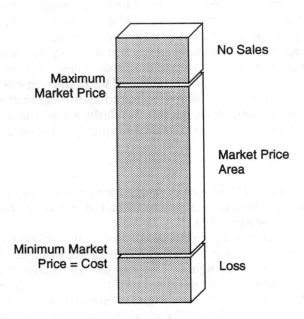

Figure 22.1: Pricing limits

22.3 The Fourth P – Promotion

The area of 'promotion' is more accurately termed *marketing communications* as it involves the communication of aspects of the organisation or the product, or both, to the market. We are all familiar with television commercials and glossy magazine advertisements, but these in fact form only a part of the marketing communications area.

The purposes of communications can also be wider than simply promoting a single product. They can be designed to inform, to remind, to educate (about the product and its use) to give a favourable image, to encourage brand loyalty and other things. Because of the variety of objectives of communication the business employs a number of techniques. These can be summarised in the following:

❑ 'above-the-line' promotions;

❑ 'below-the-line' promotions;

❑ direct selling;

❑ public relations.

22.3.1 'Above-the-line' promotions

The principal 'above-the-line' communication is direct advertising. This can take a number of forms and appear in several formats. The place chosen for the advert will depend upon the target market.

Advertising formats

- ❏ Commercial television
- ❏ Commercial radio
- ❏ Magazines and newspapers
- ❏ Buses and other transport
- ❏ Posters
- ❏ Leaflets and handouts

Because advertising tends to be expensive, it is targeted according to the market segment identified. This means that much thought goes into considering the type of customer the business wishes to reach and the messages they want to convey. The advert will then be placed in the media which will reach the market segment in the most cost beneficial way. Hence, trade suppliers of say, raw materials for the plastic industry, will principally make use of the plastic industry 'trade press'. The format of the advert will also take into account the type of interest the customer has, by, in the case of plastics, conveying mainly the technical benefits of the product.

Mass media advertising (television, radio and national press) is a big business in itself. Advertisers will buy time on in the television in order to reach their target audience. The assumption is made that viewers of a certain type of programme will represent, by and large, a certain demographic profile, and this can be made use of by advertisers.

Activity 3   *Choose a programme on commercial television and try to characterise the type of person that might watch it (such as young married couples, sports fans, children etc.). Generate a list of products that such a person might have a particular interest in. Watch the programme's commercial breaks and see how many of the products you thought of are advertised in them.*

The message the advertisement carries is oriented to the viewpoint of the customer. It will communicate the *benefits* that the customer can enjoy from the product or the desirable aspects of ownership. It is always easier to advertise a product that is in some way differentiated in that its uniqueness can be promoted. It is not uncommon for advertisers to make use of an *apparent differentiation strategy* in advertising where claims are made for products as if it were the only product with those particular characteristics. Alternatively, manufacturers with comparable products will place different emphases in advertising essentially similar products, thus achieving an apparent differentiation through innovative advertising messages.

There is a fascinating history of innovation in advertising and any number of case studies where products have been brought to public attention through the use of a successful slogan or similar 'symbol'. As a method of marketing communication, it is most appropriate in sectors which are competitive. This means that the companies who supply the market are each trying to increase their market share at the expense of the other competitors. Hence, for a market with a fairly consistent demand such as washing powder/liquid, the competitors advertise heavily in order to encourage customers to switch brands, and then once switched, to remain faithful to it.

22.3.2 'Below-the-line' promotions

Below-the-line is a term used to describe promotional drives which are used to gain customers through a less direct message than that expressed in advertising. They are often used in conjunction with above line, and in recent years, have grown in usage, especially in the retail sector. They can be conveniently divided into two factors; *'pull'* factors which are aimed at the customer, and *'push'* factors, which are incentives for salespeople.

The advantage of below-the-line promotions is that they can be targeted to provide incentives to buy (or sell) particular products or product areas. The reasons for identifying such a product might be that it has a higher profit attached to it or that it may be a new product that the business wishes to begin selling.

'Pull' factors commonly used under this type of promotion include:

❑ short-term price reductions (e.g. a loss leader);

❑ credit terms (either lower interest rates, longer credit periods or both);

❑ 'buy one get one free' offers;

❑ coupons and trading stamps;

❑ guarantees (or, more particularly, extended guarantees);

❑ point of sale displays;

❑ sponsorship of sporting occasions and the like.

Readers will realise that these are a continual feature of some sectors of the retail market. One of the best examples is petrol, where garages that *do not* give coupons or 'points' are in the vast minority.

'Push' factors are those things which encourage sales staff to sell or trade distributors to buy to resell. These can be either to generally increase sales, or to increase sales of some products. Examples are:

❑ commission for sales staff;

❑ favourable purchase conditions for staff;

❑ 'best salesman of the year' prize;

❑ increased dealer margins;

❑ demonstrations, exhibitions, training etc.

The costs of below line promotions should not be underestimated. In some businesses, they will represent a greater cost than above line, and for this reason they are targeted in the same way as advertisements. This is to ensure that the company concentrates on its areas of strategic interest.

Case Study   **Findus Lean Cuisine: marketing promotions**

The promotion of Lean Cuisine rests upon the market segmentation profile identified for it, that is; female, ABC1, 25 to 45 years. Communications are designed to gain as much coverage with this segment for the minimum cost. It is assumed that this segment contains the highest concentration of individuals who wish to reduce or maintain body weight and introduce healthy alternatives into their diet.

TV advertising has historically been used by the brand to communicate the brand's premium benefits of quality, taste and nutrition, in addition to the core benefits of convenience, portion size etc. The overriding objective of TV advertising is to have consumers purchasing higher levels of the product. This can be achieved either by increasing the weight of purchase by existing (loyal) users or by increasing the total number of people consuming the product.

Assuming the content of the commercial is compelling to the target segment, an effective campaign will balance 'coverage' (the number of consumers seeing the commercial) and 'frequency' (the number of times the commercial is seen by the consumer). For example, Findus Lean Cuisine advertising has been placed in commercial breaks of programmes like The Bill, Coronation Street, London's Burning and Brookside which have high mass market audience figures. The advantage of these programmes is that they have the potential of very high coverage among consumers. However, for Findus Lean Cuisine which is targeted at a specific segment, the danger is that whilst the total coverage is high for the target market, the advert is also being seen by a significant percentage of people who are not in the target group and who are therefore not interested in buying the product. Over-reliance on high coverage advertising is consequently expensive and is often an inefficient strategy to achieve coverage and frequency objectives.

In order to balance the campaign, the adverts will be placed into programmes which may have lower overall audience figures, but a higher concentration of consumers in the target segment. Because advertising costs are roughly proportional to audience figures, placing adverts in more specialised programmes will often represent a more cost effective strategy to gain high frequency exposure to the target segment.

TV advertising is only one tool used to communicate the benefits of Findus Lean Cuisine. The budget for this media is usually around £1 million for the brand, and other media are used in conjunction with TV to gain the maximum impact. Advertising in slimming and health magazines allows a closer targeting of the consumers who are likely to buy the product. The attraction of magazine advertising is underlined by its relatively cheap cost. An effective campaign in this media can be less than £100 000.

Brand loyalty is fundamental to the long-term success of Lean Cuisine (as indeed it is for any brand). Below the line activities like sales promotions and direct mailing are utilised by Findus Lean Cuisine to reward consumer loyalty amongst heavy users and to encourage lighter users to increase their average weight of purchase. Consumers have been invited to collect tokens and proofs of purchase for a variety of valuable rewards such as money off holidays, weekend breaks at health farms and fitness accessories.

Activity 4 Consider the consumer profile of female, ABC1, 25–45 years, list some television programmes (on commercial TV) and some magazines that might be good placement targets for Findus Lean Cuisine adverts.

22.3.3 Direct selling

The emphasis upon this type of promotion will depend upon the nature of the product and the extent of support from other promotional activities. The phrase 'this product sells itself' may be a little glib, but approximates to the truth for some well advertised products. For most industrial products, a selling operation will usually be installed and this can be done through a number of methods. They all involve a *person to person* direct communication where the benefits of the products are explained.

❑ Shops employing salespeople (as opposed to check-outs)

❑ Trade counters

❑ Showrooms

❑ Travelling sales representatives (reps) – known by a number of job titles

It is important that selling is seen in the context of marketing communications as a whole, and not as an unsupported 'stand alone' function. Sales works best when adverts have been placed in the appropriate press or other media so that the salesperson is not going in completely 'cold'. Below line support is also helpful if discounts etc. can be offered.

22.3.4 The selling process

Much has been said and written about the mechanisms of selling. The simplest model is the so-called AIDA approach. According to AIDA there are four identifiable stages in the process.

❏ **A Attention**

Gaining the potential buyer's attention is clearly the opening stage. It can be achieved through such things as adverts, displays, telephone calls, recommendations, and a whole range of 'needs identification' statements.

❏ **I Interest**

Interest is the stage at which attention is developed. It involves stimulation of the buyer's appetite for the product, usually be means of a sales presentation. Sales aids and demonstrations may be used in order to arouse the buyer's interest.

❏ **D Desire**

In order for a sale to take place, the buyer must reach a point where his objections are overcome. This occurs in this stage. The salesperson will have capitalised on the customer's interest and focused this to the point where the product is desired. The customer must be assured that the product will meet the need or want or otherwise satisfy the specification as required.

❏ **A Action**

Action occurs when the customer is fully convinced and a sale actually takes place. 'closing the sale' is a much prized skill among salespeople, and looking for 'buying signals' from customers is an essential part of every sales training course. The order is taken and the product is sold.

Any model of this type is necessarily simplified and the stages can be of varying length and significance. Some sales occur after a 'hard selling' process where the sales person engages complex techniques in order to gain *interest*. Other customers who will have researched the market, will have gone straight to the *action* stage before they meet up with the salesman (who then simply takes the order). Industrial users who take repeat orders of a certain raw material will be in the latter category, as will 'brand loyal' retail customers.

22.3.5 Public relations (PR)

We saw in Chapter 2 that an organisation will have many stakeholders. These are groups or individuals who have an interest in the affairs of the organisation. There are many reasons why the organisation will wish to maintain a good image with these people.

Reasons for PR

To encourage investors to buy shares in the company
To gain a reputation for quality, service etc. among customers
To counter suspicion about their activities, e.g. pollution or environmental issues
To encourage good people to apply for jobs
To placate and please pressure groups and other 'opinion leaders'
And many others ...

PR refers to the marketing communications of the company as a whole to the population as a whole. It is thus less focused that other communications. It is believed that by maintaining a good public image, other trading activities will be smoothed and encouraged – no organisations carry out PR for purely altruistic reasons.

Techniques for PR are well established, and again, can be expensive. Among the most popular are:

- ❐ 'roadshows' to local schools, community groups etc.
- ❐ open days
- ❐ visitor centres
- ❐ press statements
- ❐ sections of the corporate report
- ❐ charitable donations and community projects
- ❐ videos
- ❐ sponsorship of football teams, events etc.

Case study   **Sellafield Visitor Centre**

Since British Nuclear Fuels Ltd (BNFL) opened Calder Hall nuclear power station and the adjoining Sellafield reprocessing plant near Whitehaven, West Cumbria in 1956, it has been a source of controversy. Environmental groups campaigned against it on the grounds of the pollution and waste disposal issues, and local people, whilst enjoying the jobs it provided, were concerned about the health risks. Politicians argued about the costs of nuclear energy as compared to other forms of fuel. In response to this suspicion the Chairman said in 1986 'I regard the restoration of public confidence as the most important single task facing me and the rest of the BNFL team today'. After a series of minor 'radiation leaks' and the bad press for nuclear power following the Chernobyl explosion, the management decided a public relations exercise was in order.

In June 1988, at a cost of £5 million, a 'visitor centre' was opened on site, 'open every day except Christmas Day'. It contains demonstrations, displays etc. in an attempt to convince the public of the value and merits of nuclear energy. This has been reinforced by a national television advertising campaign. A wide range of literature is made available to visitors and in addition to the visitor centre, the organisation also encourages the public to take part in their guided tours of the plants themselves. Every year since the centre opened, well in excess of 100 000 people have visited the centre. The visitors figure peaked in 1992 with 161 000 people visiting the centre.

Activity 5   Suggest reasons why BNFL would place such an emphasis on 'public confidence' to undertake such an elaborate PR exercise.

Review Questions

1. What is meant by market segmentation? (22.1.1)
2. What are the most common segmentation bases for consumer goods? (22.1.2)
3. What is the purpose of the price of a good or service? (22.2.1)
4. How does a marketing manager approach the pricing of a product? (22.2.2)
5. What is a *loss leader*? (22.2.2)
6. What are the four forms of marketing communication? (22.3)
7. Define and distinguish between *above-the-line* and *below-the-line* promotions. (22.3.1 and 22.3.2)
8. Describe one useful model of the selling process. (22.3.3)
9. What are the purposes of public relations? (22.3.4)

Answers to Activities

Activity 1

All market segmentation is generalised. Some products will be predominantly aimed at one sex, but may be purchased by both. They tend to rely on typical stereotypes of male and female inclinations. Some examples might include the following:

Men	**Women**
DIY materials and equipment	Small 'supermini' cars
Cigars	Some brands of cigarette
Motorcycles	Some liqueur brands
Hand rolling tobacco	Kitchens

Activity 5

Given the Chairman's statement, the investment in the visitor centre was clearly designed to help towards restoring public confidence in the whole idea or nuclear energy. The need for such a restoration of public confidence may be due to some of the following factors:

❏ Maintaining the jobs of the many thousands of people employed in the nuclear industry. This is especially true in West Cumbria where unemployment is relatively high.

❏ Strategically, the Government may wish to maintain its energy 'portfolio' by having nuclear energy in addition to coal and other fuels.

❏ The fact that uranium is so much more plentiful than gas and coal. In the medium to long term, the Government, who owns BNFL, believes that its nuclear interests must be maintained. This necessarily means that the public must have a broad sympathy with it.

Assignment

'Marketing is not really an important part of business. Where it is useful is in advertising and coming up with natty ideas for packaging.'

Discuss the above view, and propose a more realistic approach to the role of marketing in a business organisation.

Word limit: 1500 words.

Further Reading

Lancaster G. & Massingham L., *Essentials of Marketing*, McGraw Hill Publishers.
Cannon T., *Basic Marketing (Principles and Practice)*, Cassell Publishers (Third Edition)
Oliver G., *Marketing Today*, Prentice Hall (Third Edition, 1992)
Morden A.R., *Elements of Marketing*, DP Publications
Kotler, P., *Marketing Management*, Prentice Hall (Eighth Edition, 1994)

23 The research and development function

Objectives
After studying this chapter, students should be able to:

❑ explain why R & D is essential to a business organisation;

❑ describe the classes and types of personnel employed in R & D;

❑ understand the roles of the various components of the technical work of a company;

❑ explain the function of the various parts of the technical function within the wider context of the organisation as a whole.

Featured Organisation: **Schering Agrochemicals Limited (SAL)**

23.1 Introduction to R & D

Every organisation must review its products, if not continually, then certainly at regular intervals if it hopes to remain competitive. Different companies place a different emphasis on this function. At one extreme are the large pharmaceutical companies that employ hundreds or thousands of chemists, biochemists and engineers, and at the other is the small engineering company that has an *engineer-cum-designer* who might spend one day a month in development. The purposes of the function are the same for both.

Case Study	Research and development at Schering Agrochemicals Ltd

Schering Agrochemicals Limited is a wholly-owned subsidiary of the Schering AG Group – manufacturers of a wide range of chemical products. The organisation, which was founded in 1851, is based in West Berlin, Germany. There are over 130 companies in the worldwide Schering Group and employees number over 24 000. Their business interests are divided into two main areas: pharmaceuticals (drugs) and agrochemicals. They have minor interests in industrial chemicals.

Schering Group have a number of operations based in the UK. Their British agrochemicals company is based around Cambridge and comprises two separate sites. The Hauxton site is responsible for the production and marketing of agrochemicals and their Chesterford Park site, near Saffron Walden, carries out research and development. The UK agrochemicals business employs 1 600 people of whom 450 work in R & D.

Of the 450 at Chesterford Park, 350 are directly involved in R & D whilst 100 are engaged in support administration and servicing – by any standards a sizeable R & D function. Their achievements, as well as making a key contribution to the success of the company, have been recognised in recent years by two Queens Award for Technology – in 1977 and 1984.

23.2 Objectives of R & D

Research and development (or the technical department) is an expensive but necessary part of the business, particularly in industry. In consequence, the projects undertaken are carefully selected, and the image of the 'mad professor' or the 'boffin' is far from the true picture. R & D forms an intrinsic part of a companies strategy and in effective companies, all products developed will be those identified by careful market research, so as to avoid wasting resources on developing unwanted products.

The purposes of R & D in a general sense include:

❏ increasing knowledge about the materials, processes etc. that the company utilises;

❏ testing and evaluating new materials;

❏ developing new products;

❏ modifying existing products,

    for quality improvement;

    for performance improvement;

    for cost reduction;

    to more closely match customer requirements;

❏ to improve manufacturing processes and increase efficiency.

The incentive behind R & D is simply that if there is none, there will be no new products or improvements to existing products or processes. This will result in stagnation and a loss of competitive advantage in the sector in which the company competes. The converse of this argument is that the company that is adroit in this area will achieve much from R & D. There are many good examples of companies that have generated competitive advantage from breakthroughs in the laboratory.

Objectives of R & D at SAL

Agrochemicals are synthetic (man made) products which are used to protect agricultural crops from pests and fungi which would reduce their growth and productivity. The competitive pressures and customer demands for greater product yields have meant that Chesterford Park has assumed great strategic importance in the company. It is concerned both with the search for new (novel) technologies and products and with the improvement of existing ones. In addition, the staff carry out research into new processes which will aid the production of the chemicals.

23.3 R & D Personnel

R & D tends to employ individuals from technical backgrounds. It follows that these people will tend to be among the most 'specialised' in terms of their skills, in the organisation. The particular specialists the company uses will vary according to the emphasis of the organisation, but the Technical Director will usually head up a team of scientists or engineers or both.

Type of company	Predominant R & D personnel
Chemicals	chemists, chemical engineers, engineers
Pharmaceuticals	chemists, pharmacologists, biochemists, biologists, engineers
Electronics	electronic engineers, physicists
Engineering	mechanical and electronic engineers, physicists
Food	chemists, biochemists, biologists, micro-biologists
Computing	software engineers, computer scientists, electronic engineers.
Oil/Petrochemicals	chemical, electrical and mechanical engineers, geologists, chemists

R & D departments employ a number of classes of staff. The Technical Director (or Technical Manager) will usually be a qualified scientist or engineer and he will oversee the following (usually in hierarchical order).

23.3.1 Scientists/engineers

This category of personnel will usually be graduates with a BSc degree or higher (such as a PhD) in their relevant discipline. Their training will enable them to work on projects with minimal supervision and they will 'get on' with a task and report back to the Department head when a conclusion has been arrived at. They may work alone or with a small team. Many technical professionals belong to one of a number of chartered or instituted bodies that qualify graduates who have also satisfied other professional criteria. Organisations such as the *Royal Society of Chemistry* (RSC), the *Institute of Electronic Engineers* (IEE) the *Institute of Biology* (IBiol) and others offer such an accreditation.

23.3.2 Technicians

Technicians will usually hold a scientific qualification, typically at BTEC National or Higher National level. Their responsibilities will include assisting the scientists and working with occasional supervision on their own projects.

23.3.3 Assistants

There are many tasks in R & D that are essential but do not require special scientific expertise. These may include keeping records, preparing apparatus, making up samples etc. Laboratory assistants will be qualified to GCSE level or higher and will work under a scientist or technician.

Case Study   R & D Personnel at SAL

As with all R & D functions, the types of personnel employed depend on the nature of the work and products. R & D at Schering Agrochemicals centres around three scientific areas: biology, chemistry and the discipline which falls between the two – biochemistry.

Whilst many of these personnel are professional graduates in these subjects others are at technician grade. There are also specialists within these subjects, such as plant and molecular biologists, synthetic organic chemists, and those chemists and biochemists who specialise in computer modelling of chemical molecules. All of these activities are co-ordinated by senior scientists and scientific managers in order to make sure that all necessary parts of the R & D process are carried out correctly and on time.

23.4 R & D Timescales

Technical work is often divided up according to the amount of time that any given project will be expected to take. Some laboratory projects will take just a few days whilst others will be on-going for ten years or more. Both extremes are an important part of the company's commitment to innovation and investing in the 'products of tomorrow', and neither category is 'better' or more valid than the other. Figure 23.1 shows how work fits into these timescales.

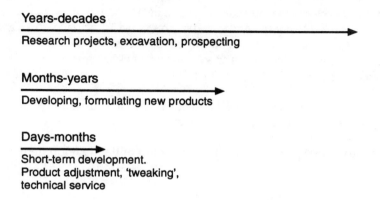

Years-decades

Research projects, excavation, prospecting

Months-years

Developing, formulating new products

Days-months

Short-term development.
Product adjustment, 'tweaking',
technical service

Figure 23.1: Time-scales in research and development.

In large companies, there will be separate departments for each of the timescales but in smaller ones, staff may 'take turns' in each area. We will briefly consider each area in turn.

23.5 Components of R & D

23.5.1 Research

Some projects involve ensuring the company has viable products and processes in the long term. In the oil industry, new oil fields must be located, test drilled etc. and this can take a number of years. Pharmaceutical companies are constantly working on improving their knowledge of the way the body works in order to make more effective drugs. These types of project tend to be on-going and continuous.

Research staff keep abreast of their respective scientific fields in order that any new developments can be considered for use by the company. They will usually read the 'scientific journals' and some may work in collaboration with universities.

Research and long-term programmes are often criticised for being costly and for not addressing the real needs of the business in its current circumstances. Other criticisms arise when the department follows a certain line of questioning or research for some time and then finds at the end that it is not viable or does not work, but this is, after all, the purpose of research – to see if new ideas are viable. Whilst it is true that research should be carefully managed, the role of these 'back room' (often literally) people should not be underestimated. All modern technology at one time began life with a researcher and some products we take for granted today are the result of years and decades of evolution.

Research into everyday products – antibiotics

In the latter half of the twentieth century, there are many illnesses which we see as minor inconveniences which our great grandfathers would fear as life threatening. Bacterial infections like pneumonia, bacterial meningitis and septicaemia can be treated quickly and totally by the use of an antibiotic like penicillin. The action of the drug was first discovered by **Alexander Fleming,** a research biologist, working in 1928. It was to be many more years before later scientists would make it into a commonly usable drug. In the middle years of the twentieth century, two research molecular biologists working in Cambridge, **Watson** and **Crick,** discovered the molecular structure of DNA in human cells, and this was the next big step which led to our understanding of how penicillin actually works at the molecular level. As a result of these two research successes, modern scientists can make modern strains of penicillin to attack the DNA of specific bacteria cells in order to achieve optimal results when treating a patient with a certain illness.

It is rare that a research project comes up with a 'finished product'. It is by nature more concerned with the conceptual, the exploratory and the principles behind things. The product of successful research is an idea, a raw material or similar that be further *developed* into a final product. This is the domain of the development people.

23.5.2 Development

The development department can be one of the busiest in the company. It will usually have formalised links with a number of other parts of the company and is concerned with taking the ideas or intermediates that research has come up with and turning them into products that can be sold. The important relationships that development will cultivate are shown in figure 23.2.

Figure 23.2: Development department relationships.

In successful companies, development projects originate in the marketing department when a need for a new product is identified as part of the market research. It is much less effective when 'the tail wags the dog' and development bring out products on their own initiative. When this happens, products tend to be over specified (better than they need to be), too complex or just not what is needed in the marketplace. The essence of most development is 'trial and error'. A number of samples will be produced which will then be tested for performance or specification, and essential to the entire project will be staying within the cost constraints as laid down by the marketing and finance departments.

Before a new product is passed on to production for manufacture, it often goes to a 'pilot' stage. This is when an intermediate quantity is made, bigger than a development amount, but not as big as a production run. The purpose of a pilot run is to see how things go when it is scaled up and to provide product samples which can be used for, say, consumer testing.

23.5.3 Short-term development

The occasion often arises when a small amount of lab time will be required for development purposes. The technical people are a major 'intellectual resource' for the business, and accordingly, they are asked to advise and support the wider activities of the company in a number of ways:

❑ production support – problems with products being made in the factory;

❑ bespoke matching an existing product to more precisely meet a specific customers requirements;

❑ customer support – either advising customers over the phone or going to visit in order to help them overcome difficulties experienced with the use of products sold;

❑ answering technical queries from customers and prospective customers;

❑ meeting up with customers, usually alongside salespeople, to discuss the technical aspects of a customers needs;

❑ monitoring the company's products being used for the first time by new customers.

In some companies, the R & D function simply allocates somebody from development for such purposes, but in larger concerns, it is formalised into a department which is called by various names, including: technical service; technical support; trouble shooting; short-term development; site support.

This part of R & D in some markets is seen as an essential part of the company's total service package to customers. It also serves to increase the sales representatives confidence, knowing that 'the technical team' are there to support him and his customers.

Case Study   **How is R & D organised at SAL?**

R & D at SAL is organised into several areas.

Under the general area of **'Research'** there are many separate but interlinked activities. These activities are divided into two broad areas. Firstly, *chemical and biochemical research* is carried out by several research groups. These groups of scientists design, prepare and test new chemical compounds which they think might be suitable for further development as agrochemicals. Their choice of projects is based upon their professional knowledge of what types of chemical might be suitable. Some projects are 'suggested' by natural processes which are seen to provide some pest controlling qualities. The second research area is *biological research*. This area focuses on the pests that the agrochemicals are designed to kill, such as fungi and micro-organisms. In addition, other biologists study weeds, insects and other living organisms for such products as weedkillers, insecticides etc.

Development involves not only turning research ideas into saleable products, but also the development of processes to spray and apply products as well as the development of new production techniques. New research product ideas are made into development products which are then extensively tested in authentic agricultural situations. SAL has 13 testing stations in various parts of the world in which they assess product performance in various climatic and soil/pest conditions. Their field testing locations are in various places from the USA to Columbia, and South Africa to the Philippines.

23.5.4 Quality control (QC)

When we looked at quality control in Chapter 20, we learned that it is most commonly part of the technical department. The reason for having the product testing carried out by a department other than that which made it is to prevent compromise occurring. QC must 'feel' more part of the technical department than of the operations function (discussed in detail in Chapters 19 and 20) and must enforce the standards set down for the products when they were developed and launched. Any change of quality standard will consequently only be allowed if it is signed by a senior person in the development department.

Most quality control involves relatively repetitive work and this sometimes involves testing batches at mid-points in the production process as well as at the end. A production run that has gone through the operations department will not be allowed to be despatched until it has passed all QC points and has been signed off as such by the Quality Control Manager.

23.5.5 Quality assurance

In recent years, as companies have come to appreciate the value of quality and conformity to specification, the issue of quality assurance has gained much prominence. As the title suggests, quality assurance is about assuring quality rather than controlling it. This is not to say that one excludes the other; rather, they work together to improve quality throughout the operation.

Some QA systems are very tight and approximate to TQM (Total Quality Management – as discussed in Chapter 20). Others concern only aspects of the flow of materials through the plant. The extent to which QA is observed will depend upon the type of business and the resources available.

In the nineteen eighties, standards were brought out by the British Standards Institute (BSI) and the International Standards Organisation (ISO) which enabled companies to meet certain QA standards and gain registration accordingly. The different Standard numbers refer to the extent to which it is implemented.

British Standard No.	Equivalent ISO No.	Extent of QA
BS 5750 Part 1	ISO 9001	Quality in product design and operations
BS 5750 Part 2	ISO 9002	Quality in operations (flow of materials)
BS 5750 Part 3	ISO 9003	Quality in the final inspection only.

QA in practice is based on *systems* and *procedures*. These state in advance how operations will be performed which are within the QA area. Again, we are talking about conformance to specification whatever 'quality' the product might be. Consistency is important, so things are done the same every time, i.e. according to the written procedure. The QA axiom is *'say what you do and do what you say!'*. Records must be kept to demonstrate consistency if the company wishes to be accredited under the BS 5750.

'Policing' the systems and procedures is usually the responsibility of a QA manager, who monitors quality and devises improvements (or tightening up) where necessary. In smaller companies the QA Manager role will be performed by somebody in the technical department on a part-time basis, but in larger companies, as would be expected, QA is a full-time role.

Case Study

Quality Management at SAL

Schering, like many other large organisations, has a full-time Quality Manager. Unusually reporting to the Operations Director rather than the Technical Director, the Quality Manager at SAL is a qualified chemist who is highly familiar with the company's products and procedures. His area of responsibility encompasses both types of quality management: QC and QA. He oversees a team of staff in each area.

Quality control is the control of the products conformance to specification as products pass through the production process. The QC processes start when raw materials are tested when they arrive on site from suppliers and before they are used in the Hauxton factory. It is their practice to test raw materials according to the degree of confidence that Schering has in the ability of the supplier to control its own quality. If Schering believes that a supplier is reliable only one delivery in ten will be tested. For suppliers which have historically supplied materials which have not been perfect, Schering tests every delivery. Complicated statistical techniques are employed to determine how frequently raw materials should be tested (under British Standard 6001 which describes statistical sampling standards).

Once the materials have begun their passage through the production process, QC takes samples at various stages and tests them for quality. This is called *in-process monitoring* and is important in ensuring that all expensive mistakes are avoided or are spotted at the earliest stage. Finally, the product, on completing its passage through the factory, is submitted to the QC lab for final testing. This is the most thorough QC analysis and involves a range of complicated tests. Tests in the QC lab will always be those which test the important functional aspects of a product. At Schering, their agrochemicals are tested for their chemical performance by using a wide range of chemical tests including *gas liquid chromatography* and *high performance liquid chromatography*. In addition, the finished products are tested for their physical properties such as viscosity ('thickness') and stability over time and for impurities which may reduce the efficiency of the product.

Quality assurance occurs differently at Schering's Hauxton production site and its Chesterford Park Research and Development centre. In 1989, Hauxton was accredited under **ISO 9002** (BS 5750, Part 2). This involved the documentation of all of the procedures that are carried out in the company. A quality manual was also written which details all of the quality specifications that the company agrees to observe. There are eighteen internal auditors at Hauxton who regularly monitor the internal procedures to check that they are constantly being observed. Every three years, the company undergoes a full audit by external inspectors. If it passes this external audit it is allowed to keep its BS 5750 accreditation; if it fails, the accreditation is taken away. On the occasion of its first triennial audit in 1993, all was well.

At Chesterford Park R & D centre, the company observes an equally rigorous set of quality procedures, but to a very different standard. It is required to abide by systems which apply to the development of pharmaceuticals and agrochemicals. The **GLP** (Good Laboratory Practice) procedures are prescribed by the UK Department of Health and backed up by a European Directive. R & D procedures under GLP are designed to ensure that there is no room for fraud in the development of these products which have a significant bearing on public health. According to GLP, all procedures must be documented and carried out in under the prescribed guidelines. Chesterford Park has four internal auditors who ensure that all systems are kept up to standard. The whole site is audited by official external auditors every two years. Continued accreditation under GLP is conditional upon a successful external audit in the same way as ISO 9002 is for the Hauxton site.

Review Questions

1. What is the purpose of the R & D function? (23.1)

2. Describe some of the objectives of the R & D function. (23.2)

3. Briefly describe the types of personnel employed by an R & D department. (23.3)

4. What factors determine the disciplines from which professional R & D personnel are drawn? (23.3)

5. Explain the different time scales involved in R & D projects. (23.4)

6. Define and distinguish between the terms *research, development* and *technical service.* (23.5)

7. Summarise the typical activities of the research component of R & D. (23.5.1)

8. What is the nature of the relationships of the development function with the rest of the functions of the organisation? (23.5.2)

9. Define and distinguish between QC and QA. (23.5.3 and 23.5.4)

10. What do you think are the benefits to an organisation of possessing accreditation under ISO 9000? (23.5.5)

Assignment

Summarise the features (advantages and disadvantages) of being a scientist or engineer actually working in each of the areas of technical work. If you are using this textbook on a science or engineering degree, it is likely that you will work in R & D when you graduate. Which area appeals to you most?

Further Reading

McLeod T., *The Management of Research, Development and Design in Industry*, Gower Technical Press (Second Edition, 1988)

Bozeman B., Crow M. & Link A., *Strategic Management of Industrial Research and Development*, Lexington Books (1984)

White P.A.F., *Effective Management of Research and Development*, Macmillan Press

Verschuur J.J., *Technologies and Markets*, Published by Peter Peregrinus Ltd on behalf of the Institute of Electrical Engineers

Holt K., *Product Innovation Management*, Butterworths (Third Edition, 1988)

Footnote: As of March 1 1994, Schering Agrochemicals Limited became **AgrEvo UK Limited**, part of a new joint venture company formed by the merger of the plant protection and pest control activities of Hoechst/Roussel Uclaf and Schering. The new company, AgrEvo, is one of the world's most significant agrochemicals businesses. This merger in no way detracts from the value of the case material presented in this chapter. All case materials in this chapter, with kind permission, Schering Agrochemicals Limited.

24 The personnel function

Objectives   After studying this chapter, students should be able to:

☐ distinguish between *personnel management* and the *personnel function*,

☐ define the terms *personnel management*, the *personnel function* and *personnel policies*,

☐ explain why the personnel function is important in an organisation,

☐ list the principal administrative functions of personnel,

☐ define and distinguish between *recruitment* and *selection*,

☐ define and distinguish between *job description* and *person specification*,

☐ explain the need for staff induction and typical procedures employed,

☐ explain the need for staff development and training and common approaches to it,

☐ describe the essentials of the 'human resources' philosophy.

Featured Organisations: **The University of Northumbria at Newcastle (UNN)** and **British Gas Plc (Northern)**

24.1. Overview of The Personnel Function

24.1.1 Personnel management and the personnel function

As its name suggests, personnel is all about the people who work in the organisation. **Personnel management** is the term used to describe the formulation and execution of the company's *personnel policies*. These involve everything from recruitment to redundancy, and are set by the management of the company as a whole. Hence, they must be carried out and observed by all managers in the organisation who have subordinates. The **personnel function** is that part of the organisation which is concerned with the *advising* of management and the *administration* of duties in connection with staffing. It is usually made up of specialists who have trained or are experienced in this area of management.

The key point about personnel is that it is primarily concerned with the people who perform the tasks and not with the operational tasks themselves. This distinguishes personnel from all other functions of the organisation.

Case Study   **Personnel Policies at The University of Northumbria**

The UNN has a formal policy covering each area of the functions work. They are expressed as procedures, which cover such areas as:

☐ recruitment and selection of staff;

☐ equal opportunities policy;

☐ health and safety policy;

☐ staff development policy;

❑ staff management (disciplinary) procedures;

❑ trade union recognition;

❑ disputes and grievance procedures;

❑ redundancy and redeployment policy.

Like all personnel policies, the details of these are observed throughout the organisation.

24.1.2 The importance of the personnel function

A good starting point in a discussion of the subject would seem to be to ask the question *why have a personnel function?* After all, as a staff department it costs a lot of money and does not directly contribute to added value or the general operations of the business. The answer to this lies on two levels: the *maintenance* level and the *strategic* level.

From a **maintenance** point of view, the personnel function is important because it is simply a fact that organisations must employ people. People always cause work for management whether it is in recruiting them in the first place, ensuring they are paid, dealing with problems or negotiating with workers' unions. There are two possible ways of dealing with such matters. The first is to make it part of the job of the line manager, i.e. each line manager is concerned with all 'people' matters for those under him. The second is to create a department for this purpose. This has three main advantages:

❑ it frees up line managers' time to get on with those things they are employed on to do – which add value for the business or directly help to meet the organisation's objectives;

❑ it helps to ensure that the personnel policies are continually up-to-date with regard to the complicated employment law requirements and with so called 'best practice';

❑ it ensures consistency in the implementation of the personnel policies in the organisation as a whole. Employees naturally wish to be treated equally and fairly by the organisation and a department that systematically enforces personnel policies helps to ensure that this is the case.

Although in smaller concerns the 'line manager' approach is adopted (due to the costs of employing a full time personnel person), larger organisations, almost without exception, opt to have a personnel department. The larger the organisation the greater the risk of variation in the way in which employees are treated in different departments. In large organisations, personnel departments can grow to be very large.

The personnel function is also important from a strategic point of view. The **strategic** or 'forward looking' approach to personnel encourages the personnel function to be proactive in its approach. This argument says that whilst maintenance issues are important, equally important is to plan and invest in people in order that the company has the best possible base of employees for the future. A business is only as good as its people, and so recruiting the right people, cultivating, training, motivating and equipping them are all seen as strategic objectives. This area is the responsibility of the personnel function.

24.1.3 What does the personnel function actually do?

The range of tasks (both 'maintenance' and 'strategic') performed within the function is broad. The emphasis given to each task will vary with the nature of the organisation and its objectives. The list will usually include the following:

❑ recruitment and selection of staff;

❑ induction of new staff into the organisation;

- training and development;
- assessing employee performance (appraisal);
- job design and specification;
- dealing with grievances and disciplinary matters;
- negotiating with employees and trade unions;
- designing and implementing salary structures;
- payroll (sometimes done by the finance department);
- succession planning;
- health and safety issues – monitoring and policing;
- redundancy – design and administration;
- welfare, pensions, health insurance and other employee benefits (e.g. cars, social clubs, canteen facilities etc.);
- work study;
- equal opportunities monitoring.

Activity 1   *Find out how many people are employed in the personnel department at the university or college at which you are studying. Which of the functions listed above does it perform?*

24.1.4 The structure of the department

The qualifying body for personnel professionals is the **Institute of Personnel Management** (IPM). The senior people in the department will usually hold this qualification, but unlike other types of professional people (especially accountants), it is not usually mandatory to be qualified under this body. The different components of the personnel function reflect the breadth of tasks it undertakes and the nature of the organisation. Figures 24.1 and 24.2 show the two featured organisations' personnel department structures.

Personnel department at British Gas Plc (Northern)

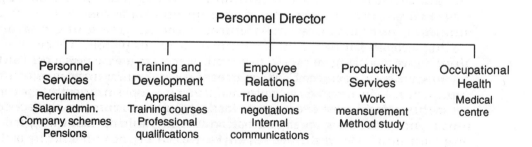

Figure 24.1

Personnel department at the University of Northumbria

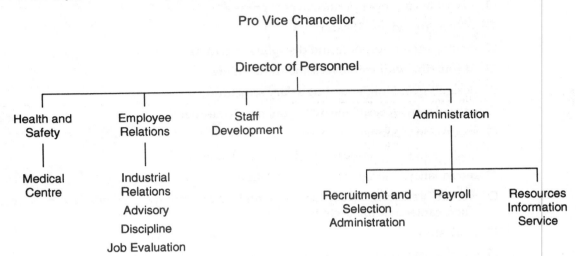

Figure 24.2

Case Study   **A day in the life of a personnel professional – Janet Copeland**

Janet Copeland is the Deputy Head of Personnel at the University of Northumbria at Newcastle. Reporting directly to the Director of Personnel, she controls a department which is responsible for all aspects of employment relations and she plays a key role in the advisory and industrial relations functions of the UNN personnel department.

On a typical day, Janet arrives at the office at 8.30 a.m. On the day the author visited, she began by collecting her mail. Some of this had to be dealt with straight away whilst she passed other items to subordinates in her department. This took about half an hour and then at 9.15 am, she held a brief meeting with the Payroll Supervisor about a query on payments to the University's security staff. This took ten minutes and was immediately followed by a further meeting with her Personnel Manager to discuss how they will approach the next meeting with the trade unions where the harmonisation of conditions for manual staff would be discussed. Janet followed this discussion by writing letters to the appropriate union representatives confirming the date and purpose of the meeting. She went down to pass these letters to the secretaries for typing and grabbed a minute on the way back to pick up a cup of tea.

At 10.00 am, Janet set aside a couple of hours for some project work she had been working on regarding the combined conditions of service for the university's administrative and technical staff. She was interrupted at 11.25 by a 'phone call from a departmental manager about the immediate future of a member of staff on a fixed term contract. One of the ProVice Chancellors arrived for a meeting at 11.50. They discussed a number of matters briefly and the ProVice Chancellor was keen to check up how a few key matters were progressing. The meeting ended at 12.15 and Janet decided that this was a suitable time to go for lunch.

On returning from lunch at ten past one, Janet picked up the messages that had accumulated while she was out. One matter needed to be answered straight away whilst another, the new 'leave card' for staff, was entered in the diary for later consideration. At 1.45 p.m., she turned her attention to preparing her notes for the 2 o'clock meeting with the internal auditors. The following meeting with the auditors included the Payroll Supervisor and was mainly concerned with discussing a draft audit report on campus services. Some useful suggestions were made which Janet noted down for further thought.

At 3 o'clock, the internal auditors left and she continued her discussions with the Payroll Manager about the most effective way of collecting information from supervisors on the adjustment of the payroll for overtime etc.

This meeting ended at 3.25 p.m. when Janet collected her afternoon delivery of mail. This contained an interesting query from a job applicant who questioned the procedures that the university followed for recruitment. Whilst musing over her response, she signed some letters that had been prepared for her which contained formal offers of employment for new staff. Just as she finished dealing with the afternoon mail, her Senior Personnel Officer called in to check the official policy on giving advice to a university manager who had some queries about a member of staff's probationary period. This took 15 minutes, and at five past four Janet finally returned to her project work on the combined conditions of service for the two staff groups (administrative and technical). At 5.20 p.m., she decided to call it a day. After making some notes in her diary, she set off for home.

24.2. Important Aspects of Personnel Management

The area of personnel is so large that a text of this kind could not possibly consider it in detail. Instead, a number of areas have been selected for discussion which illustrate the range of activities undertaken be the personnel department.

24.2.1 Recruitment and selection

All organisations must take on new employees and replace those who leave. It is hard to overstate the importance of this task as it is this which determines the quality of the workforce and management. This in turn determines the success of the business. In employing somebody, the organisation is usually taking on a long-term commitment – employees may remain with the company for as long as 45 years. To appoint the right person is therefore of paramount importance.

Recruitment and selection are two separate processes which the organisation will go through in the process of employing people.

Recruitment is the process in which the organisation generates a pool of applicants for a post. It is in the organisation's interest to give the selectors the widest choice of potentially suitable applicants. The personnel policies will often reflect this in their attempt to get people to apply for positions. They may say, for example:

❏ all vacancies will be advertised in the national and local press;

❏ all vacancies will be advertised internally;

❏ the company will reply to all applicants within 14 days of receiving their application.

Similarly, they may make efforts not to reduce the number of suitable applicants by using 'inclusive' clauses in the adverts:

❏ the company is an equal opportunities employer;

❏ the company will not discriminate unfairly against applicants on grounds of colour, race, religion, sexual orientation etc.

The emphasis in recruitment is on generating the largest pool of *suitable* applicants. In order to achieve this, adverts will be carefully worded and *targeted* so that a high concentration of people with the required skills will see the advert and be attracted to apply. The job advert market is segmented in the same way as we saw in marketing promotions (Chapter 22). Examples of intelligent targeting of adverts are:

Nature of Position	**Possible location of advert**
Accountants	*Certified Accountant*, other accountancy magazines
Teachers/lecturers	*Education Guardian* (Tuesdays)
General manual labour	Job centres, local press
General senior management	*Daily Telegraph* (Thursdays)

For some key positions, a common practice is to subcontract out the recruitment process to a recruitment consultant. Recruitment consultants specialise in generating applicants and filtering out the partly or wholly unsuitable ones (according to the person specification supplied by the company requiring the new employee. They will discuss the company's requirements in detail and interview the best of the applicants and then present the company with a 'short-list' of the best. The final *selection* will be made by the organisation itself.

After applications have been received, relevant criteria are applied and a 'whittling down' process occurs, known as *short-listing*. The criteria can be adjusted depending upon the numbers and quality of applicants, but it is important (legally) to ensure that the process is not discriminatory. Initial interviews or testing may occur at this stage in order to eliminate the weakest applicants.

Selection is the process which takes the short-list generated by recruitment and selects the best person for the job. There are a number of selection techniques available to personnel practitioners:

- interviews;

- examining application forms or c.v.s;

- psychometric testing;

- presentations by applicants;

- 'Assessment Centre' activities (in which applicants are assessed by undertaking a range of tasks that are similar to those involved in the actual job in question).

It is quite common for more than one of these techniques to be used. Companies are increasingly seeing the benefit of having thorough selection procedures, and are making use of the more modern methods accordingly.

It should be remembered that selection does not involve selecting the best person as such, but the best person *for the job*. This is very important because whilst it may be tempting to appoint a particularly able candidate, it is likely that if he is 'too good for the job' he will quickly become disillusioned or leave. The 'person specification' (see 24.2.2) should be carefully adhered to in the process. For some positions, where the criteria for appointment are not very exacting, the issue might not be finding the best person, but simply finding someone suitable.

Psychometric testing

Whilst great emphasis is still placed upon the traditional selection methods, most particularly application forms and interviews, employers are increasingly using psychometry as well – usually in addition to the traditional methods.

Psychometric tests are designed by psychologists and are designed to test certain features of the applicant's psychological profile. They ask questions, which the applicant must answer about him or herself by entering or circling numbers or letters. From these, the Personnel Manager can tell things about the person that might not be immediately obvious just by interviewing him or her.

The tests are used to check things like intelligence, initiative, analytical ability, personality, and the person's ability to lead, work with others etc. From the job description, the appointing manager will be able to identify the best candidate partly by use of data gathered from the psychometric tests.

After the choice has been made, the company must convince the right person to accept their offer of employment with the company. It must not be assumed that a person who turns up for interview will always want the job. The position can be made more attractive by stressing such aspects of the job as salary, working conditions, other benefits (e.g. car, pension), opportunities for advancement etc. The rapport that the successful applicant has enjoyed (or not enjoyed) with the interviewer can also be important, especially if the interviewer will be his new boss.

Case Study   **The recruitment and selection (R&S) process at the University of Northumbria**

The UNN employs around 2200 individuals of whom 850 are academic or teaching staff. Any organisation of this size will necessarily be continually engaged in R & S as staff need to be replaced and new appointments made. Consequently, the personnel department is well practised in this area. The university's aim in R & S is to 'attract highly qualified and highly motivated teachers, administrators and service staff'.

In order to ensure that each vacancy is treated fairly and consistently, a recruitment and selection *procedure* is followed. The stages in this can be summarised as follows:

1. identification of vacancy
2. job description is drawn up
3. person specification is generated from job description
4. decision is made on where to place advertisement for the vacancy
5. advertisement is written/designed
6. advertisement appears in relevant newspaper/magazine
7. applicants respond to advertisement
8. short-list is made up from applicants
9. short-listed applicants are called for interview
10. interview using a range of selection techniques, depending upon nature of appointment (many lecturing appointments involve applicants giving a presentation at the interview)
11. verbal offer is made and this is accepted or declined
12. health check of successful candidate
13. references are checked
14. formal letter of offer is sent to and returned by successful candidate
15. new employee starts work.

Case Study   **Recruitment and selection at British Gas Plc (Northern)**

In a letter to the author, the Regional Personnel Services manager of British Gas Northern writes:

> 'It is normal practice for vacancies to be advertised and filled internally [i.e. by re-assigning an existing staff member to the vacant position] and we rarely recruit externally. We use person specifications to identify essential and desirable criteria and this forms the basis of the interview panel's pre-interview and interview assessment of candidates. We are anxious to promote equal opportunities for women, ethnic minorities and disabled persons and we short-list applicants without knowledge of their name, sex, marital status etc.'

24.2.2 Job description and person specification

When a position becomes available, be it a new position or a replacement, the personnel department will liaise with the relevant line manager to agree on the job description and person specification for the post. These form the basis of both the recruitment and selection procedure and the contract of employment offered to the successful applicant.

The **job description** is the document that describes what the job involves on a day-to-day basis. This may be made available to applicants during the recruitment or selection stages in order for a more informed discussion to take place at interview. The description can be general or highly specific. Typical contents will include:

❐ who the position reports to;

❐ over whom the position is responsible;

❐ the limits of authority;

❐ summary of duties.

The **person specification** is a list of the qualities and characteristics that the ideal person for the job will have. The process ideally begins with an analysis of what will be required of the jobholder (the job description) and from this the specification can be drawn up. It is important that the job is not *under* or *over* specified. Underspecification may result in the appointment of a person who may not be up to all aspects of the job. Conversely, overspecification may result in the appointment of an over-qualified candidate. It is clear that specifications will vary widely – imagine the different qualities needed for an office junior and an international marketing manager.

The format of the specification may include the following:

❐ age – minimum and maximum ('it is unlikely that the successful applicant will be under 40...');

❐ qualifications – anything from 'no formal education required' to 'a postgraduate degree in biochemistry is essential';

❐ experience – both the length of experience and its relevance to the job;

❐ personal attributes – intelligence, interpersonal skills (verbal and writing ability) etc.;

❐ special abilities – foreign languages, dexterity, computer literacy etc.

Case Study **Job description and person specification for a University of Northumbria lecturer in business**

Job description

Appointees to the position of lecturer will be required to undertake any of the duties ... below...

All forms of pedagogic [teaching] work including classroom teaching, tutorial work, ...together with associated administrative work ...

Student counselling and pastoral care activities...

Curriculum development, including the planning and development of new courses...

Staff development, including participation in staff appraisal...

Research and consultancy...

Management and administration of courses...

Person specification

Possession of a degree and preferably postgraduate qualifications

Ability to teach effectively on academic and professional courses...

Ability to contribute to course management...

Ability to work as a member of a team...

Potential for successful research...

Interest in furthering his/her personal development both as a teacher and as a subject specialist.

Possession of relevant experience in business/commerce, the public sector or professional practice.

Case Study **Job description and person specification for a British Gas Showroom Sales Assistant**

Job description

To sell gas appliances, central heating systems and non-gas products ...

Use the Company's cashiering standards and procedures to effectively collect and record payments received from customers.

Provide advice, seek to resolve queries and process appropriate documentation and telephone calls to maintain an effective customer service and provide customer satisfaction.

Portray the Company image of efficient, courteous and caring service to ensure customer satisfaction.

Person specification

British Gas divide up their person specification into 'essential' and 'desirable' characteristics and qualifications. The specification contains the words *candidates who meet essential criteria should be preferred to those who do not. Exceptions to this guideline need to be justifiable and should be recorded'*. The following is a sample of criteria from the person specification.

Essential Criteria

Ability to communicate effectively and politely with a wide range of people.

Ability to portray a professional and competent image to customers.

Ability to treat customers with tact and confidentiality.

Desirable Criteria

Ability to influence customers towards the selection and purchase of gas products.

Knowledge of product prices, features and campaign offers.

Training in effective selling techniques.

Experience of working within a sales environment, handling cash and using computerised cash receipting terminals.

Activity 2   *Suggest what might form the main points of a person specification for the following occupations:*

Financial Director

Retail salesperson (consumer electrical goods)

Consultant surgeon

Building site labourer

24.2.3 Induction of new staff

The formality with which new employees are inducted into work varies considerably. Some organisations have elaborate systems while others have no formal systems at all. Broadly speaking, we can say that larger organisations with large personnel departments will have more structured induction programmes than smaller concerns. It is not uncommon in small and medium organisations for there to be no induction at all (*'here's your desk – do your job!'*).

The areas that are covered as part of a formal induction programme point to the reasons for conducting such an exercise, and would usually include:

❐ A formalised 'welcome' to the company;

❐ Answering any immediate questions;

❐ Introduction to new colleagues;

❐ Explanation of company policy:

   Health and Safety policy

   'In the event of fire…'

   'How we expect employees to behave'

   Areas associated with corporate culture

   Grievances and disciplinary procedures.

In addition to ensuring that essential points are covered, a structured induction programme has the benefit of increasing the morale and 'feeling of belonging' of the new member of staff. Notwithstanding these benefits, such a programme is observed in the minority of cases.

Case Study   **Staff induction at the University of Northumbria**

The UNN has a *personnel policy* relating to the induction of lecturers. It is organised partly by the personnel department (the 'institutional' input) and partly by the new staff member's faculty (the 'departmental' input).

Stage 1 of the process takes place between 9.00 am and 11.00 am on the first day of work. This is a general 'welcome', 'any questions' and to address any initial anxieties that new lecturers may experience.

Stage 2 is a full day programme organised 6-8 weeks into the new staff member's appointment. Like Stage 1, this is also an 'institutional' occasion. This day includes explanations of health and safety issues, equal opportunities policies, information about the university and its mission, a tour of the various quarters of the campus and lunch with the Pro Vice Chancellors.

The **departmental** input to the induction process includes the appointment of a 'mentor' – a senior member of staff who can act as a confidential counsellor and 'critical friend'. This stage tends to be more variable than the institutional procedures.

24.2.4 Training and development

It is rare that new employees arrive in a job totally qualified, fully competent and totally 'in control'. We all benefit from exposure to new challenges, new skills, new knowledge etc. Because of the strategic significance of people in organisations, it is also in the interests of the organisation that its employees are stimulated and trained in order to allow them to make a greater contribution to the business. Training and development rests upon the conviction that people are a resource to be developed and improved; a resource which is of enormous significance to the company.

Training and development is also made essential as the environment changes. When this happens, staff need to be made aware of new developments, new technologies etc. Competence must be gained as new computer software is introduced, new manufacturing systems are brought in, or when new legislation is passed requiring a change in practice at work.

Training and development needs can also be identified at the points at which employees performance is *appraised*. Some organisations have formal annual **appraisals** where each person is seen by his immediate superior to discuss issues associated with work. If a 'gap', or an area where training would be advantageous, is identified then this will be included in the forthcoming year's development plans.

The 'training equation' is used as simple guide to clarify where and what training is needed.

What the employee needs for the job – what the employee can do now = training needs

Training and development can take several forms. There are, needless to say, advantages and disadvantages associated with each option.

❒ **On-the-job training**

As the name suggests, this is training that is done while the employee is working, e.g. showing people how to operate a machine, the pitfalls of doing operations the wrong way etc. and is usually seen as essential for all but the most competent of new employees. On-the-job training of this type will constitute the on-going training for most employees as there is always something new that can be learned. New machines or equipment must be learned, as must new software etc.

❒ **In-company but off-the-job training programmes**

Companies that see the value of an on-going training schedule for all staff often hold regular seminars or similar. In these sessions, attendees are instructed in any number of things such as improving performance in their present job to learning new skills. This approach can also be used to convey 'essential' information such as the company's quality philosophy, or the legal requirements of current health and safety practice. The trainer used for this purpose can be either someone hired in from outside or, in larger companies, a member of the training department.

This format can also take on some more creative approaches, including internal secondments, special conferences away from site, team building exercises such as outward bound weekends etc. One key advantage of in-company training is that it can be specifically designed for the exact needs of the employees.

❑ **'External' education and development**

Where the company cannot meet development needs itself, it may opt to enrol the employee at an external institution. These include, most commonly, providers of further and higher education. Some jobs will have an external training programme attached as a condition of employment; most laboratory technicians will be expected to undertake an intermediate level technical qualification. Most companies are selective about who they permit to go on such programmes, as usually, not only will the company lose the employee on a 'day release' (or similar) basis, but will also be expected to pay the course fees.

This provision will be made available for those who will directly benefit from it. Because of the costs, the organisation will want to have a good deal of confidence that the training gained at the external institution will be of direct benefit to itself. Whilst the advantages of continuing education are relatively obvious, external provision such as that provided by universities has been criticised as being of only partial relevance to the real work context. Organisations also worry that if their employees become better qualified, they will leave the company to gain promotion elsewhere.

24.3 'Personnel' and 'Human Resources'

One recent development in the area of personnel management has been the rise of the so called 'human resources' school of thought. It is based on the belief that employees are primarily a *resource* rather than a *cost* and as such are to be cultivated, developed and encouraged. This is not to say that the 'old' personnel school did not recognise this, but that it is this which characterises human resource management (HRM).

It is important to understand that HRM is a *philosophy* rather than a style of management. Underpinning it is a particular view of the employees of the organisation. All of the HRM practices flow from that view – that employees are a valuable resource.

As organisations have increasingly been persuaded by the HRM approach, there has been a marked growth in such practices as:

❑ direct and regular formal communications with staff;

❑ employee involvement in decision making;

❑ staff development and training;

❑ attention to working conditions and 'comfort' issues.

The differences between HRM and personnel management tend to be somewhat exaggerated by HRM proponents, but a common list of the key emphases of HRM would be as follows.

❑ **Employee Relations** rather than *industrial relations* – seeing employees as individuals. Negotiation with Trade Unions is not discouraged, but reviewing employees conditions of employment on an individual by individual basis is seen as the ideal.

❑ HRM **comes from the top** – it ties in with the overall strategy of the organisation. It is not the domain of one particular department (such as personnel) but has the commitment of everybody in senior management.

❑ It is hard to implement as it flies in the face of many of the cultural values with which most managers have grown up. It requires a **different perception of subordinates** to that which many managers may have adopted. Staff are not there to be ruled with a 'big stick' but encouraged to adopt the same objectives as their managers.

❐ It represents a shift away from administering people from one central department and towards **empowering individual line managers** to make key decisions. A common example would be allowing line managers to negotiate training and development needs with their subordinates.

❐ HRM relies for its success on a **conducive corporate culture**. Whereas personnel management is more of a 'mechanical/administrative' approach, HRM tends to rely on staff compliance and agreement with policies.

The stereotypes say that HRM is long term, strategic and central to the entire organisation, whereas personnel management is seen as short term, *ad hoc* and marginalised to a few personnel professionals. The caricatures may tend to be unrealistic, but they do show the changes that are taking place with the introduction of HRM.

Many organisations have changed the name of the personnel department to the human resources department without necessarily instituting a HRM philosophy in the organisation. To a certain extent, HRM is fashionable, but its implementation has proved to be problematic in many organisations.

Review Questions

Distinguish between and define the following terms:

1. personnel management, personnel function and personnel policies; (24.1.1)
2. recruitment and selection; (24.2.1)
3. job description and person specification; (24.2.2)
4. maintenance and strategic issues in personnel management; (24.1.2)
5. 'personnel' and 'human resources' management. (24.3)
6. Explain why recruitment and selection is vital to an organisation. (24.2.1)
7. Name the most common selection procedures. (24.2.1)
8. Explain why large organisations have a separate personnel department. (24.1.2)
9. What are the advantages to be gained by the provision of a formal induction procedure for new employees? (24.2.3)
10. Give three reasons why an organisation might wish to provide a training and development provision for its employees. (24.2.4)
11. What are the choices in training provision? (24.2.4)

Answer to activity 2

The broad specifications for the four positions listed might include:

Financial director

❐ a formal professional accountancy qualification (e.g. ACA, ACCA or similar),
❐ at least five years experience in an appropriate accountancy position,
❐ ability to make financial decisions affecting the organisation,
❐ ability to provide correct and timely financial information to other senior managers,
❐ ability to work well with others and delegate effectively.

Retail salesperson

This will be essentially the same as that for the British Gas Showroom salesperson we encountered in paragraph 24.2.2. It may also include as desirable, a knowledge of electrical equipment.

Consultant surgeon

☐ a medical degree,

☐ a professional qualification from the Royal College of Surgeons,

☐ an appropriate amount of experience as a senior registrar,

☐ an appropriate record of research and publication,

☐ a professional approach to patient care, counselling and administration.

Building site labourer

☐ a significant level of physical fitness and strength,

☐ willingness to work outside in all weathers,

(The nature of the job means that the person specification will be less exacting than that for, say, the consultant surgeon.)

Assignment

Brown Industries Limited is a medium sized paint manufacturer. Over the past five years, it has had trouble with its sales representatives. Whilst a total of nine are needed (according to the Sales Manager) to cover the company's customers throughout the UK, the sales force has hardly ever been at 'full strength' due to losing reps through sackings for poor performance, or through resignation. This high turnover of sales representatives has had a detrimental effect on sales, as customers have switched suppliers. One important customer is reported to have said 'I haven't seen anybody from Brown for months. They never have a man here when I'm ready to place an order for paint'.

As the Personnel Manager of Brown, the MD has asked you to have a word with the Sales Manager to see if you can do anything to reverse the high staff turnover and restore some stability to the sales force. You arrange a meeting with Paul Collinson, the Sales Manager to explore how you might help.

Paul begins by informing you that he is acutely aware of the problems. 'I don't know what I am doing wrong', he said, 'it seems I am always either trying to get people to fill sales vacancies or else I am after them for not meeting their sales targets for the month'. As a good personnel practitioner, you ask Paul about the criteria he uses to choose his sales reps. 'What do you mean?', he replies, 'I advertise in the local press for a sales rep, and I appoint a person that appears to be smart and articulate – those are important in sales people'. After further discussion, it transpires that he has no firm ideas as to the qualities he is looking for in people, he just uses his 'gut feeling'. You also establish that there is a flat pay scale for reps, with no incentives for selling more paint. After quizzing Paul about how he inducts and trains his staff, he laughs and says 'Sales is the sharp end of business. You people in personnel have no idea. I don't have time for that sort of thing. On their first day, they arrive, I assign them a Vauxhall Cavalier and pack them off. They can pick up product knowledge on the job'.

Tasks

1. Tell Paul what you think he is doing wrong.

2. Outline the procedures you would recommend to Paul to ensure that he recruits the right people for the sales force and then, once appointed, how you would retain them in the company.

3. Paul asks you to give him some help on a job description and person specification for a travelling sales representative selling paint to DIY outlets. Suggest the major points you might include in such documents. (This question does not require specialist knowledge of paint selling – general points only are required.)

4. Write an advert to place in the local paper to recruit a pool of good applicants for a sales representative post.

5. Paul asks if you would mind giving him a hand selecting the right person for the sales territory of Central and Southern Scotland. Which selection techniques would you use? (hint: what are the skills you would are looking for in a paint salesperson?)

Complete the assignment in fewer than 2000 words.

Further Reading

Cole G.A., *Personnel Management – Theory and Practice*, DP Publications
Torrington D. & Hall L., *Personnel Management – A New Approach*, Prentice Hall Publishers
Thomason G., *A Textbook of Human Resource Management*, Institute of Personnel Management
Armstrong M., *A Handbook of Personnel Management Practice*, Kogan Page Publishers
Story J., *Management of Human Resources*, Blackwell (1992)
Plumbley P., *Recruitment and Selection*, Institute of Personnel Management (1991)
Mullins L.J., *Management and Organisational Behaviour*, Pitman Publishing (Third Edition, 1993, Section 7, Chapters 18 & 19)

Section 6

Markets and Structures

An important element in the running of many organisations is the competition they face from other companies. In this section we will discuss how organisations compete within industries and markets. We will consider the implications of privatisation which has become a key determinant of market structure, primarily through the elimination of state monopoly and the introduction of competition into markets where previously there was little or none.

Contents

25 Markets and market structures

Objectives

After studying this chapter, students should be able to:

- ❏ explain the common uses of the term *market* in business;
- ❏ distinguish between *industry* and *market*;
- ❏ define the term *market structure*;
- ❏ describe the factors that determine the structure of a market;
- ❏ list the principal forms of market supply structure;
- ❏ define the terms *monopoly, monopolistic competition, oligopoly, duopoly*, and *perfect competition*;
- ❏ describe the implications for pricing in each of the market structures;
- ❏ define the term *entry barrier* and give examples;
- ❏ describe the advantages and disadvantages of a monopoly structure and explain how the Government has regulated them.

25.1 What is a Market?

We use the word *market* in a number of ways and in several contexts. Two of the most common are as follows:

- ❏ A market can be a **physical place** where stall-holders gather to less their goods to shoppers.
- ❏ A market is also a defined **sector of business**. People may speak of the 'steel market', the 'petrochemicals market' or the 'textiles market'.

Both of the above are correct uses of the term. A market may or may not be a physical place, but all markets conform to one definition:

A market is place where buyers and sellers come together.

In the business sector markets, buyers and sellers make themselves known to each other, even though they may be in different parts of the world. The 'petrol' market, for example, is comprised of 'sellers' based in oil fields and refineries (at Aberdeen, Humberside and overseas) and millions of individual buyers throughout this country and abroad who use petrol in their cars.

The market comprises both the buyers and the sellers. A market cannot exist if there is an absence of either. The numbers of buyers or sellers in any sector is part of what characterises the market.

25.2 Industries and Markets

The word market is also used to describe the group of consumers who buy a particular product or service. The supply into a market is generally the output of an *industry*. We speak of the motor car industry as that sector of business that produces cars; we would not include users of cars in this industry – they would be the market for the industry.

The way in which the two sides of the market sector are structured is key to all the trading activities that occur.

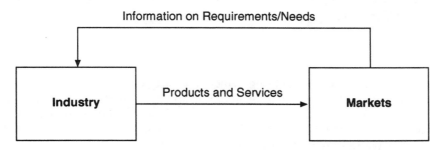

Figure 25.1: Industry and markets

25.3 What is a Market Structure?

Markets have certain characteristics. No two markets (or more correctly market sectors), are the same. Let us examine in what ways markets differ from each other.

25.3.1 Number of buyers and sellers

Some markets comprise literally thousands of suppliers, whilst others have only one. Similarly, for some products the market consists of millions of buyers, and for others just one.

Examples		
Many suppliers	Fruit and vegetables	
Few suppliers	Telecommunications services	
Many buyers	Coffee and tea	
Few buyers	Military aircraft	

We can readily understand that the more sellers there are in a sector of the market, the more competitive the sector will be. In the retail sector, intense competition can occur when there is a large number of shops supplying similar products within a close locality. Some cities around the UK have their own 'Chinatown' with a high concentration of Chinese restaurants, others have Indian restaurants, where others, such as Tottenham Court Road in London, have a high concentration of electrical goods suppliers. These situations give the buyer (customer) some degree of buying power owing to the fact that he can 'pick and choose' between suppliers. The situation is reversed when there are only few sellers and many customers.

25.3.2 Market growth

This refers to the demand for the market's goods. Is the demand growing, mature or in decline? At what stage of the product life cycle (see Chapter 21) is the product the market is selling? Some products are at the growth stage of the product life cycle and others are in decline, but at any one time, most markets can be described as mature.

25.3.3 Entry barriers

An entry barrier is something which prevents or deters would-be competitors from entering a market. We shall see in paragraph 25.4.1 that these can take several forms. If there are many entry barriers this generally means that there will be fewer sellers in the market; few entry barriers will encourage businesses to enter the market. As rule of thumb, we can say that if an industry has:

many entry barriers, there will be *few* suppliers, and

few entry barriers, there will be *many* suppliers.

25.3.4 Exit barriers

In the same way that entry barriers present obstacles to would-be entrants into an industry, exit barriers are those factors which present obstacles to companies that might like to leave. Businesses may only realise just how many barriers there are when the market begins to contract or otherwise change and they make efforts to sell a business or refocus the business into a more profitable sector. Exit barriers are usually financial, but there are such as irrevocable licences or franchises (e.g. a five year agreement may have to be honoured). For some businesses, plant and equipment is purchased on a long-term bank loan which must be repaid. If the machinery cannot be used for any other purpose, then it must be used for its original purpose until the debt is paid off – effectively an exit barrier.

25.3.5 Market concentration ratio

Concentration refers to the amount of the total market share that rests in the hands of any one competitor or of just a few large competitors. Some companies have very large market shares and others extremely small market shares. Most industries are concentrated to a degree, for example it is common to have 70% of the total market share in the hands of the biggest three or four competitors.

The way in which these factors actually affect industry is what defines the structure of the market.

The most common way of dividing up markets for this purpose is by the *number of sellers*. As we saw earlier, there can be any number of sellers depending upon the market. In some sectors there will be thousands of sellers whilst others will only have one or two. This can be shown on a simple continuum (figure 25.2). Most markets will be somewhere between the two extremes.

Monopoly   **Perfect Competition**

Figure 25.2: Market structure continuum

25.4 Monopolies and Monopolistic Competition

25.4.1 What is a monopoly?

Monopoly is a market situation in which

> *there is only one supplier of a particular product in a particular market or otherwise isolated sector.*

Monopolies exist because other would-be competitors are somehow prevented from entering the market.

Common entry barriers

- ❑ High set up costs (size of capital investment necessary)
- ❑ Unique access to a key raw material or other input
- ❑ Unique access to customers or markets
- ❑ 'Intellectual assets'

    Patents

    Licences which prevent others from manufacturing the same product

    Special expertise

- ❑ Government legislation preventing competitors from entering the market
- ❑ The amount of legislation which applies to an industry which would be costly or difficult to implement
- ❑ Intensity of existing competition

Activity 2	*Which of the entry barriers listed above would be the most relevant to an individual wishing to set up in the following industries?*
	❑ *Nuclear weapons*
	❑ *Petroleum extraction and refinement*
	❑ *Manufacture of a generic version of the patented Glaxo drug, Zantac*
	❑ *Manufacture of Coors lager*
	❑ *Fabric washing powder*

25.4.2 Monopoly pricing

The key aspect of a monopolist is that, in theory, the single supplier can charge whatever price he likes. The choice to the buyer is 'buy from us or go without'. There are no competitors against whom to compete or to match the company's prices. A true monopolist is consequently a *price setter*.

Entry barriers will prevent the emergence of competitors and so the true monopolist enjoys the right to set prices at whichever level will maximise his profits. If the entry barriers are insurmountable then technically, the monopolist is in the happy state of being able to continue his price setting regime indefinitely.

In practice, monopolies with such pricing power are rare, especially in developed economies. The term is still useful, though, because in some market sectors, some businesses are so large that they are effectively monopolists. When the majority of the market share is held by one business, it will often be the case that the big company will be big enough to dictate the market price. Such a level of influence on pricing in a market is called a *virtual monopoly*. Smaller competitors are forced to roughly follow the prices set by the virtual monopolist. In such a situation, the smaller competitor is said to be a *price follower*, and his profits will be determined by the market prices set by the big competitor in the market.

25.4.3 Monopoly – good or bad?

It might appear at first glance, that monopolies are bad if they have total price control. The implications for the consumer would appear to be unfortunate if the monopolist charges an unnecessarily high price.

It should be remembered that until the Conservative privatisation programme of the nineteen eighties (see Chapter 26), all of the utilities were effectively monopolies. Since companies like British Telecommunications Plc and the electricity generators have been sold to the public, the introduction of competition into these sectors has reduced the market concentration to a certain extent. The fact is that for forty years, the monopoly structure seemed to work, as indeed it still does in many countries.

Definition	Utilities

The utilities, in the context of the 'utilities markets' means those things that are considered as services to the home or business. They are used as fuels or means of communication and the main categories are:

Water

Gas

Electricity

Telecommunications

Like most issues in business, monopoly as a market structure has advantages and disadvantages.

Advantages

☐ Large companies such as monopolies, tend to be stable and are often able to withstand changes in the economic environment.

☐ If there is only one supplier, duplication of some activities, such as research and development, is avoided.

☐ High prices that the monopolist may charge can be used to generate high profits. These, in turn, can be used to improve service to the customer.

☐ Increased economies of scale should lead to lower unit costs. This will mean that the monopolist will have the choice of charging lower prices to the customer or making higher profits to fund expansion and investment.

Disadvantages

❐ The monopolist can charge excessively high prices. This can be highly undesirable if the monopolist is supplying an important product such as gas, electricity or telecommunications.

❐ Lack of competition can make the monopolist 'flabby' and inefficient. This may have the effect of further increasing prices as the monopolist attempts to cover his higher costs.

❐ The customer has no choice who to buy from.

❐ If the company, for any reason, cannot supply (e.g., strikes, breakdown of plant) then there is no supply to the market.

❐ The monopolist may not pass on the benefits of the increased economies of scale to the customer. This can result in excessive profits.

Key concept   Economies of scale

Economies of scale are achieved when the scale of production goes up and the unit cost (i.e. the cost associated with each item produced) goes down. Such an advantage can result from a number of sources.

❐ Raw Materials can be bought more cheaply when more is ordered.

❐ Bigger batches can be made, or a flow manufacturing operation can be set up.

❐ Fixed costs can be shared out over a larger number of units meaning that less is attributable to each one.

❐ Staff costs form a lower percentage of costs when batch size is increased.

25.4.4 Regulation of monopolies

We have already seen that in Western economies true monopolies are rare. Successive Governments in the UK have accepted that monopoly power can act to the severe detriment of the consumer and so have put a number of measures in place to restrict them.

Legislation

This is the **first** tool used to restrict monopolies. The key piece of legislation applied to market structures is the **Fair Trading Act (1973)**. This targets three areas which are seen as being damaging to the customers interests.

❐ **Monopoly**

In this Act, a monopoly is defined as occurring when one company has in excess of 25% of the total market share. This would seem to be at variance with the 'one supplier' definition, but it has some validity if the one big supplier in an otherwise fragmented market has effective control over pricing. A virtual monopoly will result where the virtual monopolist can control the market prices of goods in the industry.

❐ **Restrictive Practices**

When two or more big competitors collude in an industry, in order to agree a change in price, this can have the result of forcing others to follow. The two companies are effectively acting as a monopoly and hence this is forbidden under this Act.

❐ **Mergers and Acquisitions**

If, according to the Act, a monopoly arises with a market share of 25%, then when a company achieves this size, it falls under the influence of the legislation. Although a company can grow in size and increase market share, the Act particularly targets businesses that acquire or merge in order to grow in size. If the acquisition or merger results in a company that will control more than the 25% of the market share, then it must fall under the terms of the Act. It may or may not be allowed to proceed.

Statutory bodies

These are the **second** regulatory influence on monopolistic practices. They are QuAN-GOs (defined in Chapter 12) set up by the Government to regulate, oversee and enforce legislation within the markets. The principal bodies of this type are the Monopolies and Mergers Commission (MMC) and the various industry specific offices (e.g. OFTEL, OFGAS etc.).

The MMC sits whenever a case is referred to it by the Department of Trade and Industry. Its objectives in looking at a proposed acquisition or merger is to see if the new company that will emerge will have too powerful a presence in the market. If it finds that the company will occupy a higher than desirable market share, the MMC has the power to 'block' the proposal.

The industry specific offices, or 'watchdogs', are responsible for monitoring the prices charged and the levels of service provided by companies operating in the key utilities markets. Companies like British Telecommunications Plc and British Gas Plc are effectively monopolies, even though competitors in their fields are technically permitted. The competition offered by businesses like Mercury Communications is probably not sufficient to reduce the price setting power that British Telecommunications Plc could enjoy. The Government has taken the view that utilities are too important to leave to the markets in an unregulated form, so the watchdogs are given powers to impose price limits upon the companies in their sectors. In the late eighties OFTEL set a price increase for BT of RPI minus 6% in the interests of competition and cheaper prices to consumers. This means that their prices must rise by 6% less than the rate of consumer inflation. If inflation is less than 6% (which it usually is), then BT must find a way of actually *reducing* their prices from one year to the next. BT have responded to this by significantly reducing their workforce, centralising their computing services and implementing many other cost-saving measures. Rather than being a 'flabby' state-owned monopoly, BT have become a 'lean' competitor in the telecommunications market.

25.4.5 Monopolistic competition

One modification of the principle of monopoly is monopolistic competition. This can be said to occur when the market has been highly segmented and one product or supplier dominates the market in that one segment. Hence, the monopolist, in this context, has a high market share in a tiny segment but probably a tiny market share in the total market for the generic product.

The key to monopolistic competition is differentiation. We saw when we considered the marketing function that this is the process whereby a manufacturer attempts to separate his product from 'the pack' by augmentation of the basic product. If a product can be differentiated to such an extent that it occupies a 'niche' on its own, then it will eliminate competitive products. When this is achieved, the differentiated product enjoys the same price setting regime that the true monopolist does, only on a much smaller scale.

A common way of doing this is by branding, and manufacturers of consumer goods are well practised in promoting their brand through advertising. In aggressively promoting a product, they are attempting to build brand loyalty to the exclusion of others and to increase their market share within their particular market segment. Key technological innovations can also serve the purpose (such as a new format for music recording). Within certain geographical localities, it has been accomplished with such products as milk deliveries (where only one milkman services a certain street). As with all monopoly situations, the company's objective is to separate itself to such an extent that the customer has just one choice of product within the sector. The idea of removing customer choice within the sector is key to monopolistic competition. If companies can develop a product to such an extent that customers automatically think of their product, then they have succeeded in this regard.

The competition in this scenario from the sectors themselves which compete for business. Sellers will attempt to achieve customer loyalty within their sector. If this can be achieved, then their repeat orders will be assured.

25.5 Oligopoly

25.5.1 What is an oligopoly?

An oligopolistic market is one where the majority of the market share is controlled by a few large competitors. We can say that an oligopoly represents a high degree of market concentration and consequently sits next to monopoly on the market structure continuum earlier in this chapter.

Within the oligopoly category there are a range of degrees of concentration. The most concentrated oligopoly is when just two suppliers control the market – a scenario referred to as a *duopoly*. In others, markets may rest in the hands of up to ten big competitors, but the amount of the market held by the big players will vary from industry to industry.

It may be helpful to consider that most industries in the UK fall more or less within the oligopoly category. Each sector will have its few big players and its many smaller ones. The example of the paint industry was discussed earlier, and below are some more examples.

Sector	No. of 'big' companies	Joint market share
Domestic washing powders	2	>90 %
Food retailing	5	>50 %

Example 1   Washing powder

The supply of washing powder to the UK retail market is controlled almost exclusively by two very large competitors. Lever Brothers Ltd (part of Unilever Plc) and the US based Proctor and Gamble group together supply in excess of 90 % of the total UK market. Lever's brands in this sector include Surf and Persil, whereas P & G own Daz, Ariel and Bold. Between them they spend well over £50 million a year on advertising.

As there are two competitors, this is known as duopoly. These companies maintain their duopoly by their enormous advertising investment and by keeping their prices within a few pence of each other. Would-be entrants into the market must enter the brand identity battle. In addition they must find the capital to not only build the necessary plant, but also to advertise their brands on a comparable level with the two big players. These entry barriers have been sufficient to deter new entrants and so the duopoly looks secure.

Example 2 **Food Retailing**

The retail food market in 1991 was worth just over £55 billion and advertising on food products amounted to £559 million. By any standards, this is a large and important industry.

The majority of food sold in the UK is from the 'big five'. Between them, they control 50% of the total market share. The remainder is fought over by hundreds of smaller outlets including independent 'corner shops' and smaller chains like Marks and Spencer, Iceland and William Lows. The Big Five are as follows (1991 figures):

Company	No. of Outlets	Market Share (%)
J Sainsbury	312	15
Tesco	380	12
Isosceles Group	669	8
(Gateway, Fine Fare and others)		
Argyll Group	317	8
(Safeway, Presto and others)		
Asda Stores	203	7

(Source: Keynotes)

25.5.2 Pricing in an oligopoly

We saw that a monopolist, theoretically, can be a price setter. In an oligopoly, each competitor is *interdependent* upon the others.

For each comparable product sold in the oligopolistic market, there will be a market price. The stability of the market relies on the principle that each supplier will supply to the market at an approximately similar price. Diversions from the market price will have one of two effects, depending on the direction of the change.

❑ **Increase in price**

If one competitor 'breaks ranks' and raises its price, then customers will change supplier to one of those who still supply at the previous price. The price increase is likely to be reversed if market share is not to be irrevocably lost.

❑ **Decrease in price**

When one company reduces its price, it begins an unfortunate train of events:
a) company reduces its price;
b) customers change to the cheaper supplier;
c) competitors reduce their prices in order to win back their customers;
d) customers return to their regular supplier.

RESULT – *Everybody* ends up making less money at the new, cheaper market price, BUT, customers benefit from cheaper prices.

As a result of this price interdependence, oligopolists tend to be very careful when it comes to pricing. Price wars benefit nobody in the longer term and competition tends to occur in *non-price* areas. The tensions that exist usually ensure that prices remain relatively stable.

25.5.3 Two types of oligopoly

The large competitors in an oligopoly may or may not communicate with each other.

☐ **Competitive oligopolies** compete by attempting to take market share from each other. Because they know they cannot compete on price, they employ non-price methods. Non-price factors are those features of the product or service which describe quality, value for money, utility and similar advantages. They include claims of superior performance and a whole range of below-line promotions. Advertising is a common way of attempting to gain advantage over competitors without reducing price.

☐ **Collusive oligopolies** are those where the principal players in the market meet to agree on market shares, prices and other areas of mutual interest. Not surprisingly, collusion often results in the companies agreeing a high price structure, and for this reason they are usually illegal. Some forms of loose collusion happen in trade associations or industrial bodies in which the main competitors are represented. Informal agreements or understandings are not uncommon, and these tend to be agreed verbally and 'in the bar' rather than in the Boardroom.

25.6 Perfect Competition

The opposite of monopoly, according to the continuum in figure 25.1, is perfect competition. If it is true that a monopolist has total control over price and oligopolists have partial control, then in perfect competition, no single competitor has such power.

The distinguishing features of perfect competition in its pure form are:

☐ many buyers, each occupying a tiny or insignificant market share;

☐ many small sellers;

☐ a product which is incapable of being differentiated and where all sellers sell an identical product;

☐ all buyers have identical cost structures – they all pay the same for materials, rent, labour etc.;

☐ no single buyer or seller is of sufficient size to influence price;

☐ there are no innovations or 'secrets' which may give one buyer or seller an advantage over another;

☐ there are no entry or exit barriers associated with competing in the market.

Like monopoly, perfect competition is rare in practice – it represents the extreme. Possible examples approaching the extreme would be the provision of lots of bed and breakfast accommodation in a large town, or a large vegetable market.

Perfect competition means that there is zero concentration. Industries where there are many small businesses and fewer large ones represent an approximation to this form of market structure.

It is said that the prices for goods will be arrived at purely through the mechanisms of supply and demand. Because nobody is big enough to set the price, each supplier must take the market price – they are *price takers*. This tends to lead to medium or low profits for the supplier and relative price stability for the buyer.

Review Questions

1. Define the term *market*. (25.1)
2. Distinguish between *industry* and *market*. (25.2)
3. What factors determine market structure? (25.3)
4. What is an entry barrier? Give some examples. (25.4.1)
5. What are the market supply features that determine the following market structures?
   a) Monopoly, (25.4.1)
   b) Monopolistic Competition, (25.4.5)
   c) Duopoly, (25.5.1)
   d) Oligopoly, (25.5.1)
   e) Perfect Competition. (25.6)
6. In what ways has the Government regulated monopolies? (25.4.4)
7. Define and distinguish between *competitive* and *collusive* oligopolies. (25.5.3)
8. Why are oligopolists said to be *price interdependent*? (25.5.2)

Answer to Activity 2

Nuclear weapons

Government legislation forbidding weapons manufacture.

Unique access to raw materials (radioactive metals such as plutonium).

Access to buyers of nuclear weapons.

Enormously high capital costs (several £ billions).

Petroleum excavation and refinement

High capital costs (you would need tens of billions of pounds).

Government regulations (you would need a licence from the Government to extract oil).

Manufacture of a Zantac type drug

The patent held by Glaxo (Holdings) Plc legally prevents you from manufacturing a drug of this type.

Coors lager

Coors is made in the UK by Scottish and Newcastle Plc under a licence from the manufacturers in North America. This is exclusive to S&N and prohibits others from making it in the UK.

Fabric washing powder

The market for these products is held largely by two very large companies. These maintain the duopoly by means of high expenditure on research and development and advertising. Hence, a would-be entrant into the market would not only need to find high capital set-up costs, but also break into the intense competitive rivalry that exists in the industry.

Assignment

In oligopolistic markets, supply of the majority of market share is concentrated in the hands of a few large suppliers. However, despite the diseconomies of scale, smaller companies often make higher profit margins than their larger competitors. Discuss some of the strategies available to small companies which enable them to compete in oligopolistic markets, if possible using a named industry as an example.

Further Reading

Economics – First Year Study Guide: For first year degree students, BPP (Chapters 7 & 8)

Lipsey R.G. & Harbury C., *First Principles of Economics*, Wiedenfeld and Nicolson (London) (Second Edition, 1992, Chapters 16, 17 & 21)

Beardshaw J. & Palfreman D., *The Organisation in its Environment*, Pitman Press (Fourth Edition, Chapter 16)

Palmer A. & Worthington I., *The Business and Marketing Environment*, McGraw Hill (First Edition, 1992, Section 5.6)

26 Privatisation and nationalisation

Objectives   After studying this chapter, students should be able to:

❏ define the terms *privatisation* and *nationalisation*;

❏ describe the history of the debate in this area in the UK;

❏ summarise the arguments that have been advanced for and against privatisation;

❏ summarise the arguments that have been advanced for and against nationalisation,

26.1 Introduction and Definitions

A key determinant of market structure is the issue of who owns – or has control over – the big organisations in any market sector. There was much debate about this during the 'Thatcher years' of the nineteen eighties, and the massive privatisation programmes during that time drastically changed many markets. The overall effect of such selling off was to reduce the monopoly power of the main utilities. Let us define the terms.

❏ **Privatisation** is the selling off of government owned companies to the public. It is called privatisation because ownership is passing from the public sector (the state) to the private sector (individuals and private businesses). The Government divides up the business into individual shares and then sells the shares, through the Stock Exchange, to the public. If the Government sells more than 50% of the shares, then it loses control of the company.

❏ **Nationalisation** is the opposite of privatisation. It is when the Government takes control of private businesses and brings them under public ownership (i.e. the public sector). They would then be absorbed into a government department and run as part of the Government. This usually involves the creation of a 'government monopoly'.

26.2 A Brief History

When the Second World War ended in 1945 the Conservative Party headed by Winston Churchill was defeated by Labour. The new Prime Minister, Clement Attlee set about restoring the country's economy and infrastructure after the devastation caused during the war. One key point in Mr Attlee's strategy was to bring all of the important utilities under government control in order to exercise an increased influence over them in the national reconstruction programmes. He felt that certain things, the areas which were of strategic importance to the country's development, were 'too important' to leave to the private sector. The main targets of the nationalisation programme were energy (oil, gas, coal and electricity), railways, vehicle construction, postal services, steel and telecommunications. Nationalisation continued after the Conservatives regained power in 1951, indicating that it was accepted as sensible policy across the political spectrum.

These industries remained in public ownership until the Thatcher Government came to power in May 1979. One of the main thrusts of their legislative programme throughout the nineteen eighties was to reverse the nationalisation programme. In consequence, one by one, the government monopolies were broken up and sold off to the private sector. By the turn of the decade, the Government had divested itself of the majority of its direct interests in industry. There was a little more trouble associated with the privatisation of some of the less attractive companies and some failed to be sufficiently profitable to represent a good investment for shareholders (e.g. the nuclear power generators). These, though, were the minority.

The Conservative Privatisation Programme in the 1980's
(Principal privatisations only)

Date Privatised	Company	Value (£)
1979*	British Petroleum	7.4 billion
1981*	British Aerospace	513 million
1982	Amersham International	71 million
1982	National Freight Corp.	54 million
1984*	British Telecommunications	3.9 billion
1986	British Gas	5.4 billion
1987	British Airways	900 million
1987	Rolls Royce	1.08 billion
1987	British Airports	1.3 billion
1988	British Steel	2.5 billion
1989	Water authorities	5.3 billion

*First issue where others followed in later years.

(Source: Education Guardian, 4 June 1991)

26.3 The Debate (Advantages and Disadvantages)

There are some complex arguments associated with this area. Much acrimonious debate took place in Parliament and in the country during the privatisation programme and there emerged a broad difference along party lines. The Labour Party tended to oppose the programme arguing that the private sector could not be trusted with suppliers of strategically vital goods, and it was also concerned about possible job losses after privatisation. The Conservatives stressed the advantages of the increased competition that would result from the break up of monopolies, and that businessmen rather than civil servants knew best how to operate profitable businesses. The issues can be summarised as follows.

26.3.1 The case for nationalisation

Many of the arguments for nationalisation are the same as for monopolies (most nationalised companies will be monopolies). As we saw when we considered monopolies, these might include increased economies of scale, the avoidance of wasteful duplication of efforts when two or more companies are carrying out similar operations etc.

The more potent arguments are political ones.

❑ It allows the Government to have control over strategically vital areas. This means that supply can be guaranteed by the Government regardless of the movements of market forces.

❑ The Government can exercise a tighter control over the economy if it is heavily involved in it. A significant proportion of any company's costs will be energy, communications, transport etc. and the Government can vary its prices as part of its policy on industry. If it wishes to stimulate industrial activity it can hold utilities prices down and vice versa. Politically sensitive areas can be catered for by, say, offering cheaper electricity prices to hospitals, schools and the elderly.

❑ It allows the Government to provide goods and services which are essential but could not be provided by the private sector. This includes uneconomical provisions such as coal, health and nuclear power.

❑ Companies that must remain afloat because they supply essential goods or are big employers can be rescued by the Government putting money into them. Such companies are called 'lame ducks' and controversy always surrounds such cash injections.

❑ It provides the Government with a means of ensuring that services are equalised throughout the country. Those in favour of nationalisation argue that the outlying regions may suffer because it is uneconomical to offer the same level of service (gas, electricity etc.) to them as to those living in the major cities.

26.3.2 The case against nationalisation

The opponents of nationalisation have two principal contentions against it.

❑ Firstly, it has been argued that the traditional nationalised companies tended to be inefficient. According to this argument there was an increasing trend towards over-staffing and bureaucracy. The lack of competition in their respective markets meant that there were no other businesses against which to judge performance. Critics say that any sense of economic urgency was removed because all losses were paid for by the taxpayer.

❑ Secondly, most nationalised companies ended up costing the Government money rather than making it. This necessarily puts pressure on other areas of government finance.

26.3.3 The case for privatisation

The proponents of privatisation argue that it has several advantages.

❑ When the privatisation involves a 'breaking up' of a monopoly, then competition is increased. The former parts of the monopoly compete with each other and this, in theory, has the effect of increasing quality and decreasing costs. This will provide an improved service to customers.

❑ The sale itself generates money from shareholders which the Government can use for other purposes.

❑ The drain on government funds is removed if the loss making company is sold.

- ❏ The Government will receive tax revenues from the companies when they report profits.

- ❏ Businesses will work better when they are managed by experienced industrial managers rather than civil servants.

- ❏ It will increase the share volumes traded in the City (Stock Exchange). This in turn may have a favourable effect on the capital account in the balance of payments as foreign investors inject cash into the UK to buy up shares.

26.3.4 The case against privatisation

The opponents of privatisation have raised a number of objections both on ideological grounds and as a result of observing some of those that have occurred.

- ❏ It reduces the value of government-held assets. This has been a notable issue in the UK where the public sector was relatively small anyway compared to our main European neighbours.

- ❏ When some services are controlled by the private sector, profit will increase in importance. This may result in the company failing to serve some parts of the population which are uneconomical (especially outlying communities).

- ❏ It deprives the Government of the control of some strategically important industries such as defence equipment manufacturers, energy generators etc.

- ❏ Only the profitable parts of the nationalised industries have been sold, leaving the Government with the unattractive and uneconomical parts.

- ❏ Questions have been raised about claims that competition has been increased. After some privatisations, it appeared that a public monopoly has simply become a private monopoly. This criticism has been levelled particularly at the selling off of British Gas and British Telecommunications, although recent developments have been designed to encourage new entrants into these sectors.

- ❏ Some privatisations have resulted in increased prices. This claim is usually levelled at the water companies that project significant price increases in order to invest in improved assets and infrastructure.

- ❏ High profits have been criticised. In the year to 1992, British Telecommunications Plc made over £3 billion in profit before interest and tax. Critics argued that instead of making such profits, the company should have reduced their prices for the benefit of customers and accepted a lower profit figure.

We can see that the debates on all sides are complicated. Each privatisation is a trade off where some benefits are gained and some advantages are sacrificed. Whether the advantages outweigh the disadvantages is a matter of opinion – often arising from ones' political leanings.

Review Questions

1. Define *privatisation*. (26.1)

2. Define *nationalisation*. (26.1)

3. Why was nationalisation seen as a good strategy after the war? (26.2)

4. Explain why the Thatcher Government embarked upon its large privatisation programme in the nineteen eighties. (26.2)

5. What are the principal arguments in favour of privatisation? (26.3.3)

6. What are the principal arguments against privatisation? (26.3.4)

7. What are the principal arguments in favour of nationalisation? (26.3.1)

8. What are the principal arguments against nationalisation? (26.3.2)

Assignment

The privatisation of the **electricity industry** in the late nineteen eighties brought about significant changes in the structure of the industry.

Discuss:

The structure of the industry prior to privatisation,

The structure of the industry after privatisation,

The effects of the privatisation upon the end user (individual businesses and private consumers).

Further Reading

Economics – First Year Study Guide, for first year degree students, BPP Publishing (Chapters 7 & 8)

Lipsey R.G. & Harbury C., *First Principles of Economics*, Wiedenfeld and Nicolson (London, Second Edition, 1992, Chapters 16, 17 & 21)

Beardshaw J. & Palfreman D., *The Organisation in its Environment*, Pitman Press (Fourth Edition, Chapter 16)

Palmer A. & Worthington I., *The Business and Marketing Environment*, McGraw Hill (First Edition, 1992, Section 5.6)

Section 7

Management of Business Organisations

The management of organisations can determine their success or failure. In this section we discuss some of the more influential theories on management, and some of the techniques that have been used to improve managerial effectiveness.

Contents

27 Definition and theories of management

Objectives   After studying this chapter, students should be able to:

- ☐ summarise the principal definitions of management;
- ☐ explain why management is important in an organisation;
- ☐ summarise the contributions of F W Taylor and the proponents of scientific management;
- ☐ describe the contributions of Henri Fayol and Lyndall Urwick;
- ☐ summarise the practices of effective management from the work of John Kotter and Henry Mintzberg.

27.1 What is Management?

Management is the key to business and the 'glue' that holds all elements of business together. Good management will determine that a business is successful, bad management will cause ruin. It is as simple as that. All businesses rely on managers to run them, oversee staff, make contracts, make decisions etc. But what is *management*?

It is a concept that is easy to understand but a little harder to state. Below are a number of popular definitions.

'To manage is to forecast and plan, to organise, to command, to co-ordinate and to control.' (Fayol, 1916)

'The five essential managerial functions: planning, organising, staffing, directing and leading, and controlling.' (Koontz and O'Donnell, 1976)

'Management is a social process...planning, control, co-ordination and motivation.' (Brech, 1957)

'Managing is getting things done through other people' (Douglass, Cook, Hendricks, 1972)

One thing that quickly becomes clear is that management involves many things. It is probable that most definitions are too narrow and do not fully articulate the breadth of management as a practice. The definitions given above seem to presume that management always involves other people and co-ordinating and controlling them. However, some managerial jobs involve managing projects which may well be one person working on his own. We must be careful not to be too inflexible, therefore, when we attempt to arrive at a range of definitions. A more meaningful understanding of this complex area will emerge when we have considered the different facets associated with it.

27.2 Theories of Management

Management theory is thought to have evolved over the course of the twentieth century principally as a result of the work of a handful of influential thinkers. They can be roughly divided into the 'classical theorists' and the more recent 'modern' contributors. The people most frequently cited in the classical mould are:

- ❏ Frederick W Taylor (and the 'scientific management' school)
- ❏ Henri Fayol
- ❏ Lyndall F Urwick

We will briefly consider the contributions of each and then review the findings of two notable recent workers, John Kotter and Henry Mintzberg. There are many other significant writers on management, and interested readers should access one of the books mentioned at the end of the chapter.

27.3 F W Taylor and the Scientific Management School.

Frederick Taylor (1856-1917) was one of the earliest of the management theorists. He worked for the Bethlehem Steel Company in the USA, and it was here that he developed his theories of *'scientific management'*. He propounded the idea of applying quantitative methods to management problems. This evolved into 'work study' and the analysis of work and the rates of work. His theories were quite revolutionary at a time when the way to increase productivity was simply to take on more men and make them work harder.

He introduced the idea of comparing employee performance against standard. This involved determining the expected time for an operation to take and rewarding or punishing workers according to their performance. His work also embraced finding the optimum way for a given job to be done, such as by varying shovel size for a loading operation.

The 'scientific management' idea was further developed by later theorists, most notably the **Gilbreths** (Frank and Lilian) who concentrated on *'motion study'* and **Henry Gantt** who's principal legacy is his 'chart'.

The **Gilbreths'** contribution of 'motion study' was to analyse the way in which a worker performed a task and then to see if there was any way of simplifying it or making it more efficient. The objective of such a study was to increase a worker's actual work output within the limited amount of time in the day that he was working. The example most quoted examples of their success in this was when they worked out how to reduce the number of movements in laying a brick from 18 to 5. The outcome was that more bricks could be laid in any hour or day and the bricklayer put less work expenditure into any given number of bricks laid.

Henry Gantt is best remembered for his development of the *Gantt Chart*. He argued that time could be used more effectively if tasks in an operation were carefully planned in sequence, and the chart was originally set up to illustrate graphically the extent to which tasks had been achieved. This would have the advantage of giving management more control over events and it would prevent time 'leaking' in fruitless or unnecessary jobs. Gantt Charts are used today in a wide variety of planning and control processes.

27.4 Henri Fayol

Fayol (1841-1925) was a French industrialist who spent his entire working life with a coal mining company. His main contribution was to attempt to break down the management job into its component parts. We saw his definition of management at the beginning of this chapter, and this is a good summary of his theories.

His work is best remembered for his 'six activities' and his 'fourteen principles'. These are things he developed from his own experiences as a manager and which he worked out in his own life, with beneficial effects.

Fayol's 'six activities' are the things he considered to be the principal areas of concern to the industrial manager.

Technical activities

Commercial activities

Financial activities

Security activities

Accounting activities

Managerial and administrative activities

The tribute to the influence of Fayol's work is that his *activities* are roughly the make up of the modern Board of Directors. We would use different names today, but the tasks are essentially as Fayol described.

Activity	*In Chapters 18 to 24 of this book, we considered the various functions within a modern business organisation. These evolved from Fayol's work. Can you remember all of the functions without looking them up?*

The 'fourteen principles' were, in Fayol's opinion, the elements of good management. He himself applied them and found them to work. Again, when we consider the list, we will see that many of them are still considered today to form the basis of good management practice.

Principle	Meaning
Division of Work	One man, one job. Specialise work.
Authority	Manager must be able to give orders and be sure they will be carried out
Discipline	Respect and order throughout the workplace
Unity of command	Remove confusion by having one employee report to only one boss
Unity of direction	One boss is responsible for the planning and direction
Subordination of individual interests to the general good of the company	Employees should be prepared to put the company first
Fair pay	Pay should be fair to the employee and acceptable to the organisation

Centralisation	Management authority and responsibility ultimately rests with the management centre
Scalar Chain	The observance of an orderly hierarchy line of authority from bottom to the top
Order	tidiness and order in the work environment
Equity	Fairness and a sense of justice
Stability of tenure	As far as possible, provide job security
Initiative	Staff should be encouraged to show initiative
Esprit de corps	Encourage and develop teams and a friendly working environment

27.5 Lyndall F Urwick

Urwick worked after the Second World War, and so had the benefit of studying Taylor and Fayol. As we would expect, his ideas are built upon the early theorists are an extension of them.

The contribution of Urwick can be distilled into his ten 'principles' (1952). Some of these echo the work of Fayol and others develop his ideas.

1. The principle of the **objective**
    Every organisation (and every part of an organisation) should have a clear aim or objective.

2. The principle of **specialisation**
    Departments and individuals should specialise.

3. The principle of **co-ordination**
    All activities in the organisation should be co-ordinated, usually from a central point.

4. The principle of **authority**
    Authority must be understood and exercised. There should be a clear line of authority to every member of an organisation.

5. The principle of **responsibility**
    A departmental head is absolutely responsible for the actions of his subordinates.

6. The principle of **definition**
    Jobs and tasks should be clearly defined such that there is no room for confusion.

7. The principle of **correspondence**
    Authority and responsibility must be matched (or should correspond).

8. The principle of **span of control**
    Places upper limits on the number of subordinates any manager should have. Urwick proposes no more than six subordinates. See part 9.3 for a discussion of this issue.

9. The principle of **balance**
    The various units (departments and functions) of an organisation should be kept in balance.

10. The principle of **continuity**
    Structures should be set up so that the business can continue in any event. When re-organisation occurs, provision should be made to ensure continuity of the organisation.

27.6 Modern Thinkers

27.6.1 John Kotter

So far in this chapter we have looked at what theorists *think that managers should do*. The influence of Kotter's work arises from the fact that he looked at *what successful managers actually do*. He found that they had a distinctive person orientation and employed influence rather than autocracy in their interpersonal dealings. His summary of what successful managers do is as follows:

1. They spend most of their time working with others.

2. Most of their time is spent in short and seemingly disjointed conversations and questionings.

3. They ask a lot of questions.

4. They seldom *tell* people what to do, but they attempt to *influence* others.

5. In allocating time, they often react to others' initiatives.

In addition, Kotter identified three patterns of management behaviour that seemed to prove successful in the workplace.

1. Agenda – setting of goals and time scales.

2. Network building – establishing relationships within the structure of the organisation and with outside individuals and companies.

3. Execution – getting things done through the network of contacts established.

27.6.2 Henry Mintzberg

Mintzberg is an American thinker on management and has been one of the most influential writers among the 'modern' theorists. One of his most significant contributions to the understanding of management came in the 1970s when he continued Kotter's work when he undertook a study of what five successful managers actually do. After observing them in action, he summarised their activities into ten *good practices*.

1. Design work for the organisation or team being managed.

2. Monitor the internal and external environments of the organisation.

3. Initiate change when necessary.

4. Restore stability in disturbance.

5. Lead subordinates.

6. Provide subordinates with relevant information.

7. Develop a network of contacts.

8. Inform outsiders when necessary.

9. Serve as a 'figurehead' for subordinates.

10. Lead major negotiations.

Review Questions

1. In your own words, offer a good definition of management. (27.1 might help you)

2. What was the emphasis of FW Taylor's work on management? (27.3)

3. Name two other *scientific management* thinkers in addition to Taylor. (27.3)

4. What was Fayol's main contribution to management theory? (27.4)

5. List Fayol's *six activities*. (27.4)

6. List Urwick's *ten principles*. (27.5)

7. Summarise the contributions of John Kotter (27.6.1) and Henry Mintzberg (27.6.2)

Assignment

In this chapter we encountered Henry Gantt, who developed an important management tool which is referred to as the Gantt Chart. Find out exactly what the Gantt Chart is and in what contexts it may prove to be useful as a management tool.

Further Reading

Cole, G.A., *Management – Theory and Practice*, DP Publications (Fourth Edition, 1993, Chapters 1–10)

Mullins L.J., *Management and Organisational Behaviour*, Pitman Press (1993, Chapters 2 & 12)

Vroom V.H. & Deci E.L., *Management and Motivation*, Penguin Books (Second Edition, 1992)

28 Principles of management

Objectives   After studying this chapter, students should be able to:

- ❏ describe the advantages to be gained by managing 'the self';
- ❏ explain the two key elements of self-management;
- ❏ explain what is meant be effectiveness;
- ❏ describe the qualities that increase personal effectiveness;
- ❏ explain the meaning of the term 'time-management';
- ❏ describe some techniques that can be used to enhance an individual's use of time.
- ❏ describe Henri Fayol's contribution to the functions involved in man-management;
- ❏ understand the essentials of leadership;
- ❏ explain the meaning of the various types of power identified by Galbraith;
- ❏ describe the prominent thinkers in the sphere of human motivation.

28.1 Self Management

There are a number of good reasons why 'the self' must be managed.

- ❏ To ensure that personal objectives are met.
- ❏ To make the *best* use of personal resources (time, ability, money etc.).
- ❏ To optimise personal performance in whatever circumstances one finds oneself.
- ❏ To avoid unpleasant or otherwise undesirable situations.

Good self-management means that you can achieve more effective work per day, year etc. Individuals who are disorganised, constantly in a messy environment or who can be counted on to turn up late for meetings etc., can usually be identified as poor self managers. It is likely that such people will achieve less than others, not because of lack of ability, but because their ability is not being managed effectively.

There are two main considerations in self-management; *personal effectiveness* and *time management*.

28.2 Elements of Self-Management – Effectiveness

A common misconception is that hard work is somehow a virtue in itself. In many workplace situations, the culture dictates that if you aren't busy, you aren't achieving anything. Driven by pressure of work and guilt, many individuals work very hard, with commendable commitment for up to 50 years, and somehow the results are not commensurate with the time investment. Little may be achieved, relative to the work put in, in either corporate or personal terms.

Effectiveness is not related to the amount of work done, but how much *effective work* is done – work that achieves the objective required. A useful saying:

'It's not how hard you work, but what you achieve when you work.'

Or, put another way,

'Work smarter, not harder.'

Example	**A Poor Self-Manager**
	The story is told of a farmer who set out early one morning to plough a large field on his farm. When he arrived at the tractor, he noticed that he didn't have enough diesel, so he set off for town to get some. On his way out of the farm, he noticed that the chickens hadn't been fed. As he went to get the corn for the chickens, he passed the pig sties and saw that one of the roofs had blown in, and as it was about to rain, he decided to fix it right away. This took longer than he thought it would, so as lunch time approached, he decided to finish it the next day and get on with other jobs. Having fed the chickens, he was about to set off back to town when he noticed that one of his dogs had a sore which needed bathing. Feeling that it would be cruel to let the dog suffer, he thought he ought to do it straight away. As he was treating the dog, his wife reminded him that he still hadn't put in his already overdue tax return. He decided to start this before he went to town...
	When evening came, he had worked hard all day, and still hadn't achieved his day's objective – to plough the field.

Self management for maximum effectiveness means isolating the objective you wish to achieve, or the things for which you will be held accountable. The effective person will measure his achievement in those terms and not by any others that might seem perfectly good in their own right. It is important to learn to say 'no' to some things, in order to concentrate on the most important things in the light of your objectives. Learn to distinguish between activity and accomplishment.

There are a number of personal qualities and characteristics which increase effectiveness:

☐ clear objectives,

☐ well worked-out plans,

☐ resolve and perseverance,

☐ willingness to sacrifice some things,

☐ some degree of regimentation,

☐ discipline.

Some people seem to have these things in abundance, for others, much more effort is needed.

One key to personal effectiveness is learning to live with tension. Life is a series of difficult decisions. You can spend your time doing many worthwhile things, but the fact is that you only have so much time and energy. The effective person must keep several 'balls in the air' at once, and this may involve a continual state of psychological pressure. Constantly monitoring your efforts is an important quality. This involves ensuring that what you are engaged in doing is not only worthwhile, but the best use of your resources.

28.3 Elements of Self-Management – Time Management

Time is the one resource which cannot be controlled. It cannot be stopped, slowed down, stored or stretched. It must be used as it comes and this necessarily presents many difficulties. The simple fact is that there is not enough time to do everything we might want to do. We must decide what is important and prioritise things. The time worn phrase: *plan your time or others will plan it for you* is very true. It is surprising how time can slip away with little or nothing to show for it.

Many individuals tend to be *reactive* rather than *proactive*. The person who seems to be constantly 'fighting fires' is less likely to achieve than the one who uses his time proactively and with one eye constantly on his longer term objectives.

A number of rules are consequently used by good self-managers.

28.3.1 Decide on your long-term objectives

These will determine how you spend your time in the shorter term if you are committed to them. Once your long-range plans have been carefully formulated, you must be prepared to subordinate your short-term activities to them.

28.3.2 Schedule your time

A schedule is a formal declaration of how you intend to spend your time on a given day, month, year etc. The way time is planned in the short term will contribute towards the achievement of long-term aims. Some people use simple diaries, some planners and others a timetable type device. The purpose is to ensure that all of your time serves a purpose towards achieving your goals. This does not mean that you leave no time for recreation, but that such worthwhile activities do not encroach on time you should be working.

28.3.3 Stick to your schedule

This is where resolve and perseverance come in. If you have something in your schedule, do it and do not be diverted by other activities however important the activities might seem to be.

28.3.4 Learn to do more than one thing at a time

Be innovative in the way you reach your objectives. It might be as simple as learning a language through tapes while doing the washing up. On a larger scale an example might be doing a part-time degree whilst gaining experience in a full-time job.

28.4 Managing People

Most, but not all managers have *subordinates* – people who report to the manager on a day-to-day basis in their jobs. It is important that the manager has the ability to get things done through subordinates (to delegate work) as it will be he who will be held responsible for the objectives set for his department. The nub of the issue is how to get others to perform tasks to the required standard, consistently and continuously.

As seen in Chapter 27, Fayol would lead us to believe that the manager's job is to:

☐ forecast;

☐ plan;

☐ organise;

☐ command;

☐ control;

☐ co-ordinate.

Organising, commanding, controlling and co-ordinating are people-centred operations. This suggests that the oversight of people is the largest and most important part
of the managers job.

There are many issues with which any discussion of man management might concern itself. Fayol's people-oriented management tasks themselves conceal within them
many separate skills and competencies. Such matters can be considered as the 'nuts
and bolts' or tactics of management. One might think, for example, of the manager's
ability to organise his staff, to delegate, to instruct, to praise, to show impartiality etc.
These are all very important matters but we shall not consider these issues in detail in
this text. Overarching all these matters are the two main issues in man management.
These are the central management competencies that determine the success or otherwise of the manager. They are *leadership* and *motivation*.

28.5 Elements of Managing People – Leadership

28.5.1 What is leadership?

Most of us can look at certain political figures, either past or present, and say that they
were or are good leaders – whether we agree with their cause or not. For example most
agree that Winston Churchill and Adolf Hitler were both good leaders, whilst a more
recent example might be Margaret Thatcher. It would be helpful then to examine such
people and ask what it is about them that makes them such good leaders. They may
have been good speakers, intelligent or charismatic, but these things in themselves do
not make a leader.

A good definition of leadership is:

> '*A dynamic process at work in a group whereby one individual over a particular period of
> time and in a particular organisational context, influences the other group members to
> commit themselves freely to the achievement of group tasks or goals.*'

(Cole, G A, in Personnel Management, DP Publications 1993)

A leader, on the other hand can be simply put as:

> *someone who knows where he is going and is able to persuade others to go along with him.*

28.5.2 Components of leadership

From this second definition we can see that leadership has two essential components.

❏ **The conceptual**

Implicit in leadership is that the leader is leading people *somewhere*. This could be
something as momentous as Moses to the Promised Land or Hitler to conquer
Western Europe in World War Two. Conversely it could be a Sales Manager leading his team of reps to achieve or exceed sales targets. It involves having well
defined objectives – a mission or a vision. The leader will feel the need to achieve
this goal and this will be the driving force behind his leadership.

❏ **The interpersonal**

Leaders cannot lead unless they have followers. They may well have clear objectives and know where they want to go, but they must have the means to make people go with them. This introduces the concept of *power*.

28.5.3 Power in leadership

The nature of people is such that they act when so compelled to do by another's power over them. The fact that they may willingly submit to this power does not make it any less potent a force. John Kenneth Galbraith, a formidable thinker on management and economic issues, identified three essential forms of power:

❑ Condign Power

❑ Compensatory Power

❑ Conditioned Power

(J K Galbraith, The Anatomy of Power, 1983)

❑ **Condign Power** is that which exerts influence by offering a highly undesirable alternative to following. This is the 'do it or else' approach, and history is littered with examples of this type of power being exercised with highly effective results. It can be used where the leader has access to the means of punishment for those who will not follow. The use of condign power is broad, as Galbraith elucidates, '*it extends to power that is exercised by any form of adverse action or its threat, including fines, other property expropriation, verbal rebuke and conspicuous condemnation by other individuals or the community.*' Much of the rule of law relies on condign power in that, for example, if you do not pay your income tax, you will be punished by the state.

❑ **Compensatory Power** is loyalty 'bought', usually with money (e.g. salary) but other considerations have been known. It is the opposite of condign power in that it offers a reward if the person will follow the leader – it is a positive rather than a negative constraint. It begins with the invitation, 'if you follow me, I will give you ...' He who leads by using compensatory power must have access to the means of payment, and of course, he must reward followers according to the terms agreed at the outset if he to receive their continuing loyalty. If condign power can be considered as a 'stick' then compensatory power can be thought of as a 'carrot'.

❑ **Conditioned Power** is the willingness of followers to follow because they have been conditioned so to do. They do not expect any reward and will not follow simply because they fear the consequences of not doing so. Something within them says that they must follow; some previous conditioning makes them fall into line behind the leader. Conditioning can result from any number of previous influences, such as the expectations of society, followers' understanding of their 'role', their self image or the 'moral codes' they have been brought up with. The leader of people who are conditioned to follow need only state that his objectives are consistent with people's conditioning and he will have a ready band of followers.

From our earlier definition of a leader, we can see that there are a number of means by which a leader can *persuade* people to 'go along with him.'

28.5.4 Trait Theory

One approach to thinking on leadership, which in no way contradicts the foregoing discussion, says that the effectiveness of leadership depends on the leader's *traits*. The implication in this is that people will follow someone who has enough of certain qualities or characteristics that he is perceived as a leader. Within this school of thought, the most commonly noted traits include:

❑ intelligence;

- extroversion;
- humour;
- enthusiasm;
- fairness;
- sympathy;
- self-confidence;
- individuality;
- resolve;
- communication skills.

We all know that not all leaders possess these traits. It would seem reasonable to assume that the roots of leadership arise from a number of sources depending upon the type of leader and his situation.

Activity 1   *Consider the leadership or the nature of power that each of the following exert on their people and identify the possible sources of their influence.*

Sir Iain Vallance – Chairman of British Telecommunications Plc

Rev Sun Myung Moon – Head of the Unification Church (The 'Moonies')

The head of a household – with a large family

The Prime Minister

President Saddam Hussein – President of Iraq

28.6 Elements in Managing People – Motivation

If a manager wants his subordinates to produce effective work then the subordinates must, to a greater or lesser extent, be motivated. The manager, by virtue of his position, has a significant influence upon the level of motivation in the department. Highly motivated people will be 'self-starters' and are likely to achieve more effective work than those who must be pushed.

There have been several influential writers on human motivation and how to achieve it. Each theory has its merits and the lesson to draw from the diversity of writings is that the issue is more complicated than any one theory. Five of the most significant theorists in this area are: Abraham Maslow; Frederick Herzberg; Clayton Aldefer; D. McClelland; Victor H. Vroom.

28.6.1 Abraham Maslow

The work of Maslow, first published in 1943, remained the most influential work in this area for many years. His work rested upon the supposition that man is a being who will always want more once one type of need is satisfied. The *hierarchy of human needs*, as put forward by Maslow, is usually represented as a triangle. Figure 28.1 shows the usual form of his hierarchy.

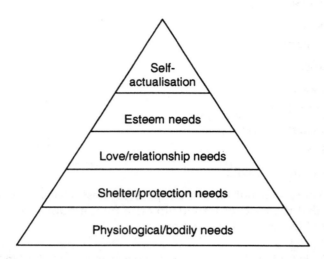

Figure 28.1: Abraham Maslow's hierarchy of human needs.

Maslow argued that humans were motivated to reach certain levels of need. Once one level of need was satisfied, his motivation would be driven by his concern for meeting the next and so on until the final level in the hierarchy was reached. The simplicity of Maslow's proposals is attractive even if they are not as coherent as some of the theories which came after it. The components of the hierarchy are:

❏ **Physiological Needs**. These are essential to the normal working of the body, and include such things as oxygen, water, food, general health etc. Some have argued that this category can also include 'quality of life' issues such as sleep, some degree of pleasure, maternal or paternal fulfilment or the satisfaction of sexual appetites.

❏ **Safety Needs**. These include a sense of security, some degree of physical comfort ('a nest'), the need for order and predictability, shelter, and protection from danger.

❏ **Love Needs**. These are sometimes called social needs as they concern the individual's need to inter-relate with others. Included in this category are a sense of belonging, friendships, affection etc.

❏ **Esteem Needs**. This category refers to the person's need to be held in esteem by himself and others. Examples are self-esteem (self image), prestige, recognition, appreciation from others and accomplishment.

❏ **Self-actualisation needs**. As the final motivating factor, when all else has been satisfied, these needs are seen as those which drive creative urges, invention and 'eccentric' behaviour. It implies doing things for their own sake and not because doing them achieves any other end.

The main critics of Maslow say that it just isn't as simple as that and that the order of needs satisfaction varies from person to person. For example, some people may be able to 'self-actualise' by inventing, creating etc., with only the most modest means of shelter and little or no social or affectionate interaction. Similarly, an individual with a serious illness (physiological needs) might have as his highest motivation to finish a book he is writing (esteem need or self actualisation need) rather than concerning himself with his illness.

Whilst the work of Maslow is seen as a valuable contribution to this area of debate, it clearly does not describe the whole picture.

28.6.2 Frederick Herzberg

Herzberg's work is particularly designed to address the motivation of people in work situations rather than on a psychological level as may have been the case with Maslow. After much research, he was able to distil his data down to two factors. These he called 'Hygiene factors' and 'Motivating factors'.

Hygiene factors are those which are important in that they prevent employees from becoming dissatisfied. They can be described as preventative measures or maintenance issues, in that they do not themselves motivate, but they do maintain the normal working of the employee. Such factors include:

- salary;
- quality and level of supervision;
- working conditions;
- interpersonal relations with colleagues.

Motivating factors, as the name suggests, are those which provide motivation to employees. Herzberg identified a number including:

- achievement and the opportunity to achieve;
- recognition of good work and status;
- the nature of the work itself;
- responsibility and power;
- opportunities for growth and advancement.

Herzberg's theories have been influential in changing management thinking over the years. They have encouraged attention to be paid to the factors according to the needs of the employees. The controversial or surprising element in the above is that salary is not listed as a motivator. Despite intuitive misgivings about this, Herzberg's findings have been reinforced by a number of studies among several types of workers. Broadly speaking, these studies have agreed with Herzberg's initial conclusions.

Activity 2   *Some critics of Herzberg have said that salary (or pay) should be included as a motivating factor rather than a hygiene factor. Do you agree or not – and why?*

28.6.3 Clayton Aldefer

Aldefer's work in 1972 post-dated both Maslow and Herzberg by many years. In consequence, his work represents a development of the earlier work. Aldefer's **ERG Theory** argues that Maslow's hierarchy is too rigid and that instead, three levels of need can be seen as a continuum. A continuum representation means that the actual state of things can be at any point along it. According to the ERG theory, the continuum has three identifiable points along it: *existence, relatedness* and *growth*.

Existence corresponds to Maslow's lower needs (physiological and shelter), Relatedness to love and attachment needs, and Growth to Maslow's higher needs of esteem and self-actualisation. Instead of moving from one level to the next (as per Maslow), individuals move incrementally along the continuum. The ERG theory is thought to be more flexible than Maslow's and more accurately represents the complexities of the various human needs.

28.6.4 D McClelland

McClelland and his colleagues at Harvard University working in the early 1960's isolated three areas of human need. They labelled these as follows:

- ❏ the need for achievement (n Ach);
- ❏ the need for affiliation (n Aff);
- ❏ the need for power (n Pow).

The study centred around the human need for achievement. The **achievement motivation theory** found that those who had a particularly pronounced n Ach factor demonstrated:

- ❏ a constant need for achievement;
- ❏ a willingness to accept positions of responsibility;
- ❏ a desire to set themselves realistic goals;
- ❏ keenness to receive feedback on their performance;
- ❏ that achievement is more important to them than affiliation needs.

It quickly dawned on personnel managers that McClelland's n Ach type of people would be ideal managers. In consequence, they sought such qualities in applicants and still use selection procedures that attempt to identify them.

28.6.5 Victor H Vroom

Vroom developed his **expectancy** (or **valence**) **theory** in the mid nineteen sixties. He presented the theory in the form of an equation:

$$Motivation = valence \times expectancy$$

According to the theory, motivated behaviour in the workplace is a product of two key factors.

Valence expresses the degree of satisfaction that the individual thinks he will enjoy as a result of the course of action towards which he is motivated. It refers to the anticipated satisfaction rather than the actual (and of course, these may differ greatly). Put simply, valence can be described as the worker's desire for the reward that will result from the action. The **expectancy** factor refers to the strength of belief that the action will lead to a particular outcome. It can be described as the strength of belief in a relationship between the effort put in and the possible rewards.

When both valence and expectancy are high, the individual, according to Vroom, will experience high motivation (which Vroom referred to as *force*). Motivation will fall off accordingly when one of the two factors weakens.

Let us construct an example to illustrate how the valence theory works. Suppose you are a director of a company and the Managing Director is due to retire in the next year. You are one of several possible successors to the top job. There are four possible scenarios based upon two variables:

Variable 1

Your desire for the job may be high or low (valence). You may want the job very much indeed or you may actively dislike the prospect of becoming Managing Director.

Variable 2

Your perception of your chances of obtaining the position may be high or low (expectancy). It may be that you have been primed for the job for some years and that your succession is almost automatic. Conversely, you may think you have no chance whatsoever of getting the position.

The four possible scenarios are shown diagrammatically in figure 28.2.

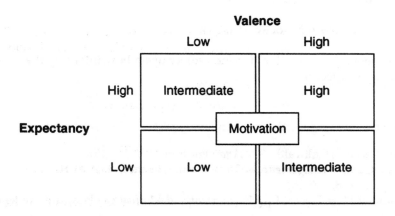

Figure 28.2: A representation of Vroom's expectancy theory.

Academic writers since Vroom have added to his theory and it can be said that it remains one of the most widely respected theories of motivation.

Review Questions

1. Describe some of the reasons for managing yourself. (28.1.1)

2. What are the two key areas to be considered in self-management? (28.1.2)

3. Describe some of the personal qualities that contribute to personal effectiveness. (28.2)

4. Describe some techniques that can increase an individual's use of time. (28.3)

5. What are considered to be the two key areas in the management of people? (28.4)

6. Define and describe the two dimensions of leadership. (28.5.2)

7. Explain the meanings of the following terms and describe what is needed in order to exercise them:

    condign power

    compensatory power

    conditioned power (28.5.3)

8. Explain the elements of Abraham Maslow's theory of motivation and how it is proposed to work. (28.6.1)

9. According to Frederick Herzberg, why is money not a motivating factor? (28.6.2)

10. Define valence in the context of Vroom's expectancy theory. (28.6.5)

Assignment

Intelligently discuss the following contentions.

☐ Leadership is simply about having firm objectives.

☐ If you want people to obey you at work, you need a big stick – punish them for disobedience.

☐ People work for money – that's all.

☐ A person's motivation depends solely upon how intensely the person wants a particular outcome to happen.

Further Reading

John Kenneth Galbraith, *The Anatomy of Power*, Corgi Books

Cole, G.A., *Management – Theory and Practice*, DP Publications (Fourth Edition, Chapters 7, 8, 9 & 26)

Vroom V.H. & Deci E.L., *Management and Motivation*, Penguin Books (Second Edition, 1992)

Mullins L.J., *Management and Organisational Behaviour*, Pitman Press (1993, Chapters 8 & 14)

Evenden R. & Anderson G., *Management Skills – Making the Most of People*, Addison Wesley Publishing (1992)

Rees D.W., *The Skills of Management*, Routledge (Third Edition, 1991)

Hunt J.W., *Managing People at Work*, McGraw Hill (Third Edition, 1992)

Luthans F., *Organisational Behaviour*, McGraw Hill (Sixth Edition, 1992, Chapters 6 & 7)

Murdock A. & Scutt C., *Personal Effectiveness*, Butterworth Heinnemann (1993)

Drucker P.F., *The Effective Executive*, Butterworth Heinnemann (1988)

Index

Elements of Marketing

A R Morden

This book provides a broad and comprehensive introduction to the principal ideas and concepts of the theory and practice of marketing.

It is known to be used on the following courses: CIM Certificate in Marketing, IIM, BTEC National and HNC/D Business and Finance, SCOTVEC, NCEA, IPS, CBSI, ICM, ACCA, CIMA, CIOB, SCIOB, ABE, BA Business Studies, BA Marketing, BA Accounting, Modular Business Degree Schemes (CAMS), Modular Combined Degree Schemes with Business (CAMS), CMS/CiM, DMS, MBA, Dip/MSc Agricultural Marketing. It is on the reading lists of ACCA, IPS, CBSI and ICM.

Review comments

'Excellent concise book which is real value for money.'

'Well balanced book, easy to understand but interesting and stimulating as well.' Lecturers

'Superb examples, new ideas, ... concepts and applications of theory are all covered in this excellent book.'

Enterprise Magazine November 1993

3rd edition • **448 pp** • **245 x 190 mm** • **1993** • **ISBN 1 85805 021 9**

Essential Elements

covering the core of modular courses

Essential Elements of
Management Accounting *Jill & Roger Hussey*

Contents The role of management accounting; Cost classification and control; Total costing; Marginal costing; Capital investment and appraisal; Budgetary control; Standard costing; Appendices.

ISBN 1 85805 103 7

Essential Elements of
Financial Accounting *Jill & Roger Hussey*

Contents The accounting framework; Users and uses of financial information; The cash flow forecast; The profit and loss account for a sole trader; The balance sheet for a sole trader; The financial statements of a limited company; Interpretation of financial statements.

ISBN 1 85805 091 X

Essential Elements of
Business Economics *Mark Sutcliffe*

Contents: The UK economy – an overview; Resource allocation; Business costs; The structure of business and its conduct; Small firms and multinationals; Wages and the labour market; Investment, R & D and training; National economic change and business activity; Money, banking and inflation; Economic policy and the business environment; The international dimension; Europe and business.

ISBN 1 85805 095 2

Essential Elements of
Business Planning and Policy *Jim Jones*

Contents The nature and importance of policy and planning; Organisation philosophy and objectives; Policy and levels of planning; Analysis for strategic planning; Choosing the strategy; Implementation of strategy; Evaluation of strategy; Framework of project planning; Project planning and control; Annual plans; Information systems for planning; Contingency planning.

ISBN 1 85805 100 2

Essential Elements of
Business Statistics *Les Oakshott*

Contents Survey Methods, Presentation of data, Summarising data, Probability and decision making, The Normal Distribution, Analysis and interpretation of sample data, Testing a hypothesis, Correlation and regression.

ISBN 1 85805 103 7

Essential Elements of
Quantitative Methods *Les Oakshott*

Contents: Index numbers, Investment appraisal, Time series analysis, Linear programming, Critical path analysis, Stock control methods, Simulation.

ISBN 1 85805 098 7

All titles in this series are approximately 128 pages long, and measure 275 x 215mm.

Finance for Non-Financial Managers

An Active-Learning Approach

A H Millichamp

This book provides a complete course of study in the areas of accounting and finance that students on many professional, vocational and degree courses are required to cover.

It is known to be used on the following courses: BTEC Higher National, NEBS, BA Business Studies, DMS, professional courses (e.g. ACCA Certified Diploma in Accounting and Finance, IPS, IAM, IM), and all courses (e.g. engineering, personnel, sales, purchasing, catering, tourism, etc.) on which students need an understanding of accountancy in order to communicate with accountants and implement necessary financial controls and plans as part of their management role.

Review comments

'Well structured, attractive layout and excellent value for money.'

'Excellent for use in a variety of modular courses.'

'Lends itself to use on student centred learning.'   Lecturers

1st edition • 352 pp • 275 x 215 mm • 1992 • ISBN 1 873981 06 6

Management

Theory and Practice

G A Cole

This best-selling book provides, in one concise volume, the principal ideas and developments in the theory and practice of management required by university and college students whose courses include an element of Management Studies.

It is known to be used on the following courses: CIMA, ACCA, AAT, IComA, BTEC HNC/D, IM, BA Business Studies, BA Accounting, MSc Information Technology, BSc Software Engineering, Hotel and Catering Management courses, CIB, CIM, IAM, DMS, CIPFA, IPS, CBA, ICM, DMS, CBSI, ABE, IPM, IOM, NEBSM, DBA, MIOM, Dip. HSM, BTEC ND, Dip. in Administrative Management, BSc (Hons) Software Engineering, MSc Computing, HND IT, NVQ 5 in Management. It is also on the reading lists of ACCA, LCCI, ABE, AAT, AEB, IAM, ICM, IPS, CIMA and CIB.

Review comments

'Very accessible to students, and forms a useful basis for lectures.'
'Excellent book, good format and easily readable.'
'Excellent content, logically and well set out.'   Lecturers

4th edition • 480 pp • 245 x 176 mm • 1993 • ISBN 1 85805 018 9

Personnel Management
Theory and Practice

G A Cole

This book is intended to meet the need of students and lecturers for an introductory text-book on personnel management.

It is known to be used on the following courses: IPM, ICSA, HNC/D Business and Finance, CNAA Diploma in Personnel Management, CNAA Degrees in Business Studies (Personnel Management Options), DMS, CIB, Institute of Training and Development, A Level Business Studies, CPP, HNC/D Human Resource Management, MIOM, IMS, BA Business Studies, IOH NEBSM, Association of Business Executives, CIPFA, Advanced GNVQ Business. It is also on the reading list of CIMA.

Review comments

'Clear, concise and comprehensive.'
'Good value all round text. Well researched and up-to-date.'   Lecturers

'Clearly presented and delightfully well written.'
Enterprise Magazine December 1993

3rd edition • 576 pp • 215 x 135 mm • 1993 • ISBN 1 85805 019 7

Strategic Management

G A Cole

This book provides a comprehensive introduction to the theory and practice of strategic management. It avoids the narrow focus and complexity of many other books written in this area, but enables the reader to identify and make connections between the key features of strategic management and the issues and choices that arise from them.

It is aimed at BA Business Studies but is expected to be used on ACCA (Management and Strategy) and CIMA (Strategic Management Accountancy and Marketing). It will also be suitable for students on postgraduate courses in Management or Business Studies, including the Diploma in Management Studies and introductory stages of MBA courses.

Contents: Part 1 Knowledge base Strategic management: an introduction; Defining mission and objectives; Assessing the environment; Formulating a strategy; Competitive advantage; International dimensions of strategy; Organisational culture.; Strategy implementation; Business planning; Forecasting the future; Managing change; Achieving excellence; Managing innovation; Managing quality; Role of marketing in strategic management; Role of personnel management in strategic management; Measuring performance and reviewing strategy; Managing success; Strategic management – a working model. Part 2 Strategic management in practice: case studies Multi-national organisations; Industrial/commercial organisations; Public sector organisations; Charitable/voluntary sector organisations; Small/medium sized enterprises. Workbook section – Exercises and questions (some with and some without answers) drawing together Part 1 and Part 2.

1st edition • **300 pp (approx)** • **245 x 176 mm** • *August 1994*
ISBN 1 85805 099 5

Tackling Coursework

Projects, Assignments, Reports & Presentations

D Parker

This book provides the student with practical guidance on how to approach the coursework requirement of a typical business studies course, i.e. projects, assignments, reports and presentations. The text makes clear the different approaches needed for the different types of coursework, with examples of each in an Appendix, and there is advice on how to conduct research, collect information and present results, in either written or verbal form. It is expected to be used on the following courses: any business studies course at undergraduate (e.g. BABS) or postgraduate (e.g. MBA) level. It would also be useful as a preparatory text for a research degree.

Contents: Introduction, Dissertations and projects, Essays and papers, Management reports, Seminars and presentations, Research methods Appendices: Further reading, Example of dissertation proposal, Example of citations, Dissertation contents, Example of an essay

1st edition • 96 pp • 215 x 135 mm • ISBN 1 85805 101 0